# The Modern Irish Novel

Irish Novelists after 1945

# For Karin

'Never die. Never die.'
*Kepler* John Banville

# The Modern Irish Novel

## Irish Novelists after 1945

**RÜDIGER IMHOF**

WOLFHOUND PRESS

Published in 2002 by
Wolfhound Press
An imprint of Merlin Publishing
16 Upper Pembroke Street
Dublin 2
Ireland

publishing@merlin.ie

www.merlin-publishing.com

Text Copyright © 2002 Rüdiger Imhof
Arrangement and Design Copyright © 2002 Wolfhound Press

ISBN 0-86327-860-4

A CIP catalogue record for this book
is available from the British Library.

Typeset by Gough Typesetting Services
Printed by Mackays of Chatham, Kent

# TABLE OF CONTENTS

# Author's Note

Extracts from work in copyright are used only where essential to the text, principally in order to underpin interpretative arguments submitted in this study. Quotations have been employed sparingly, and for those comparatively minimal quotations I have observed the guidelines relating to 'fair dealing' laid down in 1987 by the Society of Authors in conjunction with the Publishers Association.

I should like to acknowledge my indebtedness to the individual publishers of the writers discussed in this study for the use of the material from which I have quoted: Bloomsbury for Brian Moore; Faber & Faber for Julia O'Faolain and John McGahern; HarperCollins for Dermot Bolger; Headline for Jennifer Johnston; John Calder for Samuel Beckett; Jonathan Cape for Roddy Doyle; Macmillan for John Banville and Patrick McCabe; Penguin UK for Edna O'Brien, Julia O'Faolain, William Trevor, Dermot Bolger and Brian Moore; Random House for Aidan Higgins and Brian Moore; Weidenfeld & Nicolson for Edna O'Brien.

I am much indebted to Mr John McKeown, MA, and Mr Colin Foskett, MA, for reading parts of the typescript and weeding out my silly solecisms.

Grateful thanks must go to my editor, Aideen T. Quigley, for her painstaking perusal of the study and her invaluable suggestions.

**For my part, I am resolved never to read any book but my own, as long as I live.**

*The Life and Opinions of Tristram Shandy, Gentleman*
Laurence Sterne

# PREFACE

This study has been written with the clear aim of providing assistance to those who wish to acquaint themselves with the novels of twelve major post-war Irish writers more profoundly than they have, for one reason or another, been able to do so far. At the same time, each chapter has been designed to serve as an introduction to the novelistic *oeuvre* of the writer under scrutiny. The study, therefore, is not meant to be taken as part of any strictly academic agenda.

I have no intention of pandering to my peers, to readers who know as much, or even more, than I do about the writers in question as well as the Irish novel since World War II. This study was put together first and foremost with the lay reader in mind (in the very best sense of that term), while not gainsaying the possibility that even the expert may occasionally profit from the insights proffered.

The approach adopted here is grounded in the firm conviction that it is the quintessential business of literary criticism to elucidate literary texts and not to deploy or pillage them for the purpose of proving or underpinning matters extraneous to literature. To give an example, historical background research is incontestably in order if it helps to further an understanding of a specific literary text, which is mostly the case with the interpretative approach termed 'historical criticism'. Thus an Elizabethan text, for it to be truly appreciated, may depend upon an adequate knowledge of the Elizabethan world picture.

I do not want to prevent anyone from, say, analysing the characters in a novel or a play with the aim of supporting one of the principal tenets of psychoanalysis. It is not for me to query the appropriateness of L.C. Knights's notorious question: 'How Many Children Had Lady Macbeth?'[1] even though such a consideration has next to no bearing on Shakespeare's tragedy. Not for me either to scream blue murder at seeing literature employed for proving the famous, or infamous, death of the author, although one might point out that, strangely enough, it takes at least one deconstructionist author to show that there are no longer any authors around.[2] One could also, with all due respect, question the relevance of deconstructionist literary criticism, because, as is fairly often the case, exercises in the field tend to be obfuscatory instead of elucidatory. Furthermore, it is not for me to analyse literary texts, in particular Irish literary texts, with an eye to exemplifying aspects of Ireland's colonial and post-colonial history. Such an approach, apart from sometimes producing rather strange results,[3] tempts many authors to supplement the title of their treatise with the term 'nation'[4], as if it were a form of sacrilege to concern oneself with literature in its own right without roping in the whole national caboodle. One feels reminded of that old, feeble joke according to which no Irishman worth a sprig of shamrock would ever dream of writing about a piece of literature without at the same time shedding light on the Irish fight for freedom.

Let every person ride their own hobby-horse, say I; but let me, too, ride mine. Why not with honesty rejoice in the possibility of dealing with literature from a myriad different angles? Ultimately it is for each critic to decide what approach is the most appropriate and fruitful one; and ultimately it is of course for each reader of a given study to judge whether what is offered makes sense. This is the way in which I would like this book to be assessed.

The chapters that follow have deliberately been couched in a language that should be easily accessible to most readers. By the same token, I have been at pains to steer clear of the farther, crepuscular reaches of academic critical discourse. There is, possibly, one exception, and that is the chapter on Samuel Beckett. But then Beckett's novels represent a most intricate poetological examination of the nature of fiction, an examination that defies an attempt at plain fare. These novels are, some would argue, metafictions (i.e., forms of fiction used to discuss fiction itself). Which is precisely what they are — a fact that lands all those on a sticky wicket who contend that the generic form of metafiction is an integral part of postmodernist literary discourse, while in the same breath pronouncing Beckett a late modernist.[5] The point is that Beckett was writing the kind of fiction now classed as postmodernist when all the celebrated postmodernists of the second half of the twentieth century were still in their swaddling clothes. But where does that leave us as regards the argument according to which postmodernism is the most significant and most characteristic phenomenon of the last four decades? It is a question that falls outside the thematic scope of this study. May those who are interested in a conundrum of that sort have their own headaches over it, and provide their own aspirin!

The twelve novelists selected here for treatment will most certainly not be to the liking of everyone. But then there is no pleasing everyone. Each selection is bound to find its detractors. This one will definitely be no exception. That inevitable fact notwithstanding, the choice is none the less based on a few sound considerations. Books are, true enough, finite things. Space is required to cover the works of established novelists — most of whom have to date published more than a dozen novels, and mainly quite extensive ones at that — and, while doing so, pursue the aims outlined above. As it is, this study possesses quite substantial scope. To have admitted more writers would have resulted in a tome at whose sales price, to consider only one factor, most potential buyers, other than academic libraries, would surely have balked. And that would decidedly have contradicted the intention to reach the lay reader. We should not gloss over the fact that books must sell. Moreover, it would not have been a good idea to have the writers included here rub shoulders with writers whose works, when it comes to quantity and excellence, are simply inferior. There are, to be fair, a lot of interesting and exciting younger Irish novelists around these days. But it does not make much sense to exalt writers such as, say, Dermot Healy, Clare Boylan, Anne Enright, Ita Daly, Robert McLiam Wilson, Emma Donoghue, Colm Tóibín, Desmond Hogan (one could go on) to the same rank as Edna O'Brien, John McGahern, Samuel Beckett, John Banville, William Trevor or any of the other novelists chosen here by allotting a chapter to them. All these writers of a younger generation definitely warrant treatment in a study like this, but it should be a different one altogether, one that does not compare incomparables. I hope to undertake such a study, if it pleases the fountain of health to bless me long enough with life and good spirits, as Laurence Sterne put it in a different context.

The writers that figure here have been grouped into four categories in order to highlight important trends, tendencies or whatever one may want to call them that have evolved in the Irish novel since 1945. The first category is devoted to what may be termed 'experimentalists', in other words novelists such as Samuel Beckett, Aidan Higgins and John Banville, who have aimed at developing narrative discourse, at exploring new thematic areas and surmounting the comparatively narrow, nation-oriented interest of much of Irish fiction, linking up with international trends. (*Pace* all those who are inclined to regard this as a derogatory and disparaging opinion. It is not.) The second category comprises women writers who, in different ways, have investigated the role and significance of women in Irish society. Naturally enough, there are others who have done so, but they were considered to be, in various ways, of different calibres. The third group accommodates novelists who share a propensity for quintessential storytelling of the realist tradition, notwithstanding the fact that one of them, i.e., Brian Moore, occasionally employs preternatural incidents in his plots. The last category features three representatives of a younger generation of writers who, unlike their contemporaries, can already look back on a more substantial body of work. These are, in a sense, quite exciting new voices, if the epithet 'new' is appropriate for persons who have been wielding their pens for a decade or more. But compared to the other writers they do represent new voices, voices of the 1990s. Roddy Doyle and Dermot Bolger are variously credited with introducing an innovative form of realism into Irish fiction, something akin to American 'dirty realism'. Occasionally they find themselves grouped as 'Northside Realists'. McCabe is notable, among other things, for having, at least with some of his writings, helped inaugurate a neo-Gothic strain into more recent literature, one not limited to the Irish variety, but to be encountered rather frequently in it.

In the final analysis, selections of this kind inexorably have a subjective note to them. They cannot help reflecting the individual preferences of the person responsible. No one will want to claim that they have an equally penetrating and profitable access to all the different writers. One man's meat is another man's poison, of course. No one critic, moreover, can boast an intimate knowledge of all the noteworthy Irish novelists to have emerged since 1945. No man at all can be knowing it all, and we must be satisfied, to echo Maurya in Synge's *Riders to the Sea*.

Lest it be a cause for some misconception, I am of course fully aware that quite a few of the writers under discussion have, in addition to their book-length narratives, published collections of short stories. Some of them, such as Edna O'Brien, William Trevor and John McGahern, have established themselves as indisputable masters of the genre. Samuel Beckett's *oeuvre*, to give another example, also comprises such publications as the early collection of stories *More Kicks Than Pricks* and the superb later shorter narratives, including *Ill Seen Ill Said* — that unrivalled investigation of the workings of the artistic imagination as well as of the creative process. Had each chapter in this book been intended as a full-scale introduction to the writer in question, it would have been inconceivable not to cover all their works of fiction. However, I decided to restrict the focus to novels only. This may be deplorable, but there it is.

Most of the novelists discussed here will, it can only be hoped, continue to publish books of fiction. Hence, the coverage of their works cannot claim to be comprehensive. Hardly a month elapses without a new book by one of them appearing on the market. A critic trying to keep up would soon feel like poor old Tristram Shandy, who is compelled to admit to himself that, because he fails to observe the two most important rules of story-telling, viz. to alternate between the scenic method and the summary method and not to fall prey to inordinate digressions, he will never be able to overtake himself in his efforts to write down the story of his life, no matter how fast he pens. I therefore considered it a wise decision to focus only on those of the writers' novels that appeared before the end of the twentieth century. It seemed a plausible deadline, indeed.

# SAMUEL BECKETT

Samuel Beckett's artistic credo and the fundamental creative predicament underlying his seminal work can, in a sense, aptly be summed up in terms of his often-quoted statement in 'Tal Coat':

> The expression that there is nothing to express, nothing with which to express, nothing from which to express, no power to express, no desire to express, together with the obligation to express.[1]

In *Molloy*, Beckett, or his narrator, rephrases the idea in these terms:

> Not to want to say, not to know what you want to say, not to be able to say what you think you want to say, and never stop saying, or hardly ever, that is the thing to keep in mind, even in the heat of com-position.[2]

The categorical imperative to create combined with the im-possibility of creation is the principal issue with which Beckett continued wrestling in what he called 'the madhouse of the skull and nowhere else'.[3] Among all the comments made about Beckett's fiction, Anthony Cronin's are among the most lucid and insightful. Three quotations will make Cronin's point clear:

> There is on the one hand the command to give utterance, to be verbal, even loquacious — in other words, creative. But this loquacity, this creativity almost necessarily involves fictions — that is, lies. And at the same time there seems to be a command, or a necessity, to utter something important, something which once uttered will give him quittance, will restore him to his primal self.[4]

> [...] it would seem that this is one of the things the trilogy is 'about': the position of the artist — more specifically the literary artist — who has been commanded, or seems to have been commanded, by an obscure power or junta of powers to give

utterance, to create, but from whom not mere creation alone but also some sort of ultimate truth is demanded.[5]

Just as it seems that the artist who is concerned only with the truth can arrive at it only by means of a fiction, that it is lies which are seminal, even of the truth, so it is only by the adoption of a fictitious mechanism and the entry into a labyrinth which may never lead back to the self that the self can be revealed.[6]

As for his style, Beckett has developed unmistakable char-acteristics. Not all of them can be highlighted here. Four — possibly the four most important — must suffice. This passage from *Watt* may serve to illustrate them:

> [...] he once knew a priest, who on leaving with a sigh of relief the chapel where he had served mass, with his own hands, to more than a hundred persons, was shat on, from above, by a dove, in the eye.[7]

Perhaps the first thing to note is the particular brand of humour that permeates so much of Beckett's writing, which may be summed up by this statement from *Endgame*: 'Nothing is funnier than unhappiness, I grant you that'.[8] One of the Addenda in *Watt* is: 'die Merde hat mich wieder'.[9] Now, this distinctive brand of humour results from the fact that human existence 'auf der Erde' (on earth) is largely seen as 'merde'. It is, significantly, a dove, the bird symbolising the Holy Ghost, that shits on the priest who has just emerged from the chapel 'with a sigh of relief'. Why should he leave the chapel with relief? Because he found the task of saying Mass onerous, even loathsome? Because, as Hamm in *Endgame* puts it: 'The Bastard! He doesn't exist!',[10] meaning God of course? But that sigh of relief is to no avail, for the priest is shat upon none the less.

The next thing is the stylistic parallelism, the rhythmic, balanced cadence of 'was shat upon, from above, by a dove, in the eye' — a cadence clearly indebted to the King James version of the Bible, with which Beckett became thoroughly familiar at his school, Portora. One finds this kind of *parataxis*, or syntactic parallelism, everywhere in the Bible, as in David's lamentation over Saul and Jonathan:

> Tell *it* not in Gath, publish *it* not in the streets of Ashkelon; lest

the daughters of the Philistines rejoice, lest the daughters of the uncircumcised triumph [...]

How are the mighty fallen, and the weapons of the war perished!
(2 Samuel 1:20, 27)

One also finds it everywhere in Beckett.[11] Thus of *Watt* it is said: 'But having neither tie, nor collar, he had neither collar, nor tie'.[12] Beckett was a lord of language who could have said of himself, as the narratorial voice in 'From an Abandoned Work' puts it: '[...] words have been my only love, not many'.[13] True enough, he came to rely on fewer and fewer, but even in his brief later texts the stylistic peculiarity mentioned here is conspicuous.

The third characteristic is the fastidiousness of detail, as expressed through 'with his own hands'. How else than with his own hands should the priest celebrate Mass? Such overabundance of detail dominates most Beckett prose texts, particularly *Watt*, where it is heightened to a playful exhausting of possibilities in an attempt to arrive at sense and causes.

Lastly, our passage bespeaks the world view that informs almost all Beckett — a world view based on the belief in the enigmatic and arbitrary nature of things. Why, of all people, should a priest after saying Mass be shat upon? And, then again, why not? Why should one of the thieves have been saved and the other one have been damned? This is the question that causes much mental turmoil to Estragon and Vladimir, in *Waiting for Godot*. The above passage, thus, shows Beckett *in nuce*.

Was Beckett an Irish writer or, phrased differently, should he be classed as an Irish writer? It is difficult to say. Placing an author within the context of a national literature is no doubt one of the most daunting and problematic tasks that literary criticism has to grapple with, especially if the author in question represents a borderline case, as it were. One does not have this ambiguity with a writer who, having lived in his native country all his life, writes about it in his mother tongue. But what about a person like Joseph Conrad, who, born in Poland, chose to write in English about Africa or an imaginary republic in South America? What about Beckett, who, being of Irish Protestant stock, elected to write in French of incidents that seem to be situated in locations which are difficult, if not altogether impossible, to identify — locations resembling limbo?

Numerous attempts have been made to ascertain special features in Beckett's fiction and plays as quintessentially Irish, thus salvaging the writer for the Irish literary canon.[14] Vivian Mercier was particularly active in this respect. In one chapter of his study *Beckett/Beckett*, he dazzlingly manages to ferret out instances where Beckett employs Irish speech patterns or draws on geographical or other specifics of Ireland. Thus, he argues, for example:

> Foxrock Railway Station, now disused, which once served the adjoining Leopardstown Racecourse as well as the village of Foxrock, can easily be recog-nised as the setting for the concluding pages of *Watt* and much of the action of *All That Fall*.[15]

There is also the case of Molloy, who in the novel of the same name says: 'And da, in my part of the world, means father' (p. 18), which, together with the expression '[...] I have drink taken [...]' (p. 108), seems to place the events unmistakably in Ireland. But what does all this source-hunting signify? Is *Watt* an Irish novel because the railway station featuring in its concluding pages is modelled on the station in Foxrock? What is incontestable is that Beckett was born in Ireland. What is equally incontestable is that — as the Duke of Wellington put it — being born in a stable does not make one a horse. The long and the short of the matter is that Beckett may deploy various Irish characteristics in his novels and shorter narratives, yet that fact does not render them Irish, first and foremost as a result of the thematic preoccupations he pursues in his work. These constitute nothing that could be called matters Irish. Having devoted the greater part of his literary *oeuvre* to the fathoming of the potentials and limitations of the literary process, Beckett is a genuinely international writer.

But what, then, is he doing in a book on the Irish novel after 1945? He has been included because he represents a crucial phase in the development of Ireland's literature. As is the case with any national literature, it is of the utmost significance, or so I should like to contend, to observe the point where writers deliberately transcend the comparatively narrow parameters established by indigenous themes and forms by linking up with international literary trends and concerns. Beckett clearly marks such a point, and so, more recently, does John Banville — his *Athena* may be set in Dublin, but *Athena*, on the strength of what it offers thematically, is not an Irish novel. It is, rather, a novel that has come out of Ireland. Beckett had gone one step further, having written most of his fiction in France and originally published most of it there. As I have said, the whole business is daunting and problematic.

*Murphy* (1938) shows Beckett establishing the background against which his succeeding novels, primarily the trilogy *Molloy, Malone Dies* and *The Unnamable*, may be approached and assessed. *Murphy* most obviously captures a certain period of time in the life of the eponymous character, telling, among other things, of his embroilment with the woman Celia and some of her acquaintances as well as of his predilection for sitting in his rocking chair, so that his mind can come alive; for life in his mind gives 'him pleasure, such pleasure that pleasure [is] not the word'.[16] The narrative also treats of Murphy's work in a lunatic asylum and his tragicomic demise. But all this is less significant than the fact that Beckett utilises the incidents recounted to advance his own ideas about the state of novel-writing. *Murphy*, as has been noted by others,[17] attempts a reckoning-up with Naturalism, as exemplified by Zola, and the type of novel represented by Marcel Proust's *À la recherche du temps perdu*. One of Beckett's main goals is to reassess the relation between art and literature, much in the manner in which Joyce does in *Ulysses*. Whereas the fiction of a Zola, in its efforts to highlight the manner in which the individual is determined by the social factors of his milieu, must necessarily rely on the notion that there is a reality 'out there' which the nar-rative is obliged to take into account, Proust's novel acknowledges so-called reality only as a product of memory. For Proust, reality as such is not of any relevance for a narrative rendition, but the mental awareness of it is. The way reality is perceived becomes the focus of interest. Nevertheless, a relationship, if only a tenuous one, between fiction and the real is adhered to even in Proust. Beckett, however, intentionally negates the possibility that fiction may have any direct bearings on what is a given outside the sphere of literature, beating both Naturalism and Proust at their own games.

Here is the opening paragraph of *Murphy*:

> The sun shone, having no alternative, on the nothing new. Murphy sat out of it, as though he were free, in a mew in West Brompton. Here for what might have been six months he had eaten, drunk, slept, and put his clothes on and off, in a medium-sized cage of north-western aspect commanding an unbroken view of medium-sized cages of south-eastern aspect. Soon he would have to make other arrangements, for the mew had been condemned. Soon he would have to buckle to and start eating, drinking, sleeping, and putting his clothes on and off, in quite alien surroundings. (p. 5)

Here the narrator takes the averredly scientific method of Naturalism literally. He no longer evokes the context of determinacy through the delineation of a specific locale, but instead debunks the mechanism inherent in the literary method ('Soon he would have to buckle to and start eating [...] in quite alien surroundings'). If everything is really determined in life, why make the point at such great length, when it can be conveyed more succinctly in tabular form? Hence Celia is introduced in this fashion:

| Age | Unimportant |
|---|---|
| Head | Small and round |
| Eyes | Green |
| Complexion | White |
| Hair | Yellow |
| Features | Mobile |
| [...] | |
| Upper arm | 11' |
| [...] | |
| Wrist | 6' |
| Bust | 34' |
| [etc.] | (p. 10) |

Beckett transcends the Naturalist method by disclosing its aesthetic shortcoming, which resides in its pretension to being pseudo-scientific.[18]

> In Proust, there is still something like a residue of reality, as reflected through the consciousness of the perceiver, and this residue helps generate sense in the eyes of the reader. Beckett, however, rejects this manner of establishing sense through measuring matters fictional against the real, and instead refers the reader to another point in the book, chapter six, for comparison.

> He sat in his chair in this way because it gave him pleasure! First it gave his body pleasure, it appeased his body. Then it set him free in his mind. For it was not until his body was appeased that he could come alive in his mind, as described in section six. (p. 6)

Beckett thereby implies that meaning and sense can only be won from within a literary work itself and that literature refers not to something extra-literary but to itself. He of course gained this insight from Joyce. In his essay on *Finnegans Wake*, he remarks: 'His [*i.e.* Joyce's] writing is not about something, *it is that something itself*.[19] But when the reader arrives at chapter six, the final chapter he finds himself in for a surprise. For the recurrently mentioned section does anything but provide answers to the open questions and tie up the loose ends, offering instead Beckett's critical re-assessment of the traditional notion of art, according to which art's business is to convey content. Chapter six thus does little to coerce the individual parts that go to make up *Murphy* into a sense-providing whole. There is no immanent relationship between the novel's chapters.

Murphy's mind, which chapter six is alleged to explain, is divided into three zones. In Zone One, there are 'forms with parallel [...], the elements of physical experience available for a new arrangement' (p. 65). This is the world of Naturalism, the literary forms finding parallels in reality through physical experience. Zone Two harbours 'forms without parallel'; here 'the pleasure [is] contemplation' (p. 65). The idea corresponds to the notion of art and reality informing Proust's *À la recherche*, where reality gains significance as a world remembered. Zone Three represents Beckett's concept of the aesthetic. Here, there is 'a flux of forms, a perpetual coming together and falling asunder of forms' (p. 65). In other words, Beckett regards traditional ideas of art, as exemplified by Zones One and Two, as templates, so to speak, for operating freely with, and in, in order to cancel them out and transcend them. The reader, being continually offered conventional forms of literary discourse as templates, is thereby sensitised for the manner in which such forms condition his interpretive response to a text. And such an awareness results in a kind of liberation from the constraints of the literary conventions.

*Murphy* relies throughout on what appears to be an omniscient narrator. In effect, though, he is all but omniscient. This kind of narrator, traditionally, is a guarantor of integration, signification and meaning in the fictional world he creates. Not so in Beckett, where he limits himself, or rather where he is restricted to joking, punning and patter-spouting. 'The sun', he opens his account, 'shone, having no alternative, on the nothing new' (p. 5). Later he notes: '[...] night's young thoughts had been put back an hour [...]' (p. 45). At the opening of the seminal section six, he states: 'It is most unfortunate, but the point of this story has been reached where a justification of the expression 'Murphy's mind' has to be attempted' (p. 63). Why should it be most unfortunate? At the close of the chapter, one reads: 'This painful duty having now been discharged, no further bulletins will be issued' (p. 66). Of the characters in his book, the narrator says: 'All the puppets in this book whinge sooner or later, except Murphy, who is not a puppet' (p. 71). Sentences such as this one: 'Her quantum of wantum cannot vary' (p. 112) and a great many others, including some of those given above, come as no surprise. For the narrator believes that '[in] the beginning was the pun' (p. 41). His comments and reflections, unlike those of a traditional omniscient narrator, fail to provide meaning and a sense of cohesion. They remain clichés, which are comparable to the templates of how reality is rendered in the Zolaesque and Proustian types of fiction. In short, the (omniscient) narrator in *Murphy* serves the purpose of exposing his own redundancy within the context of his own narrative construct by proving to be incapable of effecting integration and signification.

Lastly, plot as a narrative device is, by and large, treated in the fashion in which the story that Miss Carridge had to tell is handled:

> The story that Miss Carridge had to tell was very pathetic and tedious. It brightened up a little with her reconstruction of the death scene, cupidity lending wings to her imagination.

> 'He gets out his razor to shave, as he always did regular about noon.' A lie. The old boy shaved once a week and then the last thing at night. 'That I do know, because I found the brush on the dresser with a squeeze of paste on top.' A lie. 'He goes to put up the tube before he lathers, he walks across the room with the razor in his hand, screwing the cap on the tube. He drops the cap, he throws the tube on the bed and goes down on the floor. I found the tube on the bed and the cap under the bed.' Lies. 'He goes crawling about the floor, with the razor open in his hand, when all of a sudden he has a seizure.' Pronounced on the analogy of manure. 'He told me when he first came he might have a seizure any minute, he had two this year already, one on Shrove Tuesday, the other on Derby Day. That I do know.' All lies. [etc.] (pp. 83f.)

Generally speaking, rudiments of plot-constituents are built up only to be cancelled at the next instant. The example quoted is quite reminiscent of the Naturalist manner of narration. But Beckett uncovers this as a mere mechanism and, by means of the narrator's injections, as lies.[20]

Through such treatment of narrative technique and narrative devices, like the omniscient narrator, plot or dialogue (which, more often than not, has the characters intentionally fail to communicate), Beckett shows up the exhaustive nature of traditional forms of narration, thus laying the foundation for his own efforts at transcending them.

In *Watt* (1953)[21], Beckett again takes the art form of the novel and wrings its neck even more relentlessly than in *Murphy*. The story it tells has been reduced more drastically than before. Watt first appears, having been tossed from a tram at dusk

> [a] motionless, [...] solitary figure, lit less and less by the receding lights, until it was scarcely to be distinguished from the dim wall behind it. Tetty was not sure whether it was a man or a woman. Mr. Hackett was not sure that it was not a parcel, a carpet for example, or a roll of tarpaulin, wrapped up in dark paper and tied about the middle with a cord.[22]

Rising, Watt proceeds to the railway station, is knocked down by a milkcan porter, gets up, takes a train, alights, goes to the house of Mr Knott, where he is to work as a ground-floor retainer, replacing one Arsene, who had previously replaced one Vincent. In time — Watt's powers of deduction lead him to believe the period to be a year — and after a series of often intriguing experiences and observations, he replaces Erskine as the second-floor servant, whose departure is compensated for by the arrival of a new ground-floor man, Arthur. After another lapse of time, logically a second year, and another series of experiences and observations, Watt comes downstairs one morning to find a new second-floor servant seated in the kitchen. It is the signal for Watt's departure. 'As Watt came, so he went, in the night, that covers all things with its cloak, especially when the weather is cloudy' (p. 214). But the story is not the point. The point is how that story is rendered.

The structure of the book is characterised by the destruction of the conventional principle of narrative order. In his Proust essay, Beckett rails against 'the vulgarity of plausible con-catenation'.[23] In *Watt* he has divided the novel into four chapters, or parts, and appended an 'Addenda' that offers suggestions as to a possibly limitless expansion of the book. Linear narration is scotched by the fact that, in strictly chronological terms, the last chapter precedes the penultimate one, describing Watt on his journey from Mr Knott's house to the lunatic asylum which figures in the previous part. The actual chronological sequence, therefore, is 1, 2, 4, 3. To complicate matters further, Watt seems to have told his story

to one Sam. (Is he Sam Beckett? That would be too neat. And yet...?)
Sam is identifiable with certainty as the narrator of chapter 3; but perhaps
he is responsible for the entire book. No matter. What is more important
for the moment is that Watt recounted his tale in a most peculiar way:

> As Watt told the beginning of his story, not first, but second, so
> not fourth, but third, now he told its end. Two, one, four, three,
> that was the order in which he told his story. Heroic quatrains are
> not otherwise elaborated. (p. 214)

Thus begins chapter 4. Why did whoever is finally responsible for the
arrangement of the chapters put the first two parts in the correct
chronological order but not the other two? And why the reference to
heroic quatrains? It is all a mystery, and 'mystery' is the apposite word
for *Watt* in its entirety.

As for point of view, for the greater part there is a quasi-omniscient
narrator, but one that does his job rather badly, not adequately
introducing the characters — as in a traditional novel — but making
them appear and disappear unexpectedly. Furthermore, this narrator's
authority is severely debunked by another narrator-figure who comments
on the narrative procedure in footnotes, as when he remarks: 'Much
valuable space has been saved, in this work, that would have been lost,
by avoidance of the plethoric reflexive pronoun after say' (p. 6). The
footnote refers to the statement: 'Tired of waiting for the tram, said[1]
Mr. Hackett [...]'. The reader must of course regard a reflexive pronoun
in this context as 'plethoric', and the question surely is: why mention it
if it is not employed? The narrator responsible for the footnote is thus
likewise exposed as not especially competent. In addition, chapter 3
provides Sam's story told by Sam himself. Incorporated therein, to make
things even more intricate, is the story of Louit as told by Arthur, a unit
that quite clearly represents a digression from both the accounts featuring
Watt and Sam's narrative. Sam recounts what Watt told him, superseding
the not-so-omniscient narrator. He also reproduces Arthur's portrait
of Louit. He thus may be considered the medium in which the various
storylines converge. Yet, in this case, they fail to converge; they run
through him and then drift apart because Sam lacks the capability of
subsumption. The incoherence of Arthur's story about Louit as given
by Sam, and Sam's own discourse about Watt, evinces that plot here no
longer functions as a means of representation. By depriving the
(omniscient) narrator of his power and preventing the individual

narrative skeins from achieving integration and coherence, Beckett generates an impression of contingency governing his novel.

Character in *Watt* shows symptoms of an incipient dis-integration of human shape, so significant in much of Beckett's writing. Watt is no more than a physical grotesque. When first mentioned, he is referred to as a neuter. Tetty is not sure whether 'it' is a man or a woman; Mr Hackett thinks 'it' could be 'a parcel, a carpet for example, or a roll of tarpaulin, wrapped up in dark paper and tied about the middle with a cord' (p. 14). Watt's way of walking suggests an automaton rather than a human being:

> Watt's way of advancing due east, for example, was to turn his bust as far as possible towards the north and at the same time fling out his right leg as far as possible towards the south, and then to turn his bust as far as possible to the south and at the same time to fling out his left leg as far as possible towards the north, and then again to turn his bust as far as possible towards the north and to fling out [etc.] (p. 28)

The concept of plot has largely been abandoned, having been replaced by numerous digressions, like the thirty-odd pages about Ernest Louit, lists of objects, parts of songs or other textual peculiarities. Action has mainly been relinquished in favour of a static situation — the situation of a character (Watt) in search of sense and meaning. But this search does not so much result in a series of incidents as in a mental process, or mental processes, on the part of Watt, who in a most elaborate way and by dint of interminable series of logical alternatives, seeks to come to grips with the enigmatic world of Mr Knott — the closed world of senselessness. It is a really incomprehensible mystery on which Watt's mind sets to work, making all sorts of guesses. He goes into calculations by series of probabilities and hypotheses, which lead him to explore the whole field of the possible, according to a logic that in this instance is derived from Rabelais or Lewis Carroll. Thus the reader is made to pay witness not so much to the hero's, or rather anti-hero's, deeds as to his mental labours, in the course of which each and every trivial event or object is subjected to an almost endless, but futile analysis. Thus we read:

> Watt wondered how long it would be before the point and circle entered together upon the same plane. Or had they not done so

already, or almost? And was it not rather the circle that was in the background, and the point that was in the foreground? Watt wondered if they had sighted each other, or were blindly flying thus [...] He wondered if they would eventually pause and converse, and perhaps even mingle, or keep steadfast on their ways, like ships in the night, prior to the invention of wireless telegraphy. Who knows, they might even collide. And he wondered what the artist had intended to represent [etc.] (p. 127)

And:

Finally, to return to the incident of the Galls father and son, as related by Watt, did it have that meaning for Watt [...]? Or did it have some quite different meaning for Watt [...]? Or did it have no meaning whatever for Watt at the moment of its taking place [...]? These are most delicate questions. [...] But generally speaking it seems probable that the meaning attributed to this particular type of incident, by Watt, in his relations, was now the initial meaning that had been lost and then recovered, and now a meaning quite distinct from the initial meaning, and now a meaning evolved, after a delay of varying length, and with greater or less pains, from the initial absence of meaning. (p. 76)

To name in unequivocal terms the world surrounding him is therefore the aim of Watt's 'pursuit of meaning' (p. 72). He adheres to a naïve nominalism and believes he can express the essence of things, the Kantian thing-in-itself, 'foisting a meaning [...] where no meaning appeared' (p. 74); and as a consequence, he must fail to find 'semantic succour' (p. 80). Watt can no longer command the services of language because, as Rilke puts it in the ninth of his *Duino Elegies*, language is an inefficacious medium for saying the things:

[...] it was in vain that Watt said, Pot, pot. [...] For it was not a pot, the more he looked, the more he re-flected, the more he felt sure of that, that it was not a pot at all. It resembled a pot, it was almost a pot, but it was not a pot of which one could say, Pot, pot, and be comforted [etc.] (p. 78)

Words fail him. Empty spaces appear in the text; question marks replace missing words and sentences; and, in Sam's part, there are completely incoherent passages and non-sequiturs. Finally, Watt turns the order of letters, words and sentences back to front into an anti-language.[24] *Watt*, especially the chapters dealing with Watt's sojourn in Knott land, mainly consists of a great many series of minute logical alternatives by which Watt attempts to come to grips with what he sees and experiences. This overabundant juggling with, or going through, every possible combination of facts and pseudo-facts in explaining things creates an effect of boredom, to which quite a few reviewers and critics have taken exception.[25] But criticism of this strategy is ill-founded; for that boredom effect is quite intended, as it works towards distracting the reader's attention from what could constitute action in a narrative to the linguistic operation that brings action about. In short, the medium of language itself is thrown into relief. Language is no longer conceived of as the medium for rendering reality; rather it becomes the medium for a manipulation of language itself. Linguistic operations, as presented in *Watt*, lose the function of signification. Hence the lacunae, hiatuses, question marks and Watt's anti-language. Language is found to be incapable of denoting an object:

> My purely mental faculties on the other hand, the faculties properly so called of
>
> ?           ?
>
> ?           ?
>
> were if possible more vigorous than ever. (p. 167)

Beckett makes language fall prey to loquacity. By relinquishing its capacity for depiction and description, language develops the mechanism through which the linguistic flow is sparked off by the first sentence uttered, which is considered a statement devoid of a true correlative and which can be manipulated since it is not constrained to account for an intended message. In fact, language is pushed into a situation where it chokes on its own loquaciousness: 'Not a word, not a deed, not a thought, not a need, not a grief, not a joy, not a girl, not a boy [etc.]' (pp. 44f.). The playful manipulation is here heightened into a rhyme pattern. The stage where the use of language is utterly bereft of sense is reached when on two pages the croaking of frogs is rendered in onomatopoeic fashion by an insipid repetition of the syllables *krak, krek, krik* (pp. 135–137). Language is directed not to what it may signify, but to how it functions in a sentence.[26] Beckett's language in *Watt*, is thus turned into a kind of metalanguage in a novel that aspires to the status of metafiction, whose playful spirit is in evidence from its first paragraph to its last, which is this one:

> Mr. Nolan looked at Mr. Case, Mr. Case at Mr. Nolan, Mr. Gorman at Mr. Case, Mr. Gorman at Mr. Nolan, Mr. Nolan at Mr. Gorman. Mr. Case at Mr. Gorman, Mr.. Gorman again at Mr. Case, again at Mr. Nolan, and then straight before him, at nothing in particular. And so they stayed a little while, Mr. Case and Mr. Nolan looking at Mr. Gorman, and Mr. Gorman looking straight before him, at nothing in particular, though the sky falling to the hills, and the hills falling to the plain, made as pretty a picture, in the early morning light, as a man could hope to meet with, in a day's march. (p. 246)

And yet that playfulness of spirit possesses the most serious thematic intent. There may be 'no symbols where none intended', as the last statement in the book warns (p. 255). But how is one to say where they could be intended? Thus, in the end, the reader may find himself in an epistemological quandary that equals Watt's, without the frogs, of course, without the frogs. And there is the addendum 'die Merde hat mich wieder' (p. 251).

 Hardly any of Beckett's narrative texts set out to tell a 'story', in the actual sense of the term, where the telling of a story is customarily the prime intent of a novel or any shorter form of narrative discourse. Instead, they seek to lay bare the narrative, or literary, process, throwing into relief the strategies and concerns of conventional storytelling, and they reflect the conditions for the possibility of composing narrative texts. If there really is such a phenomenon as postmodernist writing and if there is really such a species as a postmodernist writer, Beckett's place is decidedly among the postmodernists and not — as Hutcheon, McHale and others have it[27] — among the late-modernists. To be sure, Beckett's novels and shorter prose narratives do tell a story after all, quite rudimentary and idiosyncratic stories for the most part, but these stories are a means to a completely different end. It is consequently rather ill-advised if Beckett critics see their task as joining together the peculiar incidents in a Beckett novel so as to make them constitute a plot. Beckett himself has repudiated and surmounted narration in the traditional sense. The novels, in particular the trilogy, thematise the process of writing itself.

The narrator-figures in *Molloy, Malone Dies* and *The Unnamable* personify consciousnesses that are desperately and indefatigably trying to find the right word in order to be able to lapse into silence once and for all. At the same time, there is the problem that to be silent means death, non-existence. While this may be a consummation devoutly to be wished, it is also a condition exceedingly to be dreaded. The narratorial voices spend their time inventing stories and telling these to themselves or — like Molloy and Moran in *Molloy* — treating of circular quests that, at first sight, serve towards finding self in finding the other. However, I believe that Beckett employs such basic situations for reflecting on aspects of novel-writing.

The two parts of *Molloy, i.e. Molloy and Moran,* are related to each other in such an artificially calculated manner as to countermand any impression that something is being delineated which really occurred. What is offered in the Molloy part is trivialised as superfluous through parallelism and echoes in the Moran part. Part I deliberately leaves a whole host of questions open. Normally in a novel these would be resolved by what follows. But such reader expectation is intentionally thwarted by Part II and thus exposed as a mere convention. Beckett critically engages with the styles and thematic preoccupations of literary precursors, such as Proust and Joyce, for instance, with regard to the use of the first-person narrator, but, more importantly, with regard to the question of identity. The theme of personal identity becomes fictionalised, and the awareness of lost identity does not — as in Proust — result in a search, or a quest, for identity, nor is memory turned into the medium through which it can be found. The illusory nature of such a search is starkly laid open.

In *Malone Dies*, plot — as generally conceived — has been shrunk to a minimum. Plot here has been turned into an object of overt manipulation. Where there were two rudimentary 'stories' in *Molloy*, we now have a great many story fragments, each one of a conspicuously variable kind. The first-person narrator continually refers to himself, only to negate the reference in the same breath. Plot as a formal device of narrative discourse is first flaunted through the manner in which it is being built up and then destroyed, thus revealing it in its artificial design as a mere convention. To gear every part and every thing towards one preordained end is a cast-iron law in conventional novel-writing. In *Malone Dies*, though, such orienting is abandoned, and the concept of chronological time underlying it is replaced by the notion of time having stopped. The concentration on, as it were, the technical side of writing provides an opportunity for writing about writing, in a fictional context

In *The Unnamable*, writing about writing, or the metafictional nature of the novel, has been pushed to such a degree that plot is merely a residue of what in the preceding parts of the trilogy remained after the efforts at dismantling it. Beckett here, to a considerable extent, engages with his own writings, proffering things familiar and focusing on the process of aesthetic reception. Reader response and reader participation as part of the communicative act between text and reader is made an integral part of the narrative itself. The novel continually ponders fragments of stories that have already been told and discusses questions that must precede all writing. The medium of reflection incessantly tries to catch hold of itself. Beckett forces writing into a dead end in order to surmount the impasse through writing.

If conventional, or traditional, narrative methods are to no avail, can empirical reality be accommodated through, and in, narrative discourse at all? That, in part, is the question Beckett attends to in his trilogy. It is of course the question that dominates much of *Ulysses*. *Molloy* (1959)[28] focuses in its two parts on two characters, Molloy and Moran, who have lost, or are in the process of losing, their identities, which circumstance is expressed, for instance, through their physical disintegration. 'To decompose', Molloy comments, 'is to live too, I know, I know, don't torment me, but one sometimes forgets' (p. 26). Molloy hopes to discover himself in a quest for his mother, while Moran seeks to follow suit in his quest for Molloy. Furthermore, both characters attempt to find their identities by a process of committing their past experiences to paper. But when Moran begins his part, stating: 'It is midnight. The rain is beating on the windows' (p. 99) and finishes his account with these words: 'I went back to the house and wrote, It is midnight. The rain is beating on the windows. It was not midnight. It was not raining' (p. 189), this means several things. Firstly, it suggests that Moran's quest is circular, and the circularity may indicate futility. Secondly, the contradiction involved here casts doubt on the reliability of Moran's way of telling. If, as the last two sentences seem to imply, he lied with his opening statements, why should the rest be true? Moreover, is Moran lying intentionally throughout? Or is he simply incapable of telling the truth about periods of his past, having only words to rely on? In other words, is the quest for accommodating reality through narrative bound to fail from the start?

*Molloy* demonstrates the impossibility of discovering one's identity or transfixing reality by means of report and description as well as rational analysis and elucidation. The novel replaces the classic point-of-view of the (quasi-)omniscient narrator, operative in *Murphy* and *Watt*, with an isolated first-person stance that finds its psychologically determined means of representation in the monologue. As a result, the 'I' becomes its own subject and partner, its own medium of experience and cognition. Reduced and disconnected, it strives towards comprehending its situation. The reason for writing is the monologuist's re-assessment of himself and of a world that constantly eludes his grasp. The only fixed point is the first-person narrator who has to locate himself in space and time and who, like most Beckett characters at the start of their monologues, has to legitimise himself by a successive reappraisal of his past in order to obtain clarity about his place in the world. Molloy begins thus:

> I am in my mother's room. It's I who live there now. I didn't know how I got there. Perhaps in an ambulance, certainly a vehicle of some kind. I was helped. I'd never have got there alone. [...] What I'd like now is to speak of the things that are left, say my goodbyes, finish dying. (p. 7)

Here and elsewhere, Molloy is looking in his world and in his recollections for proof of his own existence. The apodictic note of the initial two sentences soon gives way to insecurity and doubt.

A continuous, ordered and exact rendering of things seen and lived through, of facts, is intended to stop the dissolution of the world outside. The precise dating of incidents is meant to suggest a consecutive sequence and order of things. But before long, the carefully and fastidiously introduced time and dates grow hesitant and uncertain; memory begins to fail; the occurrences become hazy and confused; mistakes cast doubt on the credibility of the account, and the narrator has to face up to the inaccuracy of his contentions and descriptions. Reality eludes his grasp:

> The pale gloom of rainy days was better fitted to my taste, no, that's not it, to my humour, no, that's not it either. I had neither taste nor humour. (p. 31)

Part of the dilemma is that the narrator has to rely on language to convey his dilemma, and the problem is that the names are not the things themselves:

> [...] there could be no things but nameless things, no names but
> thingless names. [...] All I know is what the words know, and the
> dead things, and that makes a handsome little sum, with a
> beginning, a middle and an end as in the well-built phrase and the
> long sonata of the dead. (p. 33)

Every so often, Molloy — and the same goes for Moran — has to tell
himself:

> [...] wrong, very rightly wrong. You invent nothing, you think you
> are inventing, you think you are escaping, and all you do is stammer
> out your lesson, the remnants of a pensum one day got by heart
> and long forgotten, life without tears, as it is wept. To hell with it
> anyway. (p. 33)

To be sure, there are occasionally, as at the beginning of Part I, short
sentences that appear to refer to unquestionable facts; soon, however,
statement and counter-statement confront one another: 'A little dog
followed him, a pomeranian I think, but I don't think so' (p. 12). The
narrator is incapable of coming down in favour of one version, and so
he offers them both in order to complete the picture: 'I went on my
way, that way of which I knew nothing, qua way, which was nothing
more than a surface, bright or dark, smooth or rough, and always dear
to me [...]' (p. 27). Or there is the case of Lousse's parrot:

> He exclaimed from time to time, Fuck the son of a bitch, fuck
> the son of a bitch. He must have belonged to an American sailor,
> before he belonged to Lousse. Pets often change masters. He
> didn't say much else. No, I'm wrong, he also said, Putain de merde!
> He must have belonged to a French sailor before he belonged to
> the American sailor. Putain de merde! Unless he had hit on it
> alone, it wouldn't surprise me. Lousse tried to make him say, Pretty
> Polly! I think it was too late. (p. 39)

The efforts at making the account, through supplementing and restricting
or varying what is stated, proceed in a series of qualifications and
specifications that seem to bespeak an unsatisfactory striving after
accuracy and explicitness as well as a yearning for an infallible

apprehension and a sure representation of reality. At the same time, these efforts betray an utter helplessness, an acknowledgement of an omnipresent insecurity that a restless endeavour to utter is designed to camouflage and transcend.[29] The onerous and painful search, or quest, for the exact word as suggested by the tentative, groping style of narration, corresponds to the actual quest of the characters, of course. In Beckett, particularly from *Molloy* onwards, narrative discourse that aims at verisimilitude and credibility is portrayed as futile because of its essential inability to convey truth and reality in the actual sense. Since the narrator's efforts at mimetic representation are shown to be pointless, description is occasionally dismissed out of hand from the start or postponed until a later time, them kept in suspension and finally never realised:

> The house where Lousse lived. Must I describe it? I don't think so. I won't, that's all I know, for the moment. Perhaps later on, if I get to know it. And Lousse? Must I describe her? I suppose so. (p. 37).

But the house is never adequately described, nor is Lousse, or to be exact, only some twenty pages later (p. 59). The narrative procedure is aptly characterised by Molloy himself, when he notes: '[...] whatever I said it was never enough and always too much' (p. 36).

Beckett's characters are rationalists, strange as it may sound. They are rationalists who, in their mania to know and fathom everything, are constantly reasoning, discussing and analysing. As was the case with Watt, so with Molloy (and by the same token Moran) the most trifling phenomenon in the world outside initiates elaborate intellectual processes. Thus his encounter with the two men A and C, or his release from police custody gives rise to endless deliberation and questioning; the sight of a herd of sheep or of the rising moon forces him to embark on complicated speculations that combine logical possibilities by the principle of disjunction; he embarks to such an extent that he forgets to finish the description, reminding himself: '[...] what suits me, at the moment, is to be done with the business of the moon which was left unfinished' (p. 43); or the contemplation of simple objects elicits a great many hypotheses, deductions and conclusions in an attempt to account for their appearance and use. This need for information about the world with the help of logic finds expression in two manners of abstracting from the concrete: the conversion of facts into numbers and of facts into logical possibilities. The mathematical approach signifies the narrator's desire to escape from the disordered and contingent world of empirical reality into a realm the inner relations of which are determined once and for all, where, in other words, the arbitrariness of life can be surmounted. That is why Molloy spends a considerable amount of time on working out how to distribute his sixteen sucking-stones between four pockets (cf. pp. 73–79), or how to eat five biscuits in 120 different ways. Or take the number of Molloy's farts:

> One day I counted them. Three hundred and fifteen farts in nineteen hours, or an average of over sixteen farts an hour. After all it's not excessive. Four farts every fifteen minutes. It's nothing. Not even one fart every four minutes. It's unbelievable. Damn it, I hardly fart at all, I should never have mentioned it. Extraordinary how mathematics help you to know yourself. (pp. 31f.)

In so doing, Molloy and his fellow-rationalists appear to emulate the *Discourse de la Méthode* of Descartes, who figures in Beckett's early poem 'Whoroscope'.[30] But frequently Molloy and Moran grow weary of their own method of reasoning, and their efforts at deduction run their courses like automatic mechanisms. They are empty measures of a philosophical rhetoric that has been robbed of its objective and purpose. They are in fact turned into a parody of Descartes, circling without true sense or aim around their own procedural conditions. Pedantry and over-explicitness are characteristics of a mind that engages in intricate thought processes, analysing everything without ever arriving at any results, without ever making fresh discoveries. Molloy deliberates at great length on why the policemen let him go:

> Had I, without my knowledge, a friend at court? Had I, without knowing it, favourably impressed the sergeant? Had I succeeded in finding my mother and obtaining from her, or from the neighbours, partial confirmation of my statements? Were they of the opinion that it was useless to prosecute me? [etc.] (p. 25)

But all this questioning and reasoning ends up in the admission that '[a]ll that is incomprehensible' (p. 25). Again, it is a case of '[...] whatever I said it was never enough and always too much' (p. 36). Or as Moran rephrases it: 'It seemed to me that all language was an excess of language' (p. 125). At one point, he notes:

> Oh the stories I could tell you if I were easy. What a rabble in my head, what a gallery of moribunds. Murphy, Watt, Yerk, Mercier and all the others. I would never have believed that – yes, I believe it willingly. Stories, stories. I have not been able to tell them. I shall not be able to tell this one. (p. 147)

This, with a few negligible differences, is the situation of Malone and the Unnamable.

Malone, in *Malone Dies*, is rather outspoken as to his intentions. He is certain that he will 'soon be quite dead at last in spite of all',[31] and while waiting he will tell himself stories, 'if he can':

> They will not be the same kind of stories as hitherto, that is all. They will be neither beautiful nor ugly, they will be calm, there will be no ugliness or beauty or fever in them any more, they will be almost lifeless, like their teller. (p. 8)

Deliberating further on his plan, he makes the following decision:

> There will therefore be only three stories after all, that one [*i.e.* the story about a man and a woman], then the one about the animal, then the one about the thing, a stone probably. That is all very clear. Then I shall deal with my possessions. (p. 10)

Additionally, he wants to remind himself briefly of his present state before embarking on his stories. Consequently, what he will offer is: 'Present state, three stories, inventory, there' (p. 10). In the end, he never gets round to the stories about the animal and the stone, but he does furnish the other three items.

Malone can be observed creating a world, not trying to represent the world 'out there' or to come to grips with it. He brings about this world not through a reconstitution of his objective, factual experiences, but by means of his imagination. Imagining replaces recollecting. Tentative projecting and imaginative inventing take the place of actual experiences. The powers of the imagination become operative where perception and recollection show themselves to be inadequate, even useless. Malone seeks, by means of his imagination, to create a logical universe, to constitute his own past, which his memory denies him, to write his own fictional memoir in order to make sure of his own existence. The characters he invents are projections of his own self.

The creation of this *ersatz* world is intended to effect a model of existence, and only the narrative conventions of the traditional realistic novel can guarantee the realisation of such a project. The story about Saposcat, or Sapo, whom he later renames Macmann, employs these. Malone aims at a linear, consecutive concatenation of events for depicting Sapo's youth and adolescence; he delineates the characters in a fairly meticulous manner and is precise about places and times. The biographical account of Sapo is rather obviously indebted to the *Bildungsroman* genre: the efforts devoted to Sapo's *bildung*, or education, take up the main part of the events. But the appropriate generic scheme is parodied and reversed. Sapo is not reasonable and assiduous, as might be expected, but lazy and stupid. He is not granted inner enrichment; his journey through life is not marked by positive experiences and a successful coming to terms with the world, but by a series of sorry failures leading to general decline, until Sapo finally, as a scruffy tramp, ends up in a madhouse, of all places. The carefully introduced realistic details and traditional narrative conventions are subsequently cast into doubt, at times by self-reflexive comments. Meticulous milieu descriptions turn out to be a futile extravagance. Ignorance and indifference prevent the narrator from filling in gaps in his account. But then, Malone himself said his stories would not be 'the same kind of stories as hitherto' (p. 8). Once more, the concept of the omniscient narrator is being attacked.[32] The description of his present state as well as the inventory are no longer of use to Malone in his endeavour to find himself, and so, in the end, the text ('Gurgles of outflow', p. 117) just peters out.

In *The Unnamable*, the narrative 'I', like his predecessors in *Molloy* and *Malone Dies*, is engaged in the creation of an *ersatz* world, of an *ersatz* identity. He, too, seeks to bring to life, as it were, a little creature after his own image, or to form an image of himself in order to identify with it. Like Malone, the Unnamable is forced to acknowledge that an outer reality possessive of meaning can no longer exist even in one's imaginings. He consequently tries to evoke the residue of a man, a unicellular organism, one Worm, who, caught in empty space, lacks all mental and physical abilities and whom he can at first define negatively only as a nothing, a shapeless magma. Gradually he assumes human traits, such as ears and eyes; but he will never be an image of a human being, only an unrealised blueprint, remaining pure intention. To uncover the futile efforts of Malone and the Unnamable is to deny the claim of the kind of literature represented by their storytelling, basically a realistic variety, to be able to tell the truth.

In *The Unnamable*, the detachment from a reality that is apprehensible through the senses is complete. What is left is the 'I' that cannot be defined, that cannot define itself, locate itself in space and time, because it has not been given personal dates or other aspects of existence. The questions with which the novel opens: 'Where now? Who now? When now?'[33] bespeak an utter helplessness and an awareness of complete loss. The narrator cannot rely on any concept of reality, neither a reality perceived nor a reality remembered. Only as a desire, as an unreal possibility can components of a vanished reality be conjured up, for instance a place or a part of nature. The world depicted is the world of the mind, the world of the imagination. Hugh Kenner is probably right in defining the trilogy as carrying the Cartesian episte-mological process backwards, beginning with a bodily *je suis* — represented by the factual recollections of Molloy — and ending in a bare *cogito*.[34]

Still, however, even in *The Unnamable*, literature reflects the intention to discover the truth; the outcome, of course, is an admission of failure. Paradox, the paradox of wanting to give up and yet of forcing oneself to go on, governs the entire novel and finds expression in its very title. The Unnamable is really the one who is ineffable; his attempts to win back his lost position, to constitute a world and his self are doomed from the first. The Unnamable bodies forth the restless intellect that by thinking wishes to escape thinking. The efforts, ceaseless, futile and yet desperately trying to reach an end, are mirrored by the novel's structure, the formal principle of which is a kind of accelerated progression.[35] The process in its course gains momentum. Quite early on, the text is no longer divided into paragraphs; the Unnamable's utterances, so to speak, run on faster and faster, in an increasingly more uninterrupted and unconnected manner; full stops become more and more infrequent; sentences grow longer and longer, towards the end covering five and more pages.

We observe the Unnamable in the process of naming himself, of providing answers to the questions he poses at the outset: 'Where now? Who now? When now?' (p. 7). Everything we know about him we know because he tells us. But the narrator himself is actually ignorant, or largely ignorant, of himself, of his past and his future. 'What am I to do, what shall I do, what should I do, in my situation, how proceed?' (p. 7), he queries. Should he proceed in the manner of the academics and of Descartes, '[by] aporia pure and simple?'. Or ought he to proceed in the fashion of a sceptical Socrates, '[by] affirmations and negations invalidated as uttered, or sooner or later?' 'I', he says, after the initial three questions, obviously in the belief that it is indeed he himself who says 'I', and then denies that he believes it: 'Unbelieving'. 'Can't it be [...]? Perhaps [...] Perhaps [...] I seem [...] Can one [...]? I don't know [...] The fact would seem to be, [...] if [...] if [...]', all in the same first paragraph. By the time he and the reader come to the last line in the book, neither the Unnamable nor the reader is any the wiser with regard to his spatial situation: '[...] where I am, I don't know, I'll never know, in the silence you don't know [...]' (p. 132). There have, of course, been hypotheses: he is inside a skull or a head.[36] But none of the information he supplies about his location or whatever is ultimately credible. For he either contradicts himself sooner or later, or so qualifies an assertion with sceptical amendments that one feels permitted to suspend one's belief in the assertion.

In *The Unnamable*, Beckett has stripped away every detail of particularity and has preserved only the single element that is finally important: the Unnamable's talk.[37] The Unnamable speaks because he considers himself under an obligation to do so – an obligation he personifies as a 'master'. The subject of his speech is to be himself: 'It's of me now I must speak', but he is constrained to admit that he has been able to speak of, and about, himself only in the voices of '[all] these Murphys, Molloys and Malones', the voices of the characters that his imagination has brought forth. He has no language but the language of others, but their language is inadequate to the task of speaking about himself. To make matters worse, he has no information about himself. In order to speak of that which he must speak of, the Unnamable invents surrogates, for instance Mahood, in whose voice he speaks about what is sometimes called 'the without'. In a Mahood story, there is a world, there are people who live in places and get to other places. The first such story is about Mahood's one-legged trip back home; the second is the story of Mahood stuck in a jar. The first is a metaphor for the Unnamable's method of arriving at the place where he can in fact attempt to speak of himself. The second is a metaphor for the existence to which the Unnamable has been reduced: he is little more than a thing, an object.[38] The trouble, though, is that these *are* metaphors; they speak of the Unnamable at one remove; but one remove is not close enough to the true topic of speech, which is — or should be — 'I'.

Next, the Unnamable, in his Mahood-voice, continues the narrative of the man in the jar; but this time the man is Worm and not the Unnamable himself. Soon, however, the story flags and the Unnamable declares that there will be no more Mahood stories. Yet, no sooner is the Mahood voice ended than the Unnamable seems to hear Worm's voice:

> [...] he speaks of me, as if I were he, as if I were not he, both, and if I were others, one after another, he is the afflicted, I am far, do you hear him, he says I'm far, as if I were he, no, as if I were not he, for he is not far, he is here, it's he who speaks, he says it's I [etc.] (p. 121)

The Unnamable had hoped that by naming himself Worm, and then telling himself a story about Worm, he could finally achieve his ultimate purpose: to speak of himself. But Worm upsets the plan by refusing to stay a character in the story told by Mahood and becomes himself, on Mahood's demise, the teller of a story. After dismissing his two surrogates, the Unnamable now undertakes, on some thirty pages, the narration of, not a story so much as babble, talk which now moves closer to and now more distant from his own person. And yet, in the end, he is forced to confess: '[...] I don't know, I'll never know, in the silence you don't know, you must go on, I can't go on, I'll go on' (p. 132). The point is that the Unnamable's existence is his talk. He exists only in his speech; his being is his speaking.[39] But in order to be able to speak of himself in an effort to discover himself, he must stop inventing characters; for they are 'disguises' of his own authentic being. He must, in short, stop being an artist, for to be an artist is to fail. 'Try again', as Beckett has it, 'fail better'.

Beckett tried again in *How It Is*. After having — in a manner of speaking — deconstructed the art form of the novel, he sets out to create an alternative variety of narrative discourse. Greatly augmented here is the musical quality of the language, and features of a new form become conspicuous, consisting in the effort to overcome ordinary syntax — all conjunctions are missing —, to dispense with punctuation for the purpose of not only conveying a forced kind of speech that focuses solely on the most significant issues, but also to surmount the discursive aspect of language. Language in *How It Is* represents an approximation to an abstract, associative sort of language, the language of poetry. Rhythm is foregrounded; it is a pounding rhythm that throws into relief the dynamic quality of words. The traditional elements and conventions of narration, more or less completely eliminated in *The Unnamable*, seem to reconstitute themselves again, if merely in a minimal way.[40] A character, who is named and possessive of a body and physical abilities — movement, eating, drinking —, lives through a rudimentary series of incidents in a location that is comprehensible only as amorphous material. In the course of this series, this character comes into contact with another being, and thus encounter as a theme is established once more, after it had, in the previous novels, to give way to the theme of isolation. The three parts of the novel are named after this encounter: '[...] before Pim with Pim after Pim [...]'.[41] In contrast to the Unnamable, the narrator in *How It Is* succeeds in outlining a perceptible, albeit empty world, in discovering factuality and securing a restricted sense of his own existence. The recognition of the things that, in a most substantial way, go to make up a reality previously shown to have disappeared proves to be the new subject matter; their naming becomes the first step towards winning a language back. It is a nominal style of language, consisting mostly in a juxtaposition of nouns unconnected syntactically. The predominance of concrete nouns and the nearly complete absence of verbs indicate the lack of any speculative content as well as mental operations; furthermore, they reveal the style as an adequate means of representing an objective, concrete reality reduced to its essentials. Before too long, memory begins to stir again. Moments from the past, 'images', are activated. Then language starts attaining a reporting quality again; whole sentences begin to form; adjectives are being employed. Perception settles on the colourfulness of the world. Apart from concrete objects, the body of the protagonist is invested with especial significance as the medium of perception. His sense organs, hands, fingers, mouth, tongue are recurrently mentioned; they are the means of conquering space and all that it contains, which in a way is the only obligation the 'I' has to fulfil. In other words: to find out how it is, and then to go on from there, try again and fail better. After all, as Beckett himself was so keenly aware, there is

> [the] expression that there is nothing to express, nothing with which to express, nothing from which to express, no power to express, no desire to express, together with the obligation to express.

In a way, he was, until the end of his life, like the Unnamable, telling himself: 'I can't go on. I'll go on'.

# AIDAN HIGGINS

To some extent, Aidan Higgins's best writing was done at the beginning
of his literary career, with his first book, *Felo de Se* (1960) — later re-
issued as *Asylum & Other Stories* (1978) — and *Langrishe, Go Down* (1966).
In *Bornholm Night-Ferry* (1983), the writer Fitz bears a close affinity to
Higgins himself, and, in a self-reflexive, intertextual manner, Higgins's
books and writerly activities are alluded to and commented upon. Fitz,
interestingly enough, admits to Elin: 'You are even right about my *Werke*
— the early stuff was the best. I had the excitement then...'[1] Higgins's
subsequent books gave evidence that his creative energy was dissipating.
The reason for the qualitative decline is, to a large extent, his overriding
interest in an autobiographical kind of fiction.[2] Autobiography as fiction
harbours serious dangers if the material is not, by force of imagination,
subjected to a profound metamorphosis. The early books also make
use of Higgins's own experiences, but there, unlike the work that follows,
these experiences have, by dint of creative efforts, been transformed
into fictional events, events where the auto-biographical aspect has lost
its relevance. In his more recent work, particularly *Scenes From a Receding
Past* (1977) and *Bornholm Night-Ferry*, what is told has remained
autobiographical, but in an intensely whimsical way.

Furthermore, Higgins seems to have notable difficulty with shape.
His impressionistic, often associative and thoroughly disruptive manner
of putting his narratives together leaves the reader puzzling over the
possible *raison d'être* of the whole. Several instances could be cited: *Balcony
of Europe* (1972), *Scenes From a Receding Past* and *Bornholm Night-Ferry* are
among the worst examples. Even *Langrishe, Go Down*, which in formal
respects represents the most sober-headed of Higgins's efforts, is not
totally devoid of flaws, the love-affair between Otto and Imogen having
been given too much headway.

There is something distinctly odd about Higgins's narrative, or
descriptive, style. It is a style where purple passages rub shoulders with
instances of slack and tired writing. The stories in *Felo de Se*, for instance,
contain beautiful turns of phrase, but they are also fraught with
overwritten sections that read too clever by half and show Higgins
frantically straining for effect. Most peculiar about the style, though, is
that Higgins appears to have only one style, whether he is writing fiction,

essays or travelogue. Even his reviews are penned in the same flummoxing fashion. The pieces in Higgins's most recent two books have the same desultory compositional look as have *Scenes From a Receding Past*, *Balcony of Europe*, *Bornholm Night-Ferry*, and such stories as 'Lebensraum' and 'Tower and Angels'. One would think that a piece of travelogue calls for a different descriptive technique than a piece of imaginative narrative.

Some attempts have been made to come to grips with Higgins's *oeuvre* and art. Like Garfitt, most critics have noted that Higgins has abandoned linear narration in favour of 'contrasting, densely-packed blocks';[3] but hardly anyone has been able to suggest why Higgins chops up the old-fashioned way of putting a novel or a story together. Robin Skelton regards Higgins as an experimentalist *extraordinaire* in his search for 'the Total Book',[4] meaning in Barthes's sense a book that radically explores language. Skelton finds evidence of this search in the fact that the author employs such means as (1) shifting point of view and multiperspectivity; (2) the uniting of the books through recurrent phrases, themes, echoes; (3) intertextuality. But in the final analysis, there is pretty little to justify Skelton's claim. Bernard Share thinks that Higgins, though 'he admires Joyce and Beckett and other innovators,...is not himself an experimental novelist in the accepted sense: the narrator/ observer is too firmly installed for that'.[5] Whether or not the sense given by Share is in fact the *accepted* sense of the concept of an experimental novelist is more than contestable. Anthony Kerrigan contends that in 'Aidan Higgins we have the case of the Infallible and Infeasible Artist. (And ultimately Indefensible, in the sense that this type needs no justification...)'[6] Are there infallible artists? And why should this type and his creative efforts not need justification?

*

Most commentators have seen fit to contend that the stories in *Felo de Se* 'deal with the self-destructive impulses in man'.[7] 'Felo de Se' is in fact a line lifted from Beckett's *Murphy* and it means 'felony against the self', as Higgins has explained:

> ...in the old days you couldn't be buried in consecrated ground if you committed suicide. And in *Murphy* there is a butler who commits suicide, and they ask about this, and someone says, 'Felo de Se my arse'...[8]

Just as this butler does in *Murphy*, the characters in *Felo de Se* bring about their own end, often by actually committing or attempting to commit suicide or at least by living in a way that hastens their downfall.

Many of the stories deal with frustrated and perverted sexuality, for example 'Killachter Meadow', 'Lebensraum', 'Winter Offensive', or 'Tower and Angels'. For Higgins's characters, abnormal forms of sexuality are a manifestation of an inclination towards self-destruction. As in 'Nightfall on Cape Piscator', these forms are often associated with animal sexuality and animal imagery. Herr Bausch, in 'Winter Offensive', has a bullet head whose features squeeze themselves 'together in a veritable snout, on each side of which were arranged little bloodshot eyes' (p. 131). His preoccupation is venery. For the painter Irwin Pastern, in 'Tower and Angels', himself a figure of doom, the sexual act finally comes to represent a sacrifice from which he recoils. '*I am too old for this any more*', he thinks while journeying down south to his love-nest in Hirschhorn with Annelise von Fromar.

Troubled sexuality is frequently coupled with troubled minds, such as Helen's or Emily-May's in 'Killachter Meadow', or Pastern's or Vaschel's. The characters keenly sense the insignificance of their existence. Mr Boucher, in 'Asylum', brings to a point what most of them suffer from when he says: 'Sooner or later,..., we all come to rest in the ruins of ourselves' (p. 114); and Pastern similarly remarks: '...for every human being on earth life ends in themselves' (p. 167). The characters feel alienated, like Michael Alpin in 'Lebensraum', or Pastern; they feel they are thrown back upon themselves; they become aware that all this is their own fault. The outcome is frequently — as in Alpin's and Boucher's cases — a world-weariness that leads to mental collapse. Irwin Pastern is actually linked to the French actor and director Antonin Artaud, who is said to have lost his reason in Dublin Bay (p. 152); at the end of 'Tower and Angels', things fall apart in Pastern's mind.

*Langrishe, Go Down* is a mature, cosmopolitan and yet very Irish novel.[9] A good case can be made for *Langrishe, Go Down* as the most fully realised and historically complex of the Big House novels published in the second half of the twentieth century.[10] The godmothers and godfathers of *Langrishe, Go Down* are the modernists Virginia Woolf, Djuna Barnes, James Joyce, Marcel Proust, and Samuel Beckett, to whom he once wrote praising *Murphy*. Beckett reciprocated with the advice: 'Despair young, and never look back'.[11] On a different occasion, Beckett, to whom Higgins had sent the manuscript of 'Killachter Meadow' — the story that forms the nucleus of the novel —, remarked that he felt a 'floundering and a labouring…and above all a falsening of position' in parts of the story and admonished Higgins: 'Work, work, writing for nothing and yourself, don't make the silly mistake we all make of publishing too soon.'[12] In this case, at least, Higgins did not publish prematurely. Apart from some middle sections in Part II, the novel shows Higgins at his formal best.

Langrishe, Go Down is divided into three parts. Part I takes place in 1937, Part II in 1932, and Part III in 1938. In addition to the unequivocal placing in time of the parts, there are, in the first and last ones, repeated references to actual political events during the 1930s, such as the bombardment of Madrid[13] or the final downfall of Austria (p. 245). By these means, a political backdrop is established. Moreover, Parts I and II form a frame for the love affair between Imogen and Otto. While the world around Ireland is flung into political turmoil, the Langrishes go down and Imogen experiences her Indian summer. Failing to understand the ominous significance of what is going on, Imogen asks herself: 'What did it mean? That another senseless war was about to begin?' (p. 246). German troops pour into Austria, causing its downfall. Comparably, Otto Beck invades Springfield, causing Imogen's downfall. Conqueror Hitler is equated with conqueror Beck, who is brought into sadly ironic comparison with the conquering Protestant Ascendancy: Mr Langrishe liked to suck the juice out of oranges which he then chucked into the fire; Otto sucks the life out of Imogen and, metaphorically, discards her in a similar fashion. The political events form the backdrop to a self-willed conquest.

The novel begins with a superbly realised chapter, describing Helen Langrishe in a bus on her way back home after visiting her solicitor in Dublin. The form of the description mimics the thematic pre-occupations, form being content here and content being form. Helen is seized by paroxysms of nausea and claustrophobia; she feels hemmed in, caught like a caged animal, and the feelings are appropriately expressed through circular descriptive patterns, which are, for the greater part, generated by verbal repetition. For example, the first paragraph mentions at the beginning 'opaque bevelled glass' and 'a white face' watching Helen. The last sentence of the paragraph again refers to the glass and the face. In between this frame, things occur that make Helen feel 'her stomach beginning to turn over already' (p. 11). The second paragraph opens with a reference to Helen's gloves; the first sentence of the following paragraph has her take off the gloves. The same paragraph mentions that the newspapers 'ran war headlines: Venta Deldiabolo and

Portalrubio had fallen; Madrid had been bombed again...' (pp. 11f.).
Two paragraphs later, these headlines are repeated *verbatim*. A little later,
two consecutive paragraphs contain the phrase 'uneasy in the stomach'
(p. 12). Generally, the first couple of pages, up to the point where Helen
gets off the bus, abound with such circularity of design.

Helen feels queasy in the midst of common people, experiences
them 'all about her' (p. 11). The collective human warmth is 'stifling' to
her; the air in the bus is 'nauseous' and 'foul', the light 'bilious' (p. 12).
The world is in a bad way. It is obvious that Helen is suffering from a
terminal illness. She knows that she will 'not live to see another war' (p.
12). Repeatedly, her thoughts centre on death and the transient nature
of human life. When the bus goes into low gear, she thinks 'a change
before death' and also: 'Brief life,..., brief life, breathed on for a while,
allowed to live, then blotted out' (p. 17). Life is just a 'scourge' to her (p.
12). Never having experienced the love of a man, she abhors the sex-
talk she cannot avoid overhearing: 'In like a lion and out like a lamb' (p.
13). She is afraid of being stared at and eschews looking at people.

She has never been able to establish a sound relationship towards
the people in whose midst she and her sisters have been living, nor
towards the land. Although she has lived in the county all her life, she
does not know the 'bus-route on this by-road' (p. 18). Significantly,
neither has she been able to adopt an appropriate relationship towards
the history of the land (p. 39) and the history of her family: when the
old man, in Donycomper cemetery, speaks to her, Helen thinks: 'This
old man is speaking to me, telling me all over again the history of my
home that I never bothered to know; or, if I did by chance know it
once, did not bother to remember' (p. 41). Cut off from the people, the
land, its history and the history of her home, she lastly is constrained to
acknowledge that she is likewise cut off from its religion. Watching on
her way home the Keegan family reciting the Holy Rosary, she realises
what she is lacking — 'the faith of poor and oppressed Catholic Ireland
in the penal times' (p. 19). It is surely highly noteworthy that Mrs
Langrishe converted to the Roman Catholic faith. The Langrishe sisters
are Catholics. There is a tellingly ironic reversal involved here. The
Catholic Irish no longer adapt to the English, instead the Anglo-Irish
are unsuccessfully attempting integration with the Catholic community.
They have never belonged and this has led to a loss of history and
religion as well as identity.

For Helen, everything is in a miserable state. Political events augur
catastrophe; a Dublin welder has killed his girlfriend, severing the head

from her body with a cut-throat razor (cf. pp. 12 and 14); the wind is sighing and the pines are lamenting (p. 19), with the telegraph wires adding their *miserere* (p. 18). Helen is aware that 'the old impossible life [is] ending' (p. 19). Soon they will be old, old and ill and poor (cf. p. 71), and when they die, Helen reflects in bed, no one will mourn, and they will leave no trace. At the end of the novel, after Helen's coffin has been sunk into the grave, Imogen is also painfully concerned with the sad fact that they will leave 'little or no trace' (p. 243). The Langrishe world is falling down. Even the dog, friend to man, is 'untrustworthy' (p. 20). The cats are far from healthy and are deformed — one is suffering from an abscess on one eye and the other, appropriately for the virgin-spinsterish life of two of the sisters, from an ingrowing testicle (p. 23).

The novel, like the film *Forbidden Heaven* mentioned in the book, is about romance and pathos among four human derelicts, and Helen senses the connection (p. 33). All the Langrishes are '*moribund*' (p. 33). Suggestively, it is Helen who visits Donycomper cemetery. She has an increasing loathing of all living things (p. 76). 'Those who are dead now lie in the earth', she thinks, 'the living linger here; so much the worse for them' (pp. 36f.). She is thoroughly tired of her life and decides to spend the rest of it in bed. She has never known the love of the body or of the heart; the only passion she was able to experience was vicarious. Lying in bed and ruminating, she recalls phrases she read in Imogen's love letters to Otto, which she intercepted: 'My own dearest I am no good without you. Your lovely body. If I were close enough. Love of my life and all my senses' (p. 73). Finally, after a year of wasting away, hepatitis and a stroke put an end to her life — as Imogen reflects during the burial —, Helen goes away empty-handed. But even her going away is undignified, the tragicomic nature of her life being mirrored by the tragicomic nature of the burial: her coffin does not fit into the grave, which the gravediggers have dug wide enough and deep enough, but not long enough.

In a way, Helen and her sisters are a striking replica of their father, who, like Higgins's own Da, was 'the absentee landlord permanently in residence'.[14] Mr Langrishe had at one time shown pretences of running a farm, had advanced theories about farming and had tried to put these into operation, unfortunately, or not surprisingly, without success. The estate was then managed by a landsteward. Mr Langrishe henceforth gave up all pretence and applied himself to meditation and study, 'a mild, protected life out of the way of things' (pp. 50f.). But while he was broadening his mind, the estate went to rack and ruin. The history

of the Langrishe family and estate is succinctly summed up in the
outstanding character traits of Mr Langrishe — all of them betraying
'evidence of a wasteful, erratic nature' (p. 52) — wasteful and erratic as
Imogen after him.

The title of the novel seems to hint that the decline of the Langrishe
family and estate is the result of a categorical imperative.[15] Langrishe
has to go down because of an inborn self-destructive tendency, a
sadomasochistic relish in being victim, which is coupled with languor, a
deliberate withdrawal into stasis; or, as has become fashionable since
Joyce's *Dubliners*, what is ailing the country and the Langrishe family is
spiritual paralysis. The love affair of Otto Beck, who is greedy, selfish,
obscene in his powerful habits, intelligent, scornful of his mistress, no
more considerate of the property of others than the 'tinkerman' who
has taken over the lodge at the end of the novel, and Imogen, the seedy,
unawakened, lazy, unimaginative virgin in whom he kindles sexual fire,
is rightly accorded the main position in the book because this affair
offers interesting manifestations of the self-destructive tendency of
Higgins' spinster-sisters and epitomises the causes that have brought
them to their desolate position in which the horror of barren old age
and the fear of death are predominant features.

In chapters that alternate with those featuring Helen, Imogen is
introduced by dint of two interesting as well as telling aspects. One is
the remark that she 'had a little touch of natural colour on her cheeks.
An old love had put it there' (p. 28). The love affair with Otto is
anticipated thereby. The other is Imogen's strange dream. This is what
she tells Helen of it:

> I dreamt that Christ's body was discovered in the Ural Mountains
> outside a town called Vlannick, which I don't suppose exists. But
> later on in the dream it was me they had unearthed. I mean I was
> Him, two thousand years buried under the earth. What could
> that mean, do you suppose? (p. 26)

The dream of her merging with a dead body points to Imogen's vision
of her own death during Helen's burial. It further adds to the impact of
a death-laden narrative.[16] And still, why the identification with Christ?
Does she feel as if she had taken on the sorrows of the world?

Imogen is now, in 1937, a faded and jaded woman, no longer young,
all dressed in grey. She counsels herself: Do not look back (cf. p. 46); yet
this is exactly what she does, going through old documents, and reading

old letters, love letters that were never posted, and because they were never posted, Imogen was spared humiliation. Offers of marriage did not come her way. The money she and her sisters had was let dwindle away unstoppably. Her mother, an altogether more practical and clear-eyed person than her father, had explained that the inheritance which had come from property in America would not last into the third generation.

They have to fell and sell trees, always a sign of an estate's decline. The neglect of the orchard in Springfield is one example of how the isolation of the Big House becomes symbolic of the spinster-sisters' solitude: 'The rockery and the main garden grow wild; shrubs and grass hide the pathways; weeds proliferate everywhere' (p. 78). Otto Beck, analytical-minded and unwilling to accept anything without an explanation, wants to know the cause of the ruin of Springfield House. His mind boggles at the paradox that the resources are there and still nothing is made of them. 'Why fail?', he wants to know.

> I don't understand. You have seventy-four rich acres of land, ten
> of that in tillage. You had a herd of cattle once, a supply of eggs,
> pullets, a vegetable garden, a fruit garden, an orchard. You did
> not live riotously; so why had it to fail? (p. 180)

Imogen's answer cannot satisfy him:

> It was like this, Imogen explained. We found we couldn't go on
> running the place at a loss and pay the men their wages, so all but
> Feeney had to be dismissed. Galvin and Flynn drove the remains
> of the herd to Gavin Lowe's cattle-market in Dublin. That was
> their last job. (pp. 181f.)

Her inability to respond adequately to the changes around her makes her a perfect victim of circumstances. She is a typical exponent of the feckless, passive Anglo-Irish land-owning class.[17]

Similarly, she unwittingly also becomes a victim of circumstances in her affair with Otto, 'my dearest sweetheart, my life' (p. 67), who brings her to life for two springs, two summers, three autumns and two winters (p. 217). But as Helen, languishing away in her bed, knows, 'it broke her heart' (p. 73). Or did it? 'Are the memories of things really better than the things themselves?', Imogen wonders while reading her letters (p. 67). The relationship between Imogen and Otto is such that it reflects on both the troubled relationship between Ireland and England and between Europe and Hitler/fascism. At first, she is appalled by Otto's brutality, aggressiveness and possessiveness; and yet she more and more subjects herself to his dictates, quite willingly fitting in with his wishes. Her way of submitting to Otto equates her with the way Europe submitted to fascism.

Their first encounter bears all the marks of what is to come, throwing into relief both Imogen's and Otto's character traits and behavioural patterns. His self-introduction is determined, slightly boastful and priggish, and deceptively obsequious: 'Beck is my name. Otto Beck, student. At your service, he added, bowing.' (p. 85) True to her insecure self, she fidgets, 'her hands restless, touching herself with covetous gestures here and there, on hips, throat, cheeks, tendentious, patting her hair' (p. 85). The covetous patting of her body also bespeaks narcissistic tendencies, which are manifested in Imogen's habit of taking air-baths, the outlet of her sexual longings before Otto has arrived to quench her passion. They talk about stars and planets and, from the first, Otto starts parading his knowledge — Otto, a *'mine* of information' (p. 196). She is taken by him, having sensed 'the fire of life...burning in him, — lust and cruelty, too' (p. 88), and quickly she comes to the decision that she would not mind being his trollop.

> Him to be cruel to me, as such men are reputed; he could do anything he likes with me. What else is my soft woman's flesh good for? (p. 89)

Later she deceives herself by averring that she was attracted to him because he possesses her father's eyes (p. 105).

When Otto is in Springfield House for the first time, he feels like a poacher in the house of Irish Ascendancy. And a poacher he in fact is. The idea of a poacher in a house of Irish Ascendancy has a nice ironic touch to it, involving as it does a reversal of the Big House topic. He has his way with her; she becomes the abject slave of a foreign conqueror (cf. p. 160), like the English and the Irish, the latter exploited by the former; like Otto exploiting the Langrishe account when buying a bottle of John Jameson Green Label whiskey (p. 200), or when pilfering apples or boasting: 'Here am I,..., a *battler*, a poor scholar, with free lodging, free fuel, peace and quiet, all my corporal needs attended to...' (p. 204). The Protestant ascendancy are likewise poachers, so that in Imogen's case a member of the poaching class is being poached. Otto, in

Springfield House, scrutinises a dark print and thinks 'The Sacking of Rome' (p. 92), and he practises the sacking of Springfield House and of Imogen.

After the theatre, where no less significantly they have seen a play on the theme of the battle of the sexes, they are alone in his friend's flat, Otto goes straight for it. Later he tells Shannon and Maureen Layde that when the season is right for the woman, the man is always and ever 'negotiable' to a woman's needs. All the fumblings to get there are 'all so much humbug' (p. 118). A short time afterwards, she becomes his slave and doormat and is proud of it (p. 133). The first sex is no success, but she goes through with it, casting all bashfulness to the winds. Then he can do with her what he wishes; he has his way at all costs in everything, and even though she is mortally ashamed, she does not gainsay him. She loves him to distraction — 'Oh, Otto Beck, what have you done to me?' (p. 182) —, but he realises pretty quickly that she is just 'another victim of circumstances' (p. 177).

After a little over a year, the affair deteriorates. In a series of narrative sections consisting of small units and making up the middle of Part II, the falling asunder of the relationship is shown. Words of endearment make room for criticism and abuse. First he calls her an ignoramus (p. 168), then an imbecile (p. 191); she is too soft for him, terribly soft; they quarrel over apples, which is odd because Imogen has no qualms about furnishing the lodge for him, providing food and offering herself. Otto becomes increasingly bored (p. 198); and since he has from early on established his superiority in everything, including the handling of their affair, she realises that her hold on the relationship is very frail. At last, she feels no better than a whore. Otto becomes irritated by her presence; her manner of eating oranges is irritating to him, and so is her way of dealing with spaghetti (p. 220). Finally, one Sunday in October, Otto shoulders his haversack and, as it were, ditches Imogen and leaves her for a fresh and more rewarding affair with a younger woman. Imogen feels miserable beyond words.

Once Otto told her that he would be 'most annoyed' if she found herself pregnant (p. 207). Since he decidedly refused to use condoms, this is precisely how she finds herself when he is gone. Bearing the child turns out to put an extraordinary strain on her. Then the baby dies, is stillborn, and she is now known as '*the* Miss Imogen of Springfield, the scandalous one' (p. 234). Having been made miserable by Otto, who told her his tall tales and put his invincible mailed fist on woman's weakness (p. 253), she feels utterly lost, wishing that this winter would never end. During Helen's funeral she is assailed by a vision of her crawling into the earth through a hole in the wall that separates Mangan's field and Killadoon estate. It is a vision of her own death, the Langrishes being all *moribundi* indeed. The vision also suggests Imogen's sense of claustrophobia, which she shares with Helen: both feel trapped in a world that has become unhinged.

Why should Imogen's conqueror be a German? Otto is the very essence of fascism. Otto comes into Imogen's life in 1932, the same year that Hitler came to power.[18] Otto dominates Imogen, humiliates her and finally drops her aging body when fresh sexual occasion arises. The manner in which Otto despises and oppresses Imogen is comparable to the manner in which fascism regarded Europe.

Otto says he is indifferent to politics, denigrating the Nazis as 'a lot of beer-thumping louts' (p. 142); yet he himself talks of 'culturally inferior nations' and of 'culturally insignificant' individuals (p. 159). He claims to have studied under Husserl and Heidegger, claims, too, to have led the poor life of a scholar. He is the same, front and back, palindromic Otto. Allegedly engaged in investigations into seventeenth-century Ireland and Irish customs of that time and earlier, he does not appear to make much progress in his studies. True enough, he has a piece on 'Symbolism in Grimm' published in *Fortnightly Review*, but he considers the article worthless, feeling that his career is on the downgrade. For at least two years, while staying in the lodge, he has laboured over his thesis, yet before he leaves he tells Imogen that he will need another year or two to finish it.

Otto possesses the streaks of a predator. He has wicked lizard's eyes (p. 152) and is capable of committing violent depredation on the chastity of any female (p. 153). He is a fowler, conscript, prowler, gaolbird, fisher in prohibited waters (p. 153). His odious philosophy is 'eat and the appetite comes' (p. 161); he can see poultry and game only as potential dinners, his eyes on the white breast-meat. 'And on mine, too', Imogen thinks (p. 171). Of a violent, aggressive nature, he takes delight in senseless slaughter, killing rabbits for fun, shooting squirrels for the hell of it, cutting a wasp in half with a pair of scissors just for the kick it gives him. His first sexual experiences he had when still quite young — in Munich, during the school holidays. At twenty-two, he had a love affair with a seventeen-year-old girl. A child was born, a boy; Otto did not even care to see him once. Now at thirty-five, he fathers another child with another woman, and again could not care less. Over the mantelpiece in the lodge, he has three pictures — two by Munch,

'Jealousy' and 'Nude with Red Hair', which possess a sly reference to Imogen's jealousy, permissiveness and lasciviousness, and one showing an unnamed volcano belching fire and smoke, like Otto himself. Worst of all, he is a despicable hypocrite. Irish women are so pure, he tells Imogen.

> A man might sometimes have filthy thoughts about girls. That's natural enough. But when I meet Irish girls and can recognize at once their essential purity, then I am touched, incapable of base thought. (p. 211)

He says it, has base thoughts and makes Imogen do the most unnatural things, which she does 'not at first permit', nor at any later time relish. But dissent or assent, it is all the same to Otto.

The last chapter of the novel has Imogen visit the lodge again. She notices that the place has once more been invaded; someone is living there. A scene of even greater squalor confronts her, suggesting further decline, but likewise further intrusion into the moribund world of the Ascendancy. It is a final reminder of the end of the old impossible life as of her folly. But it, as well as the entire book, is also a reminder of the decline of a significant part of Irish culture, a decline seen in connection with the decline of free Europe.

*Balcony of Europe* represents a rather hapless attempt at experimenting with narrative discourse, sequential narration having been replaced by a spatial arrangement of disparate materials.[19] For the greater part, the book is as whimsical as the decision to set the 'N' in the title the wrong way round. The chronology of events is no less whimsical — whimsical because it does little to lend additional significance to what is being offered. Part I is set in 1961, or to be more precise in the autumn of 1961. It contains a confused and desultory amalgamation of bits and pieces concerning Ruttle's parents, his adolescence and his first years as a married man in Dun Laoghaire — spitfire pyrotechnics that fizzle out as soon as they have been fired off.

Part II is set in Andalusia in the spring of 1963. Ruttle has been having an affair with a married woman, American-born Charlotte Bayless, the culmination of which lay in the winter of 1962 (Part III). Part IV takes place in the summer of 1963, and Part V ('Autumn 1963 and after') finally brings the Ruttles back to Ireland. The affair is the thing, and it is rendered in a curiously circumstantial manner, so that one is frequently tempted to ask oneself whether one really has to know all that one is being offered, rejected epigraphs and all. Even Brendan Behan is suffered to put in two appearances (pp. 90, 412ff.), and Higgins does not shy away from including a remark to the effect that 'Dev and Hirohito sent messages of sympathy when Odin died to the strains of Bruckner and Wagner's *Liebestod*' (p. 97).

All that remains in the mind after finishing the book is a variegated group of characters, some impressive and some trite. The pity, though, is that they do not add up to anything of note. Higgins's effort at emulating Ford Madox Ford's brilliant tale of passion — *The Good Soldier*, explicitly referred to in the text: 'I was finishing *The Good Soldier (A Tale of Passion)*. I was finishing with her [i.e. Charlotte] too' — must be regarded as a failure.

*Scenes from a Receding Past* is a rather Proustian book of memory without Proust's artistic verve, a book of impressions about the past that build up and fade away, at times recurring in the same or a modulated form. As the title suggests, the whole basically represents a series of scenes. Higgins's narrative style is Impressionism pure and simple — Impressionism of the kind practised by Ford Madox Ford. But whereas Ford did not merely pile up a mass, or mess, of impressions, but rather organised them so as to effect what he called a *progression d'effet*, Higgins's efforts seem to be devoid of any organisational *raison d'être*, bringing about something that, on account of its looseness and randomness, has the air of being the bookish equivalent of a novelist's notebook.[20]

The narrative falls into two parts. The first recreates an Irish childhood and adolescence in a town in County Sligo, which, as the author tells us, is really the Celbridge of his youth. The childhood is nothing extraordinary in terms of Irish childhoods —religion, nuns, Laus Deo Semper, the Bogey Man, sweaty dreams, masturbation, madness in the family. Part II offers an extension of that childhood into adult life, featuring among other things Senator Yeats in a cinema and Ralph Richardson in a black Rolls Royce. Such quirks and a quotation of the opening lines of Rilke's *Duino Elegies* notwithstanding, the highlight of the second half is Dan Ruttle's courtship with and marriage to Olivia, which fact places *Scenes from a Receding Past* in Higgins's *oeuvre* before *Balcony of Europe*. Indeed, at the end of *Scenes from a Receding Past*, Ruttle and Olivia set off for Andalusia.

Part I tries to capture the maturing consciousness of the narrator by means of his growing command of language. The attempt very much echoes back to Joyce's efforts in *A Portrait*. There is even such a Joycean passage as this one:

Dan Ruttle,
Nullamore,
Sligo,
Ireland.[21]

It looks at first as if, in the course of the initial couple of pages, there were a surreptitious development in the diction. But if there is, or is meant to be, the development is too surreptitious to become discernibly effectual. Moreover, there are some scenes and impressions that, though they may have had their moments for Ruttle, or Higgins, can scarcely claim to be of general interest.

What stays in the mind after reading this agglomeration of questionable matter are basically three things. First, the language occasionally manages to acquire a truly poetic quality, for instance at the end of Part I. Second, Wally's mental disturbance is rendered in a capturing and impressive manner. Third, near the end, when Ruttle tells of his life with Olivia, there is clearly notable an effort to revive scenes previously dealt with, impressions recurring sometimes in the same context or form, then in different surroundings. It is as if the narrator, by going back to certain impressions, is trying to get it right the second time around, or is making the point that the truth resides in the fact that impressions are deceptive, changing their constituents, appropriating aspects of different impressions.

*Bornholm Night-Ferry* is first and foremost a book about love, about the way in which two people try to come to an understanding of each other, and all the difficulties such an undertaking involves.[22] In an interview in *The Irish Times* soon after the publication of the novel, Higgins said: 'It's about love, but not a hopeful love. But I can't write about happiness, only about loss.'[23] The love aspect is predominant, but *Bornholm Night-Ferry* also shows Higgins very much concerned with his own position and activities as a writer. It is an intensely self-reflexive book, although the way Higgins puts words of approval and appraisal of his own books into the letters of Elin at times appears slightly self-adulatory. In her second letter, Elin refers to 'Tower and Angels' from *Felo de Se* (pp. 19 and 50). Also 'Lebensraum' is evoked by Elin's mention of Sevi's last abuse (p. 77), as are *Langrishe, Go Down* and *Balcony of Europe* (pp. 15, 88). Most conspicuously, the agony of the writing process is made the major theme of the novel. Fitz and also Elin are shown attempting to formulate their thoughts, trying to find the right words. *Bornholm Night-Ferry* could thus be read as a deeply postmodernist book, in spite of the fact that it is above all a love story in letters. Notably enough, the two thematic concerns are related. The struggle for fulfilment in love is linked to the struggle for creative success — quite a common linkage in postmodernist narratives. The agonised love affair equals Higgins's writerly agonies. The love affair is above all an affair of letters and words. Words become a substitute for real life.[24] The novel celebrates the power of words. As both Elin and Fitz point out, words can create illusions, build up fantasies and dream worlds, glorify the profane and mundane, but they can also lie and distort reality.[25]

In *Ronda Gorge & Other Precipices* (1989) Higgins proffers commonplace facts, sprawling and circumlocutory associations, pearls of wisdom and arcana, compelling descriptive passages, and he blends all this with forays into airy nothings. A reader must invariably come to the conclusion that Higgins is in the habit of writing down whatever comes into his mind. *Scenes from a Receding Past* and *Bornholm Night-Ferry* read as if the author had simply copied out his notebooks from start to finish. Much of *Ronda Gorge & Other Precipices* reads the same. Sections in the book, such as the reprinted 'Images of Africa', '*Sommerspiele*, Munich, 1972', or 'Berlin Days and Nights: Letters from Lindermann',[26] are constituted by brief units. There is nothing to be said against splitting up a piece in this manner. But the units should contribute to an image, an impression, an idea. Even the different images of Africa should, in the diversity of their views, cohere in some way. As it is, they drift apart and the centre cannot hold.

*Helsingor Station & Other Departures* (1989) is fraught with similar deficiencies. Take 'Sodden Fields' and the novella-length 'The Bird I Fancied'. It is all very well to string together a large number of bits and pieces which have one fact in common, as for example in 'Sodden Fields'; that is, they pertain to the same point in time. But what are they meant to signify — alone and together? In 'Sodden Fields', Higgins — or his narratorial substitute — asks:

> Are we not all somebody's rearings in the wretched bric-à-brac and rigmarole of history, of which our life may be assigned some part, however minor, if only as passive bystanders?[27]

This idea is reason enough for him to begin his autobiographical sketch with an interminable enumeration of historical events which took place in 1927, the year in which he was born, such as that in 'Trinity College, Dublin, a Bachelor of Arts degree was conferred upon Samuel Barclay

Beckett' (p. 47), or that 'King Ferdinand I of Romania, the second Hohenzollern king, died of cancer of the bowel in Bucharest' (p. 47). One is flabbergasted at the stupendous richness of details amassed by Higgins. But yet again, what are these details intended to convey? 'What do you do when memory begins to go? I spend much of my time looking back into the past. It is no longer there. It has moved. Where to?' (p. 49). Higgins once again seeks to transfix the past and by doing so find out who he is. He conjures up '*movements from the past*', and a few pictures emerge into the light 'from the shadows within [him]' (p. 44).

In the longish middle section more pictures form. They are held together — if that is the term — by the fact that the town of Kinsale features in all of them. Higgins takes an imaginary walk around Kinsale with someone he addresses as 'you', though without identifying that person. Thoughts of the Battle of Kinsale and of moments from the ancient Celtic world spring to his mind. Added to these are fictionalised sections centring upon a couple of boozers in assorted pubs, for instance Paddy Lock, who is standing 'like a horse at the bar' (p. 61). What seems to emerge here as a *raison d'être* is something akin to the idea informing the 'Wandering Rocks' episode in *Ulysses*.

In the Preface to *The Spoils of Poynton*, Henry James asserts that 'life [is] all inclusion and confusion and art [is] all discrimination and selection...' If the 'master' is right, then Aidan Higgins' latest novel, *Lions of the Grunewald* (1993), represents life in the form of a book. Here is almost everything and anything, thrown together in a carnival frolic: autobiography, fictional autobiography (for instance, the main character was born in the same year as Higgins and grew up in County Kildare), fiction, fact and faction, travelogue; Samuel Beckett (said to have sported a cockatoo hair-do), James Joyce, Günter Grass, Max Frisch, Harold Pinter (wearing a black turtle-neck sweater and demanding whisky); even I figure in it by name: in the chapter 'At the Philharmonie', where Higgins, mimicking Joyce, gives an almost interminable list of names of the persons said to have attended a series of concerts, one reads 'Imhof *und* Kamm'. Thanks, Aidan, for giving me a mention! By nature the narrative is more akin to Bakhtin's idea of a literary carnival, of the polyphonic novel or heteroglossia, which, instead of featuring just one kind of discourse, allows a variety of discourses into a textual space.

*Lions of the Grunewald* bears some resemblance to Higgins's *Balcony of Europe*, itself characterised by heteroglossia. *Lions* features an Irish writer, Dallan Weaver, of Trinity College, Dublin, who arrives in Berlin with wife and son to take up a one-year appointment as a 'professor' with an organisation called 'Deutsche-Internationale Literatur-Dienst Organisation' (DILDO for short). Weaver falls prey to the charms of 28-year-old Lore, with whom he engages in priapic fumblings in doorways and ditches. But whereas in *Balcony* Higgins was rather po-faced in presenting his material, even listing rejected epigraphs (why give them when they are rejected?), here he is unmistakably enjoying himself with words beyond words. 'DILDO' is a pointer in the direction of how the love affair is treated: as farce, though only some of the time. In places, it is also couched in the form of a courtly romance. The manner in which the affair and other matters are presented paradoxically exploits a rich variety of literary genres and styles, with the author wilily winking. There is, at the outset, a long list of the bountiful cast, which numbers a golden retriever and slyly imitates the strategy to be found in the large, loose, baggy monsters of the previous century.

But Weaver's raunchy relationship with Lore constitutes only half the book. The complementing part attempts a panoramic view of the riven city of Berlin in the 1970s, long before the wall came down. When the lovers pay a brief visit to Spain, where significantly they feel they are Hemingway characters, different local colour is added, and Weaver's sojourn in Munich during the time of the Olympic Games introduces Bavaria, with its foaming steins and eternal sausages, as Matthew Arnold had it.

The trouble with the book is that one may find oneself at a loss as to what to make of it as a whole. The main problem it poses is one of coherence. The playful spirit that suffuses it is all very well; in the end, though, *Lions* reads like a series of set-pieces, or more or less separate scenes from a receding past.

\*

The role of memory, Mmnemosyne that lying whore, is central to a good deal of Higgins's fiction, as demonstrated most recently by the three volumes of autobiography Higgins has published: *Donkey's Years* (1995), *Dog Days* (1998) and *The Whole Hog* (2000). 'Is the memory of things better than the things themselves? We will never know' (p. 100), Higgins asks in 'Helsingor Station'. Imogen Langrishe had already been occupied with the same thought. It may be true. But what is equally true is that memory alone, memory unhoned by the imagination, the skill and the sense of the artist makes for poor literature, least of all for good fiction.

# JOHN BANVILLE

John Banville was born in Wexford on 8 December 1945, and he grew up there. He was educated at Christian Brothers' schools and at St Peter's College in Wexford. He has worked in journalism since 1969 and has been literary editor of *The Irish Times* since 1988. He has published eleven books of fiction, as well as a number of short stories in literary magazines. His adaptation of Heinrich von Kleist's *Der zerbrochene Krug* (The Broken Jug) was premiered in Dublin at the Peacock in June 1994. He is a member of Aosdána, the Irish affiliation of artists who have been honoured by the national Arts Council. *The Newton Letter* was filmed for Channel Four television as *Reflections*. Among the awards that Banville's books have won are the Allied Irish Banks Fiction Prize, the American-Irish Foundation Award, the James Tait Black Memorial Prize, and the Guardian Fiction Prize. In 1989, *The Book of Evidence* was short-listed for the Booker Prize and was awarded the first Guinness Peat Aviation Award; in Italian, as *La Spiegazione dei Fatti*, the book was awarded the 1991 Premio Ennio Plaiano. *Ghosts* was short-listed for the Whitbread Fiction Prize in 1993. In 1997 Banville received the Lannan Literary Award for fiction.

Banville's first book, *Long Lankin* (1970), consists of nine short stories and the novella '*The Possessed*'. Thematically, the narratives have at least two aspects in common: they feature characters who are caught up in the hell of a peculiar guilt, and in each a particular *persona* acts as the Long Lankin figure, intruding upon human relationships and severing them. Long Lankin was a mason in an old Scottish ballad ('Lamkin' in F.J. Child's *The English and Scottish Popular Ballads*, vol. II) who, seeking revenge for not having been paid by Lord Wearie, forces his way into the lord's castle and kills Wearie's wife and son. The narratives are grouped with respect to the age of the principal characters — childhood, adolescence, middle age — and the area of public life, recalling the organising principle of Joyce's *Dubliners*. '*The Possessed*' focuses on public life. Livia Gold, who punishes herself for the death of her small son, holds a very Irish party. Present at the event, in addition to characters from the stories, are Ben White, a writer, and his sister, Flora, for whom he has incestuous feelings. Their make-believe world has maimed them both, rendering it impossible for them to act without being bruised by reality. White is in the role of a catalyst for the others, each of whom is seeking to be cleansed. The novella is indebted to Joyce and, even more so, to the great Russian novelists, especially to Dostoevsky and his novel *The Devils* (1871), also known by the title of '*The Possessed*'. *Long Lankin*, above all on account of the novella (which Banville did not include in the revised edition of 1984), may have certain flaws as a result of Banville's thinking that he was being sophisticated when he was not, but the book clearly marked the debut of a major writer.

The title of his first novel, *Nightspawn* (1971), involves a pun: 'night spawn', night's pawn', and 'knight's pawn', heralding the ludic nature of the whole book. *Nightspawn* plays with literary conventions in order to show their exhaustive nature. *Nightspawn* is an inside-out novel, one of the very few metanovels to have come out of Ireland. Ben White tells of a *coup d'état* in Greece and his embroilment therein. White is a writer; in fact, he is Ben White of '*The Possessed*', and he succeeds in working his account into a gripping thriller. But *Nightspawn* is anything but a straightforward thriller; it is rather a parody of the narrative genre. Most scenes end in farce. Behind all the parodying, behind the playful turning upside-down of conventions and self-reflexive commenting, there lies a most serious intention: the age-old desire of the artist to express things in their essence, to transfix beauty and truth. Like Beckett's narrators, White permanently urges himself on 'to express it all'. But he fails, is bound to fail, because every artist must necessarily fail in this respect, beauty and truth defying his efforts.

A similar predicament underlies *Birchwood* (1973). Like Marcel in *À la recherche du temps perdu*, Gabriel Godkin is in 'search of time misplaced'.[1] In Proust, the realisation of *temps perdu* becomes the incentive to a search for the essential nature of the past as well as of time; and memory — in Gabriel's case *mémoire volontaire*, rather than Marcel's *mémoire involontaire* — becomes the medium of finding it. Gabriel tells his stylised story in order to get to the bottom of his life in terms of sense and purpose. He tells it from memory, and that strategy brings to bear the difficulty of drawing upon one's memory as well as the unreliability of one's memory, and the teething troubles in communicating one's experience through language. Gabriel notes:

> I spent the nights poring over my memories, fingering them, like an impotent casanova his old love letters, sniffing the scent of violets. Some of these memories are in a language which I do not understand, the ones that could be headed, *the beginning of the old life*. (p. 3)

For Gabriel, the fundamental impetus to remember derives from a modified Descartes quotation: 'I am, therefore I think' (p. 3), and since for him 'all thinking is in a sense remembering' (p. 3), he is simply bound to think and in thinking to remember. With remembering, though, there comes the problem of whether or not what one recalls is in fact authentic. Gabriel denies the possibility of authenticity: 'We imagine that we remember things as they were, while in fact all we carry into the future are fragments which reconstruct a wholly illusory past' (p. 4). The epistemo-logical difficulty notwithstanding, and in spite of his professed inability 'to discern a defensible reason for [his] labours' (p. 4), Gabriel nonetheless takes them on, in fact shows himself in the process of doing so, gathering those Proustian 'madeleines' (p. 5), comparing them to his memories of them, adding them to the mosaic, for the sole purpose of arriving at 'these extraordinary moments when the pig finds the truffle embedded in the muck' (p. 3), of discerning the 'thing-in-itself' (p. 5).

Gabriel is thus the first of Banville's characters to occupy himself with a search for sense, for the whatness of things. Copernicus after him, in *Doctor Copernicus* (1976), will also be greatly pre-occupied with the thing-in-itself; and so will Kepler (in *Kepler* (1981)), Newton, the fictitious Newton biographer, in *The Newton Letter* (1982), and Gabriel's namesake in *Mefisto* (1986), and in a sense Freddie Montgomery in *The Book of Evidence* (1989), *Ghosts* (1993), and *Athena* (1995). And like all of them, Gabriel Godkin associates this search for the thing-in-itself with the discovery of a sublime form of beauty and harmony. After inadvertently stumbling upon his mother and father making love in Cotter's dilapidated cottage, he believes he has discovered not love, 'or what they call the facts of life', but 'the notion of — I shall call it harmony' (p. 25). Trying to explain this idea of harmony, Gabriel suggests:

> How would I explain, I do not understand it, but it was as if in the deep wood's gloom I had recognised, in me all along, waiting, an empty place where I could put the most disparate things, and they could hang together, not very elegantly, perhaps, or comfortably, but yet together, singing like seraphs. (p. 25)

It should be borne in mind that Gabriel Godkin's striving anticipates Gabriel Swan's Faust-like efforts in *Mefisto*. Like Copernicus, Kepler, the historian in *The Newton Letter*, and Gabriel Swan, the narrator in *Birchwood* is convinced that, even though the world is chaotic, there are moments, rare moments, when some order, some aspect of the quiddity of life shines through:

> Listen, listen, if I know my world, which is doubtful, but if I do,
> I know it is chaotic, mean and vicious, with laws cast in the wrong
> mould, a fair conception gone awry, in short an awful place, and
> yet, and yet a place capable of glory in those rare moments when
> a little light breaks forth, and something is not explained, not
> forgiven, but merely illuminated. (pp. 25f.)

Lastly, like all subsequent Banville protagonists to date, Gabriel is driven on in his endeavour by the question: 'What does it mean?' (p. 72). Kepler, near the end of his life, will come to recognise the appropriateness of what his friend, the Jew Winklemann, told him: 'Everything is told us, but nothing explained. Yes. We must take it all on trust. That's the secret.'[2] Godkin, about midway upon his imaginative journey through the foreign land of his past, realises:

> There is never a precise answer, but instead, in the sky, as it were,
> a kind of jovian nod, a celestial tipping of the wink, *that's all right,
> it means what it means.* (p. 72)

However, he continues by asking himself: 'yes, but is that enough? Am I satisfied?' It is not enough, and he is not satisfied, hence his search for time misplaced.

Gabriel's reflections and recollections are intended to make up for what he failed to attain during the time he lived through the events. He feels that life is, and has been, terribly swift. Commenting on Granda Godkin's death, he notes:

> But I felt as I have felt at every death, that something intangible
> had slipped through my fingers before I discovered its nature. All
> deaths are scandalously mistimed. People do not live long enough.
> They come and go, briefly, shadows dwindling toward an empty
> blue moon. (p. 53)

Two things are especially noteworthy about these reflections and recollections; first, the repeatedly articulated fictionality of the memories, which in turn throws into relief the fictional character of the entire account, showing Gabriel in the process of weaving a web of words; and, second, the fact that the search for sense is slyly and deftly transferred from the narrator to the reader. The recurrent questions and permeating mysteries on which the story hinges provoke him into searching for sense and a *raison d'être* himself.

Yet for the reader and the narrator alike, the issue concerning the sense of Gabriel's life remains unresolved. Gabriel at the end, as diligently and painstakingly as a sleuth in a detective novel, clears up the mysteries, solves all the riddles with which he so expertly has spiced his narrative. The most essential question, though, namely: 'What does it mean?', is left as open as at the outset. Or perhaps this is not quite true. What *Birchwood* seems to suggest is that the answer, the result of the effort, is not as important as the effort itself. Gabriel at the beginning of his search fails to discern a defensible reason for his labours but supposes 'that there must be one...buried somewhere' (p. 4); then at the end he comes to realise that this reason resides in the particular and very specific manner in which he has taken on and conducted those labours. It is the effort that counts, not the outcome, which can at best be an approximation of the quintessential nature of truth.

He may arrive at passable, even accurate views on memory, the unreliability of mnemosyne — or on time, for instance when he recalls how he became aware of the destructive as well as transient nature of time while eating blackberries (cf. p. 60). He may, furthermore, live through one of those rare moments when the pig finds the truffle embedded in the muck, and experience 'fixity within continuity' (p. 122). He may apply this insight to his whole existence, which consequently must appear to him as if he were stumbling through it for the greater part in utter darkness, except for those rare moments when something seems to have been illuminated. But time will not be conquered.

The Elizabethans, for example, believed that art could defeat the bloody and devouring tyrant Time. Although far from being an Elizabethan, Gabriel would share that belief, if only he were able to arrive at, as well as master, an art form appropriate enough for capturing his time, all time. The narrative discourse in which he features and for which he is responsible, as it were, represents a supreme effort at testing such various art forms. But as it turns out, they are ultimately all of little avail. At the end, Gabriel is constrained to acknowledge: 'There is no form, no order, only echoes and coincidences, sleight of hand, dark laughter. I accept it' (p. 171). He acquiesces in the fact that whereof he cannot speak, thereof he must be silent. His journey thus is from the (modified) Cartesian certainty of 'I am, therefore I think' to the Wittgensteinian despair of 'whereof I cannot speak, thereof I must be silent' (p. 171). But that despair emerges at the end only.

Prior to the end and within the thematic frame thus established, there is precisely form, order, echoes, coincidences, prodigious sleight of hand and copious dark laughter. In shape *Birchwood* equals a clockwork device: wheels-within-wheels, Chinese-box fashion. The wheels are, by and large, constituted by the narrative genres that Gabriel exploits in the course of his *recherche*. There is, firstly and most obviously, the Big House genre, which features prominently in Part I and, to a lesser degree, at the end of Part III. Part II develops the account into a quest romance, or a romantic mystery story with distinctive traits pertaining to the picaresque novel and the Gothic novel. It is a quest *romance* on account of the romantic search for the twin sister, whom Gabriel, who looks upon himself as 'a knight errant' (p. 112), regards as his *alter ego*. Ultimately, of course, the search is for Gabriel's own identity. Furthermore, the use of the *doppelgänger*-motif is romantic. 'There was', the narrator points out, 'something always ahead of me' (p. 119) and that something turns out to be his twin brother, Michael. Finally, the mystery story is romantic in that it *is* a mystery story and it is embellished with Gothic elements — glamour, glaver, gloom and all. The adroit manner in which, throughout the novel, anticipations, clues, mysterious hints are dropped, then later taken up and elaborated, or the way in which the strategy of foreshadowing is employed and the motif of the twin-sister quest is slyly and subtly established, all this is especially reminiscent of the rationalised Gothic and its offshoots — the tale of ratiocination and the detective story. Part III, in particular, is very ratiocinatory, assiduously tying up all the loose ends and solving all the carefully planted riddles. 'There is no girl. There never was...I believed in a sister in order not to believe in *him*, my cold mad brother' (p. 168). Thus Gabriel commences his final unravelling of the plot, and by the end of his revelation, the reader, unlike Kepler, can say: 'Everything is told us, and all is explained.' This is a supreme triumph of art, but it is a triumph that has no bearing on reality, as Gabriel himself comes to understand. The withered wizard Prospero has never existed, but Gabriel wanted to keep him, 'with his cloak and his black hat', and so he 'became [his] own Prospero, and [ours]' (p. 168) — a magician, a wizard with words.

*Birchwood* as a whole resembles an autobiographical *Entwicklungsroman*, charting Gabriel's intellectual development from certainty to despair, or, to be exact, a specific kind of despair — the despair of the artist at never being able to find the 'rosy grail' of truth and perfection. Gabriel, of course, is an artist figure. For, after all, it is he who pens 'the story of the fall and rise of Birchwood', all of it, and in a decidedly artistic vein into the bargain. Thus, in the final analysis, *Birchwood* can also be considered a *Künstlerroman*, dealing predominantly with the possibility of expressing the essence of one's life in a creative, artistic way.

The individual parts of the book as well as the various genres adopted therein are held together by an intricate system of leitmotifs, allusions, anticipations. The very first chapter presents most of the significant thematic issues; it lays the foundation for all future events, explains the fundamental narrative situation, voices the intention informing the account, plants a rich number of meaningful clues. To mention only some of them in addition to those already discussed, Gabriel informs the reader that he has 'gone down twice to the same river', slyly echoing and inverting Heraclitus's tenet about change. He goes on to remark: 'When I opened the shutters of the summerhouse by the lake a trembling disc of sunlight settled on the charred circle on the floor where Granny Godkin exploded' (p. 3), thus foreshadowing Granny's unusual death in Part I, chapter 14, and obliquely anticipating his father's death in Part III, when he discovers him, presumably throttled by Cotter (cf. p. 167). Or the passage: 'My fists were wet with tears. I was not weeping for those who were gone...I wept for what was there and yet not there. For Birchwood' (p. 4). This passage prefigures Gabriel's return to Birchwood in Part III, when for the first time in his life he weeps, having all the while been asked by various people whether he does not weep at all (cf. for instance p. 42); now his tears flow copiously while he is nearing witness to how Cotter and the Molly Maguires slaughter the Lawlesses. The mention of a photograph of 'a young girl dressed in white', which 'Mama said was a picture of her as a child' (p. 5), but which Gabriel himself assumes was of 'a lost child, misplaced in time' (p. 5), is the first in a series of references and allusions to a lost sister by means of which the leitmotif of the twin-sister quest is established. The remarks about Rose, whose 'furry damp secret' (p. 5) he fingered and 'found not so much a hole as a wound' (p. 5), heralds his affair with Rosie, while at the same time forming a link between Rosie and his alleged twin sister. Aunt Martha, when teaching him, reads out to Gabriel the story of '*The Sometime Twins*' (p. 42), which is about the twins Gabriel and Rose, 'who lived in a big house by the sea. One day, when she was very young, little Rose disappeared, and Gabriel went away in search of her' (p. 42). The story provides the basis for Gabriel's

*idée fixé* that he has a twin sister who mysteriously disappeared and whom
he has to find. On the same day, he discovers 'on a little low table by the
bookshelves...a small framed photograph of a young girl in white
standing among leaves in a garden...In one hand she held a flower. A
rose' (p. 43). Later on, when he is laid up with pneumonia, 'on the table
by [his] bed a single red rose, mysterious and perfect' (p. 78) stands in a
glass, and his

> fevered brain [goes] back through many years ... gathering
> fragments of evidence, feeling [his] way around certain
> discrepancies...collating all those scraps that [point] unmistakeably
> ... to one awesome and abiding fact, namely, that somewhere [he
> has] a sister, [his] twin, a lost child. (p. 79)

He goes on to explain:

> This discovery filled me with excitement...Half of me, somewhere,
> stolen by the circus, or spirited away by an evil aunt, or kidnapped
> by a jealous cousin — and why? A part of me stolen, yes, that
> was a thrilling notion. I was incomplete, and would remain so
> until I found her. (p. 79)

This, then, is a prime example of how Banville, or Gabriel, works by
dint of 'those echoes bound to cause confusion' (p. 9), as he terms it:
the echo of the girl in white, the rose, Rosie, his juvenile love, the circus
which he joins in Part II to search for his sister, the possibility that an
evil aunt may have spirited her away, which in turn prefigures his later
assumption that the twin sister was Aunt Martha's invention, or the
figure of the 'jealous cousin' who, one may at first suppose, is Michael,
until it is revealed that Michael is Gabriel's twin, but no less jealous for
all that. The echoes are taken up in the end in the denouement: '...so,
instead of fratricide, he [*i.e.,* Michael] played with Martha her sly game,
and between them they sent me off in search of a sister' (p. 170).

Additionally, in his first chapter Gabriel refers to 'that mighty maid
who many years later [he] met along the road' (p. 5). The mighty maid is
Mag, with whom in Part II he has, in a symbolically portentous
environment, a singularly unfruitful sexual experience. He mentions Silas
and his band, and he anticipates that situation when, after Cotter and
the circus people have left Birchwood, he finds himself confronted by
a mysterious 'creature in white', standing under the lilacs with one hand

on the back of a seat, leaning into the sunlight smiling (p. 6). At the end, this creature is identified as Michael, whom Gabriel shies away from killing with the Sabatier (pp. 163ff.).

Wheels-within-wheels, circular patterns; Gabriel's question-able quest is of course also circular, bringing him back empty-handed to where he started. These constitute the admirable form of the story which Gabriel copies, of the fall and rise of Birchwood and of the part Sabatier and he himself played in the last battle.

Circular patterns are, however, not the only salient compositional device in *Birchwood*; they are assisted by binary patterns, sets of pairs, twins, dualities, mirror symmetries. The Lawlesses used to be the masters of Birchwood before the Godkins took over. Towards the end of the book, the Lawlesses have surreptitiously regained possession of the estate, and finally Gabriel inherits all. There are two archangels, Michael and Gabriel, and a Holy family, Joseph and Martha, a servant called Nockter and a peasant called Cotter: there is a Beatrice-Sabatiere near-anagram; the circus has a Justin and a Juliette and an Ada-Ida twin; there is a Mario and a Magnus, Silas and Sybil, Angel and Sophie. Part I and Part II end in fires. At the close of Part II Magnus is killed when an exploding bullet hits the back of his head; the same thing happens to the last of the Molly Maguires. Mario loses his child in a similar way, or so one is tempted to conjecture, to how the girl in the story gets lost. Gabriel begins with the description of a girl in a white dress, at the end he sees his twin brother in a white gown. There are mirrors everywhere, literal as well as metaphorical ones.

The metaphorical mirrors consist in an impressive number of allusions to, and quotations or near-quotations from, literary works. The book opens with an inverted reference to Descartes's 'Cogito ergo sum' as well as to Dante's *La Vita Nuova*; midway upon his journey across a famine-ridden Ireland, Gabriel alludes to the opening canto of Dante's *Inferno* (p. 132); at the very end of his labours he quotes Wittgenstein's dictum: 'Wovon man nicht sprechen kann, darüber muß man schweigen'.[3] There is the inverted Heraclitus citation, and a Shakespearian Prospero who quotes from *The Tempest*: 'our revels now are ended' (p. 110). Sybil recalls Yeats's Cathleen Ní Houlihan, bodying forth 'the sorrow of the country' (p. 139). At one point, Gabriel feels like Eliot's 'Tiresias in the city of plague' (p. 70). Gabriel's family name may be a covert reference to Stephen Dedalus's description of the artist as God. In the first chapter, there is a mention of a white cloud sailing into the blue bowl of sky; a similar thing happens in the first chapter of

*Ulysses.* The photograph Gabriel notes at the start is of a girl who smiles dreamily, 'as though she were listening to some mysterious music', like Gretta Conroy, who married a Gabriel. At the narrator's birth, there is an apocalyptic moment that resembles the central scene in 'Circe', and it is followed by a policeman's skull being split by an ashplant. Gabriel, like Stephen Dedalus, goes on his quest 'in silence cunningly' (p. 104). Silas relates of a feast that his friend Trimalchio laid on for him in words supplied by Petronius arbiter; he even curses in Latin. Gabriel is referred to as 'Caligula', or little boots. The book opens with a poem by Catullus and contains many echoes of the Oedipus myth.

But *Birchwood* is in fact much richer in metaphorical mirrors than the examples listed here can suggest; it is indeed a happy hunting ground for all those who take delight in source-hunting. What all the examples go to prove is that Banville, or Gabriel, betrays himself in the act of making literature out of literature. It is one way of making the reader aware that he is only inventing (p. 13). Another is the specific manner in which he adopts and, in doing so, flaunts the conventions of extant literary forms.

The Big House section delineates 'the fall and rise' (p. 3) of a big house. The very circumstance that the customary course of events seems to have been turned topsy-turvy, that, in other words, the story is not about the rise and fall of Birchwood, points, if only in an oblique fashion, to an inversion of the genre.

It is the story of a 'baroque madhouse' (p. 7), of a perpetual lacerating battle, fired by hatred and jealousy and greed, for the possession of the estate. As such, it contains most of the thematic issues as well as compositional means that have come to be associated with the Big House novel or story, such as drunkenness, penury, incest, the boldness of the peasants (p. 44), and madness. Birchwood, in fact, bears close comparison to such exponents of the genre as Maria Edgeworth's *Castle Rackrent* (1800) and, interestingly because of its Gothic elements, Joseph Sheridan LeFanu's *Uncle Silas* (1864).

The multitudinous parallels between *Birchwood* and the (Gothic) Big House tradition have mainly been responsible for misleading inobservant readers into regarding Banville's novel as a straightforward attempt to write in this vein. The crux, though, is that the story, or a considerable part of the story in *Birchwood*, is precisely of a 'baroque madhouse', of 'the intricate *farce* [my italics] being enacted under its roof' (p. 65), featuring, no less noteworthy, Dickensian oddities.

There is, to begin with, Granny Godkin, the dominant figure at

Birchwood, who drives her daughter-in-law to madness and lives on 'only despite us' (p. 28), until the house grows tired of her and she dies of 'spontaneous combustion' (p. 75), a most extraordinary way to depart, but one that occurs also in Dickens's *Bleak House*. Doc McCabe says he has 'read of one or two similar cases, you know, in America' (p. 75), and he is right. One such case features in Charles Brockden Brown's novel *Wieland*. Or there is Granda Godkin, who has taken to drinking on the sly and slouching around the house, producing 'an odd choked cooing little noise, like a rusty hinge' (p. 29). The curious manner of his death is comparable to that of Granny Godkin, the consequence of a farcical accident brought about when Joseph pursues a poacher who, in his flight, runs into Granda and knocks him to the ground. Granda goes soft in the head and deems himself visited by God and subsequently by an enormous woodlouse (p. 51). One morning he is found in the birchwood

> curled like a stillborn infant in the grass. His mouth was open, caked with black blood, and it was not until they were moving him that they discovered, in the tree beside which he lay, his false teeth sunk to the gums like vicious twin pink parasites in the bark. (p. 54)

There is Gabriel's mother, who wanders through the rooms of Birchwood in mad Ophelia fashion.

In addition to peopling Birchwood with oddities, or stock figures — the dark, angry father; the long-suffering mother; the ghastly grandparents; the artistic son; the wild son; the strange aunt — Banville works towards upsetting, parodying or flaunting the big-house genre and likewise the Gothic tradition by the mock-heroic vein in which he adapts the conventions. A comic note pervades Part I in particular. Take the description of how Beatrice and Joseph kiss for the first time: 'they grappled awkwardly in a stunned silence, her teeth clattering against his' (p. 10). Or think of how the Lawlesses attend the wedding party (p. 11), of Angel sitting on a little antique chair inside the door, 'her arse overflowing the seat' (pp. 12f.). There is also the moment when Gabriel, engrossed in 'the startling and menacing intricacy of a daddy-longlegs going mad against the glass in the corner of the window' suddenly sees his 'own long-legged daddy approaching through the wood' (p. 20).

To give one last example, there is papa stranded on the lavatory after two floorboards have crumbled to dust underfoot:

> 'Nockter! Jesus Christ almighty, *Nok* — there you are. Get me a
> hammer, nails, a couple of planks, hurry up, we have a job to do.
> I could have been killed. Like that! Jesus can you imagine the
> laugh they'd have. *Broke his arse on his own lav, ha!*' (p. 64)

The 'intricate farce being enacted under [the] roof' of Birchwood is
thus by various means deliberately turned into a parody of the genre.
While a comic, mock-heroic note is prevalent in the Big House section
(Part I), in Parts II and III this is replaced by a terrifying, Gothic mood.

But this is not to say that humour is completely lacking in these
sections of the novel, or that the turning inside out of literary genres
and conventions has been abandoned. The romantic quest is revealed
as a vain ploy, and what may seem to be a serious description of a
specific part of Ireland's sorry history teems with anachronisms.

Gabriel is sent on his quest for his twin sister as a consequence of
the intricate plan his aunt, Martha — who is really his mother — and
his twin brother have devised in order to regain the inheritance of
Birchwood. The intricacy of the plan finds its formal expression in the
intricate way in which the twin-sister motif is built up: from a cryptic
mentioning of a photograph of a young girl, via a seemingly casual
reference to the book *The Sometime Twins*, a random coincidence in name
between his girlfriend and his sister, pervading allusions to roses, and
finally the delirious dream of his twin sister after which Gabriel is
convinced he has in fact a twin sister. The search for her is the main
subject of Part II, and it takes on the character of a quasi-picaresque
series of adventures.

Of the features that have been established as characteristics of a
picaresque story, the following are the most relevant here. The picaresque
novel is said to be partly an *Entwicklungsroman*, treating of the initiation
of the *pícaro* from a simpleton to a *schelm*, a worldly-wise person. Gabriel
sets off in a state in which he blindly believes in his twin sister. It is a
state of enchantment, similar to the enchantment of the people who
attend the performance of the circus, a fantasy necessary for lending a
feeling of sense to his life. As he notes:

> I also [like the people who visit the circus] wanted to dream. I
> knew too that my quest, mocked and laughed at, was fantasy, but
> I clung to it, fiercely, unwilling to betray myself, for if I could not
> be a knight errant I would not be anything. (p. 112)

This marks the stage when he begins to doubt the reality of a sister, the stage when his initiation begins. It is an initiation to the extent that Gabriel acknowledges the futility of his quest and the fantasy character of his sister:

> The story of my sister, the stolen child, had been laughed at. The laughter woke me from a dream. No, not a dream precisely, but a waking, necessary fantasy...I admitted at last that the search for this doubtful sister could no longer sustain me. (p. 132)

And when Rosie, as it appears, is carried to the graveyard — Rosie who by way of association is linked with the sister-quest — his dream has died (p. 147). The initiation is complete when he admits: 'There is no girl. There never was' (p. 168). Actually, the initiation encompasses far more than the shattering of a dream; it also entails the facing up to his abilities and shortcomings as an artist.

The *pícaro* relates what happened to him, while journeying from one place to the next, meeting people of all social strata from the perspective of the underdog. To be a member of a circus gang is surely to be an underdog. Moreover, it has been argued that the genre of the picaresque novel flourishes best in times of social upheaval. *Birchwood* is true to the picaresque tradition by rendering a panoramic picture of an Ireland shaken to the roots by famine.

The reference to a famine may lead to the assumption that *Birchwood* was concerned with a particular period in the history of Ireland, namely, the Great Famine of the years 1845–8. It is a misguided assumption, for the social as well as political background remains teasingly vague. The salient socio-political features are established as recurrent phenomena. A famine was also depopulating Ireland during the days of Gabriel's namesake, great-great-grandfather Godkin (p. 7). There are, furthermore, repeated references to a famine throughout Part I, and since Gabriel, on his quest, is also troubled by a potato shortage, the famine and the social picture of Ireland is generalised, or universalised. It is an Ireland permanently plagued by shortage and want. The picture given is of a Dante-esque inferno, and it is quite appropriate that Gabriel should allude to the first canto of *Inferno*.

Although most of the socio-historical phenomena have been universalised, there are some chapters in Part II that seem to fulfil the function of raising more specific issues. These concern the contrasting pub scenes. The first one (pp. 120f.) satirises one aspect of Irish life, the conviviality of Irish pub life in its 'wild mordant gaiety' (p. 121), which appears to Gabriel 'to carry the savour of the country itself, this odd little island' (p. 121). The second time the circus people come to the pub, the picture is entirely different. The place is deserted; there is no longer merriment and melancholy all in one; the silence of the dead reigns now. Gabriel feels that 'something was dying here' (p. 149). The sounds of levity of the previous scene have been turned into a 'Tötentanz [*sic*]' (p. 149). An entire era is dying, the era of the landed gentry; the 'new-found boldness of the peasants' (pp. 44f.; cf. also pp. 16, 68) has taken over.

Yet such more specific allusions notwithstanding and in spite of clear references to rebels, 'the new State' (p. 55), the Molly Maguires, and more oblique ones to the Whiteboys Movement, the Young Ireland Movement, and the Land League, the point is valid that the socio-cultural background remains obscure, schematic. It would even be true to assert that the chronology has deliberately been distorted. As Francis C. Molloy has pertinently pointed out: '...the period details which in a serious historical work of fiction assist the reader in placing events only confuse in this novel';[4] and Sean McMahon has given a summary of the historical jumble: 'Cigarettes, bicycles and telephones are in quite common use, the Molly Maguires figure in the plot and the British soldiers have rifles and refer to the Irish as 'Fucking Micks''.[5]

The universe of *Birchwood* is a timeless one that does not coincide with any one historical period. The anachronistic aspects, primary among them the quotations from, and references to, twentieth-century literature and philosophy, bring home the point unmistakably. Whether the book should be read as 'an allegory of a troubled land'[6] is rather questionable. For Banville would appear to have been aiming at an allegory of art and the artistic imagination. This possibility is suggested by the role of the circus in Part II.

The circus is billed as a magic circus, in fact as 'PROSPERO'S MAGIC CIRCUS' (p. 99). Prospero, one later learns, does not exist; he is the supreme magician and represents the imagination, from which stems the creativity of the circus members and which is also the means whereby the artist pursues Beauty.[7] The circus is the world *in nuce*, consisting, as Gabriel's world and story does, of sets of pairs, twins, Mario and Magnus, Ada and Ida, Justin and Juliette, Sybil and Angel, Silas and Prospero. Silas's band comprises magicians and jugglers; they conjure up a world that does not exist, a make-believe world, just as Gabriel himself does. Hence it is most appropriate for him to fall in with them.

Throughout the book, he has been a Prospero for himself and for the reader. His aim has been not only to find Rose, his twin sister, but the 'rosy grail' (p. 168) as well. In both he fails. The rosy grail stands for beauty and truth, the rose being the symbol of beauty and the grail of truth. Gabriel is the artist in search of order and harmony. The quest for the twin sister is a metaphor for the artistic quest for perfection. His efforts are through art, hence the exploitation of a sizeable number of literary genres and conventions. What is more, Gabriel is all the time aware of making these efforts. He shows himself in the process of writing — writing as a way of establishing sense and order.

Metafictional comments interspersed throughout the account lay bare the creative process. 'Be assured that I am inventing', Gabriel twice signals to the reader (pp. 13, 170). At one point, he comments on a passage deprecatorily: 'Words' (p. 19). Or he interjects: 'No, that is not true' (p. 33). Furthermore, he reflects on what he has written down: 'Does that seem a ridiculous suggestion? But I do not suggest, I only wonder' (p. 139); and he expressly communicates with the reader: 'Listen, listen to me' (p. 147; also p. 82), thus throwing into relief the fact that fiction, art, come about in a communicative act between a real, or implied, author and a reader. Gabriel implies that his account is a deliberate textual construct involving a certain amount of play. He also includes commentary on the conventions exploited, as when he has Sybil remark about the romantic search for the sister: 'That's very...romantic' (p. 137). Lastly, the metafictional aspect of *Birchwood* becomes conspicuous through the use of inter-textuality.

There is an Ada in the book, and like Vladimir Nabokov's novel *Ada*, itself a book about the madeleines and madlanes of memory, *Birchwood* is, in the final analysis, about the literary, or artistic, imagination and about how the artistic imagination tries to come to grips with the world, life, truth. Gabriel has, just like that paradigmatic magician Prospero, conjured up a world. He has done so by means literary. He has tried out a wide variety of different literary genres, conventions and stereotypes to see whether these could assist him in his quest for perfection, to see whether they would help discover 'a form which would contain and order all [his] losses' (p. 171). But the conventions and strategies did not stand up to the task. All they were suited for was to be parodied, in order that their exhausted nature may be discerned. At the end Gabriel resigns himself to the fact that there 'is no form, no order, only echoes, coincidences, sleight of hand, dark laughter. I accept it' (p. 171). This admission can be read in at least two different, equally valid ways. He has failed because the old forms were of no use to him, and he has as yet been unable to discover new, more adequate ones. He has also failed because each and every artistic effort to arrive at perfection can at best be an approximation. The rosy grail forever eludes the artist's grasp. Fresh attempts have to be made, and each fresh attempt will mark yet another stage in the progressive process of failure. It is an insight that Gabriel shares with quite a number of Banville's protagonists.

*Doctor Copernicus, Kepler, The Newton Letter* and *Mefisto* make up Banville's 'scientific' tetralogy. The first two novels chart the lives of the two famous astronomers, adhering faithfully to the historical facts. But *Doctor Copernicus* and *Kepler* are not historical novels in the strict sense; the historical reconstruction is just a means to a different end. Here, as in *The Newton Letter* and *Mefisto*, the main concern is with communicating a particular idea. Kepler and Copernicus are representatives of what *The Newton Letter* terms 'those high cold heroes who renounced the world and human happiness to pursue the big game of the intellect'.[8] They sought to explain the world by dint of unifying systems, gearing their whole lives towards that one goal. Finally, however, they are forced to accept that their theories are only supreme fictions, albeit of great beauty and harmony, for which they have sacrificed their humaneness. It is not enough to spend one's life gazing at stars; the most important thing is to live and establish genuine human relationships. Copernicus wants to *explain* the phenomena, no longer simply save them. Languishing away after an apoplectic stroke, he realises that, in order to do so, he had to use language, the great falsifier, for words are not the things themselves. Even more painfully, he becomes aware of never in his life having formed a true relationship with any human soul. '[W]e *are* the truth. The world, and ourselves, this is the truth. There is no other', his brother, Andreas, tells him before Copernicus dies, and he accepts this insight with redemptive despair.[9] Copernicus and Kepler are, at the end of their lives, constrained to admit to themselves that they have been unable to discern 'the thing itself'. This brief passage from *Doctor Copernicus* expresses the case well. Copernicus is here in silent conversation with the ghost of his deceased brother, who speaks first:

> You thought to discern the thing itself, the eternal truth, the pure forms that lie behind the chaos of the world. You looked into the sky: what did you see?
>
> I saw...the planets dancing, and heard them singing in their courses.

> O no, no brother. These things you imagined. Let me tell you
> how it was. You set the sights of the triquetrum upon a light
> shining in the sky, believing that you thus beheld a fragment of
> reality, inviolate, unmistakable, enduring, but that was not the case.
> What you saw was *a light shining in the sky*, whatever it was more
> than that it was so only by virtue of your faith, your belief in the
> possibility of apprehending reality.[10]

The historian in *The Newton Letter*, the third of Banville's 'cold heroes',
has rented the lodge of a big house in the south of Ireland to put the
finishing touches to his biography of Newton, yet another cold hero.
He comes into contact with the people who live on the estate and dreams
up horrid dramas around them that have no basis in fact, thus failing to
see the tragedy that is playing itself out in real life. Although he contracts
not to be known, he becomes embroiled in a love affair that is modelled
on the central character constellation in Goethe's *Die Wahlverwandtschaften*
(Elective Affinities). Furthermore, like Hugo von Hofmannsthal's Lord
Chandos, he finds himself overwhelmed by the common-place, that
strangest of phenomena, and he gives up work on his book.

Gabriel Swan's Faustian efforts in *Mefisto* aim at accounting for the
world in terms of numbers. But the chaos of life through which he is
led by the Mephistophelian Felix defies him, and he decides to leave
everything to chance. Yet, Gabriel is a cunning old fox. Like his namesake
in *Birchwood*, he tells his own story and tells it in such a way that
everywhere mirror-symmetries and parallelisms result. Thus, the novel's
two parts correspond as far as characters and events are concerned; the
opening is mirrored by the ending. The world of *Mefisto*, apart from
being a negative version of Goethe's *Faust*, is indebted to recent ideas in
computer mathematics and chaos theory (cf. fractals, binary patterns,
palindromes, chaos turning into order and *vice versa*). In addition, this
world is Mephistophelian, imbued by Nietzsche's dictum that God is
dead. Man is denied redemption, because he lacks God's mercy.

The tetralogy investigates the scientific imagination and finds it
closely related to the creative, artistic imagination. *The Book of Evidence*,
*Ghosts*, and *Athena*, the books that make up Banville's 'artistic' trilogy,
deal with how the imagination of the artist operates upon reality. Freddie
Montgomery, in *The Book of Evidence*, murders a young woman who
comes upon him while he is stealing a painting, a portrait of a Dutch
woman, with which he is hopelessly infatuated. He is now in prison
awaiting trial; and, knowing that he will not be given a proper chance to

explain his heinous deed, he writes his 'book of evidence'. Essentially, though, this book represents an attempt to bring the young woman, whom he says he was able to kill because he did not imagine her vividly enough, back to life. The manner in which Freddie goes about his task is highly significant. While in prison, he has developed into an expert on seventeenth-century Dutch painting, and to a large extent he views the world with the eye of a painter. Moreover, he transfixes his own life and that of his victim by caging them in art, literature, and films, with a large number of intertextual echoes, the most telling ones being of Vladimir Nabokov's *Lolita*. *The Book of Evidence* looks like a simple, straightforward novel: it does not seem to be as 'bookish' as the rest of Banville's work to date. But in Banville, as in life, nothing is quite that simple or straightforward. Like *Nightspawn*, *Birchwood*, *The Newton Letter* and *Mefisto*, *The Book of Evidence* essentially probes the relationship between art and life, portraying its narrator-protagonist in the act of artistic creation. In the final analysis, the novel offers a self-reflexive and self-reflective approach to a specific form of poetic sensibility.

Comparison has been drawn between Banville's novel and Wilde's *De Profundis*, Sartre's *La Chute*, and Gide's *L'Immoraliste*.[11] The most obvious parallel, though, has so far escaped those who have analysed the book. Banville's greatest indebtedness is to the Nabokov of *Lolita*, itself a 'book of evidence'. *The Book of Evidence* is only on the surface about a senseless murder and the murderer's efforts to justify his behaviour, just as *Lolita* is only on the most accessible level a narrative dealing with a nymphet, one man's passionate love for her and a panoramic journey across the United States. In essence, both books are about art.

Throughout *Lolita*, Humbert Humbert can be observed manipulating the averred facts of life through art, or literature, as when he compares Lolita to Carmen:

> O my Carmen, my little Carmen, something, something, those something nights, and the stars, and the cars, and the bars, and the barmen [...][12]

Like Freddie in so many cases, Humbert is thereby provoking the reader into viewing the events in his life in terms of a literary precedent — the Carmen situation. He is surreptitiously laying a trap, arousing distinctive expectations, but then deliberately thwarting them. At one point, Humbert notes: 'As greater authors than I have put it: "Let readers imagine'", but he tellingly continues: 'On second thought, I may as well give those imaginations a kick in the pants' (*L*, p. 67). Most of *Lolita* consists of a linguistic-cum-literary game. 'Darling, this is only a game', Humbert pleads (*L*, p. 22). Little wonder that he should begin his story thus:

> Lolita, light of my life, fire of my loins. My sin, my soul. Lo-lee-ta: the tip of the tongue taking a trip of three steps down the palate to tap, at three, on the teeth. (*L*, p. 11)

For he self-reflexively remarks: 'You can always count on a murderer for a fancy prose style' (*L*, p. 11). That fancy prose style, as fancy as Freddie's in every respect, throws into relief right at the very start that what the reader confronts is a linguistic construct — letters and words on a number of pages. Freddie, in turn, opens his account in these terms: 'My Lord, when you ask me to tell the court in my own words, this is what I shall say',[13] thereby putting special emphasis on the primacy of text, on the verbal nature of what follows. No less unequivocally, Humbert states: 'Oh, my Lolita, I have only words to play with!' (*L*, p. 34). And play with them he most certainly does: Humbert Humbert, whose name echoes that of the car which Freddie rents: an old Humber, which he finds at a garage called 'Melmoth's Car Hire' (p. 90) — an allusion that intimates the wanderings (both physical and spiritual) of Freddie as well as a nod to Humbert's own automobile: a 'Dream Blue Melmoth' (*L*, p. 229) and Humbert's reference to it at the end of *Lolita*: 'Hi, Melmoth, thanks a lot, old fellow' (*L*, p. 309).

When Humbert remarks about himself:

> When I try to analyse my own cravings, motives, actions and so forth, I surrender to a sort of retrospective imagination which feeds the analytic faculty with boundless alternatives and which causes each visualized route to fork and re-fork without end in the maddeningly complex prospect of my past. (*L*, p. 15)

he characterises Freddie Montgomery's situation in an unwittingly precise manner. Humbert's imagination invents nymphets, and constructs a similarity between Humbert's love for Lolita and Dante's love for Beatrice (*L*, p. 21). Again life is viewed through literature. Later he enters his name as 'Mr. Edgar H. Humbert (I threw in the 'Edgar' just for the heck of it)' (*L*, p. 77). 'Edgar' refers to none other than Edgar Allan

Poe, another literary precedent. Freddie, signing a document in the garage where he hires the car in the name of Smyth, thinks 'the *y* a fiendishly clever touch' (p. 99). Humbert also admits to 'degrading and dangerous desires' (*L*, p. 26), to his 'criminal craving' (*L*, p. 25), just as Freddie will after him. And like Freddie, Humbert is 'an artist and a madman' (*L*, p. 19).

*Lolita* is about the notion of man as an essentially and invisibly caged animal; but even more so, it is about art itself as a kind of beautiful caging. Nabokov's impulse seems to have been to create a portrait of a man imprisoned in passion, like the ape who is referred to in the text as having drawn the bars of his cage from the inside. Humbert is the prisoner of his past, in particular his idyllic and brutally disrupted childhood romance, which, significantly, he sees in terms of Poe's 'Annabel Lee' poem. Nabokov's method, just as Banville's, is an intertextual one, with allusions and references to Poe, Mérimée, Proust, Dostoevsky, Dante, Sherlock Holmes and a myriad other writers, in addition to, and exploitations of, literary conventions.

*Lolita* purports to be a book written by Humbert Humbert in order to eternalise his love and externalise his pain, his *Dolores*, Lolita's real name. Yet, the Lolita he writes about is not a real person, never was one for Humbert, like the maid never was for Freddie. Lolita is only a figment, a product of Humbert's imagination whose consummation he undertook for aesthetic purposes: to satisfy his sense of beauty. The act of love, for Humbert, equals an act of satisfying his sense of beauty. Humbert is an aesthete; however, his aesthetic attitude lacks humaneness, at least for the most part. Freddie is Humbert's kith and kin.

*Lolita* could be read as a lesson in the potential inhumanity of the kind of aesthetic attitude that fails to have moral com-mitment. This is also the way in which *The Book of Evidence* could, or rather can, be read. In the end, Humbert comes to acknowledge that such commitment is of the essence. The last scene showing him and Lolita together makes this point by evincing how closely Lolita is committed to her husband and her child.

The foregoing comparative comments may appear to make up rather an inordinately digressive excursus; yet, by way of analogy, they have a close bearing on *The Book of Evidence*, outlining the novel's thematic *raison d'être*. In more concrete terms, while Banville's other high, cold heroes — from Canon Koppernigk to Gabriel Swan — did not contract to be known and forfeited their humaneness and human happiness by staying aloof from life, Freddie Montgomery, at one point equally about to become 'one of those great, cold theoreticians, the secret masters of the world' (p. 65) with his proficiency in statistics and probability theory (p. 18) as a means of making 'the lack of certainty' in the world, 'an unpredictable, seething world [...] a swirl of chance collisions' (p. 18) more manageable — Freddie, then, gets horrifyingly involved, and horrifyingly involves himself, in the business of the world; and the irony of it all is that he, too, is deprived of his humaneness, ending up in gaol for a most cold-blooded murder. 'When you have once seen the chaos', Copernicus says,

> you must make something to set between yourself and that terrible sight; and so you make a mirror, thinking that in it shall be reflected the reality of the world; but then you understand that the mirror reflects only appearances, and that reality is some-where else, off behind the mirror; and then you re- member that behind the mirror there is only chaos.[14]

It is an utterly apt description of what Freddie does in 'real' life as well as in and *through* his 'book of evidence'. Freddie's mirror is art.

After the bottom has fallen out of his world, his pursuit is seen as a desire arising from the disjunction experienced between reality and the imagination's attempt to grasp it. 'What a surprise the familiar always is' (p. 40), Freddie notes, thus echoing the epistemological predicament of the historian in *The Newton Letter*. Copernicus looked at the sky and he saw the stars; they bore him upwards in a state of sublime bliss; however, they failed to make sense, or rather not in the way in which the ancients had tried to account for them — *salvare phenomena* and all. As a consequence, he strove towards reading sense into them, setting up a theory that would explain the phenomena, rather than simply save them. Although he came quite close to the truth, his concept of the cosmos ultimately remained a supreme fiction. Kepler, too, looked at the sky and perceived the stars and the planets; he heard them produce a music of divine harmony, but he likewise could make little of them, the chaos of the cosmos defying most of his efforts. Similarly, the Newton historian and Gabriel Swan yield their epistemological efforts to appearances and chance, respectively. And Freddie commits a senseless murder and subsequently attempts to make sense of a senseless crime. The outcome is, no less, a supreme fiction — Freddie's very own 'book of evidence'. That book, though, has a slightly sinister side to it, in that it shifts the task of establishing sense onto the reader. Freddie slyly manoeuvres the reader into a situation where he finds himself seeking to make sense of a senseless attempt at justifying a senseless deed.

Notably enough, Freddie presents the events of his narrative framed, or caged, by literature, film or works of art. A considerable number of such scenes are rendered as if they were animated extant pictures and paintings. For instance, the scene where Freddie, for the first time, enters the room with wallpaper the colour of tarnished gold and thinks he has 'stepped straight into the eighteenth century' (p. 77), that room in which he finds the painting, entitled *Portrait of a Woman with Gloves*, is done in terms of a description of Balthus's painting 'The Room'. The films alluded to include *White Heat*, *Blue Velvet*, and *Aguirre — Der Zorn Gottes*. Literary references are, for instance, to *Ulysses* (p. 37), *Oedipus Rex* (p. 30) and, of course, to *Lolita*. Mention is made of the names of van Gogh, Hogarth, Jan Steen, and Lautrec. As one who is inexorably turning away from the reality of life towards a fictive unreality, the confessing Freddie must create a supreme fiction to lend credence to his past, a past that itself had 'all seemed no more than a vivid fiction' (p. 150).

In the novel, there is a definite development from an initial 'nothing' in a doorway (p. 159) to an 'invisible presence' (p. 204) and a final recognition of what this door-frame should usher forth: 'a child, a girl, one whom I will recognise at once, without the shadow of a doubt' (p. 219). This desire to give life is ironically coloured by the prospect of Freddie's probable sentence — life. Freddie is condemned to create the child on 'the blank inner wall' (p. 72) of his heart, as he once failed to do with his wife.

Briefly, the idea informing this creative urge seems to be this: Freddie names his 'essential sin [...], the one for which there will be no forgiveness' (p. 215), as a 'failure of imagination'. He never imagined Josie Bell 'vividly enough, [...]never made her be there sufficiently' (p. 215): he did not make her 'live'. Freddie can see Anna Behrens in terms of the Dutch masters, and his mother as one of 'Lautrec's ruined doxies' (p. 59), or is able to evoke an extensive and empathic scene of how the woman in the painting was portrayed, but cannot adequately picture the maid's world; in fact, the only descriptive details he notes down about the maid concern her 'extraordinarily pale, violet eyes' (p. 111), 'her mousy hair and bad skin, that bruised look around her eyes' (p. 113): that is all the reader learns of her. Freddie killed Josie because he could kill her, and he could kill her because for him she was not alive. His task now, he pre-eminently feels, is

> to bring her back to life. I am not sure what that means, but it strikes me with a force of an unavoidable imperative. How am I to make it come about, this act of parturition? (pp. 215f.)

The answer is that Freddie effects this act of parturition by caging Josie in a work of art, by capturing part of her life and his own involvement in it, but even more so her death in a full-fledged narrative — a book of evidence, art.

Freddie's redemption, if redemption it is, lies in an acknowledgement of the disjunction that exists between the artistic and the 'commonplace world' (p. 108) and the impossibility of ever bridging such a gap. Through his confession, Freddie relives the words of Humbert Humbert, who admits that the only amends he can make to his victim is 'transfiguration in a work of art'. He develops from his former ignorance to an understanding of the schism between the real and the imaginary and accepts the despair inherent in this equation.[15]

In a way, all of Banville's novels are a celebration of the beauty of our brief lives. Every so often Freddie Montgomery is unexpectedly struck by that beauty, which he inevitably discovers in the commonplace. In that sense, even in Freddie there is such a celebration, if only in that he, Freddie, succeeds in bringing forth a supreme fiction in a creative process that may bring to mind Rilke's description of how an artist creates, in *Malte Laurids Brigge*:

> But one must also have been beside the dying, must have sat beside the dead in a room with open windows and fitful noises. And still it is not yet enough to have memories. One must be able to forget them when they are many and one must have immense patience to wait until they come again. For it is the memories themselves that matter. Only when they have turned to blood within us, to glance and gesture, nameless and no longer to be distinguished from ourselves only then can it happen that in a most rare hour the first word of a poem arises in their midst and goes forth from them.[16]

If *The Book of Evidence* is, to a large extent, about the world as perceived by the artistic imagination, then *Ghosts* is about the world as *created* by the artistic imagination. After his release from prison (delineated in Part II), Freddie Montgomery has come to a penitential island. There are intertextual references to *Robinson Crusoe* and *The Tempest*, for example.

Freddie is seeking atonement for his callous crime; he feels compelled
— as he puts it at the end of *The Book of Evidence* — to bring the
woman he killed back to life, and he attempts to do so by weaving a
narrative around a group of shipwrecked pleasure trippers who spend a
couple of hours on the island. A little world is gradually coming into
being, one characterised by absences and a state of suspension, like
ghosts who belong to neither the world of the living nor the world of
the dead. It is the world of art and a world grounded in art: the *commedia
dell'arte* and the *fêtes galantes* paintings of Jean-Antoine Watteau (1684–
1721), who figures as the artist Vaublin — in short, the world of romance
and pastoral.

Freddie feels that he has forfeited his sense of being through his
crime, and he seeks to find himself again by restoring the life of the
young woman. But in the course of his imaginative efforts, he learns
that he has to imagine himself first before he can imagine the woman,
impersonating himself in a work of art, much in the sense in which
being can be attained through narrative: con-fessional autobiography in
the vein of St Augustine's *Confessions* and Rousseau's autobiographical
writings. Freddie is after 'pure existence', but that can be accomplished
only in, and through, a work of the imagination, in the autonomous
world of art within our world — a world that belongs to neither the
living nor the dead. Significantly, Freddie's little world offers a negative
variant of pastoral, a dark Arcadia, in which the great god Pan is dead.
The golden world has forever been lost in a post-Nietzschean universe
governed by chaos and chance.

In *Athena*, finally, Freddie brings to life, somewhat in the manner in
which Zeus, or Jupiter, gave life to his daughter Athena in an act of
headbirth, a young woman he calls A.. At the end of the novel, A. has
left Freddie and liberated herself from him, after having entertained an
erotic relationship with her creator, as it were. Freddie is now living in
Dubin, where he is working for a shady art dealer for whom he has to
authenticate eight paintings. While going about his business, he comes
into contact with a rich number of grotesque figures, including Inspector
Hackett, who landed him in prison in *The Book of Evidence* and who is
now in search of the stolen eight pictures. The story in the narrower
sense is repeatedly interrupted by descriptions of the paintings, all of
them created by invented artists whose names are all anagrams of 'John
Banville'. The paintings depict scenes from Greek mythology and they
have multiple bearings on Freddie's own situation. Freddie decides that
seven of the pictures are fakes and only one is an original. But this

constitutes just one of the many games that the author (or Freddie) plays on the reader in this book. For in *Ghosts*, the averred original had already been identified as a fake: Professor Keutznaer (Robinson Crusoe's German name) swindled the Behrenses with it — 'Poor Miss Behrens was taken in. [...] The professor was the one who verified it. And made a killing on it, of course.'[17]

*Athena* is in the form of a love letter, which Freddie is writing to A. and of course to art. In that sense and because of the love affair between Freddie and the young woman, one of the novel's themes is 'love'. But essentially, *Athena* is about art and the nature of art. Not only are the paintings and their artists fakes or fictions, the entire book is in subtle ways exposed as a fake, as a fiction, as a textual construct. The characters are not serious fictional creations, but only exaggerated puppets that the author moves hither and thither in that sly game he plays on, and with, the reader. Art is nothing but faking, and the artist is a crafty fraud, the 'withered wizard' Prospero of *Birchwood*. Which is where, in a manner of speaking, Banville's *oeuvre* comes full circle. It is certainly correct to suggest that in *Birchwood* Banville anticipated quite a number of thematic concerns and narrative strategies which he took up again (and laboured, some would add) in his artistic trilogy featuring Freddie Montgomery.

*The Untouchable* (1997), in a sense, marked a new departure, even though one cannot help adding that here again Banville is engaging with the topics of fakery and betrayal, once more pondering the issues of betrayal, guilt and atonement and playing his usual game with the reader. It is all very well to write a novel about a character whose life is based on that of Sir Anthony Blunt. But why at the same time give that figure an Irish childhood and family modelled on those of Louis McNeice? By the same token, why allocate a prominent significance to a painting by Poussin, *The Death of Seneca*, that Poussin never painted? Of course, Seneca was a Stoic and Victor Maskell considers himself a Stoic, electing to commit suicide the same way that Seneca did. So quite naturally, the subject matter of Poussin's imaginary work should exude an extraordinary fascination over Maskell. Of course, towards the end of the book, there are insinuations that the painting may be a fake. And yet, all that clever-clever stuff which Banville has been so fond of indulging in can get a little tiresome.

But to be fair, *The Untouchable* presents an absorbing story, which, considering the paucity of plot in the previous three books, is a noteworthy improvement in Banville's art. Banville once stated that he is not interested in story.[18] That may be so. Yet fiction writing has inexorably something to do with story-telling, whether one likes it or not, and they are legion who subscribe to the idea that the better the story the better the novel. This time, Banville has concocted a fascinating account that is clearly indebted to the spy thriller formula without being a spy thriller itself. It would be quite risible to categorise *The Untouchable* as a spy thriller, however. The novel is an autobiographical memoir, and like all autobiographical writing, it represents an attempt to discover and establish selfhood. 'Call it a memoir, then', Maskell suggests, 'a scrapbook of memories. Or go the whole hog and call it an auto-biography, notes toward'.[19]

Victor Maskell has been betrayed. After the announcement in the Commons, the hasty revelation of his double, if not quadruple, life of wartime espionage, his blurry photograph is all over the papers. His disgrace is public, his knighthood revoked, his position as curator of the Queen's pictures terminated. His exposure, after a lifetime of hiding, leaves him with a painful consciousness of his age, and at the same time a curious feeling of rebirth, of being at the threshold of a new life. Maskell sits down to write his own statement, in an act not unlike the restoration of one of his beloved paintings, *The Death of Seneca*, by Poussin, stripping away the layers of grime and varnish left by a lifetime of dissembling, in order for the process of verification and attribution to begin. 'I shall', writes Maskell, 'strip away layer after layer of grime — the toffee-coloured varnish and caked soot left by a lifetime of dissembling — until I come to the very thing itself and know it for what it is. My soul. My self' (p. 7).

There are a great many admirably rendered scenes in the book, for instance the deeply moving one that treats of how Victor's maimed brother, Freddie, is committed to a home; and the whole is — as always with Banville — written in an exquisitely wrought, scintillating prose. Perhaps not least because of the particular era it captures, the book is somewhat reminiscent of Anthony Powell's *A Dance to the Music of Time*, whose title, interestingly, is derived from a Poussin picture, but a real one. Yet, the similarities, thematic as well as narratorial, between Maskell's memoir and Freddie Montgomery's trilogy abound. Even Maskell's voice is somehow similar to Freddie's. It is time that Banville made a genuinely fresh start and forgot about dual lives, betrayal, guilt, atonement, restitution, the finding of self. Certainly, the gate is open, as Maskell states at the very end of his memoir.

# EDNA O'BRIEN

Consistently in most of her work, Edna O'Brien has explored what William Butler Yeats once called 'the foul rag-and-bone shop of the heart'.[1] The longing for communication, generosity, protection, together with opposite impulses of escape, selfishness and the fear of responsibility are obviously given full rein in love, the major experience on which the majority of her novels and stories focus. Her fiction is a record of an exacting and arduous quest for love. But since love appears as an unattainable paradise, as her heroines are perpetually cheated by life, eternal losers whose illusions are constantly shattered, her works at the same time become the record of another quest: the quest for refuge, the quest for a closed world of passive quietness, of withdrawal.[2] Edna O'Brien repeatedly deals with the break from the orthodoxies of home and education and fathoms the realities of personal choices, returning searchingly, nostalgically and painfully to the roots of the self in the childhood world.[3] The memories of childhood in O'Brien's fiction effect a dialectic pattern of rebellion and love, rebellion against 'a pagan place', as the title of one of her novels suggests, the love of some paradise lost. That divided attitude sheds some light on her heroines' divided attitude towards life in general. In short, O'Brien explores the abyss of the self and womanhood in its complexities,[4] while at once dramatising the interplay of illusion and reality, showing that the dreams which we project on people often clash with what people actually prove to be.

Commentators have frequently pointed out that O'Brien's books follow the same thematic and compositional pattern. She is the novelist who seems to be forever retelling the same story of the poor Irish Catholic girl who leaves her bogs and farmhouse to look for freedom, romance and happiness in the 'neon-fairyland' of Dublin, then in the mirage of London, and who soon discovers that she is cheated by life and wounded by love.[5] Each novel turns out to be an 'Education Sentimental'. Very often, one encounters the same two types of women. One is a gentle, vulnerable and highly sensitive girl, a generous, credulous and religious girl prone to self-pity and always aware of her inadequacy. This heroine, who holds the foreground as Caithleen in the first two novels, still has the main role in *Girls in Their Married Bliss* (1964); then she reappears with variations as Ellen Sage in *August is a Wicked Month*

(1965), as Willa in *Casualties of Peace* (1966), as Stella in the screenplay *Zee & Co* (1971) and as the protagonist of *A Pagan Place* (1970). Baba, Caithleen's school friend, is her opposite: a practical, resourceful and funny girl; she is a reckless, lucid, sometimes cynical, dashing young woman, devoid of self-pity, easily scornful and cruel and always resilient. Patsy, in *Casualties of Peace*, has some of her features, and the Baba type reaches its climax in the dazzling toughness of Zee.[6]

By the same token, critics have noted the autobiographical nature of much of O'Brien's writing. Thus, the education of her heroines is a Catholic — and even convent — education like O'Brien's own. The pattern of their lives from the country to Dublin and London corresponds to her own, and the sequence of her novels broadly follows the sequence of her own life. *August is a Wicked Month*, the story of a divorced woman with a son, was published in 1965 and written after her divorce in 1964; and the main character in *Night* (1972), an older woman, has a grown-up son, reminding us of the novelist's own sons.

As Raymonde Popot has argued, O'Brien's treatment of the love theme is reminiscent of a religious pattern, a circumstance that may also have autobiographical roots. In the first two novels of *The Country Girls Trilogy* a subtle transference from religion to love seems to be increasingly at work. It is suggested for the first time when Caithleen, in love with Mr Gentleman, refers to him as 'my new God, with a face carved out of pale marble'. But a consistent use of the religious metaphor is made in connection with Eugene Gaillard, in *Girl with Green Eyes*. When Caithleen meets Eugene for the first time, his face, she says, 'reminded me of a saint's face carved out of grey stone which I saw in the church every Sunday'. When parting after their next encounter, she notices: 'I saw him as a dark-faced God turning his back on me.' Love, therefore, is felt as a new devotion, a new religion, as a quest for paradise on earth. After the failure of her marriage in *Girls in Their Married Bliss*, Caithleen will try to recapture the initial impulse and intent 'to pour myrrh on his scalded soul, ask him to forget, forget and forgive', but this will be of no avail. The religious metaphor will appear again in an obvious form in *Casualties of Peace*, but here the possible equation of love-paradise is suggested in the negative, since Willa, still unable to commit herself to love, feels that she lives in 'limbo' and mourns 'the bleakness, the loneliness, the pointless purgatory that [is] her wont'.[7] The impact of religion on O'Brien during her childhood in the west of Ireland is emphasised by her in these terms:

> Life was fervid, enclosed and catastrophic. The spiritual food
> consisted of the crucified Christ. His Passion impinged on every
> thought, word, deed and omission, and sometimes in the wild
> fancifulness of childhood it was as if one caught sight of him on
> a hill stretched out upon a cross betwixt two thieves with women,
> at the foot of it, gnashing and weeping.[8]

The Passion of Christ becomes replaced by the worldly passion of men.

O'Brien's stance is a feminist one. Her feminism is obvious because
her whole work deals with women's struggle for physical, mental and
emotional freedom as well as for a form of love that they can never
achieve. But she does not appear to be a feminist in the customary
sense; that is to say as a woman fighting for women's rights and women's
freedom in every walk of life, as a woman proclaiming a fundamental
equality between both sexes. Edna O'Brien is simply a woman. Her
protest is not so much a social protest as a despair coming from the
depths of her being.[9]

After having published *The Country Girls Trilogy* in the early 1960s,
Edna O'Brien soon found herself ostracised in her mother country.
The three books, *The Country Girls* (1960), *The Lonely Girl* (1962, reprinted
as *The Girl with Green Eyes*, 1964), and *Girls in Their Married Bliss* (1964),
constitute a socially and psychologically realistic series of novels dealing
with young women's coming to maturity first in puritan and hypocritical
Ireland and then in England, and they were — as Christina Hunt
Mahoney has argued — certainly striking for introducing fresh and
challenging thematic concerns into Irish fiction of the time:

> The trilogy was truly innovative at the time in providing a
> voice for a segment of the Irish population historically under-
> represented in its fiction. O'Brien's young women, Catholic,
> convent-educated, and coming from small country towns to work
> in lowly jobs in Dublin, are a recognizable phenomenon in mod-
> ern Irish life.[10]

Edna O'Brien achieved a literary sensation, not least because all three
books were banned under Ireland's Censorship Law. In particular, *Girls
in Their Married Bliss* contains explicit sex scenes that surely must have
stuck in the censors' craw. Reading them today, one must wonder what
all the fuss was about. But as Robert Zimmermann used to sing, the
times they are a-changing. Anyway, throughout the 1960s the name 'Edna

O'Brien' became equated with 'sex'. For Sean McMahon, this was 'an unfair mental equation'. Benedict Kiely, writing in *Conor Cruise O'Brien Introduces Ireland*, admits that Edna O'Brien's writing is 'brutally direct', but he notes that 'those moles the censors, or whoever eggs them on to their idiocies, are not able to take them'. The pathological quality of the adverse criticism, to which Kiely draws our attention, is apparent in a piece that Bruce Arnold published in *The Irish Times* of 21 November 1966:

> Edna O'Brien's concern has been with the presentation of sex as a mixture of the furtive, the absurd, the inconsequential and the humorous adjunct to human endeavour. It has rarely been a question of passion. It has been exhibitionist. It has dealt with, or hinted at, sacrilegious sex, lesbianism, venereal disease, voyeurism, fetishism, and various other forms of sexual frustration. Her novels in this respect deal almost exclusively with sexual failure.[11]

It is not at all correct to assert that in O'Brien's novels sex is rarely a question of passion. Nor is it true that they deal almost exclusively with sexual failure, even though in *Girls in Their Married Bliss*, failure, not least sexual failure, in their marriages cause the two eponymous country girls to embark on extra-marital affairs. What has emerged without much doubt during the forty years that Edna O'Brien has been publishing fiction is that of all the women writers of her generation, to which Jennifer Johnston, Julia O'Faolain and a host of others belong, she is the finest stylist, a quality already apparent in the trilogy, especially in the manner in which Baba's voice is rendered in the third novel: a supreme blend of the bored, the foul-mouthed, the cheeky, the wiseacre, the down-to-earth and the despondent. This quality can likewise be discerned in the chapter in *The Country Girls* that treats of how Caithleen Brady comes to terms with her mother's untimely death.

In *The Country Girls,* Caithleen is fourteen years old. She has grown up in a small town in the west of Ireland. Her father is a drunkard who exudes violence. With no pride in land, he allows his place gradually to go to ruin. Before too long he has to sell it and dismiss Hickey, the farm-hand, to whom Caithleen somehow feels drawn, despite the fact that he rarely washes himself and uses a peach-tin to relieve himself in at night, pouring his urine out of his bedroom window to the detriment of the plants below. When his wife goes missing, he returns from one of his drinking sprees in this shape: 'There was my father, drunk, his hat pushed far back on his head and his white raincoat open. His face was red and fierce and angry'.[12] While people are frantically searching for Caithleen's mother, Mr Brady is drinking and singing in a pub in Portumna. When a guard comes to tell him that is wife has drowned, he passes out and has to be taken to a hospital in Galway. The death of her hard-working mother marked — as Caithleen puts it — the last day of her childhood, and never mind that she is only fourteen years old. It is also the time when she falls in love with the strangely named Mr Gentleman. He is called by that name because he is a beautiful man who lives in a white house on the hill, plays chess in the evenings and works as a solicitor in Dublin.

> Mr. Gentleman was not his real name, of course, but everyone called him that. He was French, and his real name was Mr. de Maurier, but no one could pronounce it properly, and anyhow, he was such a distinguished man with his gray [*sic*] hair and his satin waistcoats that the local people christened him Mr. Gentleman. (p. 12)

Her first lunch with Mr Gentleman is the happiest day of her whole life: 'My soul was alive; enchantment; something I had never known before' (p. 56).

Then Caithleen wins a scholarship for a convent school at the other end of the county. Her friend, Baba, the daughter of the local veterinary surgeon, is also to go to that school. The time there amounts to a devastating experience. The convent for Caithleen is 'a grey stone building with hundreds of small square curtainless windows, like so many eyes spying out on the wet sinful town' (p. 64). For most of the time in the convent, she is 'waiting for something to happen in the deathly, unhappy silence' (p. 70). When Caithleen is seventeen, she and Baba have themselves dismissed from the convent school for writing an obscene note about a nun and Father Tom. Caithleen's father is in a raging temper, but Caithleen finds shelter with Baba's family. Later they go to live in Dublin. Baba will be taking a commercial course, and Caithleen will be working in the grocer's shop of Tom Burns. They begin 'that phase of [their] lives as the giddy country girls brazening the big city' (p. 121). They find a room with a 'low-sized woman' (p. 124) of Austrian extraction, who is almost the width of the dining-room doorway, her bottom like the bottom of a woman in a funny postcard. The time of their amorous adventures begins. They have a date with two rich men. Harry, Caithleen's partner, is married and simply out for a good time. But Caithleen puts up a fierce resistance to his clumsy advances. Baba fares better with her man, before she is diagnosed as suffering from tuberculosis and has to go to a home in Wicklow. Then out of the blue Mr Gentleman appears in Dublin. Caithleen and he start seeing each other regularly and their affair commences in serious terms.

Perhaps it is that very affair which somehow mars the novel by putting rather a strain on one's credulity. Thus, for example, when Mr Gentleman, who clearly is middle-aged, kisses seventeen-year-old Caithleen for the first time, this is done in the presence of Baba's family, and of course his kiss is a 'quick dry kiss' (p. 87). He shakes hands with her, but is 'shy and strangely nervous'. His eyes, though, are saying the sweet things 'which they had said before'. Shortly afterwards, he imprints a different, a real kiss on her lips which affects her entire body and they vow their love to each other. Subsequently, she sees little of Mr Gentleman; however, she is deeply infatuated with him and would always want 'to rush back to Mr. Gentleman' (p. 119), for he is so much nicer than young boys, who, according to Baba, are nothing but 'little squirts' and 'no use' anyway. When Mr Gentleman arrives in Dublin, they go out for dinner several times, and on one occasion spend a couple of hours afterwards in her landlady's house, stripping to the buff and just looking at one another. Then she dares touch his private parts; yet nothing more consequential happens. At last, Mr Gentleman desires to take Caithleen to Vienna. She is thrilled to bits; not surprisingly, though, he fails to show up at the appointed hour. Instead there is a telegram, stating:

EVERYTHING GONE WRONG. THREATS FROM YOUR FATHER. MY WIFE HAS ANOTHER NERVOUS BREAKDOWN. REGRET ENFORCED SILENCE. MUST NOT SEE YOU. (p. 175)

The second book in the trilogy, *Girl With Green Eyes* (1964)[13] focuses on the problems encountered by a young woman who strikes up a relationship with a married man in the Ireland of the 1950s. Caithleen Brady is now in Dublin sharing a bed-sitter with Baba. She is convinced that '[all] the nicest men were in books — the strange, complex, romantic men; the ones I admired most'.[14] Before too long, though, she meets such a person in Eugene Gaillard, a man twice her age. Eugene grew up in Dublin. He went through a poor childhood, had to comb the beaches looking for jetsam. His father had abandoned his wife and child, and Eugene had to go to work at the age of twelve or thirteen. Up to the age of twenty-five, while he was apprenticed to various trades — cinema operator, gardener, electrician — he could only afford to look at girls, 'the way one looks at flowers or boats in Dun Laoghaire harbour' (p. 31). Eugene married an American woman, called Laura, with whom he has a child. When Caithleen meets him, he is separated from his wife, who is living in the States. Caithleen, of course, falls in love with Eugene. Here is how the text puts it:

> My elbows touched his; and I had that paralysing sensation in my legs which I hadn't felt since I'd parted from Mr Gentleman. (p. 15)

She pays a couple of visits to him in his house in the country; but she is terribly insecure in his presence. On one occasion she is afraid Eugene might have designs on her virtue:

> 'I'm afraid I have to go now, it's eight o'clock,' I said in a slightly hysterical voice as I groped my way towards the door.
> 'Go,' he said. 'But my dear girl I haven't seduced you yet!' He laughed and I thought of a portrait of him downstairs which looked sinister. I groped for the doorknob (the wind had caused the door to slam) but could not turn it. My hands became powerless. He relit the candle and stood there, near the fireplace, holding it.
> 'Stop trembling,' he said, and then he said that there was nothing to be afraid of and that he had been joking. I realized that I was being silly and I began to cry. (pp. 54f.)

She starts sleeping with him in his bed, but is utterly scared of having sex with him. Because she is a complete failure in bed, Eugene gives her a book entitled *The Body and Mature Behaviour*.

People are scandalised that she should have an affair with a married man. Her employer warns her; her landlady, Austrian-born Joanna, who is given to exclaiming 'Mine Got' instead of 'Mine Gott' or 'Mein Gott', warns her, too. Someone even writes poison-pen letters to her father, who unexpectedly arrives in Dublin in a drunken state to fetch her home. After a harrowing time in her father's house, the father being mostly inebriated, she manages to escape to Dublin and Eugene again, casting all cautionary advice — not least the admonitions of a priest — to the winds.

She goes to live with Eugene, and slowly but surely a love relationship develops between them. Then the father and some of his cronies arrive on the scene, forcing their way into the house and beating Eugene up. The resolute intervention of Eugene's maid — she fires a shot at the ceiling, while Caithleen is hiding under a bed — drives the intruders away. These events incidentally are rendered in a very convincing and competent manner. In order to avoid further scandal, Eugene buys a wedding ring for Caithleen, and they pretend to be married. All goes well for a while; even the sex works out wonderfully.

Yet, no happiness can last forever. Caithleen has difficulty getting on with Eugene's friends and acquaintances. He wants to go to America to make a film about some irrigation project. Laura writes to him, urging him to come and see her. Caithleen wants to accompany Eugene in order to guard against Laura's machinations. But Eugene does not want her to come along, and when he becomes interested in one of his friends' female companions, things come to a head. Caithleen throws a tantrum, Eugene accuses her of being possessive, and the break-up is only a matter of time.

Finally Caithleen leaves her lover, who has reached the conclusion that the age difference is too immense anyway and that she is too immature. At last she and Baba depart for London. At the close of the book, Caithleen is working in a delicatessen in Bayswater and goes to London University to study English, while Baba is training as a receptionist in a big hotel in Soho.

The title of the third novel in the trilogy, *Girls in Their Married Bliss*, is mischievously ironic. For Baba and Caithleen, marriage has all but bliss in store. Caithleen, heavily pregnant, married Eugene Gaillard (who, accidentally or not, has the same initials as O'Brien's former husband Ernest Gébler), and — as Baba, who tells part of the chapters from her own first-person point of view, puts it — they 'lost no time making puke out of it' (p. 381). Baba herself married Frank, a rich builder, whom she met in an Irish club. Sex for her was not a success, as Frank turned out to be a typical Irishman: 'good at battles, sieges, and massacres. Bad in bed' (p. 384). Yet Frank proved a lot nicer than 'most sharks' she had been out with,

who expected you to pay for the pictures, raped you in the back seat, came home, ate your baked beans, and then wanted some new, experimental kind of sex and no worries from you about might you have a baby, because they liked it natural, without gear. (p. 384)

And so she married him.

The story told is largely about Caithleen's and Baba's extra-marital affairs. Caithleen meets another man and falls in love with him. The upshot is the usual mess that such a move entails. Eugene discovers the letters of Caithleen's lover and turfs his wife out. The lover breaks up the affair. Caithleen has to find a place to stay. Baba cannot put her up because her husband dislikes Caithleen. Meanwhile Eugene has left London with their son. Caithleen gets a part-time job so that she does not have to take her husband's charity. All humiliating attempts on her part to patch up the marital rift fall on stony ground. Gradually, her interest in life and the will to fight diminish. Though young, she has no longer 'the energy to coax, and woo, and feed, and love, and stroke, and cosset another man, beginning from the very beginning' (p. 455). She suffers a nervous breakdown and in the end needs the help of a psychiatrist. Her life may be in tatters, but at least she is all of a sudden able to see her mother in a different light: where formerly she had cherished her mother's kindness and her love of her had been unchanged and everlasting, she now recognises in her mother

> [a] self-appointed martyr. A blackmailer. Stitching the cord back on. Smothering her one child in loathsome, sponge-soft, pamper love. (p. 477)

And she winds up still hankering after 'the De Luxe Love Affair' (p. 501) that, of course, will never come.

Baba in turn strikes up with a drummer called Harvey, who initially she gives the come-on to in the hope that he will rent a flat to Caithleen. Her husband has become impotent. Then she finds herself pregnant by her lover. When she and Caithleen break the news to him, Frank first flies into a tantrum, but later agrees to let Baba stay on with him and pass the baby off as his. Sitting in a gynaecologist's chair and being examined for her pregnancy, she becomes aware of what she considers the essential predicament of women:

> I was thinking of women and all they have to put up with, not just washing nappies or not being able to be a high-court judge,

but all this. All this poking and probing and hurt. And not only
when they go to doctors but when they go to bed as brides with
the men that love them. (p. 473)

*Girls in Their Married Bliss* and therefore the whole trilogy in its original
form ended with Kate, as her name is now spelled, having herself
sterilised in order to eliminate 'the risk of making the same mistake
again' (p. 508). O'Brien appended an 'Epilogue' when the three novels
were published in one as *The Country Girls Trilogy*. This epilogue closes
the narrative on a shatteringly poignant note. Kate, so Baba lets us know,
committed suicide, eventually having broken down under the weight of
her fate. Together with Kate's son Baba attended her funeral, carrying
the urn before scattering Kate's ashes. Baba herself had her share of
misfortune when, while holidaying abroad with a lover, she received a
telegram informing her that her husband had suffered a stroke.

  In order to do full justice to it, one has to assess the trilogy as a
literary product of the 1960s, not as the facile study of 'affairs of the
heart' for which it is often taken, but as a daring analysis of the
predicament of young Irish women who escape the stultifying impact
of life in narrow-minded, parochial Ireland fleeing to London only to
be crushed there by their own romantic aspirations, which clash with
the baseness and imperfections of life in general. The writerly qualities
of the trilogy are highly commendable, some technical shortcomings
notwithstanding. For example, it may be contestable whether the alternate
use of the omniscient and the first-person perspectives in *Girls in Their
Married Bliss* is an altogether satisfactory idea. True enough, Baba's voice
lends an unmistakable freshness to the narrative; but little else is gained
by the deployment of two different points of view. Nothing of note
would be different if the account were entirely rendered from either
Baba's angle or that of the objective, omniscient narrator.

  Ellen Sage, in *August is a Wicked Month*, represents another instance
of the quintessential O'Brien woman:

> 'Irish, cottage, poor, typical, pink cheeks, came to be a nurse in
> London, loved by all the patients, loved being loved, ran from the
> operating theatre because one of those patients who had cancer
> was just opened and closed again, met a man who liked the nurse-
> maid in me, married him in a registry office, threw away the faith,
> one son soon after. Over the years the love turned into some-
> thing else and we broke up.[15]

Ellen, 'twenty-eight and [with] skin like a peach [...], a free woman with long rangy legs and thick, wild hair, the colour of autumn' (p. 15), is separated from her husband. Their seven-year-old son is shared between their two homes. When her husband goes on holiday with the boy, she feels her time has come for free love:

> She longed to be free and young and naked with all the men in
> the world making love to her, all at once. (p. 27)

She does not take long to get a first male companion into bed with her, christening 'him foxglove because he too grew high and purple in a dark secretive glade' (p. 19). Next she flies to the south of France to enjoy herself. Every man she encounters is a potential love object for her: the Frenchman she gets to know on the plane ('She could make love to him there and then, lie down and love this total stranger. She'd always wanted to' [p. 31]); a violinist in the hotel orchestra, who turns out to be a sex maniac interested in photographing her and entering filthy words in his notebook; the room waiter, who wants to have a 'quickie'. She then falls in with an American actor, called Bobby, and his entourage. But death is never far off. One night during a pleasure trip they see a dead motor-cyclist a few yards up the road from where they have to stop their car, which experiences leave the party numbed. Still, '[a]ll her outings and hopes [are] veered towards being with a certain kind of man that [controls] and [bewitches] her. Bobby [is] such a man' (p. 81). But for the time being, she fails to land Bobby in her bed or herself in Bobby's. He meanwhile frolics about with the woman Ellen has become acquainted with and she has to content herself with Bobby's older friend Sidney. Ringing her husband in England, she learns that their son was killed by a car that ran over him and mutilated his body. Of course she is deeply shaken, but instead of hurrying home to England she stays on in France and finally is rewarded with being able to enjoy a few happy days and one passionate night with Bobby, before he disappears unexpectedly, leaving her with a secondary infection, 'but no gonorrhoea infection' (p. 168), as the gynaecologist in London informs her.

The instances of death in the narrative would seem to be intended to induce a sense of guilt in Ellen. Thus, having been notified of her son's death, she feels

> that she killed her son. The logic was simple: if she'd never left

> her husband they would have holidayed together and she and the
> child would have gone for the milk and they would have stood,
> hands held, waiting for the car to go by and it would be some-
> thing that flashed by leaving a cloud behind and they would have
> then crossed the road. (p. 122)

When back in London she finds out that her husband has gone away
with a nice, young woman, she admires him for possessing the strength
to start afresh out of his pillaged life, 'to lay his head on some pure
green breast where the milk might be wholesome', and she feels grateful
to him in some strange way. 'He had freed her of the responsibility of
feeling eternally guilty for him' (p. 160). Guilt plays a significant role in
O'Brien's fictional world. But there is also the redemptive insight that
forgetfulness and forgiveness will enable one to go on:

> in time those people who meant everything to her and consumed
> her thoughts and inflamed her passions, those same people would
> become fragmented too and days would go by and she would not
> think about any of them. Her son would be the last to be relin-
> quished but he would go, just as he would have gone of his own
> volition, if he had lived. (p. 161)

*Casualties of Peace* (1966) is not among O'Brien's best novels. The book
is shoddily put together and has grown dropsical with agonising
reflections about the plight of women. The men are mostly bastards,
and the women are inevitably victims. The decision on the part of the
author to have Willa McCord's experiences at the hands of the villainous
Herod conveyed in a series of letters at the close of the narrative is not
a particularly satisfactory one, not least because it leaves the numerous
previous references to Herod teasingly vague.

Willa has remained the 'oldest twenty-six-year-old virgin'[16] because
of her having been mangled by love. She has lived through a devastatingly
traumatic time with Herod that has caused her to be haunted by terrifying
dreams of being murdered. Herod was a man 'punishing himself for a
crime that he could not conceive of, Herod twice destroyed, not a
German, not a Jew, a nothing' (p. 53). He told her: 'You do not go
because you would rather have a man that punished you than one who
did not, because you are a woman' (p. 132). Willa has found a peace of
sorts, living together with Patsy and Tom and working in glass — a
creative occupation that is surely meant to signify something, but what

that something could be remains altogether unclear. Patsy turns out to be another casualty of peace, or rather love. She has an affair with another man, a 'Kerry tiger', and wants to separate from Tom, who, when he is told, first beats her up and then forces her to make love to him.

Tom's revenge on Patsy has fatal consequences for Willa: he mistakes her for Patsy and strangles her to death just at the moment when with the help of her black lover, Auro, a sensitive, though married, man, she has liberated herself from the psychic lacerations inflicted by Herod, feeling that '[s]omething had been accomplished' (p. 124).

*The Love Object* (1968) deals with the typical O'Brien predicament of women *in nuce*. Thirty-year-old Martha has an affair with a married man, a lawyer, who uses her and abuses her as a love object. One morning he tells her he adores her and the next he discards her. His departure dements her, and yet she persists in remembering his pale blue eyes, his tongue that liked to suck, his whole presence. She tells herself that she remembers these details because, were she to forget them, there would be nothing to hold on to:

> I suppose you wonder why I torment myself like this with details of his presence but I need it. I cannot let go of him now, because if I did, all our happiness and my subsequent pain — I cannot vouch for his — will all have been nothing, and nothing is a dreadful thing to hold on to.[17]

*A Pagan Place* (1970) offers a diary-like stream of image, im-pression, expression, experience and bitter facts of life addressed by the unnamed female narrator to herself. This represents a narrative procedure that was to lead to the expertly rendered stream-of-consciousness technique of *Night* (1972). The first eighty or so pages, Part I, constitute a reconstruction of a child-hood experience and, together with the remaining two Parts, lend heartfelt expression to the pain of memory. They light on incidents such as the narrator's first Holy Communion, life at home, a day spent at the sea-side, a man dying from a haemorrhage after having his teeth removed, the excitement over a banana found in pre-war Ireland, a teacher's losing her wits and drowning herself, a visit to a friend who had consumption, a row in the family that led to the mother's leaving the house for a brief period of time and her eventual return. The whole, one feels sorry to say, proffers pretty slim pickings, conveying a life that may be summed up in these terms:

Sacco began to describe the marriage pattern. He said it was love at first, frequent journeys to the bed, matinée and evening performance, the hay not saved, the calves not fed, then after the first child a bit of a cooling off, the man going out nights and the subsequent children begotten in drink, then squabbles, ructions, first Holy Communions, shoes having to be bought, a lot of troubles and late in life the man back at his own fireplace spitting and banging and grunting inanities to his own wife.[18]

Part II centres mainly on the narrator's sister, Emma, who arrives back home and turns out to be pregnant after having had numerous affairs with a string of men. There is, understandably, a fracas in the family on account of the pregnancy, not least because it is difficult to identify the father of the child. Emma then gives birth to the baby, who is handed over to the State a few seconds after the birth, and disappears. The subsequent search for her finally leads to her discovery. The highlights of Part III include a priest's interfering sexually with the narrator and her decision to become a nun. We are, of course, firmly located in O'Brien country. The question, though, is whether what the author has chosen to show of it is in fact compelling enough to warrant two hundred pages, the pain of memory notwithstanding.

O'Brien has frequently confessed to a fascination with James Joyce and his writings. This has recently manifested itself in O'Brien's biography of Joyce. Earlier on, in anticipation of the narrative technique operative in *Night*, there is here in *Casualties of Peace* Patsy's interior monologue (pp. 13ff.), which is clearly indebted to the 'Penelope' episode in *Ulysses* and is an expertly wrought passage.

*Night* (1972) is contestably one of O'Brien's best novels — quite challenging in narrative technique and managing to put her familiar thematic arsenal to invigorating effect. The book offers Mary Hooligan's young night thoughts. Mary is lying 'in bed, a fourposter no less'[19] in a house of a befriended couple, who are away on holiday and for whom she is looking after the place, and her life passes by before her mind's eye in fits and starts:

There is so little and so fucking much. Half a life time. Felt, seen, heard, not fully felt, most meagrely seen, scarcely heard at all, and still in me, rattling, like a receding footfall, or Count Dracula's swagger. (p. 7)

*Night* is in the form of one long, uninterrupted interior monologue that clearly testifies to O'Brien's admiration for Joyce. Mary's monologue may not be as syntactically disruptive or otherwise iconoclastic as Molly Bloom's, in *Ulysses*; but here as in Joyce's chapter the tendency is discernible to link individual thoughts, or trains of thoughts, in an associative manner. Thus, for example, Mary at one point reflects on '[a] hard ebony cock, secure within the lassies and the myriad others, that is to say the poor male human rejects, displayed upon a clothes-line [...]', and in the next paragraph she recalls that they 'had a clothes-line in Coose [...]' (p. 9). Moreover, Molly's life-embracing 'yes', with which she ends her stream of consciousness, is emulated by Mary's final statement: 'let's live a little before the all-embracing dark descends' (p. 122).

On her course to that final affirmative remark, Mary remembers formative events and important people in her life:

> I've met them all, the cretins, the pilgrims, the scholars and the scaly-eyed bards prating and intoning for their bit of cunt. More of them anon. (p. 8)

Thus she recalls her life in Coose, her father and mother, her mother's death and funeral, her son, her time in Liverpool, her sojourn in New York, where she went to promote Coose, the occasion when she posed naked for a group of amateur artists, and a visit to Coose last Christmas when she saw her father. At times small things help her get through the night, as they help Winnie get through her day in Beckett's *Happy Days* (cf. p. 49). And of course Mary vividly remembers her affairs and the men in her life.

> I have had unions, tête-à-têtes, ripping times, gay collisions. All sickeningly predictable, like a doh ray me fa. Simply did they start up the perturberations, the spring-time spawn, the yea-nay, the boogie-woogie. Result, more blasted birth more blasted arrested birth. (p. 9)

There was, for instance, her spouse, Dr Flaggler, 'one of the original princes of darkness' (p. 80). Or there was a man called Nick; with him and his wife Mary enjoyed a threesome. A man and a woman, called Daphne, came and made love in her presence. Another man called himself the 'Duke' and went so far as to propose to her; and, to end, there was a Finn, who had a blind wife. But all these represented only 'shadows of love, inebriations of love, foretastes of love, trickles of love, but never yet the one true love' (p. 121).

The life that Mary presents is in many ways a botched one. 'Still [she] wouldn't have it any other way. The raptures make up for everything, even the doldrums' (p. 105). The upshot of her reminiscences is that she becomes aware of this inescapable fact:

> Still, little by little the circle dwindles. One has to admit that thing are thinning out, handshakes getting more limp, [...] people dying or emigrating to Australia, people going bonkers, or taking umbrage for the remainder of their lives. (p. 108)

One must, as Mary does, resign oneself to the truth that '[a]s it faws to one, it faws' (p. 113). And Mary, in the end, finds herself in a position where she can say good riddance to the past:

> Au revoir Tig, au revoir Jonathan, au revoir Boss and Lil and all soulmates, go fuck yourselves. I have been saddled long enough. It is time for memory to expire. (p. 121)

*Johnny I hardly knew you* (1977) has a woman, Nora, in jail for murdering her young lover, her own son's friend, pleading her case from her own angle:

> Tomorrow I shall have to tell them. I shall have to stand in court and tell them why I did it. [...] So I will try to tell them as best I can and perhaps ask them to fathom it, to piece it together.[20]

The account falls into two compositionally different parts: in the first she hopscotches about in her past, detailing above all her various sexual affairs — with a man called Jude and another one named Dee and even a woman; the second consists of rather more consecutive coverage of a time spent in Tuscany, a subsequent stay in Edinburgh, culminating in the fatal event. Nora is the paradigmatic O'Brien heroine who, after a marriage that foundered — 'I can hardly think of the marriage bed, my mind shudders, or rather slinks away' (p. 34) — gets embroiled with various men. The way Nora finds herself 'entering the mad bazaar of love again' (p. 117) with the young man Hart is delineated with O'Brien's customary panache. What may possibly not be quite satisfactory is the aspect of why in fact she suffocated her lover with a pillow. In other words: the initial question 'why I did it' does not receive a wholly adequate answer. 'Because of course fear it was that had turned me into instant murderer' (p. 139), she states, but that is not really borne out by her statement. Such deeds as Nora's may be perpetrated without premeditation, without the perpetrator's clear insight, so that Nora is probably right when she comments:

> I do not know what I shall say and as it gets nearer it seems to me that I may be able to make no sense at all, that I may say incomprehensible things, gibberish, even obscenities. (p. 69)

All she can say in her defence is:

> I do not want to strike them as a crazed woman. [...] Nor seek pity. Let pity not be dragged into it. And for a very sound reason: I still do not think that I was wicked. Rash maybe, and racked by the impossibility of a fruitless love, and chiefly putting my own case before that of another. But killing him was an aberration. It was not a crime. (p. 69)

The blurb speaks of 'Dostoyevky's *Crime and Punishment* and Camus's *The Outsider*' as literary progenitors of Nora's story. Nora herself mentions Dostoyevsky's *Notes from Underground* (p. 40) as a book that she was reading at a time: 'a cry from the dark unloosened zones'. But the implication of the blurb's contention is vastly overreaching, because it is simply risible to compare O'Brien's modest — and for all its modesty quite commendable — achievement with Dostoyevsky's and Camus's masterpieces. Moreover, Nora's 'unloosened zones' may not be dark enough for her cry to have reverberations comparable to those of the cry in *Notes from Underground*.

*The High Road* (1988) opens with a roar, 'a remembered summons',[21] and the principal character thinks she hears her name — 'Anna, Anna — being uttered with malice' (p. 1). It is a situation that finds its counterpart near the close of the book, when Catalina, Anna's lover, roars out before being killed by her incensed husband. O'Brien is at pains to emphasise the fact that the narrative begins on Easter Sunday, the day of Christ's resurrection, thereby possibly suggesting her heroine's own spiritual and emotional resurrection after disappointment in love. Early on, Anna meets David Anthony Ignatius Donne, better known as D'Arcy, a defrocked Irish priest and now a painter, who tells her about 'another Catalina stigmatist and saint [...]. Catalina...the Beata whom Satan tempts with sugar' (p. 4). Later Anna's Catalina will, in the eyes of the villagers, have been tempted by Satan.

Anna, like most of the other female characters in the novel, is a mendicant from love. She has come to Spain to forget the man who, she believes, has broken her heart. She met this man on her lecture tour of the US and in a 'snow town in the Midwest' (p. 16) he threw her off like an old garment. Yet at one point it comes to her in one of those dreadful revelations 'that [she] feared [she] had not loved him enough [...]' (p. 123). Wanda is another 'mendicant from love, from disappointment' (p. 10). She came to the place over ten years ago and has never regretted it. Her husband went off with a dancer from Seville while she was away. Subsequently, she had a few amorous affairs, but there is 'no numero uno or numero dos for that matter', as she admits 'with a tinge of bitterness' (p. 75).

Wanda finds Anna a house, which she has to share with an English woman who calls herself Charlotte, but whose real name is Portia, whom Anna used to know in London. Portia married a man, grandiloquently called Pirate, who after the ceremony in the registry office did a bunk. She later married another man who betrayed her with an au pair girl. Iris, a rather eccentric woman whom Anna befriends, suffers at the hands of her South American paramour, who leaves her for Cannes and 'cheap little bitches, starlets, pseudo-starlets, models, tarts, the lot' (p. 88). Subsequently, she has an utterly abortive fling with D'Arcy. He tells the story of that debacle to Anna, although he later relativises the authenticity of his account in a note to her: 'not a word of truth in anything I said' (p. 134). The Swede, D'Arcy's drinking partner, with a moody wife in Malmo, has his own marital problems, and he concedes 'that all scheming and dreaming on this planet [concerns] man and woman' (p. 73). The only reasonably happy — if that is the term — man seems to be 'Scottie, Jnr., the agonised artist', who 'is enjoying a renaissance of conjugal rites' (p. 67), since his wife has followed him to Spain.

When Anna attends the party of the fashion photographer from Cologne, the make-up artist of the group paints her face, and she thinks 'I shall escape being me for this night at least' (p. 24). At the end of the night, the photographer tells Anna 'fucking is very overrated and coming is overrated too' (p. 26), and she reflects that 'this would be enough forever, this moment of pure life, this stream of abstract love' (p. 27). But it is not enough, this stream of abstract love. Anna will indulge again in corporeal passion. As rendered by O'Brien, this affair is a blissfully innocent one, tainted only in the eyes of Catalina's family and fellow-villagers.

Meeting and getting to know Catalina in the hotel that she goes to stay in after leaving the house she had to share with Charlotte/Portia cause in Anna 'this trickle of happiness, thinking to myself that I knew someone even as slightly as this' (p. 50). Before too long, she has fallen in love with Catalina, who makes her forget her misery. But Catalina has herself experienced disappointment in love. She threw herself at a man with 'El Greco eyes and [a] long beautiful El Greco face' (p. 135), a married man, who in the end turned out to be impotent, as Catalina avers. The two women spend a passionate night in a cave in the mountains. Afterwards Catalina is branded a lesbian by the villagers. D'Arcy successfully alleviates matters by scrawling the word LESBOS on various houses, including the spinsterish postmistress's house. In the end, though, Catalina's husband, whom she had denied all the time, avenges himself on the two women: he tries to arrange a meeting with Anna that Catalina prevents by going herself to the appointed spot, as a consequence of which she is killed by him. D'Arcy rescues Anna from being lynched by the angry villagers and then sets off for home.

Significantly, all this takes place in a world of disaster, tragedy and a general displacement of things. A man with a scowl on his face frightens Anna out of her wits and out of the house that she has been staying in. The sirocco causes a catastrophe, wreaking havoc on nature. A man suffers a heart attack as a result of unrequited love. The news on television reports that a woman was raped. A small boy drowns in a swimming pool; his parents are devastated. It is a world that O'Brien conjures up with aplomb.

*Time and Tide* (1992) represents a sprawling narrative affair. The Prologue opens with crisis: the question 'Do you believe her?'[22] has caused a breach between mother and son. With it, she has made Tristan set out for the girl Penny, who occupies the top-floor flat of the house and who told him that she was pregnant, probably by his brother, Paddy, who is at the bottom of the Thames. It is an effective opening by any standard.

Flashback to Part I. The two boys are still quite small. Nell and her husband are living in mortal enmity. If asked, she could not say exactly when things went wrong, so wrong that they were no longer retrievable. Formerly, he had had his huffy periods, but after a few days he would relent, and those moments reminded Nell of what it must have been like for Jane Eyre when she sensed a certain thaw in Mr Rochester. Now, however, things have come to a head. There is open war and a rank poison permeates through the house. Not yet thirty, Nell finds herself in this situation: 'She could not leave him, that was certain; she could not stay with him, that, too, was certain' (p. 27). A battle of over three years begins for custody of the two sons. Physically assaulted by her husband, who thinks that all women are bitches, Nell leaves the house and goes to live in a rented flat and to fend for herself. No stops are left unpulled by the contending parties to win over the sons. Nell catches her husband having an affair with a young woman, but fails to make a case out of this against him. Eventually, she is awarded custody by a court; her response, though, to the decision is anything but happy:

> [...] she felt not the glorious surge of victory that she had antici-
> pated but instead a great onset of sorrow, as if in the years to
> come the true consequences of it all would unfold and the heart-
> break she had been party to would live like a ghost in whatever
> room, whatever country she happened to be in. (p. 62)

Part II sags considerably, proffering too much inconsequential matter: obscene phone-calls, Tristan's bad dream, the two boys' jealousy over who is their mother's favourite, Paddy disappearing during his birthday party and being thought to have drowned before he is at last found, a holiday in Italy bringing both disappointment and happiness, a dinner with an old codger, her falling in love with a man called Duncan — one could go on listing the string of events that O'Brien has tied up. But there would be no real point in doing so. The main thematic thrust of the novel, which unfortunately is for long stretches overshadowed by the variegated incidents, is the estrangement between mother and sons. Why does Nell lose the affection of her boys? Can the reader comprehend why Nell and Paddy and Tristan fall out? Are the reasons for the estrangement to be sought in the marital break-up, in Nell's own chaotic life, in certain forces of society? Possibly in a combination of all these? Or is it impossible to pinpoint a reason? These are questions that the author has failed to answer satisfactorily. All that can be stated with certainty is that Paddy becomes a drug addict and falls in with a strange crowd. He slips away from Nell and she realises with infinite sadness that 'he has now entered a labyrinth of untruth where I will never find him, and worse, where he will not find himself' (p. 232). She feels utterly helpless, wishing 'if only she could be omnipotent, as she had once seemed' (p. 250). When he decides to leave her to live in the country, Nell understands 'that the love they once had, the sweet vital reserves of love, had vanished' (p. 254). Paddy then drowns in the Thames when a pleasure boat collides with a tug. Of course, understandably Nell is devastated. A well-written and pacy chapter conveys the bedlam surrounding the search for the victims. It brings out the best in O'Brien, while the whole sequence of chapters devoted to the aftermath of the accident evince the weakness of the entire novel by simply spinning out the occurrences and adding more material. Tristan returns from Turkey after Paddy's death and informs Nell that he and Penny will be living together, she having confided in him that she is pregnant. We and the narrative have come full circle: we are back at the 'Prologue', as it were. A young man who was on the boat with Paddy and who has come to terms with his grief over having lost three friends helps Nell to countenance her own mental and emotional turmoil. Walking away from him, she experiences a great silence:

> 'You can bear it', the silence said, because that is all there is, this now that then, this present that past, this life that death, and the involuntary shudder that keeps reminding us we are alive. (p. 326)

One reviewer, discussing O'Brien's *House of Splendid Isolation* (1994) in a London weekly, commented that the book was to a large extent a Big House novel and chose to point out that this was a narrative genre the Irish had appropriated from the Russians at the end of the last century. *O sancta ignorantia!* It is of course true, Russian fiction, particularly in the nineteenth century, shares with its Irish counterpart a conspicuous preference for the Big House subject; but it is equally true that Ireland saw the first specimen of the genre in 1800 with Maria Edgeworth's *Castle Rackrent*. Without undertaking a comparative study of the matter, we have no way of saying whether the Irish stole from the Russians or *vice versa*. Most probably, both literatures, for comparable socio-political reasons, developed the same thematic narrative genre and did so quite separately.

Nor is it correct to assert that *House of Splendid Isolation* is a Big House novel at all, or even to a large extent for that matter. The Big House subject is not even of foremost significance. There are some of the familiar generic features all right. For, after all, the chief protagonist, Josie O'Meara, lives in a decaying mansion in the Republic of Ireland to which she came as a bride many years ago. She is now old and ill, alone with her recollections, her dissatisfactions and guilt. The servants are long departed; her hated husband is dead. She has been left childless and is only kept alive by memories of her brief, intense passion for a local priest.

Enter McGreevy, an Ulster terrorist who is on the run. Wanted for murder, his photograph flashing across the nation's television screens, he holes up in Josie's house to plan the assassination of an important Englishman who is due to arrive at a nearby fishing lake. Taciturn and bedraggled, McGreevy first petrifies, then inadvertently beguiles his hostess. While he goes about his grim preparations, coming and going at all times, Josie watches, frets and relives her buried past. Gradually the two are drawn to one another, as they metaphorically step outside their 'houses of isolation'. She arrives at an understanding of the motives for his passionate commitment, and he evolves from a ruthless killer into a sympathetic human being, with a pitiable personal history of his own: his child is dead and his wife was murdered. One may perhaps feel this is overdoing it, pointing to the myriad cases of extremely brutal people in history nonetheless capable of showing humane feelings towards selected individuals.

Yet, *House of Splendid Isolation* is a highly commendable novel, beautifully written, superbly paced and imbued with admirable empathy, whereas some of O'Brien's previous books indulged in unmitigated romanticised agonising. It incontestably marks a major achievement on the part of its author. Which is not to say that the novel is completely devoid of flaws.

There are quite a number of excellent, engrossing scenes, some of which are very amusing. So is a good deal of the conversation between the policemen who, in the second half, are on McGreevy's trail, squelching about in the cold and the dark. Josie's marriage to James and her subsequent relationship with her husband, which somehow resembles the one between Marie-Lousie and Elmer in William Trevor's *Reading Turgenev*, are expertly rendered. When a local half-witted boy hands him the new pink corset that Josie discarded while waiting, flushed with passion, for her priest-lover who did not turn up, the husband finds out about her down-by-the-sally-gardens tryst: he beats the living daylights out of her and then makes her fry sausages for himself and his cronies. Or there is a marvellous scene in which two policemen are keeping a watch on the big house; Josie and McGreevy are in the living room, and from the policemen's angle it looks as if the two are making love, which they find repulsive; but Josie and McGreevy are only chasing two wasps.

The way Josie falls in love with the priest is reminiscent of Emma Bovary's falling for Leon or Monsieur Rodolphe: there may be romanticism involved, but romanticism of the Flaubertian kind. It is here that O'Brien is at her very best.

Nor can one say anything against the novel's compositional design, which is shrewdly intricate. It is when it comes to assessing the book as a novel about Ireland's blood-soaked present, which obviously *House of Splendid Isolation* aspires to be, that one begins to have reservations. The reverberant opening suggests a serious elucidation of historical processes: 'History is everywhere. It seeps into the soil, the sub-soil. Like rain, or hail, or snow, or blood. A house remembers'.[23] Subsequently, though, the history of the nation — though not Josie's — is strangely neglected. The conversational exchanges between Josie and the terrorist achieve little towards shedding light on the problems of a divided Ireland and the Northern 'Troubles'. Least of all is one convinced of the appropriateness of the author's apparent suggestion for a solution to the disastrous state of affairs: 'To go right into the heart of the hate and the wrong and to sup from it and to be supped. It does not say that in the books. That is the future knowledge. The knowledge that is to be' (p. 216). Well, yes, but how does one go into the heart of the hate etc.? That of course remains the question. Unfortunately, *House of Splendid Isolation* offers too little in the way of an answer, excepting the idea of metaphorically leaving one's house of splendid isolation. Sartre may have had a point when he suggested that hell is other people; he forgot to add that too often one is oneself the devil. Still, anyone who sincerely cares for fiction will find the book a joy to read.

*Down by the River* (1996) begins with a chapter written in a prose of a pretentiously poetical kind. In its last chapter, the novel will resort to that style again, with faint echoes of the ending of Joyce's 'The Dead':

> Across the land the snow is falling, the silver-thorn flakes meshing and settling into thick, mesmerising piles, sheeting the country roads, looping the winter hedges to a white and cladded stillness [*etc.*][24]

Sandwiched in between is an exceptionally good narrative about child abuse and the way such an issue is handled in Ireland.

At the very beginning, James MacNamara interferes sexually with his daughter, Mary. She is in her early teens. Later on, James will tell a guard that she is fourteen (p. 136). Significantly, after that unspeakable

experience, Mary is made to watch a stallion covering a mare and the
stallion's owner asks her: 'Did you enjoy that', nudging her and adding:
'The mare gets most of the fun' (p. 14), in order to see how she is taking
the joke. Tears are trickling down Mary's cheeks and she wants to explain
that it is not from fear, that it is something beyond fear, 'something else,
but she cannot, because she knows that no matter what words she uses
he will not understand' (p. 14). He laughs loudly, commenting:
'Christ...You must live in a doll's house'. If only she did! Well thought
out by O'Brien, the next important scene features a gathering of women
who, led by the militant Roisín, a staunch defender of the Holy Father's
*Evangelicum Vitae*, are discussing the problem of unwanted pregnancy.
'What if a girl is raped?', one woman queries. 'An abortion won't unrape
her, all an abortion will do is compound the crime', Roisín replies, nettled.
Another woman points out that scandals happen to families everywhere,
so that one reads of girls drowning themselves, or giving birth in
graveyards and leaving infants to die. 'Oh, the incest tosh', Roisín is
quick to counter. Little wonder that Mary will not receive much support
from people of that sort.

The father may, with caring attention, help his mare to foal; yet
after his wife's untimely death he continues to abuse his daughter. Neither
he nor Mary can, quite understandably, unburden their minds. Then
Mary finds herself pregnant and runs away to Galway, where for some
days she camps in the filthy flat of a bodhrán player, Luke, with the
future 'a big hole' to her (p. 90). Luke is one of the very few people to
offer her genuine help. Back home, she unsuccessfully tries to drown
herself.

When an understanding neighbour, a woman called Betty, takes her
to England, so that she may have an abortion, a gossip-mongering village
woman discovers the plan and threatens James with the police:

> 'If you don't tell the guards I will.'
>> 'You will not...I'm her father...Ask a guard to come and see
>> me...This is my business.'
>> 'This is not your business...It's the whole country's business.'
> (p. 134)

Betty is scared out of her wits as a doctor friend rings her in London to
tell her that the country is up in arms about their move and that his
practice is finished if they do not come home. So they fly back to Ireland,
where Mary will be made to run the gauntlet. Her friend's mother breaks

the news about Mary's pregnancy to the headteacher, and he sees beneath the outrage 'the jealousy of a thwarted woman seething over her own lost, never-ever-tasted delight of being thirteen and fourteen and fifteen' (p. 150). A doctor in a Dublin hospital tells her: 'You should have told someone, you should have told your daddy or your friend, people are there to help.' 'They are not', she retorts (p. 153).

Eventually, the Attorney General is made to take up the case, while Mary is being looked after consecutively by various well-meaning women. Listeners call the radio station that has taken up her plight for a phone-in programme, most of them expressing disgust at what she has done: 'All you people with liberal tendencies is what's destroying the country...It gives me the gick' (p. 187). However, two solicitors can be won over to represent Mary in court. One of them, Cathal, is able to sense who the father of Mary's child is. He confronts James without being able to get the truth out of him. Nor are the guards more successful. Yet, feeling that he has been run to ground, James finally hangs himself. In court, the judges decide in Mary's favour. The irate women who have gathered are beside themselves, and when shortly before legal judgement is passed Mary suffers a miscarriage, Roisín, ever her true self, bursts out: 'May you rot in hell...You have murdered it' (p. 259).

The incidents at the close may be rather too melodramatic and pat for everyone's taste, and the last chapter, which has Mary sing 'a paean of expectancy into the gaudy void' (p. 265) may be unconvincing. Yet Mary's frightful agonies and, for that matter, also her father's predicament are expertly rendered. Moreover, in quite a number of scenes, for example one in which a group of lawyers have dinner and another in which James is questioned by two guards, O'Brien shows her fine ear for dialogue. *Down by the River* confirms brilliantly what was apparent from her previous novel: that O'Brien has sure-footedly broken fresh thematic ground.

*Wild Decembers* (1999) concludes what is apparently intended as the author's latter-day Ireland trilogy, the series also including the preceding two novels, *House of Splendid Isolation* and *Down by the River*, and representing a rather idiosyncratic stocktaking of the state of affairs in O'Brien's native country during the second half of the twentieth century. We are in Cloontha, 'a locality within the bending of an arm', where fields 'mean more than fields, more than life and more than death too'.[25] It is difficult to place the events in a particular time, for the author takes no trouble to authenticate the period. Girls wear platform shoes and talk of hot pants, and one character owns a mobile phone. Most anachronistic of all, everyone in Cloontha is obsessed with sex. The women talk openly about it and speculate about the romantic entanglements of their friends and acquaintances. Two sisters, called Reena and Reeta, run a kind of brothel from their tiny cottage. O'Brien may deliberately have obscured time in this love-hate story, which — according to the blurb — 'explores the depth and darkness at the root of all possession', in order to imbue her narrative 'with the permanence of myth'.[26] Nevertheless, the averred mythical quality of the incidents in *Wild Decembers* remains contestable and, this apart, the atmosphere in the novel is that of middle Ireland mid-1960s: cattle markets, dinner dances in the local town, and life on the land.

Joseph Brennan has a smallholding on the side of a mountain and a beautiful, shy, passionate 22-year-old sister, Breege, who cooks for him, keeps the house and feeds the chickens. Enter upon the scene tall, dark and handsome Michael Bugler, returned from life on an Australian sheep station to claim his inheritance of the land adjoining the Brennans'. With him comes 'the first tractor on the mountain and its arrival would be remembered and related; the day, the hour of evening and the way crows circled above it, blackening the sky, fringed, soundless, auguring' (p. 3). Joseph and Michael get on reasonably well at first, but before too long old family feuds are reignited:

> The families, though distantly related, had feuds that went back hundreds of years and by now had hardened into a dour sullenness. The wrong Joseph most liked to relate was of a Bugler ancestor, a Henry, trying to grab a corner of a field which abutted onto theirs and their uncle Paddy impaling him on a road and putting a gun to his head. (p. 4)

Bugler is engaged to be married to one Rosemary, who is still in Australia waiting for the moment when he finishes their house. After Rosemary's arrival in Cloontha, Breege, who is in love with Bugler and has spent one passionate night with him ('For one night I knew I had found happiness' (p. 216), she later confesses to someone), is momentarily unbalanced and has to spend some time in a mental home. But Breege's situation notwithstanding, a fierce legal tangle ensues between her brother and Bugler. Letters are sent flying back and forth between the lawyers of the two parties. A bona fide right to go up and down a corridor of the mountain held by one of Bugler's ancestors, a certain D'Arby Bugler, who had lost the right to that part of the mountain to Joseph's grandfather, is declared null and void. Finally, Joseph becomes a man possessed by irrationality and with a craziness in his eyes, as one acquaintance puts it (p. 220). And so he shoots Bugler dead, winding up in Mountjoy Prison. Breege, bearing Bugler's child, can see the lights in the windows of Bugler's house each evening, and she knows that Rosemary is within, and she finds herself wondering 'if the old wars are brewing again and will they, as women, be called on to fight the insatiate fight in the name of honour and land and kindred and blood' and hoping that there 'is communion between living and dead, between those, who even in their most stranded selves are on the side of life and harbingers of love' (p. 244).

There is some experimenting with point of view: whereas most chapters are rendered from an objective, quasi-omniscient angle, some feature a first-person stance offering Breege's voice, presumably in an effort to invest the narrative with a personal note of some emotional depth expressive of love and devotion, a note that is pitted against the all-prevailing hatred and resentment which trigger off the behaviour of Bugler and, in particular, Joseph Brennan. Nothing, it seems, has changed in Cloontha in the course of hundreds of years. This is made apparent for instance through the alternate use of the past tense and the present tense: 'the wrongs of years and the recent wrongs all lumped together' (p. 66). Feuds over land are still fought; deadly hatred still quenches all love; the meek are still those who suffer the most. Yet, if *Wild Decembers* is really meant as a state-of-the-nation novel, then the account lacks some credibility on account of some of its characters, for example the spiteful Crock and the two sisters, Reena and Reeta, who could be straight out of a Somerville and Ross story involving an Irish RM and are damagingly reminiscent of stage-Irishry.

The title of the novel is taken from the third stanza of Emily Jane Brontë's poem 'Remembrance', the appropriate part of which O'Brien quotes at the outset — incorrectly as some commas and a colon are missing. The stanza reads:

> Cold in the earth — and fifteen wild Decembers,
> From those brown hills, have melted into spring:
> Faithful, indeed, is the spirit that remembers
> After such years of change and suffering![27]

The poem has some bearing on the narrative, in particular on Breege's predicament. In it, the lyrical 'I' bemoans her 'only Love', who has been cold in the earth for fifteen wild Decembers, asking herself whether she has 'forgot [...] to love thee,/Severed at last by Time's all-severing wave'. She goes on to plead:

> Sweet Love of youth, forgive, if I forget thee,
> While the world's tide is bearing me along;
> Other desires and other hopes beset me,
> Hopes which obscure, but cannot do thee wrong!

After all, she admits that:

> No later light has lightened up my heaven,
> No second morn has ever shone for me;
> All my life's bliss from thy dear life was given,
> All my life's bliss is in the grave with thee.

It was only when 'Despair was powerless to destroy' that she learned 'how existence could be cherished,/ Strengthened, and fed without the aid of joy', and she resolved to 'check the tears of useless passion' and to wean her 'young soul from yearning after thine'. For she became aware that she could never 'seek the empty world again' if she dared to let her young soul languish and 'indulge in memory's rapturous pain'. The lines do indeed fittingly sum up Breege's situation at the close of *Wild Decembers*.

*

In the Yeats poem alluded to at the beginning of this chapter, the poet states at the outset: 'I sought a theme and sought for it in vain', and he comes to realise that '[h]e must be satisfied with [his] heart'. He then goes on to ask himself: 'What can I but enumerate old themes?', or to be more precise: 'Themes of the embittered heart, or so it seems,/ That might adorn old songs or courtly shows'. These sentiments are, in a fairly accurate sense, applicable to a great many of Edna O'Brien's novels. They are, in a manner of speaking, about her heart. One must note that fact with the necessary circumspection that the pitfalls of the biographical fallacy command. O'Brien, furthermore, has, in a considerable number of her full-length fictions, enumerated, or rather elaborated on, old themes, themes of the embittered heart that might adorn old songs or courtly shows or, more precisely, novels. But equally clearly, in her last two novels, O'Brien, apart from achieving a highly commendable artistic density and narrative elegance, has broken new thematic ground. Such new-found qualities combined suggest that, just as for Yeats, so for O'Brien, too, '[i]t was the dream itself enchanted [her]', meaning of course that latterly it has been her art itself that has enchanted her. 'Players and painted stage took all my love', Yeats goes on to specify, '[a]nd not those things that they were emblems of'. The embittered heart as a predominant thematic concern has yielded its significance to a wide-angled focus on the human condition, and O'Brien's art has attained a profundity that some critics may have found missing before. And yet, as again Yeats knew, those masterful images that he refers to may have grown 'in pure mind'. But 'out of what' did they begin? They began out of a mound of refuse or the sweepings of a street:

> Old kettles, old bottles, and a broken can,
> Old iron, old bones, old rags, that raving slut
> Who keeps the till.

And so, in the end, they all grew in 'the foul rag-and-bone shop of the heart'.

# JENNIFER JOHNSTON

Jennifer Johnston's works of fiction have, almost unanimously, met with extraordinary praise and pronounced admiration. *Shadows on Our Skin* (1977) was shortlisted for the Booker Prize, if that is anything to go by. *The Old Jest* (1979) won the Whitbread Award for Fiction, and *The Invisible Worm* (1991) was shortlisted for the Sunday Express Book of the Year. The comment on the cover of her latest novel, *Two Moons* (1998), states that Jennifer Johnston 'is recognised to be one of Ireland's finest writers' — an appreciation underpinned by numerous articles about her *oeuvre*. Yet what in the face of all this eulogy may be surprising is that none of the studies written so far has anything to remark on the glaring deficiencies in the novels. Still, it is rather odd that she should seem from their comments to be among the most consummate of stylists and artists. Seán MacMahon, for instance, argues:

> Her technical skill, her handling of dialogue, her tact when writing of youth and age, her detachment and humour, her quality of imagination, and above all her economy [...] all mark her out as a writer who may some day be great.[1]

The tentative note in MacMahon's verdict is due to the fact that it was made early on in Johnston's career. Writing some five years later, Mark Mortimer, with far fewer doubts, asserts:

> Now that she has established herself as a novelist of great and varied gift — admirable in constructing her plots and portraying her characters. Showing, as Minnie says of herself at school, 'remarkable genuity in phrase making' [...] she brings to her work many of the qualities that make a novelist's work memorable: precision in handling the army of words implanted in her mind [...][2]

Similarly, Heinz Kosok finds evidence in her work of a restless search for *le mot juste*.[3] But there are occasions, too many in fact to justify such praise, where Johnston's *mots* are anything but *justes*. Anthony Burgess even had no qualms in evaluating *Shadows on Our Skin* as 'unique and perfect art'.[4] While he was penning his review, Burgess must, for a moment, have forgotten what perfect art is. After all — *indignor quandoque bonus dormitat Homerus*, as Horace so sapiently suggested.

Johnston's works of fiction, to offer a summary critique, are self-deflatingly schematic: just too many of them rely on the same compositional pattern and concentrate on the themes of initiation and the sad plight of, frequently adolescent, would-be writers. Johnston's novels, furthermore, betray deficiencies in narrative style and technique as well as an unsure hand at what may be termed metaphorical enrichment, or metonymy. Lastly, they show the author's propensity for simply overdoing the coincidences in her plots and burdening her narrative accounts with intolerably melodramatic elements.[5]

There are many ways of indicating the schematic nature of the novels. One would be to ask why if anyone in Johnston's fictional world plays, or listens to, a piece of music, it has, without fail, to be something by Chopin. In *The Captains and the Kings* (1972), Mr Prendergast immerses himself in the playing of Chopin's *Nocturnes* shortly before he dies;[6] Alec's mother, in *How Many Miles to Babylon?* (1974), has a penchant for Chopin, and so has Maeve, in *The Old Jest* (1979);[7] *The Christmas Tree* (1981) yet again carries a reference to the Polish composer, but there, by way of compensation, Beethoven, Brahms, and Liszt get a mention as well.[8] In *Fool's Sanctuary* (1987), the principal character is, as so often in Johnston, an adolescent girl with a propensity for playing the Joanna. She, too, is fond of Chopin; but unlike Mr Prendergast, she is not particularly good at playing his music, having opted for Debussy instead.

Or, one may ask, why it is that so often in her fictional world raindrops have to 'burst' on some character's cheek (e.g. *Shadows* and *The Old Jest*), or why so frequently her characters have to stare 'inimicably' (*Shadows* and *The Old Jest*). The best way of indicating the schematic nature of her novels, however, is by pointing to the structural similarity of the books. In most of them, Johnston has favoured two compositional designs: either a combination of diary entries in the first-person and narrative sections in the third-person, or a circular narrative pattern, utilising a framing device.

The first group consists of *The Gates* (1973) and *The Old Jest*, very similar books also in respects other than purely structural. In fact, *The Old Jest* cannot pretend to be much more than a *réchauffé* both of thematic matters and structural patterns tried out in the previous fictions, most notably in *The Gates*. An eighteen-year-old girl, Nancy Gulliver, with aspirations to become a writer, narrates certain allegedly crucial events that span a couple of days in her life, adopting a third-person point of view. Once again, as in *The Gates*, each narrative section is prefaced with a diary entry. These entries are intended to record 'passing thoughts that give impressions of [Nancy]' (p. 6), and their *raison d'être* is simply 'that in forty years...[she] can look back and see what [she] was like when [she] started out' (p. 6), or so Nancy wishes the reader to think. In spite of this explanation, though, it remains teasingly unclear, here as in *The Gates*, what the strategy of combining diary entries with narrative units is meant to convey. For, apart from being from the same pen, the two have little to hold them together thematically. Thus it would have been feasible to have the entries reflect on the narrative parts, or *vice versa*. Besides, why should someone who believes she has it in her to become a writer and wishes to fictionalise aspects of her own life preface her account with unfictionalised diary entries, or undisguised addresses to the reader concerning her whereabouts, before embarking on her narrative enterprise? In slightly varied form the same problem arises again in Johnston's *The Railway Station Man* (1984), where it is, as in *The Gates* and *The Old Jest*, linked with a shift in narrative point of view, quite a questionable shift, to be precise, as will be argued later.

As for the reliance on a framing device, *The Captains and the Kings* marks the beginning of this trend. The novel starts off on the afternoon of 20 September, with Guards Devenney and Conroy on their way to Kill House. After two pages, this unit is left undeveloped and unresolved, and the reader is kept guessing as to what the guards' business may be. Only at the very end does the account pick up from there to divulge that the two men are on their way to summon Mr Prendergast to the police barracks. Within this frame, the story is told of what happened between 'late May' (p. 8) and 20 September, involving Mr Prendergast and the boy, Diarmid Toolish. Intriguing though a framing device may be, the trouble is that in *The Captains* it fails to have any real thematic consequence; it is just an empty ploy. In her third novel, *How Many Miles to Babylon?* (1974), Johnston once again resorts to a framing device as well as to a circular course of events. Alexander Moore has been sentenced to death and will soon have to face the firing squad for shooting his friend, Jerry Crowe. While he is thus waiting for his execution, he spends his time writing, committed to no cause and knowing that 'for the waiting days [he has] only the past to play about with' (p. 5). His juggling 'with a series of possibly inaccurate memories' (p. 5) leads him back to his childhood in Ireland, and proceeding from that period in time, he gradually unfolds the story of his friendship with Jerry. The next novel to openly make use of a narrative frame is *The*

*Christmas Tree*. While it therefore belongs firmly to the group under discussion, the book at the same time shares certain structural characteristics with *The Gates* and *The Old Jest*. The frame is formed by the letter Constance Keating pens to Jacob Weinberg at the outset, urging him to come and see her before she dies, and by Jacob's belated arrival at Constance's house in Ballsbridge near the close. This apart, the story consists of sections told from a first-person viewpoint and recording the events during the last eight days of Constance's life. Intercalated into these are units presenting scenes from a receding past and constituting those 'thousand pieces of a jigsaw puzzle' mentioned by Constance herself. This compositional scheme not only recalls the narrative texture of *The Gates* and *The Old Jest*, but is essentially similar to it, the present sections in the first-person corresponding to the diary entries, and the past sections in the third-person to the straight narrative passages in the other two novels. *The Railway Station Man* (1984) yet again employs a framing device, and yet again has a circular course of events, while at the same time exploiting the narrative procedure of *The Gates* and *The Old Jest*. It begins with Helen Cuffe, in the first-person, filling the reader in on her past life before she came to live in a cottage in the northwest of Ireland, near Sligo. Unlike most of her fellow-protagonists in Johnston's world of fiction, Helen had, until quite recently, no aspirations to become a writer. A painter of sorts, she exchanged brush for pen after a disastrous event in which her son, Jack, and the eponymous railway station man were embroiled. The last section of the book closes the ring-like frame; it belongs to the same level as the opening passage, again presenting Helen directly addressing the reader in the first-person. Within this frame, reminiscent of the procedure in *The Captains* and, especially, in *How Many Miles*, Helen tells the story of her involvement with Roger Hawthorne and of the explosion cryptically mentioned at the start. The references to the explosion at the beginning and the end thus reinforce the circular pattern, as does the device of starting and finishing the account with a single word. At the outset it is the word 'isolation', at the close it is the word 'running'. It seems as if Johnston deliberately chose to begin and end her novel thus in order to further enhance the circular course of events, to indicate (say) that the story moves from the 'isolation' which characterised Helen's life before she got to know the titular hero, via a brief period of friendship, even love, happiness, and involvement, to — well, yes, 'running'. But where to and what from? There's the rub. Apart from the fact that the novel begins and ends with a single word, the idea does not make much sense. Why, one may wonder, did Johnston not select a word for the close that fitted better the otherwise meaningless pattern?

In Johnston's previous books, whenever there was a would-be writer giving a fictional account of her, or his, life, it was done from a third-person viewpoint. That is, at least partly, again the case in *The Railway Station Man*. But whereas previously the perspective remained the same throughout, namely that of the teller, now, in the third-person part of the novel, the point of view changes between that of Helen and that of Jack, so that, taken together, the narrative presents three different perspectives: Helen in the first-person, Helen in the third-person, and Jack in the third-person. Thus, as mentioned, the prefatory section has Helen state, for instance: 'At this moment, as I write these words [...]'.[9] The first and second units of the fictionalised part are seen through Jack's eyes, while the next one shows a change to Helen's. The strategy is later repeated. Why should that be so? Is the change in point of view thematically necessary, or significant? This much is certain: since Helen states of herself that it is she who is writing everything, this means that whenever the reader is asked to assess the incidents through Jack's eyes, Helen assumes cognisance of her son's thoughts. There is nothing odd about the procedure because, after all, the greater part of the novel represents a fictionalised version of recent events in Helen's life featuring Helen the writer taking on the role of omniscient narrator. The trouble, though, is that *The Railway Station Man* is so centred, for its effect, on Helen (most narrative units are from her point of view), and Jack remains such a marginal figure in the Helen–Roger drama that the change in perspective must appear entirely arbitrary. Why, for instance, if there must be viewpoints other than Helen's is the reader never allowed to enter into Roger's, or Damian's, mind? Why are the events not mirrored through the consciousnesses of all the main characters, in the manner employed by (say) Joseph Conrad in *Nostromo*? The question must remain unanswered. And so must the related one of why Johnston adopted the policy. In fact, the whole strategy becomes nonsensical if one takes the following into account: in her first couple of paragraphs, Helen states: 'To be accurate, and it is in the interest of accuracy that I am struggling with these words [...]' (p. 1). How can she be accurate about Jack's thoughts, unless he told her himself, which is wholly unlikely as he was blown to smithereens in the explosion?

In *Fool's Sanctuary*, the narrative present forms a framing device for a recollective account of past events. The frame is quite promising.

Miranda, late in life — in fact, she is on her deathbed in 'Termon' (an anglicisation of the Irish word for 'sanctuary'), a Big House somewhere in County Cork, a situation comparable to Constance's in *The Christmas Tree* — is playing '[her] play for the last time'[10] in her head, a play focusing on a stormy weekend and involving her father, her brother Andrew, Andrew's British soldier friend, Nanny, her youthful sweetheart Cathal, and members of the IRA. The style of the first pages is almost scintillating and the subject matter seems compelling. But as early as page 7, when Miranda's 'play' commences, it becomes only too apparent that a sour disappointment is afoot. Cathal, son of a Catholic worker at Termon and now a student in Dublin and associated with the fight for freedom, has come from 'the real world' to visit Miranda in order 'to breath the same unreal air as [she]'. Also on a visit is Andrew, a sort of glorified spy for the British Army, whose life in Britain has taught him to despise the Irish and their fight for independence. He is haunted by the 'ghost' of his mother and has never been able to hit it off with his father, Mr Martin, who dreams of repaying his debts to a country exploited by his ancestors: thousands and thousands of acres of derelict land must be given new heart, he believes, through 'planting combined with major drainage schemes' (p. 65). Andrew is accompanied by his officer friend Harry Harrington, who complicates things at Termon by falling in love with Miranda, thus becoming a rival to Cathal, who is already hard put to it to stand his ground against attacks from his erstwhile friend Andrew for stepping out of his class. While Harry is making sheep's eyes at Miranda and Andrew is quarrelling with his father and getting drunker and drunker, Cathal comes with the news that the IRA have sent some hitmen down from Dublin to assassinate Andrew and Harry. After some poking around in Mr Martin's antediluvian car, the British 'intruders' are packed off to Dublin, and Cathal is later taken away by the IRA men and shot for betraying the cause.

The blurb claims that *Fool's Sanctuary* is about 'loyalty and betrayal, and the thin line that divides them'. If it is, then the realisation is severely marred, most devastatingly by the reliance on worn-out features of the big-house novel: the ineffective, philanthropic father; the soldier son, who has turned to drink and despises his father's idealism; the stuttering, likeable Englishman who has no clue about Ireland; the no-nonsense Nanny; the overpowering mother, albeit now a 'ghost'; and the Catholic patriot who goes to his death for a grand gesture. There is also the problem that the novella is too much centred on Miranda for the themes of loyalty and betrayal to come into their own. The way that Miranda, imprisoned in the unreality of her fool's sanctuary and stunted in her emotional growth by the hapless immaturity of her consciousness, comes to terms, or rather fails to come to terms, with the disruption of her 'Indian summer of illusions' is not worked out properly. In fact at times it is made preposterous. For instance, when Cathal meets Miranda, she suggests, quoting the line from *Richard II*: 'Let's sit upon the ground and tell sad stories of the death of kings'. This is completely out of context. In its over-reliance on dialogue the narrative reveals its origin in a stage play, *Indian Summer*, first produced in Belfast in 1983.

*The Invisible Worm* (1991) yet again employs a framing device, confronting past and present. The novel is about guilt and atonement, about the laying of ghosts from the past. It is the story of 37-year-old Laura Quinlan and how the invisible worm of memory 'doth [her] life destroy', to adopt a line from Blake's 'The Sick Rose'. Laura is given to standing by the window and seeing scenes from the past in her 'X-ray eyes', scenes that reverberate and conjure up other scenes. In them, her father, with whose funeral the account opens, figures prominently. While kneeling in church, Laura reflects: 'I can't. I cannot forgive. Forget it, God.' What it is that she cannot forgive is left vexingly vague at this stage. Nor is it any clearer why she 'will infect this race [with] her hatred'. But not to worry, all is revealed in the end.

The past may preoccupy Laura a good deal, but so does the present: for example, in the shape of Dominic O'Hara, a spoiled priest and a teacher of classics who comes to tea when Laura's husband, Maurice, is away and noses about in Laura's gargantuan collection of memorabilia amassed by her forebears. A bloody museum is what Maurice calls it. Dominic is an oaf and an obnoxious inquisitor who elicits the secret from Laura that she is afraid of her late father — at times even feeling his hands around her neck.

Basically, the account is made up of two stories. The narrative present is generated by a series of quite inconsequential events, showing Jennifer Johnston not at her best in trying to get Maurice off the stage in order for Laura to fall in love with Dominic, who has problems of his own: his father is dying and his family want him to stay away. 'Barge in. Fight' is what Laura advises. And that is what he does. There is also much ado about restoring a summerhouse, overgrown with weeds, brambles and dry grass. The summerhouse is the link with the past. Every so often, Laura envisages scenes featuring a woman running. It is herself. Or so it turns out when she divulges to Dominic the reason for her mental preoccupation with *temps perdu*. Her father raped her when she was still a child, stealing from her the expectation of love, joy and peace. Her mother, when told by Laura afterwards, killed herself in her boat. In the end, having recovered from a nervous breakdown, Laura sets fire to the summerhouse and unburdens her traumatic past to Dominic.

This is ample stuff from which to weave a good narrative. *The Invisible Worm*, though, is an uninspired novel. The main shortcoming is the inexpert way in which the past has been incorporated into the present. Of course, memories sometimes do occur in random fashion; mostly, however, they are generated by optical and audible impressions or through associative thinking. The modernists knew this intimately. Here, memories too frequently happen out of the blue. The affair between the oafish Dominic and guilt-ridden Laura is completely unconvincing, and so is her ambivalent relationship with her husband.

The inevitable framing pattern is also employed in *The Illusionist* (1995). The main character, Stella Macnamara, is once more a writer and the narrative that constitutes the novel is meant to be from her pen. But Stella does not match her Johnstonian fellow-writer-*personae* in the number of imbecilities she perpetrates, even though she is given to dancing around the house, coughing up lines from songs whether appropriate or not and filling her head with silly words, such as 'Tararaboomdeay', in times of crisis, thus, in a way, anticipating Grace in *Two Moons*. The frame-story has Stella's daughter, Robin, visit her mother in Dublin after her father's funeral in London. The father, the eponymous illusionist, was killed by an IRA bomb in his station wagon with 150 white doves neatly caged in the back. Mother and daughter are estranged; in fact, Robin seems to hate Stella's guts, particularly because Stella ran away from the illusionist when their marriage was on the rocks. The story accommodated by the frame, which in brief episodes is kept up and elaborated throughout, is the story of that marriage.

Stella met the illusionist on a train. At that time, she was working in the publishing business. The couple married, lived in a dingy flat in London at first, then bought a grand house in Suffolk. She left her job, despite a tempting offer to become a partner in the publishing firm, gave birth to a daughter and lived the life of a housewife. Then, one day, her former boss visited her and presented her with a portable typewriter. For he knew that she had it in her to be a writer. Her first efforts with the machine yield only 'QWERTYUIOP', but she made quick progress and before you could say 'Jack Robinson', her first novel was completed. Now, at the age of fifty-eight, Stella has been writing fiction for fifteen years. While she was pottering about the house and getting keyed up for her writing career, the illusionist, Martyn (with a 'y' to the chagrin of Stella's mother), was busy taking his illusionist act to the Continent and all over the place. Stella never knew where he went or what exactly he was up to. For Martyn was an egregiously enigmatic man. He is in fact allowed to be enigmatic to such an extent that he is hardly a real presence in the book. His act is a bit of an enigma, too. Apparently, Martyn on stage has doves all over him and, flapping his arms about, is transformed into an angel that hovers above the darkness of the world. It is all done with mirrors, of course. Eventually, the marital relationship deteriorated because 'secrets seemed to be everywhere'.

What is somehow disappointing about the novel is that Stella's development, or growth, into a writer, as that of the other would-be writers in Johnston's canon, is not in the least made evident and consequently remains unconvincing. We only have Ms Johnston's word for it. The reader may be somewhat at a loss to say what the illusionist business is all about. But perhaps it is significant that Martyn was an illusionist. For, as one learns at the close of the book, as do Stella and Robin, he successfully created the illusion that he was deeply in love with his wife and his daughter when, in truth, he entertained a fancy woman, his secretary, with whom he sired a second daughter. Which only goes to show that one should not put one's trust in men who keep their pasts a well-guarded secret and perform with birds.

Johnston's reliance, for purposes of structure, on framing devices and circular plot-patterns is thus obsessionally overriding. Even the storyline of *Shadows on Our Skin* is no exception. For it could be argued that the incidents chart a way from humdrum, stultifying routine, via a brief exciting period of time in which Joe Logan, by befriending Kathleen Doherty, is jolted out of the monotony of his existence, back to an even bleaker sort of humdrum, stultifying routine. But enough on that score. There are other considerations that now call for attention, such as the deficiencies in Johnston's narrative style and technique.

In the very first of her published books, Johnston seems to have developed and exploited the narrative method that best suits her talent. It is here, as in most of her other works of fiction, basically a scenic method that depends for its effect on dialogue. The descriptive passages betray an unmistakable heavy-handedness and lack of control. But even the conversational sections often have an imbecile ring about them, for example in *Shadows*. While one could excuse some of them, allowing for Joe Logan's age, there is one instance especially that is difficult to accept.

Coming back from Grianan, Joe notices his brother, Brendan, 'standing by the corner of the garden shop'.[11] He hopes Brendan cannot see him; however, in order to make sure, he ducks down his head. Now, this is how the incident is rendered:

> ...perhaps Brendan couldn't see him.
> The ostrich principle.
> 'Hello.'
> He heard Kathleen's voice tentatively speaking.
> 'Hello, Miss...', Brendan hesitated.
> The ostrich never wins. (p. 97)

Ah, well, the ostrich leads a hard life! Or take the manner in which the love affair between Helen and Roger is presented in *The Railway Station Man*. The affair is of exceptional importance to the novel, for it entails Helen's relinquishing her chosen life of isolation for the love of another human being, of Roger, but with the sad result that, when this love seems in full bloom, Roger becomes the victim of some hare-brained political action and Helen is left to 'mourn the needless dead' (p. 186). To begin with, the love affair is pitifully implausible. Why should Helen, a woman in her fifties, become attracted to a man who is not at all physically attractive, unless, of course, he had an intriguing personality? Of that, however, there is next to nothing. In fact, Roger's preoccupation with restoring yet another railway station on a closed-down line unequivocally singles him out as a nutcase. On the first two occasions when they meet, his behaviour towards Helen is rather rude. But the next thing that happens is that they go on a picnic and end up first in his bed, then in hers. A transition from the status quo, as laid down when they first get to know one another, to their mutual infatuation is simply missing.

And what preposterous features, downright imbecilities, this affair contains, implausible as it is! At the end of one evening, before he leaves Helen, Roger feels it incumbent upon himself to tell Helen, entirely out of the blue: 'I've had women you know. I'm not...' (p. 121). Well, of course, naturally; after all he is a man well advanced in years, and he was not born a cripple either. Or here is how the first advances in this extraordinary love affair are described:

> He moves his cheek against hers and the sudden scratch of stub-
> ble made her heart thud. Oh no God, please God, don't let

anything stupid happen. (p. 153)

Of course, something stupid will happen. Yet wait, relish this, just moments later:

> He kissed her. He held her tight with his hands on her back so that she could feel his hardness. The stubble scratched, oh God, she thought again, where are You now? Why didn't You do something before it was too late? (p. 155)

God does not seem to have been much interested, for 'ten minutes later' they are 'upstairs in his bedroom' (p. 155). Next morning, Helen questions herself about what happened the night before: 'Was what happened last night love? Desperation? Alcohol?' (p. 157). She is inclined to say 'Yes to all three' (p. 157). Her son, Jack, believes it 'is some sort of menopausal madness' (p. 127). Matters become even odder when menopausal madness in a woman of fifty and more is coupled with a kind of outlook appropriate only for a teenager. The morning after they have next had sexual intercourse, Roger urges Helen to stay in bed with him and let 'the bloody Aga go out'. Helen, however, retorts: 'Even for Paul Newman I wouldn't let the Aga go out' (p. 169). And when, shortly after, Roger asks her to marry him, Helen rejects his proposal, justifying her decision by noting that she would 'say the same thing to Paul Newman' (p. 175). Would any woman of Helen's age who claims for herself the sensitivity, the creative and intellectual capacity of an artist as well as a writer, respond, *in earnest*, by dragging in Paul Newman?

Since in *The Christmas Tree* she chose to have the story told, for the greater part, by the principal character, in order to include her death, Johnston was of course in need of someone else as the recording authority. It would, at first glance, seem an expert solution to have Bridie take on this role. Thus Bridie notes: 'These last few pages are written by me Bridie May, beginning on Christmas Eve 1978. I have made nothing up, nor have I left anything out [...] at least I don't think I have' (p. 158). There is, however, something quite inexpert about this solution. One would expect that there should be discernible a distinct change in narrative voice between Constance's and Bridie's pages. For after all Constance likes to think of herself as a failed writer with three unpublished novels behind her, and Bridie is a girl of all but ebullient linguistic skill. Self-defeatingly, the novel does not contain any such change in tone and style. To have the doctor referred to as 'Dr Bill' is about all there is in this respect, and it simply will not do.

The next point of criticism concerns the melodramatic elements and the overdoing of coincidences in plot development. The love affair between Helen and Roger is of course highly melodramatic. All too often these melodramatic elements go hand in hand with vastly implausible coincidences. This rather deplorable state of affairs is noticeable in all of Johnston's novels. In *The Captains*, Mr Prendergast is given to pondering why, in contrast to his brother Alexander, he has never been able to master the piano accompaniment of Goethe's 'Der Erlkönig':

> Wer reitet so spät durch Nacht und Wind?
> Es ist der Vater mit seinem Kind.
> Er hat den Sohn wohl im Arm,
> Er fasst ihn sicher, er hält ihn warm. (p. 111)

It must surely be counted as a pretty preposterous concretisation of the sentiments expressed by these lines, when Mr Prendergast is placed in a situation where, as some sort of father surrogate, he can, or could, hold in his arms and keep warm the boy who intrudes into his curious privacy. Of the instances of melodrama in *The Gates*, by far the most telling ones can be found in the section describing how Minnie and Ivy try to get the inebriated Major up the stairs into his bed, with the Major in a drunken stupor begging them not to let on to his niece, Minnie. The whole passage reads like an involuntary parody of Tristram Shandy's difficulty in getting his father and uncle Toby down the stairs. Yet another example occurs in *The Christmas Tree*, involving Jacob Weinberg's arrival at the side of Constance's deathbed as a result of Constance's letter to him. When she sends it, she is altogether ignorant of his present whereabouts, but she is hopeful that, wherever he may be travelling, the letter will follow him around the world and that he will come to Dublin before her life is ended. And Jacob does come, never mind that he arrives too late — the morning after the night in which she died, on Christmas Day, like one of the Magi. His arrival represents one turn of the narrative screw too many. Tracing a man whose address is unknown outside Ireland, in under six days, is no mean feat, in fact it *is* a miracle. *The Christmas Tree* would have been a better book if Jacob's arrival had been left suspended, so to speak, as a mere thematic potential.

The examples could easily be multiplied, but these will suffice. I will now turn my attention to Johnston's misfiring attempts at metonymy, at embellishing her narratives with metaphoric connotations. Again many examples could be cited, but, due to lack of space, one must do. The use of the swan metaphor, near the end of *How Many Miles to Babylon?* before Jerry is shot by Alex, is certainly rather inexpert and objectionable. Particularly during the big-house part, the two friends are associated with swans: swans fly above their heads while they are taking a swim; and Jerry, minutes before his death, remarks to Alec:

> 'Remember.'
> 'I can remember nothing.'
> 'The Lake. The swans...'
> 'Only that their wings sound like gun shots.' (p. 140)

Later, before we know what will happen to Jerry, who has just returned to his regiment, Alec observes two swans: 'They were flying low, their wings fanning with dignity the air around' (p. 136). While he raises his hand in greeting, the sound of a shot reaches him. 'The front bird's neck swung for a moment from left to right and then drooped' (p. 136). One of his soldiers has shot the bird for a lark. But does this incident not foreshadow the fate of Jerry? Yes, yes — but rather too obviously. Even without reading on, one can — by courtesy of this pointing with a bargepole — guess that Jerry will be sentenced to death. Nothing substantial would be missing if those wild swans at Coole were not in the book.

Most puzzling as well as self-defeating about Johnston's novels is surely the fact that in so many of them their author persists in concerning herself with would-be writers, quite a number of whom are adolescents. Minnie, in *The Gates*, is the first of these principal characters. Why, upon returning to Ireland, she should decide to become a writer is a surprise, a mystery even. She claims that a novel is growing in her head (p. 81). But the only explanation for her decision could be that her father had been a writer of sorts himself. He never wrote a novel, though, only 'Bolshevik rubbish in the newspapers' (p. 92), as a former friend of his puts it. The next writer-*persona* is Alec, in *How Many Miles*. Then follow the poetising Joe Logan, in *Shadows*; the novel-writing Nancy, in *The Old Jest*; Constance, in *The Christmas Tree*; Helen Cuffe, in *The Railway Station Man*, and, last in the line, Stella, in *The Illusionist*.

The questions to be answered in connection with this repeated choice of writer-protagonist are these: Do all the characters really represent artists? Are Johnston's novels therefore *Künstlerromane*, as some critics think? Are their experiences, artistic as well as initiatory, compelling at all?

As for the mental agonies of adolescent protagonists, did not Aldous Huxley have Mr Scogan, in *Crome Yellow*, express the view: 'Why will you young men continue to write about things that are so extremely uninteresting as the mentality of adolescents and artists'?[12] The same would seem to apply to some women writers too, this especially so if the mentality portrayed is in no way exceptional, in spite of Johnston's implicit claim that in *Shadows*, as elsewhere, we are after all concerned with the mentality of a potential poet, or writer.

There is good reason to suppose that Johnston wants the reader to regard Joe Logan's frame of mind as somehow akin to that of Stephen Dedalus, for instance with regard to Joe's preoccupation with the sound and meaning of words. Instances such as these:

> Sugar, gritty crystal in a blue bowl! (p. 18)

> 'Obscure!'
>> The word came into his mind and he said it out aloud.
>> 'Obscure. Ob...scure...lure...pure...hoor.' He laughed to himself. 'A pure hoor dressed in velour is pretty obscure.' (p. 68)

> Hallowed...hallow was a lovely word...Hallowed be Thy...(p. 127)

do of course recall Stephen's musings on 'Tower of Ivory', 'God' and 'Dieu', 'suck' and 'kiss'. Similarly, Joe's deliberations on how he can make words express what he is seeking to express (cf. p. 139) are reminiscent of Stephen's pondering on matters aesthetic and creative. But what a difference there is between the delineation of the two artistic, adolescent consciousnesses! That Joe should be concerned with such issues is quite in order, after all he is endeavouring to write verse. Where Joyce incorporates only one sample of Stephen's poetising, the one about 'ardent ways', Johnston offers several specimens of Joe's poetic efforts, which are presumably meant to chart his artistic progress. Here is one:

> My brother has come home.
> Why?
> That's what I would like to know.
> That's what I ask myself from time to time.
> He has money rattling in his pockets.
> Money that folds in his wallet.
> He says he earned it by working hard.

Over there he worked.
Making a packet.
How?
My mother says I shouldn't believe everything I'm told.
Why not? (p. 47)

It may be easier 'if you [don't] have to make rhymes' (p. 47), as Joe
reasons, but he goes on to ask himself: '[Is] it poetry at all?' Well, the
simple answer is: No. It is, among other things, rhythm that matters, as
Joe is rightly aware himself, 'so that it [doesn't] sound like ordinary
sentences' (p. 47). His sentences are pretty ordinary, though. After the
trip to Grianan he pens another 'poem', which he recites to Kathleen,
once more stressing: 'You don't have to rhyme' (p. 85). Indeed not, but
the long and the short of it is that Joe's efforts do not add up to much.
In fact his forays into poetry bring to mind the wise reflections on
poetry of Rilke's Malte Laurids Brigge:

> Ah! but verses amount to so little when one begins to write them
> young. One ought to wait and gather sense and sweetness a whole
> life long, and a long life if possible, and then, quite at the end,
> one might perhaps be able to write ten good lines. For verses are
> not, as people imagine, simply feelings (we have these soon
> enough); they are experiences...it is the memories themselves that
> matter. Only when they have turned to blood within us, to glance
> and gesture, nameless and no longer distinguished from ourselves
> — only then can it happen that in a most rare hour the first word
> of a poem arises in their midst and goes forth from them.[13]

One does of course not become a writer by merely putting pen to paper
while one is waiting for the bullet, like Alex. Nancy's endeavours, in *The
Old Jest*, are scarcely less pathetic than Minnie's, in *The Gates*. Constance
Keating, in *The Christmas Tree*, may be an exception. In spite of some
melodramatic coincidences, the way in which she pieces together the
jigsaw puzzle of her life shows a fair amount of novelistic skill. But
then, mercifully, she is no longer an adolescent girl, and, equally mercifully,
she is well past the stage at which she entertained pretensions to be
much of a writer. As early as her sojourn in Italy she told Jacob that,
although she left Ireland for London to become a writer, it was hopeless:
'I suppose I didn't have anything to say. Not enough talent...perhaps no
purpose' (p. 52). The case of Helen, in *The Railway Station Man*, is

different. The ado about her art, her sudden burst of creative energy do pose severe problems; and so do her efforts at writing, as witness the examples discussed earlier. Additional problems arise as far as the portrayal of Helen's consciousness is concerned. Here once more, despite her being a woman in her fifties, the theme of initiation looms large. And that is, not least, because her reflections, as offered in what for better or for worse must be termed her interior monologues, are more akin to a teenager than to a woman of Helen's age. Her deliberations on art are of the Simple Simon variety. Her mental reaction to seeing Damian jogging in the raw on the beach: 'I hope to God he doesn't catch pneumonia' (p. 105), is quite laughable. Or take her thoughts immediately after she has been informed about her husband's death: 'I remember that I hadn't got a handkerchief and wondered would I need one. Uncheckable tears flow in the cinema. Maybe at any moment that might happen' (p. 9). Would anyone at such a moment really be reminded of the tears that flow in the cinema? Or would a woman in her fifties, unless she were dotty, mentally refer to her bicycle, which she has to leave by the side of the road because someone is offering her a lift in his car, in the following manner: 'Goodbye, old faithful' (p. 68)? It is in such interior monologue passages, but also in the way in which, in many cases, she makes her characters respond mentally to certain incidents, that Johnston could do with more imaginative resources. The personalities of her would-be writers are frequently at odds with the kind of consciousness they have been equipped with.

The prime instance of this shortcoming is probably to be found in *The Old Jest*. From what is shown there of Nancy's mental activities, or reactions, one cannot but conclude that hers is a rather retarded consciousness. For would an eighteen-year-old girl really agonise over unrequited love as Nancy does, wishing 'the same wish that she had wished for years, that Harry might one day love her' (p. 120)? Would an eighteen-year-old girl, upon hearing that her rival, Maeve, is not present, react thus:

> Fingers crossed tightly in her pocket. Not coming. What bliss! Never coming again. Found beautifully drowned, like Ophelia or the lady who went to call the cattle home across the Sands of Dee. Hair floating, lilies, ever so romantic. What bliss! A beautiful corpse [...] (and so on) (pp. 45f.)

Would an eighteen-year-old girl who is intent upon starting 'to become a person' (p. 6), absent-mindedly pick her nose in the presence of a stranger while telling him about her grandfather (p. 52)? Would an eighteen-year-old girl really ask the man she desperately hopes will one day love her whether he has 'fucked' (p. 79), and then go on to tell him that she will 'have done it by the time [she's] twenty-six'? *O tempora, o mores!* Does an eighteen-year-old girl really talk to her sponge and really say to the cat: 'I really want him [*i.e.* Harry] to love me' (p. 79)? Does an eighteen-year-old girl respond to being told what a good thing it is to be a freedom-fighter by ejaculating: 'Tomorrow I'm thinking of starting a life of crime. Maturing crime' (p. 116)? Not very likely.

And yet, Shari Benstock has approached Johnston's novels as portraits of artists as young men, or women, believing that their subject matter is fundamentally 'the act of writing and the motivation for story-telling'.[14] The books, according to Benstock, portray boys, or girls, who, having discovered in themselves the vocation to become writers, are trying to come to grips with the creative process. Admittedly, if viewed in this light, the weaknesses and shortcomings discussed here would take on a new significance. They would not so much reflect on the artistic ineptitude of Johnston herself, as on that of her writer-protagonists in the individual books. Thus, for example, the mistake of introducing Christopher Boyle in *How Many Miles,* and the failure to inform the reader about the relationship he had with the Moore family could be laid at Alexander's door. It is a nice thought, but hardly a true one. If one compares these weaknesses and shortcomings and also the tones and styles of the fledgling writers, one will conclude that they are always more or less the same, a fact surprisingly acknowledged by Benstock herself.[15] Does this mean that the juvenile writers in Johnston's world of fiction all share the same artistic difficulties, all grapple with the same creative problems, all adopt the same tone of voice? This would surely be a ridiculous state of affairs. No one would seriously want to submit that every aspiring adolescent would-be writer finds himself, or herself, in a predicament shared by every other adolescent would-be writer. As Benstock goes on to note, these would-be writers all have come to terms with social, parental, familial, and other forces that impinge on their personalities, no matter whether they live in Derry or on some Big House estate in the Republic. These forces are, furthermore, said to have the same effect on the sensitivity and mentality of the would-be writer. Does this mean that Johnston believes all writers have the same kind of sensitivity and mentality? It is not easy to subscribe to such a disparaging idea. The crux of the whole matter seems to lie elsewhere: in Johnston's inability to differentiate her writer-characters sufficiently. Her novelistic efforts should not bring forth such similar results.

There is also something quite wrong with Johnston as a literary artist, and this something can aptly be characterised by referring to one of William Golding's statements on the nature of the artist, literary or otherwise. Golding has remarked that the artist, any artist, must remain a moving target. To be precise, he has said of himself: '[...] as for me, I am a moving target'.[16] It is true, artists worth the name must remain moving targets. Their artistic conscience must compel them to develop their art. They must keep themselves as well as their readers and critics on their toes by observing the need for innovation, variation, change of technique and subject matter. They must not let their art grow stale, but keep it alive.

There is a difference, though. That difference is represented by Johnston's latest novel, *Two Moons*, a book about missed opportunities and relationships jaded because things remained undiscussed that should have been discussed while there was still time to do so, or because of an overriding concern with one's own interests. The narrative thrives on dialogue and interior monologue or free indirect discourse. Whereas on previous occasions, Johnston's deployment of these two techniques, particularly of interior monologue or free indirect style, betrayed an unsure hand, here this has greatly improved, a few lapses notwithstanding.

The novel focuses on the lives lived in a house in Killiney, covering a period of about three weeks.[17] Eighty-year-old Mimi Gibbon all of a sudden receives a messenger from the land of the shadows, someone like the spirit of Hamlet's father, who of course remains unseen by everyone else, even though he occasionally leaves some of his accoutrements lying around the place. The messenger, or angel, has come, one supposes, not least because, as he remarks, Mimi is someone who is able to 'see beyond reality' (p. 8). He is one Bonifacio di Longaro, who was born in Borgo Sansepalcro in 1429 and died forty-two years and three months later from a 'plague you might call it of mosquitoes' (p. 106). Bonifacio fills the old woman with a fresh, quite pleasant and invigorating sense of life. Thus, for example, the pain that she feels at times in various parts of her body disappears in his presence. She enjoys going on walks with him, whereas BB (that is: Before Bonifacio) she spent her days sitting in her garden or staggering laboriously around on her walking stick. Additionally, he makes her relish the purchase of sinfully expensive Italian suede boots, this being a consequence of the fact that Bonifacio used to be a shoemaker in fifteenth-century Italy.

Most importantly, though, Bonifacio causes Mimi to think about her late husband, Benjamin, 'not something she did very often' (p. 31) or used to do BB. Benjamin led a strange life, cooped up within himself and drowning his never-disclosed sorrows and pains in gallons of whiskey. He was like a man 'in a locked room banging his body and his spirit against the wall' (p. 59). In the end, he took to silence. The marriage had been reasonably happy for a brief period of time; but after the birth of a daughter it deteriorated quickly. Mimi did not run away from what she experienced as hatred out of consideration for this child. Bonifacio helps Mimi come to terms with the past. 'It's so hard to get rid of the past. [...] It's like a web all around me. I keep trying to escape and I can't' (p. 44), she admits. Bonifacio likewise assists Mimi in coming to grips with her misspent life and in arriving at an understanding of her husband. In fact, Bonifacio, first claiming to have been summoned by Benjamin, turns into Benjamin near the ending of the novel, where the husband unbosoms the secret of his life that marred his relationship with his wife. Before he came to know Mimi, Benjamin was passionately in love with another man who suddenly left him after making love to him at the Pine Forest. He kept this hidden from Mimi, fearing that otherwise she would have deserted him. 'I was so disgusted with myself. Neither prayer nor drink saved me from that disgust. And I saw [...] how I was destroying your life [...]' (p. 213). After Benjamin's confession, Mimi can say: '[...] you've lifted some burdens from my back' (p. 214).

Mimi's fifty-year-old daughter, Grace, an actress currently playing Gertrude in a production of *Hamlet* at the Abbey, also lives in the house in Killiney. (Hence the reference to the spirit of Hamlet's father earlier on.) Grace is given to spouting some of Gertrude's lines throughout the book, apparently so as to show the full extent to which she is preoccupied with her work, which indeed is the only plausible reason for having her do so. '[...] I am steeped in omelette' (p. 10), she explains to her daughter, Polly, when Polly is a bit miffed at not being greeted with the expected enthusiasm upon her arrival from London. The 'omelette' is of course meant to be funny, in case you hadn't realised.

The phrase most employed by Grace throughout her adult life as well as in the course of the book whenever someone, especially Mimi or Polly, approaches her for comfort, help or advice is: 'Not at this moment' (cf. for instance p. 13). At one point, appropriately, while noticing her mother's sulking face, Grace wonders: 'Is this my fault [...] Am I not giving her her fair share of attention? I used to wonder that about Polly too' (p. 20). She presently finds herself in a situation where '[her] inertia or carelessness has caught up with [her]' (p. 130). As Mimi correctly comments, Grace's problem has always been that she puts her work first (cf. p. 149). Thus, when Polly desperately tries to seek succour from her mother after Paul has broken off his engagement to her, Grace is, as usual, otherwise engaged. Neither Polly nor Mimi nor any man could ever mean as much to Grace as her work. Her marriage came to an end after fifteen years. There was a divorce and John, her former husband, married again. Polly is now living in the basement of his house in Hampstead, feeling neglected and pushed around.

The title of the novel is a reference, firstly, to the two moons that Grace sees outside her window: 'one suspended in the globe of blackness, the other flickering in the sea below' (p. 26), and secondly, it is a reference to her personal approach to life, Grace being suspended 'between Gertrude and I [*sic*]', between her work and her role in a clearly defined social context.

What may somehow stretch one's credulity about the skein involving Grace is her affair with Polly's lover, who is about thirty years her junior. Paul arrives late one night out of the blue. Polly had told her mother that her new lover would arrive on the next day. Possibly, Polly, like Grace, is so self-centred that she is unable to attend properly to matters concerning other people. The following evening, Grace and Paul go for a swim in the sea and without as much as a by your leave he pulls Grace against him and begins to kiss her. Grace's first reaction is to give him a good whack on the ear. But he keeps persevering, pestering her with phone-calls from London and telling her that he does not know what to do. 'I am so sorry. My darling Grace' (p. 100). For the most part, she is fully aware that '[this] is all totally absurd' (p. 155) and that she is too old for 'this sort of nonsense' (p. 155). But eventually he succeeds in having sex with her at the Pine Forest after the first night of the *Hamlet* production.

There is a coincidence involved here. Grace's father, Benjamin, made love to his male lover at the Pine Forest. Mimi never went to the Pine Forest with her husband and never lay with him under the trees (cf. p. 233). Grace grants Paul her favours at the very same place before sending him packing for good, saying: 'But there is Polly. I love Polly. I couldn't do that to Polly. I couldn't build that wall between us' (p. 225). Has Grace finally overcome her self-centredness? Or is she only trying to have her cake and eat it? It is difficult to tell; and so is it to interpret the significance of the coincidence.

In the end, the strand featuring Mimi is altogether satisfactory and offers some good writing. But the Grace parts of the book fall flat in comparison, mainly one feels because of the love affair, which is implausible simply because next to nothing is provided that could suggest the development of the relationship. So one is landed in a position where one can either take or leave the entire business. The Polly skein, lastly, is left too underdeveloped to impress.

Of course, one has, in evaluating *Two Moons*, to make allowances for a number of things, for certain supernatural occurrences, for example, things like

> I am thy father's spirit,
> Doom'd for a certain term to walk the night,
> And for the day confin'd to fast in fires,
> Till the foul crimes done in my days of nature
> Are burnt and purg'd away.
> (*Hamlet*, I, v, 10–13.)

One has also to make allowances for other elements that for different reasons beggar one's credulity, such as the love affair or the fact that Grace is given to quoting not only Gertrude's lines, which is quite warrantable in her situation, but also lines from songs at the drop of a hat. If, however, one draws the line at suspending one's disbelief to a degree of that sort, then perhaps there is after all not such a great difference between *Two Moons* and Johnston's other novels.

# JULIA O'FAOLAIN

Julia O'Faolain's thematic concern as a writer has largely been with social issues, primary among these the position of women and its various complexities. However, as with *Women in the Wall* (1975) and *No Country for Young Men* (1980), her most convincing pieces are those in which O'Faolain has tried her hand at larger canvases, relegating the theme of women's challenges to a position of one among many. Overall, her involvement with questions of female liberation has been thoughtful and circumspect — perhaps too thoughtful and circumspect for vindictive viragoes and their *saeva indignatio* — but it has led her, together with Lauro Martines, to edit *Not in God's Image*,[1] a study of women in history from the Greeks to the Victorians. Her narrative work to date is rather mixed. The efforts to express in fictional form the condition of the female sex have at times been rather hapless. Furthermore, some of the issues she has focused on are too fatuous to appeal. The narrative strategies employed tend to repeat themselves. A couple of her characters remain quite wooden. Some of the dialogue passages betray a lack of proficiency. The frequent shifts in point of view, for which O'Faolain appears to entertain a particular fondness, are sometimes devoid of any discernible *raison d'être*. A few of her books have something *dèja vu* about them, as for instance her first novel *Codded and Godded* (1970).

This novel exploits the familiar topos of the innocent abroad. Making liberal use of Joycean interior monologue, the account charts the education, in several senses, of Sally, an Irish woman in Paris, proffering numerous occasions for burlesque comedy, such as Fintan McCann's 'spontaneous picture' before a respectable bourgeois audience, which is incontestably a comic *tour de force*. But Sally's involvement with three lovers (the book's American title), her pregnancy, the Christmas visit to her parents in Ireland, the circumstances that have made her what she is — all this is ground too well-trodden to be of general interest. It is surely something of a pity that, given this fact, O'Faolain should have found it necessary to return to some of these thematic issues in her subsequent work. Thus, for instance, the later story 'Lots of Ghastlies' transplants to an English bourgeois setting the theme of a return visit to the parental home.[2]

Before *Women in the Wall* appeared in 1975, O'Faolain had mainly concentrated on writing short stories, which were published in two collections, *We Might See Sights! and Other Stories* (1968) and *Man in the Cellar* (1974), by and large mediocre perform-ances, quite light-weight stuff, somewhat vitiated by her lack of control over the short forms of narrative discourse. Things changed markedly with *Women in the Wall*, which, together with *No Country for Young Men* and *The Obedient Wife* (1982) — if one disregards certain deficiencies in the latter book — seems to prove that she is more at home with this type of full-fledged narrative. *Women in the Wall* offers an imaginative reconstruction of certain extraordinary incidents 'in the Wild West of dark-age Europe',[3] being a historical novel in the best sense of the genre.

One of the women in the wall is Radegunda. After most of the members of her family have been murdered by Clotair, the king of all Gaul, she and her brother, Chlodecharius, are brought to live at Clotair's court. Later she becomes one of his several wives and yields to the temptations of the flesh. But when Clotair has her brother murdered, she leaves him to become a deaconess and found a convent, which she runs with a determination as dogged as that of Clotair in his pursuit of women and slaying of his opponents. She convinces herself that she is one of the elect, mortifying her flesh with live coal and envisaging a corporeal union with the Heavenly Bridegroom.

Another woman in the wall is Agnes, whom Radegunda brings with her into the convent, leaving her little choice to follow her own inclinations. Agnes becomes abbess. She does not succumb to the Heavenly Bridegroom, but to the seductive efforts of Fortunatus, 'a most verbal man',[4] whom words inflame as no reality unfiltered by them could do and who lives in the convent as Radegunda's biographer. They have a girl-child, Ingunda, who, after being raised by foster-parents, is admitted to the convent where, in atonement for her mother's lapse, she decides to become an anchorite, spending some years immured. She is yet another woman in the wall, the most literal of them all.

The mental turmoil suffered by Radegunda, Agnes and Ingunda within the convent is matched by the political and social turmoil without. The reconstruction of the turbulent, partly barbaric, partly Christian world of nuns, bishops and kings is splendid. Fury and frenzy prevail. Paradox is central. The haven of the convent becomes a hothouse of intrigue. Radegunda, the foundress, endeavours to break the cloister rules in a doomed attempt to establish the Kingdom of God on earth.[5] The bishops are all scheming devils. The only reasonably human character is Clotair, despite his cruelty and dissipation. There is a moving scene involving him and Radegunda. He has come to persuade her to return to him (pp. 117ff.). But his pleading is to no avail, and dropping his suppliant pose he reasons: 'You are too generous, Radegunda. You care more for your own salvation than mine. Maybe holy people are never generous that way.' (p. 131). She still feels the fire of lust burning inside her, but she seeks atonement by mortifying her flesh.

The catastrophe at the end is finely handled. Less satisfactory is the use of different levels of time. The time-shifts are indicated by dates specified in the margin. This strategy is unnecessarily bothersome and lacks any discernible *raison d'être* other than to present one and the same event from different angles. Thus at the start we have Ingunda's view of certain incidents in the convent. Then Radegunda recalls her time with Clotair. The account moves backwards in time to describe the slaughtering of Radegunda's family. Later Agnes remembers the killing of Chlodecharius and their leaving Clotair. After that Fortunatus's perspective becomes dominant for a while as he recollects a visit to a brothel where he helped with an abortion. Before too long, though, the change in perspective is discontinued; the time-shifts, however, remain operative. One wonders whether the same effect would not have been achieved without those temporal signposts.

One reviewer has seen fit to remark that O'Faolain uses the history of Queen Radegunda 'to try to answer fundamental questions about woman's role in society, and to discover the reason behind vocations'.[6] The idea is highly contestable, representing as it does a case where the wish is father to the thought.. No less contestable is the notion according to which Ingunda 'serves [...] as a symbol for the buried individuality of womankind'.[7] The point about those women in the wall is that each one, for very different reasons, betrays her true self and shores up empty pretences against her ruin. Radegunda sublimates her inborn lust and sexual desire, turning them into a questionable yearning for a union with the Bridegroom. Moreover, she becomes guilty of getting involved in political intrigue. Agnes's sin consists not so much in her sexual intercourse with Fortunatus, but in the shirking of her responsibility for Ingunda, who, in turn, becomes the self-appointed victim of Agnes's neglect. Chrodechilde is driven by hatred and a hunger for power, whereas she should have let herself be guided by love and submission. With her as abbess, the convent of the Holy Cross has perverted its true aim and purpose: she pays lipservice to, and becomes the handmaid of, political and worldly power.

*No Country for Young Men*, its title inverting Yeats's famous phrase 'no country for old men' in 'Sailing to Byzantium', is a novel of mixed modes. As Patricia Craig notes in her review, it is not a political thriller, not a stark comedy, not a documentary of social behaviour, not a story of personal relations, not a family saga, not a piece of historical fiction.[8] Nor is it a novel of ideas, nor a novel of character. But to its detriment, the account contains elements of all these.

Most accessibly, *No Country for Young Men* is a novel-with-a-secret, quite reminiscent of those popular Victorian tales. Unlike a good many of its precursors, the secret in O'Faolain's piece, when it is at long last revealed, is too tawdry to bear out the significance that it is intended to carry throughout the at times overbearing narrative. In her efforts to make the point that Ireland past and present is no country for young men, the author heaps up an enormous amount of material, parts of which may have served for a number of books in their own right. A good deal is going on in the novel, but O'Faolain has not always been successful in avoiding disaster. The contrasting delineation of Driscoll's and Duffy's fates comes off at times; just as often, however, it seems laboured. The ending is decisively disappointing for being hopelessly implausible; and the character of gaga old Judith O'Malley, who links the two periods covered in the book, is altogether ruinous to the narrative. Her memories are supposed to be disordered or non-existent; much of the strategy of withholding the solution to the riddle on which the book thrives depends on Judith's inability to recall what happened in 1922. And yet her memories are presented as straightforward narrative. A couple of scenes are quite awful (pp. 98f.), showing not infrequently an unsure hand at dialogue (pp. 229f.), as when James and Gráinne are in bed for the first time (p. 178). The love-talk is pretty inane (pp. 198f.); at one point James is made to say: 'I want to eat pineapple chunks out of your cunt' (p. 240). As they say, there is no accounting for taste. One of the worst things in the book is this missive that James pens home to his wife. It contains the following lines:

> Love is possessive. I rebel against the impossibility [of sharing his joy with her] and feel that if you too could climb over the barriers of everyday logic, then somehow we could all benefit from this source of warmth and happiness. [...] my impulse in writing what may be clumsy and hurtful letters is not to boast or hurt but to bring you into the orbit of this delight which I am experiencing. (pp. 351f.)

Imagine receiving a letter like this! Would you not think that the writer had lost his marbles? You would probably have no doubts about it if you saw him shred his missive into his whiskey and water and drink down the concoction, which is what James does (p. 352).

The basic narrative strategy informing the novel is mytho-poeic. *No Country for Young Men* very much relies on the famous Diarmuid and Gráinne myth on at least two levels. As Ann Weekes has admirably shown,[9] the myth is operative on the level of the 1921/22 skein involving Sparky Driscoll and Kathleen O'Malley, and on that of the 1979 skein featuring James Duffy and Gráinne O'Malley. By exploiting motifs of the Diarmuid and Gráinne myth and by establishing many parallels between her novel and the myth, O'Faolain uncovers a destructive pattern that persists throughout myth and history into the present time in Ireland. But in her retelling of the myth there is one significant difference: Gráinne O'Malley does not capitulate in order to restore the 'order' derived from male principles.[10]

O'Faolain's main concern seems to be with probing the sources of the political conflict in the Republic of Ireland today, a conflict that was born in 1922, when some members of the Irish government repudiated the Treaty signed with England. These members and their followers took up arms against the Treaty forces, thus beginning a protracted and deadly civil war.[11] Men like Sparky Driscoll were sent to Ireland from the American aid organisation to monitor the situation and recommend groups for financial support. Winning Sparky over to the anti-Treaty cause was very important to Owen O'Malley. In 1922, after months of fighting, the leader of the anti-Treaty party agreed to rejoin the government, but some of their followers refused to accept the decision and resorted to guerilla attacks against both the Republic and the Six Counties. These men, the IRA, have been active ever since.

In 1979, James Duffy is sent over from America to record stories of the earlier troubles. His employers intend to make a propaganda film to increase American financial contributions to the Banned Aid organisation, whose goal it is to undermine both the Six Counties and the Republic. Owen Roe, Gráinne O'Malley's uncle, is the contemporary counterpart to Owen O'Malley. Although a member of the present government, he secretly works towards toppling it when the time is ripe.

As O'Faolain, perhaps in a somewhat one-sided fashion, diagnoses it, the source of Ireland's troubles is to be found in the frail morals of women, at least this is what Judith O'Malley, who links the two periods, is told in her history lesson: from Dervogilla, via Mac Murrough's daughter, Eva, and the mythic Gráinne, to Gráinne O'Malley. Or perhaps this is not quite what the account suggests. For at bottom it is less the frail morals of women, but the peculiar attitude of the men in Ireland towards the role of women. The long history of English involvement in Ireland shows that the seizure or exchange of land and of women are balanced, the two commodities being regarded as equal. Gráinne O'Malley recognises that even today most Irishmen think of women as chattels.

As in pagan religion and as with the Fianna warriors, twentieth-century Ireland is fundamentally androcentric. Judith recalls the priest, home from World War II, counselling the young girls to go forth as inspiration. Owen Roe, in 1979, and Gráinne's husband, Michael, who, like most men young or old, is only interested in the past (he wants to write the history of his grandfather), look upon women as either a source of physical satisfaction or as clay — a functionary in her relation to man. Michael, though, is cute enough to sense that, since he cannot, or is unwilling to, satisfy Gráinne, she needs another relationship, which she finds with James Duffy, whom she finally decides to follow to America, thus making a moral choice.

The trouble, though, is that James is killed in the end by Owen Roe's mindless follower, Patsy Flynn, in order that the honour of the O'Malley family may be preserved. But in that, too, history repeats itself. The Diarmuid-Gráinne constellation in the 1920s also came to a sad end. Judith realised that her sister, Kathleen, was more attracted to the American Sparky Driscoll, a full-blooded man of passion, who reminded her of animals, than to the cold fish Owen O'Malley, who did not care for individual human beings, only for the 'cause'. When Sparky kissed her, Judith experienced a burgeoning of sexual emotions that she felt must be repressed. Alarmed by her own responses, fearing that Kathleen would leave Owen and go with Sparky, and afraid that Sparky might report unfavourably about Owen's plans, thus threatening the supply of American funds Owen needed to continue his fight against the Treaty, Judith killed Sparky. Her action had to be hushed up: she was spirited away into a convent by Owen O'Malley, and Sparky's murder was blamed on the British forces. This is the secret on which the novel pivots.

It is a sad and saddening tale, the numerous re-enactments of the Diarmuid and Gráinne myth offering a depressing comment on Ireland's history. Sexuality is still condemned. Patsy Flynn, the present-day counterpart to the young Judith, in one of the last scenes in the book, sits locked up in the lavatory, waiting to kill the 'Californicator' (p. 363), who, so he thinks, is making love to Gráinne in an upstairs room. He feels the emotion of James and Gráinne 'locked into his own, maddeningly like the pedal of someone's bike getting locked into yours' (p. 360). But political concern takes precedence over his emotional involvement, and some time later he pushes James and his car into the canal. The senseless fighting is still going on. Cormac, Gráinne's fourteen-year-old son, has been won over to the 'cause' by Owen Roe. Perhaps Ireland will 'be a country run by young men' (p. 213), but these young men will be like the old men. As Michael rightly sees it:

> Our grandparents were chameleons on tartans. They were idealistic and thuggish, cunning and mad, politicians and fighting men according to need: variegated. Then came our parents who made money. Solid-coloured individuals. Green for them meant pound notes and government contracts. You and I, the chameleon grandchildren, didn't know how to react and keep our individuality. Cormac's gone back to the tartan. (p. 327)

In the end, Gráinne is left standing alone, waiting unknowingly for the dead James, and as Ann Weekes remarks: 'The text, not the woman, then disappears'.[12] Thus there would seem to be hope still, or does there? For essentially nothing much has changed. O'Faolain's use of the Diarmuid and Gráinne myth appears to make this point:

> The same arrogance that allows these men to dictate women's actions also abrogates the rights of an entire nation, decreeing bloodshed and violence to restore a principle they believe in, thus confusing in their madness the country with themselves.[13]

O'Faolain's Ireland, therefore, is not only no country for young men, but for young women either.

In the Los Angeles of *The Obedient Wife*, things are sliding perilously downhill — marriages, morals, mud and all. The thematic set-up of the book may, at first sight, appear to be intended as a salute to the preoccupations of feminist fiction. The narrative's ending, though, must leave every feminist sorely disappointed: the obedient wife remains obedient, choosing to go back to her family and prop it up. 'I want to make pasta and give dinner parties and contribute to order',[14] she tells her lover over the phone before calling her husband to say that she will return to him.

Carla Verdi, thirty-six years of age, has been left in Los Angeles by her husband, Marco, who is back in Italy. Their marriage, like the marriages of her friends, has grown sour over the years. She feels he has been overbearing, he thinks she has gone frigid. They have agreed on a trial separation, and Marco's idea is that Carla should get herself laid (cf. p. 35) by another man to broaden her mind, gain experiences, liven things up between themselves again. But in a world fraught with lovelessness (p. 7) and endangered by a symbolic mudslide that threatens the safety of the houses — in short, in a disaster area (p. 39), her newly gained freedom is like that of her rabbit, whose escape from its hutch results in its death. Carla does not suffer actual death, but a moral and emotional death none the less: in a way she, too, gets mangled like her pet.

While the dog she buys and grandiloquently names 'Carlomagno' throws a fit of happiness when freed from the leash, she is at heart incapable of enjoying her freedom, the acquisition of the dog pointing to her essential lack of self-sufficiency. Her friends are of little use to her, having troubles of their own. They either live separated from their husbands with frantic drug-pushing lovers, or have just fallen for another man, like Sybil, who confides in Carla that she is in love with a priest, Father Leo Hausermann. "Go to bed with him. [...] Then you'll be free' (p. 25), Carla recommends, thus laying the basis for a case of involuntary irony of which she will soon become the victim. For she, too, gets involved with leonine Leo, but is long in arriving at the same conclusion with regard to herself.

She is flung into an excruciating emotional turmoil over whether she should have an affair with Leo, who is prepared to leave the Church for her, even marry her. The turmoil business would not be so bad if it were not rendered in such an abominable manner. The reason for her procrastinating behaviour is, the reader is meant to understand, her belief in chastity. 'Carla, raised on Boccaccio, had no belief in clerical scruples. Women, in her view, took chastity seriously. Not men' (p. 42). But then, while running her hands over the flat surface of the mattress 'on which she and Leo had not lain' (p. 19), she asks herself what silly scruple had held her back. She makes up her mind to succumb to his advances, this especially in view of the following consideration:

> 'I'll be thirty-seven next year, forty in no time, older and older! I'll get varicose veins, flab, wrinkles, hair on my chin, menopause,

hot flushes, brittle bones. [...] What's the good in surviving your best self?' (pp. 191f.)

Before she can consummate her relationship, Marco comes back from Italy. His body, when she feels it in bed, brings 'back moments in early marriage when he and she had lost their separate selves in a surge of blind tenderness' (p. 193), and she makes love to him, not once but twice, giving 'herself back to his conjugal amenity to which she had every right since she had not sought satisfaction elsewhere' (p. 193). Such explanation would do in a pulp novel, but in a more ambitious piece of writing, for which *The Obedient Wife* obviously wishes to be taken, it is quite preposterous. No less inconsistent is her post-coital insistence on a divorce. After her sexual bout with Marco, she has another with Leo, to whom she says, while running her hands down his body: 'What a waste, keeping this for celibacy! All those years' (p. 206). There is, in fact, quite some running of hands down bodies involved. Her affair makes her realise that fifteen years with Marco have deformed her, 'so that now she saw delicacy as weakness whereas, surely, it was strength? What was special about Leo *was* his delicacy' (p. 209). But for all his delicacy, in the end she decides to leave him for her husband. Again, the reason she gives is somewhat implausible after all the ado previously made. 'You're self-sufficient' (p. 228), she tells him, adding: 'You're my lover. I need a husband' (p. 229). That, however, is exactly what Leo wanted to become: her husband. But maybe she realised that with him she could not 'make pasta and give dinner parties and contribute to order' (p. 230).

The reviewer in *TLS* claimed that *The Obedient Wife* was 'an exceptionally polished work'.[15] One has difficulty ascertaining what is meant here by 'polished'. In its general sense the term does not readily suggest itself in connection with this book, which is too long, dithering too often and spreading itself out by including material of dubious relevance. As quite frequently in her other pieces, O'Faolain employs numerous shifts in viewpoint. That of Carla's son, Maurizio, features prominently. The passages rendered through his eyes focus largely on his agonising over the fate of Evie, the daughter of Carla's friend Wanda, with whom he is in love and whom he wants his parents to adopt lest Wanda's crass lover, Cass, should molest her. Possibly some of these units find their justification in being manifestations of genuine love of, and concern for, another person against which Carla's world of lovelessness may be judged. But there are too many of them in the novel, whose title suggests that it is about an obedient wife. Once more, as in previous narratives, the sentiments expressed by the characters in their conversational exchanges are too trite or eccentric to ring true. Here is one of them:

> 'Leo, it's hard to know what you want. A declaration of friend-ship? OK I enjoy your company. I wouldn't have you here if I didn't. So does Maurizio and so does the dog. I can't answer for the orchids. (p. 118)

The lines are part of a serious conversation about Carla's and Leo's relationship. What are those orchids doing in it?

*The Irish Signorina* (1984) is, according to the *Sunday Telegraph*, a 'fascinating sortie into a romance of secrets'.[16] In point of fact, however, the novel is a far cry from that, being muddled, cliché-ridden, and teeming with half-baked views on love and terrorism.

Take a young Irish woman who pays a visit to a family villa in Tuscany where her mother, lately deceased, spent some time as chaperone to the daughter of an Italian aristocratic family. Let the mother have committed adultery there while her young husband was in the UN forces in Africa, and make the daughter want to find out what was so special about mummy's lover for her to betray her husband so soon. Guido, the marchesa's son and a man of 'forty-five or so',[17] is supposed to have been a witness. Let the girl fall in love with Guido because he exudes an attraction hitherto unencountered by her in other men, and let her love be requited. There is surely sufficient stuff for romance here. Throw in Guido's son, who is involved in shady political issues. Make the girl become embroiled with him, helping him to get rid of a terrorist he is hiding in the villa and succumbing to his sexual advances. Spice the whole with more or less contrived instances of mystery that climax in an ominous warning by the marchesa at the request of the girl to stay clear of Guido. Leave the reason for the warning open until the end. That way you have romance and secret all in one. Then, finally, spring the surprise on the girl as well as on the reader: she is Guido's daughter. All that is now left to do in order to complete a novel such as *The Irish Signorina* is to let the account peter out without further ceremony.

A number of things are especially execrable about the novel, apart from the nonsense that Guido spouts about love (cf. pp. 86ff.) or such tripe about politics as this:

'We believe that when it comes to conspiracy and terrorism the people are never users, always the used. It doesn't look that way, of course, so that what we're trying to do is show up the *government's* conspiracy. (p. 136)

Or there are the various shifts in point-of-view that do not add anything of consequence to the narrative. The characters fail to come into their own: they remain wooden for the most part, and their relationships are left either too obscure and obfuscatory — for instance the relationship between Guido and his son — or too trivial, as that between Guido and his wife, whom he had been forced to marry by the marchesa; needless to say the marriage did not work out.

Least convincing of all is the principal character, Anne, herself. Her consciousness is too childish and immature by a long chalk. This becomes most noticeable in her attitude towards love and sex. When she ponders her mother's having fallen for a man in Italy, 'arguing with a ghost who was by now an extension of herself' (p. 17), she asks herself: 'Would I have behaved differently? Am I like her?' (p. 17). Only the most undiscerning of readers will not instantly suspect that she will not behave differently, that she is like her. Before too long, Anne reflects: 'She wanted what her mother had wanted and failed to hold on to: a fiery thrilling love with a happy ending' (p. 74). In her sleep that night, she dreams of one of Guido's ancestors who fittingly merges with Guido, and the reader is tersely told that Anne was now in love with him and in her mind 'he had loved her back' (p. 75). So much for her falling in love. Suitably enough, upon awakening she finds Guido's face bent over hers. 'I was thinking of kissing you', he tells her, and she asks back: 'Why didn't you?' He kisses her, and this is her reaction: 'I wish I were a boa-constrictor. Then I'd cripple you and hold you forever' (p. 76). But wait! There are further imbecilities in store. The reason why he was thinking of kissing her was — yes, precisely! — so that he could see her mother in her. 'So that was all?', she retorts, and Guido launches forth into one of his abstruse panegyrics on love and youth:

'Don't say 'all' as if all were nothing. It's a breath-taking phenomenon: the fallen blossom afresh on the branch. A miracle. You're too young to know what I'm talking about. You provoke the sensation but can't feel it.' [...] 'Fair is youth and void of sorrow. [...] Yet it hourly flies away.' (p. 77)

To top it all, the sequence ends with Anne embarking on one of her intolerable flights of insipid fancy:

> Anne, though ready to melt, remembered an old determination never to be a man's plaything, not engage — if in love herself — with less than all of him. [...] Wouldn't it be the loneliest of fates to find yourself gravely in love — at last, Anne — with someone who had lost touch with his own deep feelings? Were men of Guido's age necessarily mean in their commitments? (p. 78)

Maybe they are, but do young women with a BA think like that?

There is one scene in the book that is especially awful, involving as it does some heavy-handed dialogue and horseplay of the Keystone Cops variety. Anne goes into the library of the villa and discovers a young man there holding a book in his hands. He is Neri, Guido's son, and he is equipped with a torch. 'I'm the lightbearer', he explains, and Anne is quick to associate him with Lucifer (p. 58). Neri has sneaked into the library to fetch a book by one of his ancestors.

> 'As I'm interested in what may be the last of the Italian Republic, I thought I'd check out analogies. Our ancestor was one of the *Arrabbiati*: men held in much the same esteem by conservatives then as my grandmama holds today's activists.' (p. 59)

Neri goes on to tell her that property is theft and that power and money interest him and his cronies. Then, unexpectedly, the marchesa enters the library and Neri manages to duck behind the sofa unseen. The old lady sits herself down on the sofa and while she is talking to Anne, Neri's foot first simply sticks round the end of the sofa, then is drawn back, sticks out again, does 'an ironic little dance in the air' (p. 62), nods unctuously, 'nod, nod' (p. 62) and — well, never mind. The marchesa leaves, and Anne returns to Neri only to be told that what has attracted him to politics is 'the challenge to put their rotten world to rights' (p. 64).

At one point, when she is with Guido, Anne longs 'to shout "cut" like a film director. But she wasn't in control here' (p. 159). I likewise frequently longed to shout 'cut', but I was not in control either — other than electing to slam the book shut.

O'Faolain's latest novel, *The Judas Cloth* (1992), is a voluminous historical work, in narrative method somewhat reminiscent of the writer's efforts in *Women in the Wall.* On an extraordinarily large canvas, O'Faolain evokes the years of Pope Pius IX — Pio Nono (1846–1878) —, starting in 1881 with the late Pope's proper burial three years after his death, years during which his household had not dared cross the hostile city of Rome and bury him where he had asked to be laid to rest, and then backtracking to 1831, the year in which Pius IX, then still Archbishop Mastai-Ferretti of Spoleto, issued this proclamation:

> Following our provinces' happy restoration to their lawful Sovereign and trusting in the pious submission of our flock, we wish to have known our concern that respect be shown to all rebels who hand in their arms in token of their intention to return to the paternal embrace of the Supreme Pontiff...[18]

Turbulent times of rebellion and political strife had, it seems, been overcome. But peace, it turned out, was short-lived during the remaining years of Gregory XVI's popedom. When he was succeeded by Mastai-Ferretti, who — as O'Faolain remarks in her 'Note' — took to polemic as salamanders do to flame, Italy and Rome especially were flung again into political turmoil. As O'Faolain goes on to note:

> His invective was biblical, and his enemies gave back as good as they got. Caught between their cartoons and his anathemas, the Catholic world was pushed ever further towards polarisation.

The Pope's politics were in fact so contentious and caused such a schism in society that when Pius's corpse was transported across Rome, people could be heard shouting: "Pitch the swine in the Tiber" and "*Carogna!* Into the river with his carcass!" (p. 1).

O'Faolain has peopled her imaginatively reconstructed world of Pius IX with such a vast cast that she found it necessary to preface her account with a 'LIST OF THE PRINCIPAL CHARACTERS' that comprises no less than forty-seven names. And these forty-seven names do not actually include all the principal characters. The reader can look here in vain for some who figure quite prominently. So the actual cast is far richer, and here lies one of the problems connected with the book. As with quite a number of historical novels that rely on a myriad of fictional *personae* and attempt to reconstruct a specific period in massive detail, travelling the madlanes of history as well as the main roads, *The Judas Cloth* puts rather a strain on the reader's efforts to keep track of what is offered. Chances are that he, or she, may get lost at times. The point could be made that *The Judas Cloth* would have profited from pruning. Some parts that deal with matters rather perfunctorily could certainly have been jettisoned.

Any attempt at summarising the multifarious ramifications of the plot, which is spread out over some 590-odd pages, would most decidedly go beyond the scope of this chapter. The following remarks must suffice, and they will do so not least in view of the fact that a sizeable part of the narrative is pretty straightforward and therefore in no need of further elucidation.

When Mastai-Ferretti was picked as a compromise candidate to succeed Pope Gregory XVI, hopes were raised that Mastai would reconcile the ideals of 1789 — the ideals only: liberty and fraternity, not the guillotine — with the gospel's message, and the Church with the world it had shunned for forty years. But things took an entirely different turn. A new nationalism surged and ran rampant. Rumours abounded that the Jesuits were plotting against the new Pope, and as a consequence the Jesuits were chased out of the papal city. The official terminology called it euphemistically 'exiling them'. Spies were ubiquitous. Both France and Austria had designs upon Italy. When the Pope used the words 'God bless Italy' — harmless words, one might think — they were twisted to mean that to bless Italy was to curse Austria, whose presence in this peninsula made a free Italy impossible. A nationalist and Liberal preacher and chaplain in the army, arguing that the Pope had thereby launched a crusade, recruited young men to fight in it and then told the Pope that it would be dangerous to check the tide of patriotism that he himself had unleashed. Rival groups fought for possession of a revolution that had not yet happened. A deployment of Roman troops along the Austrian border was turned into a crusade. A manifesto, issued by one of the Pope's generals and containing the words 'God wills it!', committed God and His Vicar to making war on Catholic Austria. In Bologna a war was waged. The Austrians crossed the Po and marched through the Pope's land, mopping up the remnants of the defeated Roman army. Highly influential people, such as Count Pellegrino Rossi, Pio Nono's chief minister, were murdered in broad daylight. Then a republic was declared in Rome and the Pope dethroned. Pius IX was spirited away to Gaeta, while in Rome a new government, a democracy, was to be established.

The events centre on Rome, but they are made to stretch to Bologna and later to Paris. The papal city, bewildered by nationalism and revolution, is powerfully evoked: an insidious place of intrigue and corruption, of denunciations and anonymous letters, a city of blackmail peopled with aspiring monsignori and iniquitously scheming lesser mortals. In a sense, O'Faolain's main interest is focused on three young men whose lives she interweaves with that of the besieged Church. Prospero is the son of a liberal count and he ends up among the most resolute of the Ultramontane bishops. Flavio, a streetwise orphan, discovers that he is the son of his mother's brother and inherits the dukedom of his nominal father. Nicola, in many respects O'Faolain's principal character, is another supposed orphan. He spends much of his time pondering the identity of his parents. In the end, he finds his mother but refuses to reveal himself. As for his father, he speculates about various people, including a cardinal, a Bonaparte, and his mother's uncle, before he finally finds out.

The novel's real protagonist, Pope Pius IX, rarely appears in the flesh. He is the hope of the liberals on his election, subsequently he develops into the despair of all liberal Catholics on account of certain disastrous decisions, which have bedevilled Catholicism ever since: the dogma of the Immaculate Conception, the Syllabus of Errors, the megalomaniac proclamation of infallibility. O'Faolain clearly sides with the Catholic moderates, who lost out under Pio Nono and have lost out so often since, men who believed and have believed that the modern world must not be denied. As one Cardinal puts it shortly before his murder, repeated prohibitions to think will not defeat modern science and put out its light. At the Vatican Council, the elections to the commissions are rigged and the Pope forces the dissentient bishops into line. Nicola, who is now the titular Bishop of Trebizond, is tormented by the infallibility debate. He cannot come to terms with the evils of papal politics. It is all too much for him and he goes to pieces. The novel ends during the aftermath of the Paris Commune. Nicola gets caught up in its savagery and this makes him pull off his cassock, the 'Judas Cloth', and renounce the Church. In layman's clothes at his father's funeral, he rejects the handshake of Bishop Prospero. In other words, Nicola must have succeeded in finding out who his father is — none other than Pius himself. It is a fictional coincidence that may be stretching things a bit; but this is possibly the only major deficiency in an, all in all, intelligent and impressive narrative performance. And yet, there is, as always, no pleasing everyone. Readers who are loath to go in for things like immense historical novels of the kind represented by *The Judas Cloth* may be put in mind of Abraham Lincoln's comment on the

*Memoirs* of one G.W.E. Russell: 'People who like this sort of thing will find this the sort of thing they like'.

Julia O'Faolain has noted that the 'freeing of the female imagination' is an exhilarating side-effect of the women's movement.[19] Taken as a creative manifestation of this kind of imagination, her work as a whole leaves a good deal to be desired. The majority of her topics are not especially compelling. Her sorties into aspects of human love, aberrant or otherwise, are at times not penetrating enough to command unflinching attention. Her craftsmanship shows considerable shortcomings.

As a writer born in Ireland, she has frequently tackled non-Irish subject matters. Her writing has a cosmopolitan touch, featuring locales in Italy, France and the United States of America and quite often focusing on matters Italian, which may be the result of her own experiences abroad. Her very first collection of stories, *We Might See Sights!*, by being divided into Irish and Italian stories, reflects her interests well enough. *The Irish Signorina*, too, spans Ireland and Italy. O'Faolain's efforts to open up the comparatively narrow thematic confines of contemporary Irish fiction are commendable. Her imaginative reconstruction of sixth-century Gaul, in *Women in the Wall*, is well-equipped to bear comparison with the more successful attempts that have recently been made as a consequence of a wide-spread concern with bygone days. Even if her Irish stories add little to the long tradition of the Irish short story, being too conventional in form and too whimsical and wilful in thematic preoccupation, she has so far been at her most convincing in a genuinely Irish novel, *No Country for Young Men*, which wisely eschews labouring the point about women's plight in the world, while at the same time giving evidence of the freeing of the female imagination.

# WILLIAM TREVOR

Increasingly throughout his career as a writer, William Trevor has focused his thematic interest, in almost all of his novels and quite a few of his stories, on the exploration of evil. What possibly fascinates most is the light-hearted manner in which he does so, effecting an almost inimitable blending of the hilarious with the poignant, of farce with tragedy, in the general sense of that term. This blending clearly works towards a mutual intensification of the comical and the dreadful. Thus, for instance, the death of Mr Obd, in *The Boarding House* (1965), is the more heart-rending for forming the climax of a series of laughter-inducing incidents in which a number of eccentric characters are involved: so eccentric that they are little short of being Dickensian oddities. That Trevor should people his novels, particularly his early English novels, with eccentrics is not at all surprising, given the fact that English eccentricity was what first attracted him to writing — 'it was that that made me wonder and muse about this country'.[1] Comparable set-ups invariably play an important part in Trevor's work to date.

The first novels that Trevor published in the 1960s are set almost entirely in England, with English characters; they are comic in manner, grotesque in characterisation and plotting, and generally apolitical. From the 1970s on, humour is softened by pathos; more Irish characters and settings are employed and political and domestic problems interconnect. In the 1980s and 1990s, four novels (if *Reading Turgenev* and *Nights at the Alexandra* are classed as such) are set in Ireland, three in England and one, *My House in Umbria*, in Italy; events and manner of presentation are usually serious, the tone often despairing.[2]

Trevor published his first novel, *A Standard of Behaviour*, in 1958, two years before his decision to end his career as a sculptor. He had, in a manner of speaking, embarked upon this career at the age of sixteen, when he became interested in sculpting while at St Columba's College, Dublin. *A Standard of Behaviour* contains several violent events of a serious nature (date rape, suicide); but its real concern is with the unnamed narrator's near-picaresque progress from schoolboy loves and a sense of accidie to a collapse of faith in 'a certain standard of reasonably intelligent behaviour'[3] in the face of a world that appears to render that standard irrelevant.[4] The plot, which moves from youthful misery through bohemian experimentation, erotic success, and lost love followed by new love, tends to be episodic, each incident a kind of dramatised joke.[5] It is a slight work, in which Trevor fails to turn even such a promising set-piece as a nudist party with a clergyman present in full attire to the best effect. Trevor seems to have repudiated this novel, by dropping it from lists of his published work. In a letter to Kristin Morrison, he dismissed it in parentheses with the single word 'worthless'.[6]

*The Old Boys* (1964) is most apparently concerned with the efforts of the elderly Mr Jaraby to secure his election as president of an Old Boys Association. It employs — as Schirmer has shown[7] — a wide variety of comic modes, from the relatively crude comedy of slapstick to the more sophisticated humour of puns and word-play. Despite the comic surface of the novel, generated not least by its partly hilarious cast of characters, *The Old Boys* is informed by an essentially bleak vision that throws light on serious moral issues, thus introducing the interplay of the comic and the poignant, which has come to characterise so much of Trevor's art.

There is, for instance, the Jarabys' failed marriage, which, to some extent, culminates in Mrs Jaraby's killing her husband's cat, Monmouth, and which expresses the idea of disconnection on the private level of human affairs. The theme is likewise worked out in the troubled relationship between Mr Jaraby and his son, Basil. After Basil has been arrested for child-molestation, Jaraby, fearing that his chances to be elected president may be jeopardised, goes so far as even to deny his paternity. 'He is not my son', he tells the members of the association. 'My wife's only. By a previous marriage' (p. 183), and the men stare at their hands, embarrassed by the pathos of the lie. Mrs Jaraby's efforts to restore Basil to what she considers his rightful place in the family bespeaks a deep-seated sense of loneliness. Her fantasies about her son's coming to live with her and her husband reveal her desperate need for some kind of human connection.

Even minor characters whose roles seem basically comic contribute to the novel's dark side. Their actions are quite often hilarious and pathetic at the same time, for example Mr Sole's and Mr Cridley's attempts to increase the amount of corres-pondence by soliciting junk-mail. Mr Turtle is a glorious figure of farce in the early parts; later he develops into a sympathetic embodiment of the feeling of loss associated with old age. Trevor expertly modulates between comic surface and psychological depth. No character in the novel expresses the idea of alienation with more conviction than does Mr Turtle.[8]

Another hallmark of Trevor's subsequent novels is that an undercurrent of violence runs beneath their comic surfaces. Such an undercurrent also permeates *The Old Boys*. Many instances could be cited, such as the beating of Nox when he was a schoolboy or Mrs Jaraby's drowning of Monmouth. The primary agent of this dark force, though, is unquestionably Basil Jaraby, seemingly a harmless eccentric, a lonely, frustrated man preoccupied with raising pet budgerigars, who is in fact a child-molester. Trevor tellingly reveals Basil's criminal proclivity from the young man's own point of view:

> And the little girl hadn't been frightened. She had done what he had asked her to do, and only afterwards — when he had led her back to the playground in the park, fearing that she might not know her way; when her mother had shouted at her and him — only then had she said that she was afraid. (p. 125)

While it conveys the full horror of Basil's actions, the passage also manages to generate some sympathy for Basil and so implicitly raises the question about whether characters such as he are more victims of a society that has abandoned the principles of compassion and connection than victimisers.[9]

In formal terms, *The Old Boys* is organised around multiple centres of consciousness. Trevor builds up a network of varying points of view, colouring the narrative voice with whatever character is functioning as the scene's centre of intelligence. This strategy works towards bringing about a balance between sympathy and irony, intimacy and distance, assertion and qualification.[10] It marks yet another characteristic of Trevor's subsequent novels and stories. Schirmer also appropriately draws attention to another narrative device employed for maintaining ironic pressure on his material. He calls this device 'panoramic perspectives [...]. A sudden pulling-back of the point of view to a remote, bird's-eye position [...]', employed to introduce 'ironic qualifications by forcing the specific character and events of the novel into a large, deflating context of indifference'.[11] One example of this occurs after Mr Jaraby has denied that Basil is his son. The next chapter opens with a reference to rain that 'came on the night of the committee meeting' and fell in Somerset, in London, even in Rimini (cf. p. 184), sounding the note of death and decay that runs through the whole book and pointing, in spite of all the comic incidents, to its bleak ending. Mr Jaraby does not become president, Basil is arrested, and Mrs Jaraby, a frustrated agent of compassion and connection, comes away empty-handed, with nothing but the old routine to pass the time.

Kristin Morrison has drawn attention to certain other literary devices employed in *The Old Boys* that have also become a hallmark of much of Trevor's subsequent work: the use of comic tag names and tag behaviour; the use of comic ironies and reversals; and, most distinctively, what she calls 'that special technique of Trevor's, "significant simultaneity"',[12] as when the central heating salesman and the bossy charwoman sit in different bars of the same pub in Barking, strangers to each other but having interacted earlier with some of the same crazy 'old boys'. Trevor is always fascinated by such hidden connections and often weaves them into his plots.

In *The Boarding House* (1965) the titular house is the world in miniature, filled with cranks and misfits whose lifelong process of development has led them into a thicket of errors and misunderstandings.[13] The focus once again is on a group of people who have been brought together because the proprietor, Mr Bird, is interested in observing certain characteristics that they all share: loneliness and an inability to tell the truth. The plot of the novel, which at first glance seems merely episodic, is in fact circular: it opens with Mr Bird's death and concludes with Mr Bird's comic apotheosis in a second death.

Among the Dickensian oddities that people the book, there is, for example, Mr Scribbin, the railway enthusiast, alone in his darkened room playing his train records. Listening to the sound of trains brings solace to Mr Scribbin, while causing severe disturbance to his housemates. Through such ironic effect, but also by means of frequent repetition, Trevor manages to make obsessive behaviour of this sort increasingly funny. Or there is the Nigerian, Mr Obd, who has been crazily in love with an English girl, bringing her expensive flowers every day and writing her long letters, a total of 1,248, unable to take No for an answer. Mr Bird himself is no less eccentric, with his *Notes on Residents* and his decision to will joint continuance of the boarding house to two people who hate each other's guts, Mr Studdy and Nurse Clock, and whose hatred is responsible for the eventual destruction of the boarding house and the severance of all the characters from each other for the future. Did Mr Bird compose his will out of benevolence or malignancy? Was it an act of charity to save the inhabitants from something worse, or a diabolic act aiming to preserve them in their misfortunes?

In J.S. Studdy, Trevor for the first time supplies a major character who is Irish. He is a small-time conman, hilariously unsavoury. In Mr

Bird's *Notes*, he is described as 'a species of petty criminal, with his hair-oil everywhere and his great red face'.[14] He is a red-haired man of fifty-three, who wears in his left lapel 'a small religious badge, the emblem of the Sacred Heart' (p. 38) and is said to make the 'sign of the cross' (p. 13) upon seeing the corpse of Mr Bird in evidence of his Catholicism; winter and summer alike, he is given to wearing 'a thick, black, double-breasted overcoat' (p. 38), recalling Beckett's Irish derelicts.[15] Studdy is nicely balanced by Nurse Clock. Her sadism is just as manipulative as Studdy's petty thievery, but she stands upright while he slinks; she is antiseptically clean, in light clothing, while he is dirty and dressed in black.[16]

Between the death of a white man at the outset and the death of a black man at the close, the novel uncoils itself as a tragicomic study of related loneliness and interconnected isolations. Notably, what for the greater part reads like undisguised farce suddenly near the end transmutes into tragedy, which, in turn, is imbued with a sense of the hilarious by being a parody of something else: Mr Obd's death, though dreadful as suicide is, is a type of ritual sacrifice — as Morrison points out:

> The primitive man (for so he has been presented) arranges a blazing pyre on which to consummate his frustrated love, on which to climax his ruined life, and none of his self-superior English observers (themselves potential victims) understands what is going on.[17]

With *The Love Department* (1966), Trevor overworked his by now familiar formula. In particular, the set-up of events rather defies credibility. The quirkiness on which the narrative thrives is decidedly a shade too quirky. There are, for instance, Lady Dolores Bourhardie, 'four and a half feet high but [...] never [...] classified as a dwarf',[18] and her love department, the aim of which is 'the preservation of love within marriage' (p. 14). Furthermore, there is Edward Blakeston-Smith, with his fear of posters on hoardings and his attempt, in accordance with his father's (and now Lady Dolores's) persistent advice, to 'be [his] age' (cf. p. 107). To Mrs Poache, one of the fallen women of Wimbledon, Edward remarks:

> I'm trying desperately to take a place in the world, and to grow up into an adult. I feel a child, Mrs Poache: inept and suckling, three years old. (p. 154)

Believing Edward to have been sent to her by Almighty God, Lady Dolores takes Edward into her employ for the purpose of making him put a stop to the despicable adulterous doings of Septimus Tuam. Septimus to her is 'an enemy of love' (p. 37), wriggling his way into various marriages in Wimbledon, 'peddling love' (p. 52), seducing the wives and persuading them to offer him money. In the end, he has amassed the total of £4,742.17 (cf. p. 221). At the opening of the novel, slick Septimus has caused the split-up of the FitzArthurs' marriage, and soon he will make Eve Bolsover enter into an affair with him.

The Bolsovers have made a 'balls-up' of their marriage. On their tenth wedding anniversary matters come to a head. James Bolsover believes his wife considers him 'a species of a bore' (p. 45), spending his time at home doing nothing but drinking brandy. To a large extent, he is the victim of his stultifying work as a member of a board consisting of eight fat old men whose sole interests are central heating systems and door-handles. The Bolsovers' marriage has drifted into boredom, but Eve, after her abortive affair with Septimus, is made fully aware that it is her own fault as much as James's.

The skein of the plot focusing on the Bolsovers introduces a poignant note into the otherwise farcical sequence of incidents and this has a somewhat jarring effect. Kristin Morrison refers to 'a mix of realistic and cartoon characters [...] much like that of a Disney movie', and she considers 'such a contrast [...] especially appropriate',[19] given the subject of the novel. There is reason to contest this view. Of course, Trevor's comedies are almost exclusively dark comedies, where, in other words, farce may suddenly turn into tragedy. In *The Love Department*, though, the impression remains that the straightforward Bolsover plotline has been developed alongside the farcical rest without any appreciable increment of either the serious or the hilarious. The latter never ceases to hold sway, to the detriment of some more serious issues, which are overshadowed by, for instance, the machinations of bald-headed Lake, who is out to discredit James Bolsover in the eyes of his board colleagues and flings flour at the back of his coat, in order to gain James's post. 'Brownie', James's secretary and the woman madly in love with Lake, assists him, hoping thus to further her marriage plans. Mrs Hoop, the Bolsovers' charwoman, tries to make old Beach sign his will in her favour. Meanwhile, James's father is dying somewhere in Gloucestershire and driving the nurse who is attending him crazy with his talk about being 'in love with a dead wife [...]. I am', he says, 'keen to join her. We will be together on a marble ledge' (p. 85).

There is a lot of funny business involved that certainly brings out the best in Trevor: the case of mistaken identity, when Edward remains firmly convinced that Mr FitzArthur is really Septimus Tuam; or the havoc wrought by the Clingers' monkey in the Bolsovers' home during a dinner party; or even the affair with Lake's broken dentures, when Lake seeks to persuade old Beach to lend him his set of false teeth for his appointment with the board members on the next morning. Kristin Morrison notes that with *The Love Department* 'Trevor has constructed a much more ambitious plot than in any of his previous work',[20] one relying on the tying-up of several lines of action. But all the hilarious episodes and the allegedly ambitious plot cannot camouflage the novel's deficiencies: its ending, for instance, is especially unconvincing. Edward returns to St Gregory's hoping soon to become Brother Edward, and Septimus is killed by a taxi-cab when the driver tries to avoid running into a man who has bent down to pick up the gloves that Edward has discarded in the course of his bicycle journey to St Gregory's. Thus Edward, against all odds, is responsible for Septimus's demise and Lady Dolores is deprived of the punishment intended for the enemy of love. All is too much of '[a] farce in a vale of tears' (p. 262), as Edward unwittingly puts it.

Trevor shifted the location of the events in one of his novels to Ireland for the first time in *Mrs Eckdorf in O'Neill's Hotel* (1969). But it was only subsequently, with *Fools of Fortune* (1983) and *The Silence in the Garden* (1988) that he began to engage with topics of an essentially Irish nature. Gap-toothed Mrs Eckdorf, an English woman in her late forties from Maida Vale, with two failed marriages to her name, one to a man named Hoerschelmann, the other to Hans-Otto Eckdorf, and with no illusions about herself,[21] is on her way to Dublin by plane. She has travelled the entire world seeking faces and the stories they tell, photographing people, thereby attempting to lay bare the unvarnished truth. She calls herself 'a merchant of truth' (pp. 11f.), imagining herself to be a photographer of 'human stories of quality' (p. 16) with a number of coffee-table books to her credit. She is flying to Dublin in order 'to photograph a tragedy that took place thirty years ago' (p. 12), as she tells a fellow-passenger on the plane, who really could not care less for Mrs Eckdorf and her doings.

In O'Neill's Hotel lives 91-year-old Mrs Sinnott, the owner of the place, a deaf and dumb woman who converses with people by writing everything down in exercise books. A person famous in her time for her love of orphans, she took in Agnes Quin, now a prostitute, ferret-

faced Morrissey, who is now in his mid-thirties and acts as a pimp for
Agnes, and some other women who are mostly quite long in the tooth,
as well as O'Shea, the hotel's solitary porter. Her son, Eugene, has no
interest in the hotel, and has allowed it to go to seed. Instead he spends
his days in the nearby Excelsior Bar of Mr Riordan's public house,
consuming large quantities of sherry, as if to corroborate one of Mr
Riordan's principles, which holds 'that only in intoxication were people
truly happy' (p. 85). Twenty-eight years ago, Philomena, yet another
beneficiary of Mrs Sinnott's solicitousness and the woman whom Eugene
had married, left Eugene, taking from him their baby son. Twenty-eight
years ago the daughter of the hotel also ran away and married a man
named Cregan. Twenty-eight years ago a tragedy occurred the result of
which can be seen today, and Mrs Eckdorf means to uncover the truth.
A barman, who had been shown round O'Neill's and told about the
deaf and dumb owner, communicated the story to Mrs Eckdorf and
whetted her appetite for a further feat of truth-finding.

Employed here once more is the customary formula of gathering a
number of characters in one place, not in a boarding-house, as in a
previous novel, but in a hotel; and once more the characters are the
customary Trevor eccentrics, above all Mrs Eckdorf herself. But there
is also Mr Smedley, a travelling salesman, who is in frantic search of a
woman and later ends up with Morrissey and one of his women in a
room in O'Neill's. He has his clothes hidden away by Mrs Eckdorf and
takes his revenge by beating up Morrissey. Mrs Eckdorf is a crackpot,
of course, with her tenet that everyone is the concern of everyone else
(cf. p. 14) or that '[we] are the victims of other people' (p. 241), her so-
called intuitionary powers, her visualising while still in Munich that
twenty-eight years ago a tragedy had taken place in the hotel, and her
intention 'to tell the documentary truth that only the probing of a camera,
enriched by compassion and perception, [can] supply' (p. 140). She has
come to photograph the faces of the relevant guests at Mrs Sinnott's
ninety-second birthday.

At one point, Mrs Eckdorf senses that she may have made a sorry
mistake, that all might be wrong.

> She was in a city she did not wish to be in [...]. She had consorted
> with beggars and card-sharpers, and had ridiculously moved into
> a disgusting hotel. She had listened to the obsessions of two
> women who were as ordinary as the pavement she stepped on.
> She had wasted her time with a preposterous hall-porter, she had

said to an inebriate [*i.e.* Eugene] that he had gentle eyes. [...] Was this the end of a woman's life, that a farce should drift into madness? (p. 169)

But in spite of her severe misgivings, Mrs Eckdorf plods on and does indeed drift into madness. She stays maddeningly intent upon finding out 'what happened in O'Neill's Hotel to cause Eugene Sinnott's wife to leave him' (p. 179). It is Morrissey who realises that they are 'all being drawn into a stranger's lunacy for no reason whatsoever' (p. 196). Mrs Eckdorf finds herself wading into the lives of all these people and yet discovering nothing of what she expected. Instead the whole process teaches her, or so she convinces herself, that she 'had been punished by her disgraceful mother, by the predatory Miss Tample, and the bitter failure of her marriages' (p. 211). What she feels is absolutely necessary for her to do is to 'learn forgiveness' (p. 212), and she believes that through the example of the people in the hotel and the goodness of Mrs Sinnott she has herself been given the strength to forgive those who have victimised her. She arrives at the decision to wash and anoint Mr Smedley's feet. Before that, however, she goes to confess to Father Hennessey. It is in the conversation with the priest that the full extent of Mrs Eckdorf's delusion, even derangement, becomes apparent. 'It is the needy who have made your God' (p. 261), she tells him. Father Hennessey is deeply shocked. 'God is a disease in all your minds' (p. 264), she adds. The woman repels Father Hennessey, who puts his finger on the sore spot when he argues:

> O'Neill's Hotel cannot be called a bawdy-house. [...] Nor do those people for a moment believe that God acts particularly and directly through Mrs Sinnott. You are dramatising everything, including your own state of gracelessness. [...] You act in pride and bitterness. You are telling lies. (p. 265)

The rest of Mrs Eckdorf's life is a descent into madness. Yet in her deranged state, visited by Father Hennessey, she says something that, some might say, is not entirely devoid of appropriateness:

> How could your God create that life for Morrissey or have the parents of Agnes Quin throw her away? How could your God give that life to O'Shea or that one to Eugene Sinnott? We arrive alone in the world, Father: your God's another word for human comfort, and maybe it's enough. (p. 299)

Maybe, too, Mrs Eckdorf has indeed discovered the truth, disclosing 'the myth of God' (p. 295). What Mrs Eckdorf and the occupants of O'Neill's Hotel — like all other Trevor characters — are doing is 'struggling against the difficulties of existence' (p. 41). It is probably interesting to note that his own fellow-countrymen seldom fare well at the hands of Trevor. Some of the characters in *Mrs Eckdorf in O'Neill's Hotel* are certainly cases in point. Earlier, in *The Love Department* there had been Septimus Tuam, one of those slick and deceitful Irishmen. He is never expressly identified as Irish; but when he tells Eve Bolsover that he loves her he does so in a 'Celtic voice' (p. 156), and, additionally, certain Irish speech patterns give him away. Later, in *Elizabeth Alone* (1988), there will be the slippery Declan and the shady Mr Maloney. Furthermore, the picture evoked of Dublin is not an especially commendable one:

> 'Charming,' said Mr Smedley, and went on to consider that of all the cities he had ever visited this one [*i.e.* Dublin] was the most unfriendly, the most unenterprising, the rudest, the ugliest, and the stupidest. There was litter everywhere, he noticed, and poorly-clad children, and a pity in the eyes of the people that wasn't at all to his liking. It was not a city, decided Mr Smedley, that he would ever wish to return to. (p. 144)

Mind you, this is Mr Smedley's view, and Mr Smedley is not an especially commendable person either.

*Miss Gomez and the Brethren* (1971) is in many ways a companion piece to *Mrs Eckdorf.* It is another of Trevor's studies of evil, in particular the evil of prejudice — prejudice against all foreigners in London, especially, though, against blacks and the Irish. A crew of demolition workers razing whole neighbourhoods and creating '[a] wilderness of wastelands'[22] is composed of colonials from all over the world, but 'mainly from the provinces of Ireland' (p. 74). Among them is red-haired Atlas Flynn from County Cork, who seduces the English publican Mrs Tuke, a comic adulteress whose chief point of humour lies in her deliberate self-deception. Her main objective of contempt has to do with race and nationality. Of black-skinned people she says:

> The sun affected their brain as well as blackening their skins: she'd heard that said and after all it stood to reason, intense heat like that and most of them not possessing the intelligence to make use of a hat. (p. 41)

Her attitude towards foreigners is echoed by London at large. Alban Roche, another Irishman, is widely suspected of being the murderer of Mrs Tuke's daughter, with whom, it turns out, he is entertaining a most happy liaison.

Racial hatred is a powerful symbol of disconnection and alienation in this novel, and so is the corruption of sexual relations, as becomes evident in Miss Gomez's work as a stripper in the Spot-On Club and a prostitute in Mrs Idle's 'pleasure house' (p. 14). The aberrant nature of sexual congress in such circumstances is fully thrown into relief through the deadpan manner in which Trevor renders a scene such as the following one:

> In a cold room the man knelt down and put money in a gasmeter so that they could light the fire. He took his overcoat off and by way of conversation said he was in the advertising business. He showed her an advertisement in a newspaper that he took from his briefcase and said that it had been composed by the firm of which he was the managing director. A large picture showed a man and a woman putting paint on a wall of a room. It was, the man said, an advertise-ment for a brand of tea.
>
> When the room warmed up they took their clothes off and lay together in bed. They smoked cigarettes after the man had satisfied himself [...]. (pp. 12f.)

Racism and sexual deviancy are part of an entire pattern of morally voracious behaviour, against which Miss Gomez, in a ludicrously inefficacious manner, attempts to preach the gospel of the church of which she becomes a member.

The main object of prejudice is, of course, the Jamaican Miss Gomez. Mrs Tuke, for example, believes that she is 'ridiculous and half-baked and half-witted and probably half human [...] a black savage who'd cook you and eat you as soon as she'd look at you' (p. 52), and she accuses her of breeding wild cats that terrorise the demolished neighbourhood and kill Mr Tuke's dog. Finally Inspector Ponsonby blames the Alban Roche fiasco on her. But Miss Gomez is highly prejudiced herself. Trevor moves the whole issue into the realm of the problem of evil. The origin of evil, here as elsewhere in Trevor's *oeuvre*, is to be found in childhood mutilations, physical or emotional, which then set off a chain of related evils. Miss Gomez grew up in an orphanage, where, aged two and a half, she was the only survivor of a fire. The

experience haunts her, making her incapable of feeling affection or believing in God. In the orphanage she is alienated and destructive; with
indifference, she allows the caretaker, Mr Kandi, 'small, elderly liberties'
(p. 14); then she runs off to Kingston and from there to London, earn-
ing her money as a prostitute. She herself does not know what she
wants, but Trevor makes it clear that she wants love and a feeling of
belonging, both of which she believes will be offered her by the Church
of the Brethren of the Way, paradoxically back home in Jamaica.

The events again constitute a circular pattern, beginning and ending
in Jamaica. In between, Miss Gomez moves from atheism and a feeling
of non-existence to faith and an unshakeable sense of identity and
purpose. And little difference does it make that when she returns home
she is forced to discover that the Church of the Brethren is non-existent,
a confidence trick perpetrated by a ganja-smoking Englishman, who
has absconded with all the money. Her faith remains unaffected by the
experience, whereas in other novels by Trevor this comforting faith is
of questionable validity. Miss Gomez is clearly a disturbed person,
something of a fanatic, something of a crackpot. After her
disillusionment about the Church of the Brethren, she notices the
signboard for another church in Kingston and carefully marks its address
and telephone number. The novel, thus, ends on a note of folly, but
folly that possesses its positive aspect. Miss Gomez has found meaning
in her life; what used to be chaos now has pattern, and death, the greatest
of evils, now makes sense as part of God's mysterious plan.

*Elizabeth Alone* (1973)[23] basically relies on the narrative pattern established with *The Boarding-House*: a number of characters are assembled
in one location and then the author painstakingly, patiently and sympa-
thetically surveys their lives and those of their family members or friends,
all of them somehow jaded. We have the usual group of eccentrics:
crackpots, oddballs, conmen and failures. Here it is a ward in a women's
hospital to which Elizabeth Aidallbery is admitted for a hysterectomy.
So is Sylvie Clapper, with false teeth and bleached hair, young, witless,
cheery. She lives with a slippery Irishman: no children yet, and now no
chance. Likewise confined, devout Miss Samson, with the raw black-
berry birthmark and one bad eye, worries about her boarding-house,
for believers only, and the discovery that her Christian mentor, with
whom she believes she was in love, died in utter unbelief. Lily Drucker,
after several miscarriages, is in for childbirth, while her obnoxious
mother-in-law tries to bait her son with sausage rolls and Lincoln Creams.
As Kristin Morrison notes, like *The Boarding House* and the three novels

preceding it, *Elizabeth Alone* shows lonely and eccentric people managing to cope with the evils that plague them while simultaneously
contributing to those evils and perpetrating further evil on others.[24]

The narrative starts off with a brief, straightforward summary of
Elizabeth's previous life. There was a marriage that failed since she did
not want to share a bed with her husband, whom she had married when
she was aged nineteen because beneath his elegant exterior this man
was very like her father. She eventually had had an extra-marital affair
with a married man, and then there was the break-up. However, farce
soon takes over when Elizabeth's daughter Joanna and her weirdo friend,
Samuel, are introduced, which is as early as the end of chapter 1. A
couple of pages later, we read about a woman 'who had persuaded her
bank to issue a chequebook to her cat' (p. 20).

The typical situation of a Trevor character, especially in the early
books, though frequently also in the later ones, is reflected in the way
Elizabeth views herself:

> Dwelling now on her past, with its friends and incidents and the
> beginnings of this and that, Elizabeth could make little sense of
> her life as so far it had been. She saw mistakes mainly, made by
> herself. She saw her life as something that was scattered untidily
> about without a pattern, without rhyme or reason. She often
> wondered if other people, examining their lives in middle age,
> would have preferred, as she did, to see something tidier and
> with more purpose. (p. 8)

Elizabeth is alone, as the book's title suggests, because

> [...] it's lonely when you're forty-one and your children are row-
> dily growing up, when Joanna's gone with a Jesus freak, and your
> mother's packed away in a Sunset House. (p. 245)

Trevor is almost unsurpassably brilliant at analysing human behaviour,
as when he shows how in Miss Samson's boarding-house religious
fervour can easily foster hatred and bedlam. Or take Lily's husband,
Kenneth, a lanky-looking man, who before his marriage was driven by
the treatment he received at the hands of his redoubtable mother to
consorting with prostitutes, accompanying them to their flats and
watching them take off their clothes. Or there is Elizabeth's friend from
childhood, Henry, the vending-machine operator. He is one of life's all-
time losers, with a broken marriage behind him, now trying to grow

mushrooms under the staircase in his house to improve his dire financial situation, and brewing his own beer in his bathroom. Henry changes his job to become an area sales executive in the fish division of a sales firm and to his great dismay is issued with a Vauxhall Viva that has an enormous fish on top of the roof. One drunken night, he and a casual acquaintance, Maloney, an Irishman and a conman if ever there was one, barge into the home of one of Henry's friends and wreak havoc there. Completely unfit to drive, he is stopped by the police on his way home by car and the Viva as well as his driving licence are confiscated. The next day he buys a bottle of whisky, drinks most of it and gasses himself inadvertently while trying to make some dinner. As so often, it is the way in which Trevor succeeds in rendering the incident that commands admiration for its marvellous blending of the comic and the deadly serious: Henry is lying drunk on the floor of his kitchen, finding it hard to move. There is a strange smell around him, but he is of course unable to identify it. He is laughing loudly and delightedly, hearing his own laughter bouncing about the room. People in his life are going through his mind, and he is laughing at 'the whole bloody lot of them'. And Trevor ends the chapter laconically stating: 'He was feeling great, he said to himself' (p. 210). The next thing we hear about poor Henry is that he is dead.

*The Children of Dynmouth* (1976) opens with a panoramic description of an apparently tranquil and idyllic seaside village on the Dorset coast. Dynmouth used to be renowned for its lacemaking and its turbots and 'later developed prettily as a watering place'.[25] That was years ago. Now, things have changed somewhat for the worse. Industrialisation has left its traces. There is a sandpaper factory, a tile-works, a fish-packing station, and quite soon plastic lampshades will be manufactured in a new factory, and the Singer Sewing Machine organisation is thinking of developing a plant there. Trevor, significantly, also stresses the effects that the class system has on the housing situation — from the solitary houses of the well-to-do to the cramped terraced houses so near the river that people consider it a disgrace. Still, Dynmouth seems, on the surface, to be an ordinary provincial village. But that ordinariness masks a community that is morally bankrupt, crippled by the class system and governed by deceit. The true children of Dynmouth are the adults, living in a moral world carefully designed to hide the truth.[26]

Dynmouth is the place in which Timothy Gedge, now fifteen years old, has grown up. He is the product of a broken marriage, a failed school system, and a culture defined by daytime television. As Mr

Featherston, the local rector, reflects:

> [...] the boy was increasingly becoming a nuisance to people, end-lessly friendly and smiling, keen for conversation. He was what Lavinia [Featherston's wife] called a latch-key child, returning to the empty flat in Cornerways from the Comprehensive school, on his own in it all day during the school holidays. Being on his own seemed somehow to have become part of him. (p. 14)

Timothy receives no encouragement in school, where he finds no subject interesting. There was one exception, when a teacher called O'Hennessy was at the Comprehensive; he told his pupils that everyone was good at something: 'it was a question of discovering yourself' (p. 23). But interest-ingly, O'Hennessy fell out with his fellow-teachers over his ideas and had to leave the school after only six months. Timothy — as he is aware — is without prospects for the future other than working in the sand-paper factory. Little wonder that his principal motivating force is distrust.

Timothy may be on his own for the most part, but he has a habit of following people around, sniffing out their secrets. His knowledge of what certain inhabitants of Dynmouth carefully seek to hide stands him in good stead when it comes to organising materials and gadgets he needs for an act he is planning to put on at the Spot the Talent competition — 'Brides of the Bath', three women killed by a murderer called George Joseph Smith. Timothy dreams of being propelled by his act into Hughie Green's television show *Opportunity Knocks*. He is in need of, among other things, curtains, a bath-tub and a wedding dress, and he approaches certain people, blackmailing them by threatening to disclose the truth about them. He becomes a catalyst for these people's character deficiencies, self-doubt, self-deceit, marital problems and infidelities. The Dasses have so far deluded themselves about the problems they are having with their nineteen-year-old son, Nevil, who stays away from Dynmouth because he rejects his mother. Commander Abigail has camouflaged his homosexual leanings, and Mrs Abigail has, for thirty-six years, deceived herself about the emptiness of her marriage, which was never consummated. Mr Plant, the owner of a local pub, is having extra-marital affairs with several women, including Timothy's own mother. Quentin Featherston is brought by Timothy to the awareness that he is 'an ineffectual clergyman' (p. 117), 'a laughable figure, with his clerical collar, visiting the sick, tidying up' (p. 179). His wife, Lavinia, ostensibly a model rector's wife, is on the verge of a psychological breakdown, because she can have no more children.

While what, for his own profit, he discloses about the Dasses, the Abigails and Mr Plant is true, the story he plants in the minds of step-siblings Stephen and Kate Fleming in order to obtain the wedding-dress hidden in a box in the Flemings' house is a wicked lie. Timothy insinuates that Stephen's father murdered his wife so that he could marry Kate's mother, with whom he had been carrying on an adulterous affair. In truth, Stephen's mother, having known of the relationship, committed suicide. It is probably correct to suggest that Timothy is largely a victim of the class system. His victims are all higher up on the social ladder than he is himself, and in his dealings with Stephen and Kate, whose privileged upper-middle-class lives are everything that Timothy's life is not, he is at his most malicious,[27] deliberately sowing discord into the intensely close relationship of the two children.

Not only, however, are other people made to face the facts; Timothy himself is brought face to face with the truth about his future. Asked by Mr Featherston to leave Stephen and Kate alone, Timothy replies: 'They are no use to me [...]. Opportunity won't knock, sir. I'll get work in the sandpaper factory. I'll maybe go on the security. My dad scarpered.' (p. 171) Not many take pity on him or try to explain the reasons for his behaviour. In fact only Lavinia Featherston is made to feel compassion for him, possibly to compensate her sense of deprivation at not being able to have a son herself. She in the end cannot believe 'that the catastrophe of Timothy Gedge [is] not somehow due to other people, and the circumstances created by other people', and she wonders 'if Timothy Gedge's future [will] be as bleak as her husband has forecast' (p. 181), which is this:

> The boy would stand in court-rooms with his smile. He would sit in drab offices of social workers. He would be incarcerated in the cells of different gaols. By looking at him now you could sense that future, and his eyes reminded you that he had not asked to be born. (p. 177)

However, Trevor does not end on the reconciliatory note introduced by Mrs Featherston. Throughout, Timothy had promulgated the idea that a Miss Lavant had been fancying Dr Greenslade for twenty years, wasting herself on a married man. Now at the close of the book, he is pretending that he is the child of Miss Lavant and Dr Greenslade, given to Mrs Gedge to bring up. It is a preposterous illusion, but one that seems to indicate that life for Timothy in Dynmouth, as shown in the novel, is too bleak to be endured without escaping into fantasy.

The most accomplished conman among Trevor's characters is probably Francis Tyte in *Other People's Worlds* (1980). Tyte wriggles his way into the worlds of other people, exploiting them with a vengeance and wrecking their lives by malevolence, a man 'with a particular English charm and a smile that stayed in the mind'.[28] Francis is thirty-three years of age and not for nothing an actor. He is an inveterate liar who, during his first conversation with Julia Ferndale, subsequently his bride-to-be, and her mother, transforms his dingy room in Folkestone into a magnificent flat with a pleasant view of the sea. That his relationship with Julia should end in catastrophe is a foregone conclusion. There have been other such relationships — with two elderly sisters called Massmith; a doctor and his wife in Lincolnshire; the exceedingly rich Kilvert-Dunnes, with whom he stayed on the Isle of Wight; a fourth couple, with whom he remained for almost a year, and other couples as well. All of them came to a disastrous end, always through no fault of his, according to Francis's own view of things. During that first conversation with Julia and her mother, as in the course of his other relationships, he invents the tragedy of his parents' death in a railway accident when he was eleven. In point of fact, his parents are still very much alive and living in an old people's home. Francis thus concocts an existence for himself out of the figments of his imagination. 'Real people', the text suggests, 'had rarely matched the shadows of his make-belief' (p. 38).

But there are of course real people in his life, such as his wife, the dressmaker, thirty years his senior and living in Folkestone, or Doris, a girl in the shoe department of a store in London, who has a child by him. And there is of course Julia Ferndale of Swan House in Stone St Martin, Gloucestershire, a widow in her forties with two grown-up daughters. Julia is a Catholic, not especially devout, but never able to think of life without God, without the sacraments and Mass. However, hers is a childhood vision of God, 'greyly bearded and venerable in a tropical garden' (p. 14). Julia is an innocent, as her mother is aware, with quite a collection of what the older woman defines as 'lame ducks' (p. 19), men, in other words, unsuitable for her daughter, in short: an ideal prey for a person such as Francis. Tyte proves to be no exception where suitability is concerned, leaving Julia during their honeymoon in Italy after only one day there, taking with him her jewellery and some money, both of which she gives him voluntarily when he tells her that he is already married. But at one point, Julia herself realises that:

> she was a silly kind of person, deserving of what had happened
> to her. Every single word Francis Tyte had spoken she had be-
> lieved; his caresses had easily enticed her; she'd longed to be in
> bed with him. (p. 141)

Doris has been driven to drink by Francis and is rarely sober these days, entertaining frantic hopes that Francis will eventually marry her. But he keeps on making excuses, arguing that his ailing wife in Folkestone is an insurmountable hindrance. Nor is he able to visit her in the evenings since he has, or so he claims, to attend to a non-existent uncle from Manchester who is in a home and has problems with his water-works. Her daughter, Joy, is completely neglected, fending for herself and slowly going to the dogs. She plays truant at school and spends her time in front of the television set, while her mother is drinking herself senseless. The last time Doris had forced him into a sexual encounter with her, Francis had wanted to commit murder. When she had leaned forward to seize him, her breasts had loosely dangled, reminding him of 'freshly plucked chickens' (p. 72). Doris is more and more caught up in her drunken fantasies and in the end she commits murder by battering Francis' wife to death with a teapot. The Constance Kent film, which is frequently mentioned and in which Francis performs a minor role, is of course about childhood abuse and a need for revenge. In that, it forms a parallel to Francis's life story: Francis, too, was sexually abused as a child by a lodger in his parents' house, and his exploitive treatment of women is born out of his need to seek revenge on society.

   Notably, Julia, in her despondency after her devastating experience with bigamous Francis, which is further aggravated when her association with Tyte brings Doris into her life, questions the possibility of a benevolent God, thus recalling Mrs Eckdorf. Her bearded God, who saw her through her childhood and her widowing, has dwindled into 'a wisp of nothing' (p. 179). But the people involved with Francis compel her to ask Father Lavin: 'What was God thinking of, for heaven's sake?' (p. 178), adding: 'Why does it always have to be the innocent?' (p. 180). Father Lavin cautions: 'You're being extravagant and dramatic. You're finding meanings where there aren't any.' (p. 181); but his words fail to convince. The world is a terrible place; Calvary has become remote for Julia, 'just another distant act of violence' (p. 181). Julia, like Mrs Eckdorf and Miss Sampson in *Elizabeth Alone*, has lost her faith in view of the evil that she sees in her world and that has affected her. Spiritual counsellors are usually unable to offer a satisfactory answer, leaving their confidants bereft.[29] But unlike the other characters, Julia moves beyond her lost faith to struggle with evil in whatever way she can. In the end, she has learned to forgive Francis, sending him more money, and she is able to pray for him and all the others who have been involved with him. She even wishes 'to rescue him at last from this awful world' (p. 196). Moreover, when Susanna Music turns out not to have been murdered by Doris in an act of vengeance, Julia believes 'her prayers and Father Lavin's had been answered. "Thank You," she said. "Thank You for that."' (p. 213)

*Fools of Fortune* (1983) marks a significant point in Trevor's work where the interest of his novels begins to focus more on matters Irish, throwing light on aspects of Ireland's troubled history by engaging with the topic of political violence as well as deploying narrative conventions of one of Ireland's oldest novelistic genres: the Big House novel. *Fools of Fortune* opens by contrasting two houses — Woodcombe Park in Devon and Kilneagh in County Cork. In the first of these, history is sold to paying tourists; in the second, the place has lapsed into economic and cultural silence, its sorrow-laden history being evoked in the elegiac voices of the narrative. Kilneagh, the Quinton estate built in 1770, represents the emotional focal point of the three narrative consciousnesses. Willie Quinton spent his childhood and adolescence there and inherited the estate. Marianne Woodcombe, his English cousin, identifies the place with Willie; her love for him has, in spite of many reasons to the contrary, bound her to the almost completely gutted house. Finally Imelda, the daughter of Willie and Marianne, vegetates in Marianne's care in what appears to be a mentally deranged state; in her, the terror and the glory of the family's history unite.

*Fools of Fortune* is divided into four parts, the first and last rendered from Willie's point of view, the second from Marianne's, and the third being devoted to Imelda. Willie and Marianne address each other directly, as it were, in letters and diary entries. Imelda's thoughts, into which are incorporated quotations from statements of her aunt's, are communicated by an omniscient narrator. In Willie's recollections (he was born in 1910 and now narrates from the perspective of a septuagenarian), with which the story proper starts, Kilneagh stands for a sense of order, safety and harmony — a sense that has also left its mark on Willie's own character. The scarlet drawing room, warm in winter and fragrant in summer with the scent of roses, used to be the centre of his world when he was a child. It was in this room that he was first told about

Irish history. A kind of near-pastoral idyll prevailed in what was believed to be an intact world. Here the first word of Latin he learned (*agricola*: farmer) reminded him of his place in life. But this idyll found its abrupt end after Willie's schooldays, with the inadequacy and insufficiency of his educational instruction being fully thrown into relief. A similarly sudden destruction of idyllic happiness had also occurred in the two previous generations of the Quinton family.

Willie's grandmother, Anna Quinton, whose name permeates the novel in leitmotif fashion, had tried to alleviate the horrific suffering of those stricken by the 'Great Hunger' of 1849, but she had died of famine fever. She had attempted to extirpate the guilt with regard to the Catholic part of the Irish population that, in her view, the Protestant Ascendancy (of which she was a member) had incurred. Her English relatives had reacted with a lack of understanding, even ridicule towards her behaviour and considered her a madwoman. Anna Quinton had sought to eradicate one of the prime causes of political and social unrest in Ireland by making her husband promise before her death that he would work to overcome the institutional hegemony of the Irish landlords. But after his wife's demise, he had locked himself into his room at Kilneagh and done nothing.

Willie's mother, Eva, succeeded Anna as mistress of Kilneagh. She combined in herself support for Home Rule and Irish independence with a demand for militant action, urging her husband to aid Michael Collins. In response, he offered financial help but would not allow Collins to use Kilneagh to train soldiers. His caution, though, did not prevent disaster at Kilneagh. After the war he reluctantly hired the veteran Doyle, who had in fact been a spy for the Black and Tans. In retaliation for his betrayal, the Irish nationalists hanged him on the Kilneagh estate and cut out his tongue. Because the Black and Tans were loyal to their spies, they took vengeance. Under the direction of the British soldier Sergeant Rudkin, Kilneagh was burned down and Willie's father and sisters were murdered. Unable to forgive and forego violence as a means of resolving conflicts, Eva passed on her hatred of the man allegedly responsible for the cruel deed to Willie, who, after his mother had committed suicide out of bitterness and despondency, carried out the wished-for act of vengeance, with the consequence that he had to seek exile from Ireland and his beloved Marianne and to live in Italy for the best part of his life. Marianne came to Kilneagh after her child was born and has elected to stay on there into the narrative present. The house is now presided over by Aunt Fitzeustace.

Notably enough, among the Quintons it has always been the women who set the tone. Marianne equals Eva in that she, too, defends blood revenge as well as the necessity for armed action and contends fatalistically that '[d]estruction casts shadows which are always there [...] We will never escape the shadows of destruction that pervade Kilneagh'.[30] It is Imelda to whom it falls to break the vicious circle of violence breeding violence. She immerses herself in the incidents that make up the Quintons' past; she digs into the secrets of Kilneagh, unearthing details which she relives with such intensity and empathy that eventually her fantasies take over completely and she withdraws into an exceedingly private world, envisioning paradise regained — a reconciliatory experience that goes hand in hand with Willie's return and the reunion of the lovers, Willie and Marianne. Imelda's spiritual and mental peace is interpreted by the Catholic people as a sign of divine delight. In the end through Imelda, a symbol of healing and redemption,[31] the guilt of the Quintons has been expunged:

> Imelda is gifted, so the local people say, and bring the afflicted to her. A woman has been rid of dementia, a man cured of a cata- ract. Her happiness is like a shroud miraculously about her, its source mysterious except for her. (p. 192)

*Fools of Fortune* concerns itself with the thematic paradigm of innocence and experience. At its centre lies the tension between history and the individual, between political ideology and personal values. Willie and Marianne's relationship plays itself out against the backdrop of political and historical events which cause Willie to sacrifice his love and take on a role foisted upon him by certain forces over which he has no control. While it thus seeks to fathom the extent of the sacrifice that political commitment imposes upon human love, the novel also highlights the moral obligation of the individual to act as Willie did. Finally, *Fools of Fortune* hints — albeit implicitly — at a way of solving some of Ireland's major politico-historical conflicts. The innocence/experience paradigm works towards painting an almost tragic picture of men and women as 'fools of fortune', especially if these find themselves caught in a certain political context. In the end, though, the power of love and the imagination wins out over history and political ideology.

In the novella *Nights at the Alexandra* (1987), the narrator, Harry, 'a fifty-eight-year-old cinema proprietor without a cinema',[32] recalls his time as an adolescent in a grubby provincial Irish town. His father owned the local timber yard, having worked his way up from low origins: 'We were a Protestant family of the servant class which had come up in the world [...]' (p. 3). Harry's father, his family, the family business, the town itself constitute an existence as drab and paralysing as any confronting the youthful protagonists in Joyce's *Dubliners*.[33] In sharp contrast to this world of dreariness and routine, there is the mysterious life of the newly arrived Messingers, which Harry becomes familiar with through running small errands for Mrs Messinger, an Englishwoman, her husband a German. The time is during what used to be referred to in Ireland as the 'Emergency', that is to say: World War II. The Messingers have come to Ireland, purchasing Cloverhill, a spacious house on the edge of the town, because she could not live in Germany and he found it impossible to live in England. Despite a considerable difference in age, the Messingers are devoted to each other and lead a happy married life, unlike Harry's father and mother, who can frequently be heard quarrelling in their bedroom. The Messingers inspire powerful ambitions in Harry, which he hopes to realise some day. Part of his hopes, though, become thwarted when Harry discovers that the young woman is dying. Prior to her death, Mrs Messinger asks her husband to build a magnificent cinema, the Alexandra, in the town, and this becomes a symbol of the husband's devotion to her, but also of the selfless impulse to reach out beyond the confines of one's individual life and to 'bring pleasure', as Harry puts it, to other people.[34]

The novella, as Schirmer observes, maintains a fine balance between disillusionment and hope, resignation and determination, alienation and connection,[35] a balance that characterises not only the Messingers' life, but also Harry's own existence. Harry has become a figure of loneliness and alienation, a man who never married, who has no children (cf. p. 1), who lives on the edge of society. 'I am', he says, 'pitied because I am solitary and withdrawn, because I have not taken my place and am left in the end with nothing' (p. 71). But from his own subjective point of view, his life looks completely different. He has his memories of the Messingers, his imagination and his faith in the power of love. As he puts it, '[...] memory is enough' (p. 71).

*Nights at the Alexandra* is a fine example of Trevor's use of the garden motif.[36] Trevor frequently employs this motif, again for instance in *My House in Umbria*, to evoke ideas that refer to the Biblical Garden of Eden. Mr Messinger significantly has turned the overgrown wilderness around his house into a respectable garden. He has undertaken the task for his wife, as evidence of his love for her. The garden becomes an emblem of their harmonious, even blissful relationship. In *My House in Umbria*, the creation of the garden by the two men represents an act of gratitude, signifying also the bonding between the characters gathered in the eponymous house.

*The Silence in the Garden* (1988) engages with aspects of the violence and division that are seen to characterise Ireland's troubled history. Principles of compassion and connection have been sacrificed for political and religious fanaticism.[37] It is a notable feature of Trevor's art that the treatment of so relentlessly sombre a subject should involve one of the funniest scenes in all of his writings to date: the scene showing Mrs Moledy at Villana Rolleston's wedding breakfast. Mrs Moledy arrives at Carriglas well-oiled with a few glasses of whiskey. She keeps drinking more and finally takes a seat at the table:

> Mrs Moledy sat down on a chair and carefully placed her glass on the table. The female had gone all right, she said; one minute she was there and the next she'd walked off. She closed one eye because all of a sudden there appeared to be two of the old grandmothers in front of her. She wondered if the female was suffering from toothache, which would account for being so serious in the face. She asked about that, but although she could see the women's lips moving, she couldn't hear what they said. She couldn't understand why none of these people would speak up, and then she wondered if they were able to hear what she was saying herself.
>
> 'Excuse me, were we ever introduced? Moreen Moledy, originally of Cahir.'
>
> She held out her hand in the direction of the two women, but by mistake she closed her eyes for a minute and the next thing was they weren't there any more. She felt tired so she went to sleep.[38]

Later she starts a conversation with the Bishop of Killaloe:

> 'Well, isn't this great?' she remarked to the Bishop.
> 'Isn't what great?'
> 'Errah, go on with you!' She nudged his elbow with her own. (...)
> (p. 151)

Her intention had been to hide among the bushes in order to give the

money for the French car to her lover, John James Rolleston, unobserved
by the wedding-guests. But all that whiskey, in the end, makes it
impossible for her to stand up: 'She'd have stood up only she was afraid
of feeling groggy due to the sun. 'I was drinking Paddy,' she explained
to the brother.' Yet this does not deter her from conveying jumbled
facts of local history to the Bishop, most of which escape him:

> She wondered if the man was affected in the brain. She watched
> him eating his fish, the fork going up and down, the single face
> becoming two and then one of the faces sliding away altogether.
> It was Dowley who killed the butler, she explained in case the
> man was ignorant. (pp. 154f.)

The events that go to make up the tragic picture of Irish history are
separated from each other by long periods of time and references to
them are meticulously scattered throughout the account. They are
brought together to form a meaningful pattern only in the consciousness
of old Mrs Rolleston, and many of them are preserved in the diaries
kept by Sarah Pollexfen. The first entry is for 1904; most entries, though,
are for 1931. Sarah originally came to Carriglas as Villana's tutor. Later
she worked at the Misses Goodbody's School for Protestant Girls. When
her mother died, Sarah left the school and returned to Dundary Rectory
to look after her father. When her father died in 1930, she was invited
back to Carriglas by Mrs Rolleston, who feared that Sarah would be
penniless. In 1931 she returned to the island off the Cork coast. At the
heart of the island there is a ruined abbey and there are also some
standing stones to be found. The standing stones are remnants of the
warring pre-Christian civilisations that once inhabited Ireland. The ruined
abbey is a relic from Ireland's mediaeval Christian period and a reminder
of the ancient conflict between pagan and Christian. The Rolleston
house is thus steeped in a past of violence and usurpation.

The present-day Rollestons are an impoverished Protestant
Ascendancy family, living in a 'big house'. At the close of the novel,
after Sarah's death, the house has become Tom's property, Tom
significantly being the illegitimate son of Catholic servants, who will
not allow the place to be turned into a hotel or be sold in an auction.
The days of the Protestant acendancy are, as shown in so many 'Big
House' novels, over for good. A bridge is being constructed that will
link the island with the mainland, thus suggesting that the insularity of
life on Carriglas can no longer be sustained in twentieth-century Ireland

and, since the town has decided to dedicate the bridge to one Cornelius Dowley and not to one of the Rollestons, suggesting too that the Rollestons' status in the community is no longer what it used to be.[39]

The Rollestons originally arrived on Carriglas 'in the wake of Oliver Cromwell' (p. 41) in the seventeenth century. They dispossessed the family who then lived on the island, sending them on their way to the stony wilderness of Mayo. The Rollestons came 'to the island with slaughter in their wake' (p. 188), as Sarah puts it in one of her diaries. During the Great Hunger, though, one generation of the Rollestons, known as the 'Famine Rollestons' (p. 42), showed compassion for their tenants, finding work for them and waiving monies and title to land. The immediate history of the Rolleston family has been overshadowed by a childhood cruelty that, as Mrs Rolleston remarks to Sarah, 'has turned around and damned a household' (p. 186). Once the Rolleston children — John James, Lionel and Villana — hunted a child ('As of right, they hunted', p. 184), a red-haired child, who turns out to have been none other than Cornelius Dowley. The Rolleston children thus re-enacted the original sin of colonialism.[40] Cornelius was subsequently responsible for blowing to pieces Tom's father, Linchy the Rollestons' butler, at Lahane crossroads in mistake for members of the Rolleston family. The deed was intended as a retaliatory measure. That incident happened in 1920, 'in the time of the Troubles' (p. 26). Dowley, then a member of the IRA, was himself in turn murdered by the Black and Tans in retaliation for an attack on them and the raiding of their barracks. Dowley's mother, having been informed of her son's death, had walked into the sea and drowned herself.

All these occurrences have drawn extraordinarily long shadows. Thus, for instance, as a consequence of the Linchy murder, the engagement of Sarah's brother, Hugh, to Villana was broken off. But the lives of the Rollestons were crippled by other events, too. Colonel Rolleston fell in action at Passchendael. John James was wounded in the First World War shortly after his father's demise; he now leads a life of inertia. In fact, all the Rolleston children lead lives damaged by the events of the past. Sarah records in an entry for August 25th, 1931:

> Yet neither he [*i.e.* John James] nor Villana — and certainly not their brother [*i.e.* Lionel] — seems able to escape from the shadow of their abandoned lives. (p. 152)

The damage is, among other things, reflected in the deviant love relationships that they have entered into. Villana marries the much older Finnamore Balt, a dry stick of a man and a solicitor whose only world is the law and who dreams of restoring Carriglas to its former glory with the help of the law. 'Marriage', Villana softly promises to Finnamore, 'would not mean children' (p. 44). The Rollestons will leave no heirs. Villana has consented to marry Balt not least in order to forget her attachment to Sarah's brother, to put an end to her 'dream of Hugh returning to Carriglas' (p. 94). Most people believe that she is after Finnamore's money. There is also Sarah's unrequited love for Lionel, who largely avoids human contacts by immersing himself in farm work. John James entertains a tawdry affair with plump, simpering Mrs Moledy, the proprietress of a boarding-house called, of all names, the Rose of Tralee.

But the child Tom is living under a shadow, too. He feels alienated from the community for having been conceived out of wedlock. Holy Mullihan, the religious fanatic, is trying his best to put the fear of God into him by haranguing him with remarks to the effect that Tom's mother committed the sin of having sexual intercourse with Linchy. 'It's like you'd walk up to the Cross and spit on Our Lord', he tells him (p. 87). The nuns at the convent school exacerbate his feelings of being ostracised. In school, Brother Meagher keeps the memory of the incident at Lahane crossroads alive and bombards Tom and his fellow-pupils with names of heroes and martyrs, which they have to learn off, and if they fail to present the facts properly they are given the strap. Thus, Tom, too, is living very much in the shadow of a past over which he has no control and which has been coloured by the political and religious violence that has engulfed Carriglas.[41]

Mrs Rolleston, who is approaching ninety when Sarah returns to the island in 1931, shows compassion, thus recalling the Famine Rollestons. She shares acutely Brigid's distress over the killing of Linchy, and she shares the distress of Kathleen Quigley, the woman who was close to Dowley. On one occasion, Mrs Rolleston remarks to Sarah: '[...] no one can do without love. It is the greatest of all deprivations not to know love in some wise, either to give or to receive. It hardly matters which' (p. 93). She it is who urges Finnamore to see to it that papers are drawn up that ensure provision is made for Tom (cf. p. 172). And of course it is Mrs Rolleston who wants all the facts written down in Sarah's diaries, 'so that the truth could be passed on. Or left behind, whichever way you look at it' (p. 183). The devastating truth about the Rolleston family and Irish history, as incidentally about myriad other families and the history of other countries, is summed up by Mrs Rolleston:

> Chance had supplied a gruesome plot: in another place and an-
> other time they would have grown up healthily to exorcise their
> abberations by shrugging them away. (p. 187)

Trevor, thus, imbues an intrinsically Irish topic with international
significance. Reflecting the international through the parochial is no
doubt the prime characteristic of all worthwhile art.

*Two Lives* (1991) wonderfully proves the richness and fecundity of
Trevor's creative imagination. He quite obviously can afford to offer his
readers two full-blown novels in one where other writers would have
taken occasion to bring out two separate books. Reviewers of *Two Lives*
have frequently referred to its two constitutive parts, *Reading Turgenev*
and *My House in Umbria*, as novellas.[42] But these are rather too long for
that literary concept to qualify. There is no real reason why one should
not categorise them as novels.[43]

The two pieces that go to make up *Two Lives* are excellent examples
of Trevor's fascination with jaded characters and lives. They show two
women withdrawing from a harsh reality into a world of the imagination.
*Reading Turgenev* offers the story of Mary Louise Dallon, 'not yet fifty-
seven',[44] who, in the narrative present, is staying in a home for the
mentally insane to which she was sent after she allegedly attempted to
poison her husband and her two sisters-in-law with rat-poison. The
home is intended to be closed down and turned into a hotel, and the
inmates whose condition is not too worrying are destined to be released
into their families. Mary Louise is one of them. As she tells the priest at
the end of the narrative, for the last eight years she has flushed the
prescribed drugs down the lavatory and she does not take them now
because they are not necessary. She also admits to not having used the
Rodenkil at all, instead having stained green with Stephens' ink the
rissoles her husband and her sisters-in-law ate. For more then half her
life she has been living in the world of the novelist Turgenev into which
her deceased cousin, Robert, invited her. The tragedy of her life, if one
can call it a tragedy, began with her agreeing to marry Elmer Quarry, as
four-square a character as his surname suggests.

One of the most exquisite things about *Reading Turgenev* is the way
in which Trevor has rendered Mary Louise's story — gentle, sure-footed,
unassuming and doubly effective because of its gentle and unassuming
nature. Mary Louise left school with no greater ambition than to work
in the local chemist's shop, but in that she was frustrated and
circumstances obliged her to stay at home, helping in the house on her

parents' twenty-seven-acre farm in the townland of Cullen. Elmer Quarry, a bulky, entrepreneurial presence, invariably attired in a nondescript mud-coloured suit, owned the drapery store in the town. In 1955, when aged thirty-five, he was still a bachelor; but that was nothing out of the ordinary because for more than a century the inheritors of Quarry's drapery had married late. Elmer was the only well-to-do Protestant for miles around, the fact notwithstanding that his business had slumped.

The courtship began on 11 January 1955, when Elmer invited Mary Louise, twenty-one at the time, to the pictures the following Friday. To the Dallon household, the invitation came as a surprise. Mary Louise's brother declared it an affront and her sister warned Mary Louise about what might occur under cover of darkness and advised her to keep a safety-pin handy. Mary Louise herself was terrified. But they went nonetheless and saw the film *The Flame and the Flesh*. Elmer did not in the least enjoy it, and in the end the safety-pin was not opened. Yet the courtship ran its strange course and eventually the wedding took place on 10 September 1955, nine months after the visit to the Electric Cinema. Theirs was a marriage of convenience: she knew it and Elmer knew it; 'the curiosity of affection was not present on either side' (p. 31). Matters came to a head when during their honeymoon Elmer showed himself to be impotent. This is how Trevor, true to his mastery of narrative technique, describes the scene. Elmer, one should add, who up to this point in his life had abstained from drinking alcohol, has had a few whiskies:

> Mary Louise put her nightdress over her petticoat and then slipped off the petticoat and the rest of her underclothes, and her stockings. [...] Elmer tried to watch, but his efforts at concentration caused a visual confusion he had not experienced before. A second image of his bride floated out of the first, precisely the same outline, hands and head, the white nightdress picked up from the bed, the body bent, then turned away from him while some sort of groping took place, stockings in her hands. He wanted to tell her she was great, but when he tried to his voice wouldn't work properly. (pp. 47f.)

Mary Louise went to live in the Quarry house over the shop together with Elmer's obstreperous sisters, who could only find fault in all her Ladyship, as they dubbed her, did. Gradually she took to slipping up the steep uncarpeted stairs to one of the attics, sitting in an armchair and closing her eyes. Then one morning, when the marriage was just over a year old, she awoke to find tears on her cheeks. Elmer, in turn, developed the habit of frequenting Hogan's bar, instead of playing billiards in the YMCA room; for he discovered that the whiskey he drank deadened 'an ache that oppressed him' (p. 66).

It was in this situation that Mary Louise started cycling around the countryside and on one of her journeys she came near her Aunt Emmeline's house and remembered her aunt's invalid son, Robert, with whom she used to be quite close when they were both still children. She paid him a visit and the visits became regular. He introduced her to the novels of Turgenev, reading from them to her in a churchyard next to the grave of the Attridge family. A tender love developed between Mary Louise and Robert, and once more it is the manner in which Trevor handles the affair that commands admiration. At the height of the relationship there is this scene: Robert, having kissed Mary Louise for the first time, at which she experiences 'neither regret nor the shadow of guilt' (p. 106), is sleeping in his bed and dreaming of his beloved:

> He put his arms around his cousin's waist and as they walked on the strand they talked about his father. In that moment Robert died. (p. 107)

When her aunt's house was put up for sale in an auction, Mary Louise bought some of Robert's belongings with money she had taken from Elmer's safe, thus causing a fracas in the family. She furnished her attic room with them and withdrew there, more or less permanently, leaving her husband to his own alcoholic devices. She went on visiting the graveyard and kept up reading Turgenev, in particular *On the Eve*, significantly a novel about a dead lover, the character Insarov, for whom she once mistook Elmer when he came to visit her in the home. In brief: Mary Louise built up an imaginary world that she believed she was sharing with Robert. The members of her family, Elmer's sisters, in fact almost everyone in the town noticed that Mary Louise had developed strange habits. Most of the people believed that Elmer had taken to drink as a result of her eccentric behaviour. And there was of course the fact that the marriage had remained childless. Yet Mary Louise kept on hearing Robert's voice: 'His voice continuing, and hers embracing it, was their act of love' (p. 187). So, before too long, she purchased the Rodenkil and stained the rissoles green with Stephens' ink.

Finally, after having been sent home from the asylum, her first thought is to visit the graveyard where her love for Robert had first begun to blossom, and all she wishes for now is to be buried together with her departed lover in one grave. 'All it is', she tells Elmer, 'is moving the remains from one graveyard to another. I want to be buried with him, Elmer' (p. 211). The clergyman to whom she confesses her love in the end, reflecting that Mary Louise will outlive the Quarrys, promises to arrange the mutual burial, 'There is the burial, and then the lovers lie together' (p. 222). This is the ending of the story.

The frame, describing events set in the present and treating of Mary Louise's release from the asylum, and the story of the marriage effect a contrast between past and present. The past is quite unequivocal, but the reader's appreciation of it would be entirely different without the level of the present. Without it, we would have an inadequate notion of the depth of Mary Louise's attachment to Robert as well as of her miserable existence in the Quarry household. In short: we would not know how strong the need was for her to escape into an imaginary life. At the same time, without the present, the idea conveyed of Elmer's character would be just as one-sided. This is the figure he cuts now:

> He was a seedy figure now, cigarette-burns on his clothes, his shirt-collars frayed, portions of his jowl forgotten when he shaved. Guilt has made him take her in; guilt made him visit her and pay a little so that she wouldn't have to drink out of an enamel mug. He'd be ashamed of himself if he'd struck her. (p. 192)

He, too, is a pitifully broken person. In the end, he emerges as not at all too bad a spud, one who cannot withdraw into the happiness of an imaginary world, but simply drowns his sorrow in whiskey. Lastly, the frame enables the reader to form the right view of the relationship between Mary Louise and Elmer. To his sisters' reprimands, he replies: 'She's my wife' (p. 192), and Mary Louise says notably enough to Elmer: 'I'm sorry I caused you trouble. [...] I'm sorry I made things worse' (p. 193).

*My House in Umbria* represents the attempt by Emily Delahunty, also known as Gloria Grey, Janice Ann Johns and Cora Lamore ('Names hardly matter, I think', p. 225), to set the record of her life straight, after '[r]umour and speculation — even downright lies — have abounded since [she] was sixteen years old' (p. 225). And what an eventful life hers has been! Emily Delahunty has now reached her fifty-sixth year. She is the proprietress of a small hotel/*pensione* in Umbria (although it was never known as such, cf. p. 230) and the author of a series of fictional romances. The latter career she embarked upon in her middle age after her arrival in the house.

Emily Delahunty was born in an English seaside resort to parents who owned a Wall of Death, the mother standing upright on the pillion of her husband's motor-cycle while he raced it round the rickety enclosure. Soon after her birth, her parents gave her away to a Mr and Mrs Trice. When she was eleven years of age, Mr Trice assaulted her sexually. Not much time went by before other men besides Mr Trice desired her. At the age of eighteen, 'green as a pea' (p. 337), she started an affair with a Mr Chubbs, who took her to Idaho, promising to show her the Wild West there. She worked as a stewardess on the S.S. *Hamburg* and eventually ended up as a prostitute in the Café Rose in Ombubu, Africa, where she met the Irishman Quinty, who is a bit of a conman and now acts as her handyman in the *pensione*.

The event that features prominently in her account concerns an outrage that took place in the summer of 1987. Emily was travelling by train to Milan. With her in the compartment were the German Otmar and his girlfriend, Madeleine; the English General, his daughter and his son-in-law; and the American girl, Aimée, her brother and her parents. Suddenly a bomb exploded, killing Otmar's girlfriend, Aimée's brother and parents as well as the General's daughter and son-in-law. While she is lying in her hospital bed, scenes from her romances, dreams and real experiences blend together to form a phantasmagoric mish-mash. 'Faces and words and voices flowed over me' (p. 244). The house that figures in one of her books, Mara Hall, is more vivid to her 'than the shadows of nurses whose speech [she does] not understand' (p. 245). In the end, Emily takes the three surviving victims into her care and allows them to stay in her house.

To understand Mrs Delahunty's behaviour and comprehend what *My House in Umbria* is trying to convey, one must take into account that Mrs Delahunty is the author of romances. '[...] in my works I dealt with happiness ever after' (p. 228), she notes. On the train to Milan, she is conceiving another romance, *Ceaseless Tears*, and out of nowhere these words come to her:

> In the garden the geraniums are in flower. Through scented twilight the girl in the white dress walked with a step as light as a morning cobweb. That evening she hadn't a care in the world. (p. 238)

But the image freezes in her mind, and she is unable to continue with the story. Much later, she believes that the girl in the scented twilight is Aimée. Mrs Delahunty has always been a sucker for romance:

> When I was in the care of Mr and Mrs Trice I longed for a cow-boy to step down from the screen of the old Gaiety Cinema and snatch me on to his saddle, spiriting me away from 21 Prince Albert Street. When I was a girl, serving clerks in a public-house dining-room, I longed for a young man of good family to draw his car up beside me on the street. When I was a woman I longed for a different kind of stranger to appear in the Café Rose. That summer in Umbria, I had long abandoned hope. In my fifty-sixth year I had come to terms with stuff like that. My stories were a help, no point in denying it. (p. 233)

From the misery that she believes surrounds her she escapes into the harmonious world of her romances. Otmar and the General tell her of their pasts. She learns of events in their lives. But what is of greater significance is that she starts weaving stories around the two men, fictionalising reality, or seeing certain events in terms of her own novels. Thus we have, for instance, this passage:

> I smiled at him again. He needed an excuse, a cover for what he saw as cowardice. 'When in distress, pretend, my dear,' Lady Daysmith pronounces in *Precious September*, and I pretended now [...]. (p. 272)

The verb that is quite conspicuous in its frequent use is 'to imagine'. Every so often Emily Delahunty writes: 'I imagined [...]', for instance how Otmar met his girlfriend in a café, and even though Otmar never told her, she is as convinced as one can only be about real occurrences that Madeleine 'said exactly a month later': '*Otmar, ich liebe dich*' (p. 276). By the same token, real people in her life, like the Sunday-school teacher Miss Alzapiedi, get turned into fictional characters: Miss Alzapiedi becomes Lady Daysmith.

Mrs Delahunty's imagination runs rampant and before too long she has concocted a fantasy according to which Otmar was asked by his fellow revolutionaries to plant the timed device in the train. Similarly she dreams up a story about the General and his dislike of his son-in-law. After Mr Riversmith has arrived to fetch his niece, Aimée, to the United States, she starts imagining his life back home with — in her view — his termagant wife. Or she invents Mr Riversmith's strained relationship with his sister, Aimée's mother. Matter-of-fact Mr Riversmith, whose pro-fessional interest is in bark-ants, cannot follow Mrs Delahunty's rambling stories and dreams, putting them down to a hyperactive imagination that is, more is the pity, befuddled by quite a high intake of alcohol. Mr Riversmith is also taken aback by the large number of drinks Mrs Delahunty keeps pressing on him at all hours of the day.

Either she is constantly imagining things, or 'vivid pictures' keep coming into her mind. For her, there can be no doubt that 'we are all inside a story that is being composed as each day passes' (p. 353). Emily Delahunty keeps on dreaming up horrid dramas around the people who are staying with her, all the time failing to comprehend the reality that is unfolding itself. At one point, she tells Mr Riversmith about 'the feeling I continued to experience — of a story developing around us, of small, daily details apparently imbued with a significance that was as yet mysterious' (p. 335). She of course also fails to apprehend her existence correctly because she is for the most part under the influence of alcohol, while at the same time blaming people like Mr Riversmith for not having so far 'displayed [any] signs of awareness what-soever' (p. 345). Mr Riversmith certainly is right when he says of Mrs Delahunty: 'Her imagination has consumed her' (p. 346).

It is noteworthy that Mrs Delahunty is the implied author of the account that constitutes *My House in Umbria*. Additionally, she comments, for example, on the manner in which one composes a romance: 'To compose a romance it is necessary to have a set of circumstances and within those circumstances a cast of people [etc.]' (pp. 269f.). She also includes excerpts from her fan mail, thus demonstrating how readers mistake fiction for fact, quite in the manner of Jane Austen's Catherine Morland in *Northanger Abbey*. Furthermore, Mrs Delahunty exemplifies the process of fictionalisation.

Now, enthusiasts of postmodernist literary criticism would probably jump at the idea of classing *My House in Umbria* as metafiction; but nothing could be more misguided. In the novel, the narrative process is never laid bare in the ontological sense in which this occurs in metafiction. Instead, *My House in Umbria* is about the power of the imagination and the need to leave the harsh world of commonplace reality for an illusory one. As Mrs Delahunty notes: '[i]llusion came into it, of course it did. Illusion and mystery and pretence: dismiss this trinity of wonders' and what is left indeed! She finishes her account with these words: 'I haven't learned much, only that love is different among survivors' (p. 374). It is a nice thought, but one not borne out by the actual events in the house in Umbria.

In *Felicia's Journey* (1994), Felicia, a gawky slip of a girl, is, at the end of her tether, embarked on a fruitless journey, aimlessly roaming around from one town or city to the next, eating in charity halls and lugging her few belongings about in carrier bags: a down-and-out. At the opening of the book, she has taken herself off — as her father would put it — to the Birmingham area in search of her boyfriend, who has got her in the family way and has told her he is working in a lawn-mower factory somewhere in the Midlands. Her efforts remain despairingly futile: Johnny Lysaght cannot be tracked down. While traipsing from place to place or lying awake in sordid digs at night, Felicia broods on events pre-dating her journey to England, thereby offering Trevor the opportunity of weaving the past into the narrative present. She may not find her Johnny, but she runs into Miss Calligary, a religious fanatic intent upon 'gathering in for the Lord' (one of the inimitable crackpots that have been strutting the pages of Trevor's novels from *The Old Boys* onwards).

And she comes to know Joseph Ambrose Hilditch, an obese 54-year-old catering manager, who of all things in the world loves eating — suitably enough. Mr Hilditch is given to accosting women for what turns out to be predatory purposes. Essentially, though, he is leading a vicarious existence; he is one of Trevor's loners, set upon by life. Mr Hilditch intentionally steals the money that Felicia has stuffed into the sleeves of a navy-blue jersey, making her utterly dependent upon him. Feigning sympathy, compassion and concern, he takes her under his wing, ingratiating himself with her. He allows her to live in his house, even persuades her to have an abortion. Then something horrifying happens that causes Felicia to bolt from 3 Duke of Wellington Road, where Mr Hilditch lives. Following the young woman's disappearance, the food-lover Hilditch loses his appetite. He neglects his work and agonises until he 'is capable of suffering no more',[45] as the text laconically refers to the man's demise.

It would somewhat spoil the fun to reveal what precisely happens between Mr Hilditch and his prey. Suffice it to note that it has something to do with the six women the creepy catering manager previously elected to cater for, as also with something that took place when Joseph Ambrose was still a boy: apparently his mother had some hanky-panky going on with his uncle; the knowledge of the affair wrecked Joseph Ambrose's personality. Followers of the man whom Vladimir Nabokov dubbed the Viennese quack would no doubt have a field-day illuminating the darker aspects of the depths that lie within Mr Hilditch. But let them lie. The novel is about evil and goodness, mercy and disdain; 'and always, and everywhere, the chance that separates the living from the dead' (p. 213). *Felicia's Journey* proves Trevor's admirable adroitness at drawing memorable characters with a few deft strokes and shows the novelist registering human and social aberrations in a pungent style; for instance, the manner in which he maps the industrial wasteland of present-day Britain is expertly done.

If *Reading Turgenev* and *My House in Umbria* are classed as novellas, then Trevor's *Death in Summer* (1998) has every right to be grouped in the same textual category, relying as the book does on basically one single situation: the abduction of Thaddeus Davenant's baby girl, Georgina, by Pettie, a young woman of dubious upbringing who applies for the position of the baby's nurse. She is turned down by Thaddeus's mother-in-law and as a result develops a severe hatred of her.

Most importantly, she becomes besotted with Thaddeus himself, believing that by kidnapping the baby she will prove the older woman's incapacity for looking after the infant properly and ingratiate herself with the father. Pettie is another of Trevor's riven personalities in search of love and affection, which is why she loses herself in fantasies of living together with Thaddeus Davenant in Quincunx House, more as a lover than as a baby-minder.

The novel is notable for relying on some of Trevor's familiar thematic interests, recurrent motifs and specific character constellations that effect that characteristic amalgam of the hilarious and the poignant. To begin with the latter, *Death in Summer* would not be a typical Trevor novel if the treatment of the sudden death of Thaddeus's young wife, which leaves him with having to look after his months-old baby, did not involve the introduction of some grotesque characters. Mrs Ferry, the wife of the manager of the Beech Trees Hotel with whom Thaddeus had an affair in 1979, is one such grotesque, with her coloured beads that 'lollop over double chins and reach an artificially deepened cleavage, exposed between mammoth breasts'.[46] So are Albert and Pettie, the latter in a frightening, sinister way. Albert is a worrier, not exactly the full shilling, 'a few marbles short' (p. 182), the text has it. At night he works in Underground stations, erasing graffiti when the trains are not running; during the day, when he is not in the Soft Rock Café — as distinct from Carole King's Hard Rock one — he attends to his landlady's needs. Secretly, he dreams of joining the Salvation Army. Pettie, small and just into her twenties, is a tearaway, a kleptomaniac and a fraudster: 'Taking possession of things touches a part of Pettie she does not understand, stirring an excitement in her that never fails to brighten up the day' (p. 58).

Trevor once more explores evil or abnormal impulses that stunt the growth of a personality, and he traces them back to childhood mutilations. Thaddeus is a solitary figure, incapable of feeling any affection, incapable even of loving his young wife, 'this the legacy of an unusual childhood' (p. 2). But after his experiences surrounding the abduction of his child, the death of his wife and, in particular, the news of Pettie's death, Thaddeus wonders what will become of his house and garden, envisaging that offices or a supermarket may be built in the place. Significantly, he asks himself whether anyone will know among the tins of soup and processed peas 'that death was a balm here when it came', and 'feelings he has never before experienced invade Thaddeus's solitude' (p. 212). 'Tonight', the text concludes, 'he pities, and is angry' (p. 212).

Both Pettie and Albert grew up in a home, the Morning Star, from which they eventually ran away. Pettie was sexually abused during her childhood by a 'Sunday uncle' and other men. That has turned her into what she is. She meets her death when the Morning Star is razed to the ground, with her inside hiding from the police. She leaves Albert on his own; but Albert, tellingly, takes it upon himself to go and explain, as best he can, to Thaddeus and his mother-in-law why Pettie kidnapped Georgina, trying to make them understand and, possibly, forgive. Moreover, his dream has come true: he has joined the Salvation Army, and at the close he meets up with an old acquaintance, Bev, who will take Pettie's place.

Finally, Trevor employs again the garden motif. Thaddeus has for long been growing fruit and vegetables in his garden, eking out a meagre living by selling the produce. His wife, Letitia, brought some money into the family. Now, though, 'his garden is suffering from the drought' (p. 140), in evidence of the fact that the harmony in people's lives has been disrupted. The Garden of Eden has vanished, they say; yet in the end a future for Georgina is conjured up, with 'dancing on the lawns [...] music and voices on the cool night air [...] the laughter of Georgina's friends' (p. 211), and of course those 'feelings he has never before experienced invade Thaddeus's solitude' (p. 212). It is an elusive future, and Thaddeus may only derive small comfort from it; but that seems to be all people can expect in Trevor's world of fiction.

# BRIAN MOORE

Brian Moore started his career as a pseudonymous thriller-writer. Among the pulp-novels he published between 1951 and 1957 and which basically served to finance serious work are *The Executioner* and *Wreath for a Redhead* (both 1951, under the pen-name Michael Bryan), *French for Murder* (1954, under the pen-name Bernard Mara), *A Bullet for My Lady* (1955, again as Bernard Mara), *The Gun for Gloria* (1956, once more as Bernard Mara), *Intent to Kill* (1956, under the pen-name Michael Bryan), and *Murder in Majorca* (1957, again as Michael Bryan).[1] It is probably a fitting coincidence that he should have brought his writerly activities full circle by again resorting to the thriller formula with novels such as *The Colour of Blood* (1987), *Lies of Silence* (1990), *No Other Life* (1993) and *The Statement* (1995). His first piece of serious writing was a story, entitled 'Sassanach', which was published in *Northern Review* in 1951. His first serious book-length narrative appeared in 1955 as *Judith Hearne* (American title *The Lonely Passion of Judith Hearne*, under which the novel is now known). For many admirers of Moore's achievement, *Judith Hearne* remains one of the most impressive books,[2] both in terms of powerful character delineation and literary craftsmanship.

Having just moved into her new bed-sitting-room in a house in Camden Street, in a run-down part of Belfast, Miss Judith Hearne unpacks the silver-framed photograph of her late aunt and the coloured oleograph of the Sacred Heart: 'He had looked down on Miss Hearne for a long time, almost half her lifetime'.[3] In fact, the two of them have looked down on Miss Hearne for a long time, having exerted the two authoritative influences over the greater part of her existence: family and religion. 'When they're with me, watching over me, a new place becomes home' (p. 20), Miss Hearne ruminates, after placing her aunt's photograph on the mantelpiece in her room and hanging the Sacred Heart on the wall at the head of her bed. The same thought will be in her mind at the close of the book, after Aunt D'Arcy's sepia-toned picture and the Sacred Heart have been put on the dressing-table in the sanatorium room where Miss Hearne has resigned herself to stay for a while.

But much later Bernie Rice, the obese son ('fat as a pig he was', p. 9) of her landlady, Mrs Henry Rice, will tell her: "Religion is it? And what has religion ever done for you, may I ask? Do you think God gives a damn about the likes of you and me?"(p. 182) Bernie ranks at the opposite end of the religious scale. He is indolent, lazing about in his mother's house and claiming to be working on 'a *great* poem' (p. 178), and he fornicates with the sixteen-year-old serving girl of the house. His view about God is simple and utterly dismissive:

> 'Why does He allow all this suffering in His world? Why doesn't He answer your prayers, my mother's prayers? Has He ever repaid your faith in Him? Has He some secret reason for behaving the way He does, some reason He can't tell us? All right! Then why should I be expected to know His secret reason? Why should I be expected to understand Him when an omniscient, omnipotent God can't give me the answer? It's stupid, stupid!' (p. 182)

When Miss Hearne tries to defend her own faith, crying out: 'God's ways aren't our ways. This life is a cross we have to bear in order to store up merit in the next. Don't you know your Catechism at all?' (p. 183), Bernie readily scotches the notion by arguing: 'You and your Sacred Heart. What the hell good has it done you? It's only an idealized picture of a minor prophet. [...] Your God is only a picture on the wall. He doesn't give a damn about you.' (p. 183).

Aunt D'Arcy took in the orphaned Judith Hearne and made her utterly dependent upon her. All the men Miss Hearne ever got to know, not many by any standards, were declared unsuitable by the redoubtable aunt. Then the older woman suffered a stroke and since she drove each of the hired nurses to distraction with her incessant, curmudgeonly demands, it was in the end left to Miss Hearne to sacrifice her own life to the nursing of her relative until the woman mercifully passed away, leaving her only a little money. Consequently, Miss Hearne had a hard time of it eking out a living. While her aunt was still alive, Miss Hearne could only dream about her own happiness: 'Mr Right, a Paris honeymoon, things better not thought of now, all these things were slipping farther away each year a girl was single' (p. 131).

The only friends Miss Hearne has, if that is what they truly are, are the O'Neills, whom she goes to visit every Sunday after church. When one of the O'Neill children sees her approach the house, he says: "Let's say ten minutes at most before the advent of the Great Bore" (p. 79). And boring Miss Judith Hearne certainly is, always coming out with the same utterances, 'saying something she always said' (p. 88), and causing most of the members of the family, especially Professor O'Neill, to beat a hasty retreat prior to her arrival. His wife, Moira, has to suffer her presence, offering her cake and sherry.

Observing herself in the mirror in her room, Miss Hearne sees 'a plain woman' (p. 23), but in her view time has not run out just yet. For she finds herself

> changing all to the delightful illusion of beauty. There was still time: for her ugliness was destined to bloom late, hidden first by the unformed gawkiness of youth, budding to plainness in young womanhood and now flowering to slow maturity in her early forties, it still awaited the subtle garishness which only decay could bring to fruition [...] (p. 23)

Mr Malloy, cashier at the Ulster and Connaught Bank, confronting Miss Hearne on the occasion of her withdrawing all her money from her account, thinks: '[...] that one wouldn't be an occasion of sin for any man. [...] On the wrong side of forty with a face as plain as a plank [...]' (pp. 201f.). Bernie Rice plainly spells out Miss Hearne's problem: "[...] you're no beauty and this is a hard country to find a man in" (p. 182). So when she encounters Mrs Henry Rice's brother, James Patrick Madden, who has just returned from the States after having lived there for thirty years, she instantly starts romancing about him, imagining herself sailing with him from Southampton to New York as 'Mr and Mrs James Madden' (p. 33).

James Patrick Madden is one of life's losers. He used to be a doorman in a hotel on Times Square. He had held other jobs, but that was his last one. Mr Madden becomes attracted to Miss Hearne because he senses that she is a woman with money. He finds her friendly and educated, but her rings and her gold watch impress him the most. 'They are real', he reflects, being of course pitiably ignorant of the fact that the watch has for long been out of order. 'A pity', he adds in his reflections, 'she looks like that' (p. 39). Having lived for so long in the States, he takes rather a dim view of Ireland and the Irish: "The Irish, I'll tell you the trouble with the Irish. They are hicks" (p. 45). In other words: they are unsophisticated, uncultured and ignorant people. A fellow-lodger tries to chastise him for this statement, pointing out that he was a hick once himself, but Mr Madden repeats, smiling happily:

> Hicks. [...] They think everybody is interested in their troubles.

> Why, nobody cares, nobody. A little island you could drop inside
> of Texas and never see, who cares? Why the rest of the world
> never heard of it. (p. 45)

But things had not gone too well for Mr Madden in the land of unlimited
opportunities. Walking into the city he remembers that, unlike Belfast,
New York at ten-thirty would be humming with the business of making
millions, but he was refused his share of the gigantic cake. He is just a
'returned Yank', with a bad leg, 'who didn't make his pile, a forgotten
face in the great field of Times Square' (p. 46). He was involved in an
accident; a City bus ran him over, and by way of compensation he was
given ten thousand dollars for his pains. Moreover, he had not got on
particularly well with his son-in-law ('That Hunky', p. 49), nor had his
relationship to his only daughter, Sheila, been all peaches and cream.
His bitter feelings with regard to Sheila surface when Madden flails the
bottom of the serving girl after catching her and Bernie in bed together:
he gets completely carried away because in his mind's eye he mistakes
her for his daughter, whom he surprised in a compromising situation
with his future son-in-law in the woodshed. Later he forces the young
servant girl to have intercourse with him to assuage his sexual urges.

   Having decided to return to his native country and his native city,
he finds himself with plenty of time on his hands and little to do with
himself, apart from drinking with old codgers in assorted pubs. So having
met Miss Hearne and imagining her to be a woman of some means, he
conceives the plan to open a real American coffee shop (he later tells
Miss Hearne it is going to be a hamburger joint) in Dublin, because in
his view what Dublin needs is a good American eating-place.

   Miss Hearne and Mr Madden go out together a number of times,
to the cinema mostly, and little wonder, given Miss Hearne's situation,
that she should expect him to declare his love to her and ask her to
become his wife. Yet, the words she is so eagerly waiting for remain
unspoken. Even so, for her they *were* said, despite all evidence to the
contrary:

> He was lonely, he had said he was lonely and he wanted her to
> shape his life. It had been said, she felt, although it had not been
> put into words. That would come later. (p. 103)

But it does not come later. Instead, he asks her, in a roundabout fashion,
to become his partner in his business venture. Worse still, Mrs Rice

reveals to her that her brother, instead of having been an influential and successful person in the hotel business, was merely a doorman. Miss Hearne imagines her dear aunt chiding her for becoming involved with a man of that class: 'Imagine! Common as dirt' (p. 109). It is then that Miss Hearne severely hits the bottle.

A friend had introduced her to alcohol, purely as a remedy for bronchitis, and of course Miss Hearne drinks not to forget but to put things right:

> A drink would put things right. Drink was not a help to forget, but to help remember, to clarify and arrange untidy and unpleasant facts into a perfect pattern of reasonableness and beauty. [...] She drank to be able to see these trials more philosophically, to examine them more fully, fortified by the stimulant of unreason. (p. 122)

After a noisy binge in her room, things for Miss Hearne begin to go seriously downhill.

Of course, Mr Madden never intended marriage, as he confesses to Bernie: 'I'm not marrying anybody [...]. This is a business deal, purely business. (...) There's nothing between us, not a thing' (pp. 116f.). Miss Hearne is aware that '[t]he male must pursue' (p. 152). But what can you do if nothing is coming from that corner? In the end you have to take matters into your own female hands. And so Miss Hearne pursues the male and forces things to a head by confronting Mr Madden with the marriage business.

The nature of the religion that has held sway over Miss Hearne becomes stridently apparent during Father Quigley's hell-sermon, a dead ringer for Father Arnall's condemnatory diatribe in Joyce's *A Portrait of the Artist as a Young Man*. Here are some of the Reverend Quigley's sentiments:

> Plenty of money! Plenty of time! Plenty of time! Yes, people of this parish have both of these things. Time and money. But they don't have it for the church! They don't even have an hour of a Sunday to get down on their bended knees before Our Blessed Lord and ask for forgiveness for the rotten things they did during the week. They've got time for sin, time for naked dancing girls in the cinema, time to get drunk, time to fill the publican's pockets and drink the pubs dry, time to run half-way across the town and stand in the rain watching a bunch of dogs race around a track,

time to go to see the football matches, time to spend hours making
up their football pools, time to spend in beauty parlours, time to
go to foreign dances instead of *ceilidhes*, time to dance the tango
and the foxtrot and the jitterbugging, time to read trashy books
and indecent magazines, time to do any blessed thing you could
care to mention. Except one. (pp. 72f.)

And that one thing is: 'They-don't-have-time-for-God.' Since Father
Quigley has noticed some young people standing in the church 'like a
bunch of hooligans [...], waiting their chance to run out at the Last
Gospel', this has put him in mind to introduce rather a drastic measure:

Beginning next Sunday, I'm going to order the ushers to close the
doors at the Offertory and not open them until Mass is over. If
anybody is sick or has some reason, he or she will be let out.
Otherwise not. (p. 74)

It is quite a forbidding sort of religion, one based on punishment and
the suppression of everything that makes life on earth worth living,
because everything that makes life on earth worth living is deemed sinful.
Consequently, Miss Hearne feels 'closer to fear than exultation as the
Mass [ends]' (p. 75).

The Belfast of Miss Hearne is much in the grip of religious bigotry.
Even Professor O'Neill, who presumably considers himself an
enlightened man, has so far refused to read George Sands because she
is on the Index. When Judith remarks that, though it may have been
disgraceful for Chopin to live as a Catholic 'with a woman who smoked
cigars', he was a great artist after all and 'we must allow great leeway for
the artistic temperament' (p. 170), she is rebuked by the professor, who
believes that "[b]eing an artist does not absolve a man from his religious
duties [...]".

Her devastating experience with Mr Madden not only makes Miss
Hearne fall back on alcohol after six months of abstinence, but
additionally and more seriously causes her to question her faith in God,
in fact question the very existence of God. While sitting in her parish
church, she ruminates:

The lights were out, the people had gone home, the church was
closing. In the tabernacle there was no God. Only round wafers
of unleavened bread. She had prayed to bread. The great

ceremonial of the Mass, the singing, the incense, the benedictions, what if it was show, all useless show? What if it meant nothing, nothing? (pp. 140f.)

If there is nobody above her, watching over her, then nothing is sinful. There is, therefore, no sin. Miss Hearne feels cheated. Immediately erotic thoughts fill her mind. She recalls a handsome boy she saw one day at Greystones, standing up in his tight bathing trunks, 'his bump of virility sticking out' (p. 142). And she remembers the occasion when she lay on the examination couch in Dr Bowe's surgery, her breasts bare. The doctor approached and bent over her, and she could feel 'it, his thing, swelling there soft' (p. 142).

Once again she reasons:

No hell, no purgatory, no responsibility to God. If all the priests were wrong and you died and slept into nothingness, what point, then, in all of that? The community, it can go hang, what did the community ever do for me that I should help my fellow men? (p. 143)

Pouring her heart out to the Reverend F.X. Quigley in confession does not lend any succour to Miss Hearne. In fact, the Reverend is of little help to her. After having said five Our Fathers, and five Hail Marys as penance for her sins, she still surmises that there is only bread behind the tabernacle door. A sign is what she demands, a sign from God to prove that he exists in the face of her doubts. But such a sign fails to manifest itself. And so once more she seeks the assistance of Father Quigley, who tells her: 'go home and sober up and examine your conscience while you're at it' (pp. 235f.). Quite inebriated, Judith Hearne runs through the church towards the Holy of Holies; she tears at the small golden door of the tabernacle, screaming: 'Open. Let me in!' But the door rejects her: it will not open. This is the horrible climax of Miss Hearne's monstrous predicament. The bottom has been knocked out of her world.

After that incident Miss Judith Hearne is admitted to a sanatorium, her private rooms being paid for by Professor O'Neill. There she will finally try to settle in after the photograph of her dear Aunt D'Arcy and the Sacred Heart have been put up on the dressing-table in her room. So the two authoritative influences over her life have squarely been re-established. Her religious scruples and doubts seem to have been overcome. After all, 'in God's house [she] defied God. And nothing happened. [She is] here' (p. 251).

The events are masterfully rendered. Most impressive perhaps is Moore's use of the stream-of-consciousness technique. There are quite an impressive number of interior monologues worthy of anything to be found in that great hunting-ground of interior monologues, *Ulysses*. Many of the respective passages read like Leopold Bloom's streams-of-consciousness. Here is one:

> This was religion. Religion was begging God's pardon on a morning like this one when the drink had made your mouth dry and the thing that happened last night with the serving girl was painful to think about. It was making your Easter duty once a year, going to Mass on Sunday morning. Religion was insurance. It meant you got security afterwards. It meant you could always turn over a new leaf. Just as long as you got an act of perfect contrition said before your last end, you'd be all set. Confession and resultant absolution were the pillars of his faith. He found it comforting to start out as often as possible with a clean slate, a new and promising future. (p. 66)

Quite obviously, the syntax of the passage is not as shattered as in most cases it is with Bloom, but Mr Madden's ruminations are rendered so as to allow the reader a perfect insight into the man's consciousness.

A great many of the problems Judith Hearne is carrying around with her stem from her incapacity to face up to life and find a proper place therein, escaping instead into fantasy. Perhaps one should not go quite as far as Jeanne Flood, who argues that 'Miss Hearne is victim *because* she is child'.[4] Miss Hearne may be a stunted personality, but that does not make her a child. There are, as shown, numerous reasons why she behaves the way she does. What, after all, is adequate adult behaviour? If Judith Hearne is to be regarded as a child then most of the other characters are, too.

More to the point is Flood's contention that Miss Hearne has modelled herself on Christ.[5] This association with Christ, as well as an inability to confront the adult world, with the concomitant possibility of still being rooted in adolescence Judith Hearne shares with Diarmuid Devine, the protagonist of *The Feast of Lupercal* (1958).

Diarmuid Devine, BA (Junior and Senior English), teaches at Ardath College in Belfast. He is 'a man whose appearance [suggests] some painful uncertainty',[6] an uncertainty which manifests itself in that Dev, as he is commonly called, has formed the habit of turning his signet ring round and round in moments of anxiety. Somewhat incongruously, as a young man he had fancied himself 'an Irish Baudelaire' (p. 55), 'a man who'd been a hellish sinner but who'd come back to the Faith in the end' (p. 55). From then on, he decided to live the life denied him by his Catholicism, or so he thinks, in his imagination: '[...] he decided to content himself with sinful thoughts. He'd had some shocking sinful thoughts in his day' (p. 56).

We meet him first as he is caught in a lavatory cubicle, while two colleagues whom he does not wish to meet discuss him outside. From what he hears he tellingly concludes that they believe him to be 'some ninny, incapable of getting a girl' (p. 14). In the course of events he will become involved with the twenty-year-old niece of his friend, champion and colleague Tim Heron. When he encounters Una Clarke, a vivacious Protestant girl, he recognises at once the possibility of enjoying what he has so far missed. The exciting sense of Una's freedom causes him to fall in love with her, but at the same time it brings disaster. Even so, for most of his life he has felt 'like a flower that had never opened. [...] He had been afraid to open, afraid' (p. 124). In fact, 'afraid' is the word employed most frequently to characterise Dev's behaviour, for instance during his abortive attempt to have sexual intercourse with Una.

Una Clarke has been sent up to Belfast by her mother to stay with her uncle before taking up nursing in the Memorial Hospital, because she was mixed up with a married man in Dublin the year she left school. Dev's reaction to her is quite significant in its ambivalence. On the one hand, he rejects her, abominates her and is afraid of her as a result of her being a Protestant. For in Mr Devine's world, Protestants are the hostile Establishment. He fears them

> as a Spanish Protestant might fear cardinals: their power was great, their intolerance absolute [he reflects]. To them, Catholics were a hated minority, a minority who threatened their rule. (p. 37)

At the same time, he is aware that things are different in England, and even in Dublin. 'There, Protestants were unbigoted pagans, enjoying a freedom which Catholics would never tolerate' (p. 37). On the other hand, it is precisely that freedom, her appertaining to the world of this pagan Protestantism that attracts him.

After it has been decided that Una will take part in the production

of the play *Mulligan's Will*, Dev offers to coach her for she is a completely
inexperienced actress. The rehearsals offer ample opportunities for the
two to get to know one another better. Lines such as: "I love you. [...] I
want to marry you, so I do" (p. 69), have to be spoken, first in jest, as it
were, before they are eventually uttered in earnest for their importance.
The relationship finds its pathetic climax during the night that Una
spends in Devine's flat. In Dev's solitary bed where he has sinned a
thousand times in sinful imaginings, real sin is about to be consummated,
but Dev feels shame, shame for his naked body, for looking like a
'comedian in long drawers, someone to be laughed at' (p. 146), and he
prays:

> Never, oh God, in thought, word or deed, will I sin again, if
> tonight, in Your Infinite Mercy, You will spare me this. (p. 146)

Little wonder that he shows himself to be impotent. Part of his dilemma
is that he can take his wanton pleasure with an imagined woman in his
lewd fantasy, but is unable to deal with a real woman in life. His
imagination, as the text puts it, atrophies reality (cf. p. 150). Una and
Devine are utterly incompatible. As Una notes in a clear-eyed manner:
'I want to fight against what life's doing to me, and you're afraid to. Live
and let live is your motto' (p. 189).

Dev behaves like a spineless boy who, after having perpetrated some
mischief, does not have the guts to assume responsibility. His relationship
with Una comes to the notice of Tim Heron, and Heron, remembering
Una's affair in Dublin, is incensed. He repeatedly questions Dev in order
to get to the bottom of what really happened; but each time Dev lets
Una down, not speaking out in her defence (pp. 88, 157, 205, 209). Dev
is aware of his cowardice; yet he cannot help it. Even when Una
desperately begs him for help (p. 176), he shirks his responsibility.
Significantly, the discussion between Una and Devine about their
relationship takes place in a playground for children (pp. 181ff.). That
Dev should, in a sense, behave like a child has many reasons, the two
most important being, firstly, the influence that his deceased parents
still hold over him, and, secondly, the impact that the school he teaches
at has on him.

As Jeanne Flood has noted,[7] Dev is associated — and associates
himself — with Christ. Notably enough, he has two pictures in his
living room. One is of the Divine Infant of Prague, which was bought
by his mother. An Irish Sweepstake winner had cited devotion to the

Divine Infant as the cause of his winning the lottery. After the picture was purchased, family prayers in the Devine household regularly implored a repetition of that good fortune. But the Infant never completed the double, and Dev, the member of the family who sinned by secret, lustful thoughts, knew why. Years later, he kept the picture out of some vague need for penance. The second picture is a reproduction of *Ecce Homo* by Guido Reni, which Dev's father had greatly admired. It shows the thorn-crowned, lacerated head of Christ, and Mr Devine senior had intimately associated himself with sweet, suffering Jesus, particularly when severely troubled by his migraine headache. Dev had at the time felt that there was something absurd in comparing a migraine headache with the real pain a crown of thorns must cause. So he kept that picture, too, as an act of making amends. Jeanne Flood has cogently argued that

> the divine baby in the robes of the priest embodies sexual innocence and a purely spiritual conception of power; the thorn-crowned [...] head, submission and obedience to civic authority and to the will of the divine Father.[8]

But Dev submits not only to the divine Father and to civic authority, he likewise still submits to the authority of his parents: he has so far kept the two pictures that show the prevailing influence of his mother and father, and he wears his father's signet ring. He only gets rid of the pictures, thus in a way shaking off the parental sway he has lived under, after getting to know Una.

The religious implication of Devine's character is also hinted at when Tony Moloney, punning on his name, calls Dev 'Divine Devine'. Another instance should be noted to which Jeanne Flood has drawn attention.[9] Forced to acknowledge to her self that Dev is impotent, Una twice screams at him: 'Oh, Christ!' (p. 149). One should probably not attach too much importance here, given the fact that this exclamation is quite common among Irish people who, of course, do not readily associate the person addressed by it with the son of God. Finally there is this situation: while Devine is explaining the Feast of Lupercal to the boys in his class, someone giggles. 'Some boy, among the twelve, had stifled a short, obscene chuckle' (p. 211). Devine is here like Christ among his Twelve Disciples.

After the Dean, Father McSwiney, whose name surely is a telling one, has browbeaten him into organising the revival production of *Mulligan's Will* to raise funds for the Foreign Missions, Dev walks away, thinking:

> Dammit, he was a grown man now, why should a priest still make
> him feel a wee boy? Why should he be afraid of Father Mac? He
> should have refused point-blank [...]. (p. 45)

But that is precisely what is wrong with Devine: he cannot put his foot
down.

The college where Dev teaches runs on the principles of punishment
and submission to hierarchic authority. In the refectory the motif of
hierarchy is emphasised by life-sized oil paintings of four robed and
solemn Irish bishops who stare down from the platform, challenging
the wickedness of any boy who dares to look. The long wooden trestle
tables at which the pupils sit stretch in prison rows from entrance door
to staff platform. In Ardath College, 'force must be met by force' (p.
81). That is the prime maxim, one that also holds sway over Devine's
entire life. He therefore reasons: '[o]ccasions of sin must be rigorously
guarded against [...]' (p. 81). In college, every misdemeanour is met with
flogging. Father Mac, notably called the Dean of Discipline, embodies
the merciless and unrelenting power of authority. At the same time, he
stands for personal drive and ruthless ambition, gunning as he is for the
position of the present President, the Very Reverend Daniel Keogh,
MA, DD, rather a lenient man of advanced age. Repeatedly, Father Mac
convinces himself that

> it was unfortunate that a man who had [...] admin-istrative talents
> should be forced to take a back seat because some old fellow
> would not step down. (pp. 99f.)

In Ardath College the rule of teaching is 'boys [respect] the cane, the
cane [is] what [gets] results [...]' (p. 161).

In the final confrontation between Tim Heron and Devine, in which
the whole business of Dev's involvement with Una is intended to be
resolved, Heron treats Dev as if he were one of his unruly pupils,
accusing him of being a 'useless snivelling liar' (p. 218) and slashing his
cane across Dev's cheek. Devine's glasses fall in tiny fragments to the
path.

> Blinded, he knelt to grope for them, presenting to Heron's frenzy
> his long back in abject posture. Again Heron raised the cane

striking the kneeling figure in his path. (p. 219)

In this position of abject submission Dev receives his punishment. Later before the President, who, contrary to Father Mac, forgives Dev and keeps him in his job, Devine offers a feeble statement of defiance: 'I'm a grown man, I will not be treated like a schoolboy. This is my private life you are discussing' (p. 228, see also p. 231). Yet he feels:

> He had thrown himself off the cliff; but by some miracle he was still hanging to a rock on the cliff face. The President was that rock. (p. 230)

The image in which he envisions Father Keogh's action towards him shows that he sees it as protection from the terrors of chaotic space.[10] It also bespeaks a desperate fear of abandonment to the wide world without paternal protection, a fear that has survived in Dev's habit of turning his father's signet ring in every situation of stress.[11]

The Feast of Lupercal is referred to by Marullus in Shakespeare's *Julius Caesar*, I, i., and as Devine explains to his pupils:

> The Feast of Lupercal was a feast of expiation celebrated on the fifteenth of February in honour of Lupercus, the god of fertility. It was remarkable for the number of ancient rituals which were observed. The chief of these was the course of the Luperci, or priests of Lupercus, who, after making their offering, ran from the shrine of the god on the Palatine through the streets of Rome, their only clothing being an apron cut from the skin of the slaughtered animal. They struck all they met with thongs [...]. Barren women [...] placed themselves in the path of the flogging priests, believing that by means of the strokes, the reproach of barrenness would be taken away from them. As a day of atonement [...] this day was named *Dies Februatus*. (p. 211)

As Jeanne Flood notes, the members of the community portrayed in the novel transform physical paternity into a spiritual relation by envisioning sexual intercourse as an act in which the male expresses moral authority. This community conceptualises intercourse in terms of the Lupercal ritual, a fact that explains the boy's obscene chuckle and Dev's instant understanding of the significance of that chuckle: 'But they were not listening. His private life was a dirty joke. They were not listening. He was no longer master' (p. 211). Moore's Belfast Catholics see copulation as corporal punishment presided over by a priest. The cane and the phallus are identical. The punitive dimension abstracts and spiritualises the sexual act, intercourse is the expression of moral force rather than of natural generative love.[12]

In *The Luck of Ginger Coffey* (1960), James Francis (Ginger, because of his red hair and red moustache) Coffey is shown to be yet another of Moore's characters who have opted to withdraw from the harsh everyday world they find themselves in to live in a dream world. Furthermore, he, too, has as yet not fully managed to escape childhood. Thus when beating a hasty retreat from the restaurant where he has caught his wife, Veronica, with his friend, Gerry Grosvenor, Coffey feels like 'a boy escaping a pair of bullies'.[13] A short time later, he thinks: 'Oh, to be a boy...tears one moment, all wiped away the next. A world of toys. Nothing so terrible a kindness would not change it. Oh, to be a boy...' (p. 77). For most of his life, Ginger has dreamed of paddling down the Amazon with four Indian companions, of climbing a peak in Tibet or sailing a raft from Galway to the West Indies (cf. p. 15). Jobless and almost broke, he still regards himself as 'an adventurer, a man who had gambled all on one horse, a horse coloured Canada, which now by hook or crook would carry him to fame and fortune' (p. 13). Ginger is a person who will not and cannot face and tell the truth, as his wife is only too aware. For example, when he arrives home after his interview at the *Tribune*, he first tells her patent lies about his salary and his new job in the Dante-esque inferno of the proofreaders' room. Notably, Fox, one of his immediate colleagues, quotes from Dante's *Inferno*: 'All ye who enter here' (p. 62).

Ginger, his wife Veronica and their daughter, Paulie, live in the lower half of a duplex apartment in a shabby Montreal street, 'dark as limbo [another reference to Dante's *Inferno* to characterise Ginger's existence as an immigrant in Canada], jerry-built fifty years ago and going off keel ever since' (p. 8). Now in his fortieth year, he considers himself 'a fine big fellow with a soldierly straightness, his red hair as thick as ever and a fine moustache to boot' (p. 10). But when we meet him first, he is on his way to the Unemployment Insurance Commission because he is out of work. The past has not been too kind to him. He failed to finish his BA at University College, Dublin; in the jobs he held after his stint in the Irish Army from 1940 to 1945 he proved a sorry failure. More is the pity, he has never had a great hand for money. It was only because his father, when he died, left him two thousand pounds that Ginger was able to pay the debts that he and his wife had incurred and make a fresh start in Canada.

Coffey and his wife had agreed that, if he did not land a job by Christmas, they must go home on the first ship in the New Year. They had six hundred dollars put aside for the passage home; but of course Ginger has not succeeded in landing a job, and he has spent most of the money: fifteen dollars and three cents are all that is left.

And so he takes the low-paid job as proofreader on the *Tribune* and accepts another one with *Tiny Ones*, a diaper service. During the early years of his marriage he did not want diapers; instead he craved adventures. Yet he has ended up delivering just that — diapers, 'a regular member of the shit brigade' (p. 98), as Corp puts it at *Tiny Ones*. His wife, thoroughly fed up with Coffey's way of handling their affairs, is threatening to leave him for another man and requesting a divorce. Although he agrees to cooperate in a false adultery scene set up by Gerry Grosvenor, the man who wishes to marry Veronica, in the event he does not go through with the arrangements, walking out on the woman hired to act as his *amorata*, being firmly convinced that somehow or other he must try to get his wife back. In the end, having lost both his jobs — the one rather unfortunately because he was precipitately expecting promotion in the other —, having also, as he must presume, lost his wife and having become estranged from his daughter, he gets drunk with his proofreader colleagues and relieves himself in the dark doorway of an hotel, for which 'act of indecency' he is apprehended by the police, put on trial and given a suspended sentence of six months in prison.

Coffey left Ireland for Canada because, first and foremost, he sought to escape the influences of the Catholic church and the family. There was, for example, Father Cogley, who used to inveigh from the pulpit against the boy who thinks he is different and wants to go out into the great wide world to find adventures; this boy is like Lucifer and will end up 'at best a twopenny penpusher in some hell on earth' (pp. 18f.); for this class of boy has no love of God in him. While delivering his sermon, Father Cogley had looked into the eyes of young Ginger Coffey, and Ginger had been made to feel that he was that kind of boy. Up to the present day, he has not forgotten those words of clerical warning. After all, his six months in Canada have borne out the priest's condemnation.

To some extent at least, Coffey has associated his wife with some of the hostile forces that he felt were impairing his life in Ireland. Veronica is, notably enough, his 'Dark Rosaleen' (p. 56), one of the numerous female impersonations of Ireland. Early on in their marriage, she still was a devout Catholic, obeying her priest's warning against practising birth control. 'Once I was very holy, do you remember?', she says to Ginger (p. 106). Consequently, before too long, she 'blew up' (p. 28), reminding him that his duty was with his family when he wanted to see some action: 'Family! He wanted adventure, not diapers' (p. 28). Little wonder that he hankers after 'entering a world where no earthly women are' (p. 36).

Ginger repeatedly glimpses himself in a mirror and he certainly does not like what he sees. These are rare, painful moments during which he is made to confront his true self. They mark the beginning of the process of change that he is compelled to undergo. At one point, he catches sight of this mirror-man:

> He looked at him. A stupid man, dressed up like a Dublin squire. Looked at the frightened, childish face frozen now in a military man's disguise. He hated that man in the mirror, hated him. Oh, God, there was a useless bloody man, coming up to forty and still full of a boy's dreams of ships coming in; of adventures and escapes and glories yet to be. When, what were the true facts of that big idjit's life? Facts: James Francis Coffey, failed B.A.; former glorified secretary to the managing director of a distillery; former joeboy in the advertising department after he was kicked downstairs; former glorified secretary to the manager of a knitwear factory; failed sales representative of three concerns in this new and promised land. Facts: husband of a woman who wanted out before it was too late; father of a fourteen-year-old girl who ignored him. Fat-head! Great Lump! With nine solitary dollars between him and all harm. (p. 81)

And a lousy nine solitary dollars they are to live on in a country like Canada. His colleague Fox lectures Coffey on the importance attached to money in Canadian society. 'Why, money is not evil, Paddy my boy', he says. 'Money is the Canadian way to immortality. [...] Money is the root of all good here. One nation, indivisible, under Mammon, that's our heritage' (p. 62). Time is money, they say. So Coffey is forced to note how everybody is in such a frightful hurry in Canada.

> Everybody shoving and pushing you aside! Cana-dians had no manners! Raw, cold country, with its greedy, pushy people,

grabbing what didn't belong to them, shoving you aside! Land of opportunity, my eye! (p. 72)

The events that befall him convince him to a certain extent that Fox is right. 'Money, that was Our Saviour', he reflects. 'Not love, mind you, not good intentions, not honesty nor truth' (p. 84).

In the end, though, he comes to change his view. On one of his delivery rounds, Coffey encounters old acquaintances from his Dublin days, and he considers this a most humiliating experience, believing that the story of his fall from grace will make the rounds back in Ireland and that everyone will enjoy a hearty laugh at him. It is then that he knows that 'sink or swim, Canada was home now, for better or for worse, for richer or for poorer, until death' (p. 112). After his trial he senses 'his ship would never come in' (p. 184), whereas at the start of the book he is fully convinced that it will. He also realises that a 'man's life [is] nobody's fault but his own' (p. 185). Moreover, he is constrained to acknowledge to himself that his hopes, his ambitions, his dreams are but shams (cf. p. 191). The only person, he comes to understand, who has ever meant anything to him and who has suffered with him because of the ties between them was his wife. And so in the end all's well that ends well: Veronica and Ginger will not separate; the family is re-united; the power of love, earlier on averred to have been sacrificed to Mammon, is reconstituted. 'Life was the victory, wasn't it?', Coffey tells himself. 'Going on was the victory' (p. 202).

Wallace Stevens, in his poem that has lent the title to Moore's next novel, *The Emperor of Ice-Cream* (1965), notes that 'The only emperor is the emperor of ice-cream'.[14] While working in the morgue, young Gavin Burke sees the horny feet of a female corpse protrude from under the sheet that covers it. It is one of many references to Stevens's poem, where one finds the two lines: 'If her horny feet protrude, they come/ To show how cold she is, and dumb'. Jeanne Flood is inclined to attach no real importance to the intertextual parallels, commenting that '[the] poem itself seems awkwardly used in the book'.[15]

At the centre of *The Emperor of Ice-Cream* is again the conflict between the fantasiser-son and the rigidly authoritarian father. This time, though, the conflict is resolved through the reconciliation of father and son and the father's acceptance of the son's triumph. The novel's eighteen chapters proceed chrono-logically through the months between November 1939 and the bombing of Belfast in April 1941. Moore counterpoints Hitler's conquest of Western Europe with Gavin Burke's struggle against the emasculating paternalism of Belfast, represented concretely by three father-figures. One is Mr Burke, Gavin's father, the centre of order and stability in the Burke family. Stern and pious, he rules his children and his wife with absolute authority. Craig, the commander of the Air Raid Patrol post where Gavin works, personifies the sadistic component of paternal authority, revelling in the arbitrary exercise of power. The doctor, John Henry Moriarty, seems, as Jeanne Flood suggests,[16] to be the father as oedipal rival: he competes with Gavin for the affection of Sally Shannon.

Significantly enough, paternal power is ironically counter-manded in this novel by Moriarty's cartoon doll appearance and his lips, by Craig's speech mannerisms and the fact that Craig's despotic behaviour is a bizarre annoyance to those under his power, and, lastly, by the discrediting absurdity of Mr Burke's political views. Unlike the earlier Moore male protagonists who live under their fathers' thumbs, Gavin is shown to be a decent, good-natured lad who is able to view himself with a kind of ironic detachment. He has the mental habit of envisioning himself in a struggle with two guardian angels: 'The White Angel sat on his right shoulder and advised the decent thing. The Black Angel sat on his left shoulder and pleaded the devil's cause'.[17] As Jeanne Flood has suggested, the angels look suspiciously like Superego and Id, and when they are replaced by 'a new voice, a cold grown-up voice', a voice that he will henceforth heed 'as he had never heeded the childish voices of the angels' (p. 252), we have, in a manner of speaking, the Ego.[18] At the opening of the novel, Gavin expects his release from the world dominated by the father to coincide with the destruction of the old order, prophesied by the champions of the subversive world of the imagination — Yeats, Auden and MacNeice — and about to be carried out by Hitler. At the close, he is fain to enter the generational order as an adult male, forgiving his father, who is pitiful and broken and who at last confesses his love for his son. Gavin has attained psychological maturity against the formidable opposition of his family and the Church. His sexual problems constitute a relatively minor aspect of that rather complex mission.

Early in the novel, Gavin muses over two lines from the Stevens poem: 'Let be be finale of seem./ The only emperor is the emperor of ice-cream'. He is quite uncertain as to their meaning, except that they seem 'to sum things up' (p. 12). His growth to an understanding of himself is paralleled by his gradual and implicit understanding of these lines. In the closing scenes he is in a very real sense translating them into action: no longer is his emperor the authority of the past or the future, but simply the exigencies of the moment. His emperor now is the overriding priority of the here and now, and the realisation that everything is in a state of flux.[19] Perhaps the relevance of the Stevens poem is, after all, of greater significance than Jeanne Flood is prepared to concede.

In *I am Mary Dunne* (1968) Moore has taken some risks where the technical presentation of the narrative is concerned. Always a dab hand at interior monologue, as *Judith Hearne* already showed, he has here, unlike in previous cases, employed the stream-of-consciousness technique almost entirely throughout the whole account, as the eponymous heroine ranges over her past. Additionally he has supplemented the interior voice by what may be termed a more objective, matter-of-fact narrative stance. The blending of the two manners of representation recalls Virginia Woolf's *Mrs Dalloway*. The strategy in its combined effect has as its aim the evocation of the intensity and frequent irrationality of Mary Dunne's guilt and memories.[20] The narrative is deliberately made to appear fluid, even haphazard, so that it mimics the workings of the mind. Mary Dunne, who is the narrator of her own life and the interpreter of her own feelings, draws attention to the apparent randomness by trying to impose coherence on her thoughts.[21] These are framed by the actual narrative of her day, a Thursday in New York, which is completely logical, proceeding through the morning, through lunch, to the afternoon, then dinner and the evening. The actual events of this Thursday cover just over twelve hours, from Mary's hairdresser appointment at 11:30 a.m. to her midnight contemplation of suicide and eventual resolution. During that period she undergoes some fifteen experiences, some trivial, some disturbing, which, as she contemplates them in her mid-night pre-menstrual tension, assume overriding and ominous significance and evoke confused recollections of her past, so that the very question of whether she has an identity is put in doubt.[22] The story she tells within this frame may give the appearance of randomness, skipping backwards and forwards in time, here and there in location; but the different strands are skilfully interwoven by Moore. Mary's life has been lived under a suffocating cloud of guilt: guilt by association with her father, guilt about Jimmy, about Mackie, about Hat. As if she did not already feel enough guilt, Janice Sloan and Ernie Truelove make her feel more. The moral resonance carried by the novel is that the individual's perceptions are formed, not just by the quantifiable degree of culpability, but by all the elements that influence the human psyche, including heredity, memory and religion.

Her methodical re-ordering of her past is a process deriving from a philosophical speculation Mary had first indulged in at the age of fifteen in a Catholic convent school in Nova Scotia. Mother Marie-Thérèse had written the Cartesian maxim on the blackboard: '*Cogito ergo sum*', and Mary had wondered whether it would not have been more correct for Descartes to have said: '*Memento ergo sum*', 'I remember, therefore I am'.[23] Now sixteen[24] years and three marriages later, she puts this process to the test. The two seemingly discrete events that usher in Mary's calamitous day are in actual fact closely related to the duality of her identity problem. The social threat inherent in the receptionist's forgetting Mary's name is counterbalanced almost immediately by the stranger's blunt recognition of her sexual identity. He says: 'I'd like to fuck you, baby' (p. 12). The obscenity of that proposition offends her, but its import is essentially the same as the function she demands of her husbands. In this respect she is assured that in at least one dimension she is unchanged. But as a result of her pre-menstrual depression, the confusion is already upon her, and by the time she arrives back at her apartment she has gone through all three of her married identities.[25]

In her marriages Mary changes her name and her circum-stances three times and she does so through a more or less calculated use of her husbands. She married Jimmy Phelan not because she loved him, but to escape from Butchersville, Nova Scotia. She married Hat Bell, trading a drab life with a dull man for a glamorous one in Montreal and New York with a successful, though alcoholic, journalist. She then married Terence Lavery to get away from Hat, thereby causing his suicide. Mary exists in a world where every person is subject and object, exploiter and victim.[26]

Mary is a classic neurotic and the novel is an almost Freudian case study. Sigmund Freud actually gets a mention in the book.[27] Two scenes in her past life have especial relevance for her present state. Repeatedly she returns to her discovery at the age of fifteen that her father, Dan Dunne, died in a hotel room while in bed with a prostitute who abandoned him in death. She dreams of the scene, thinks of it, and more than once enacts it in her own sexual life. Additionally, Mary remembers her first experience of the loss of identity, which occurred in a public square in El Paso after her Mexican divorce from Hat Bell. Her panic began when she reflected that for that moment, between marriages, she had no appropriate name. She ran until she came to the door of her hotel, where she found her identity, seizing on the name her father gave her: '*I am Mary Dunne*' (p. 96).

The eponymous hero of *Fergus* (1970) shares with other previous male protagonists in Moore's *oeuvre*, like Dev in *The Feast of Lupercal* for instance, that he, too, has retreated into a world of the imagination and lives very much under the influence of his late father. The California to which Irish-born Fergus has come is an unreal world, a waste land,[28] an *ersatz* world of make-believe, where essence is subordinated to appearance, reality to fantasy. Fergus is hard-pressed at times to ascertain who has the most reality: the ghosts of his past that assail him on the particular day which the novel charts, or the living characters with whom he is in contact during his twenty-four-hour ordeal.[29]

At thirty-nine, living with 22-year-old Dani Sinclair, he is under contract to adapt one of his two successful novels into a film script, under the direction of two Hollywood producers, Norman Redshields and Bernard Boweri. He needs the money for his work to pay alimony and child support to his first wife, but he is reluctant to change his manuscript to satisfy the popular market. When the novel opens, he has not heard from his producers for three weeks and he has just had a row with Dani, and thus the fit comes upon him: he is visited both by a procession of ghosts from his past and by various individuals from the real world of California. In a series of scenes ranging from warm and teasing reminiscences to vicious kangaroo court proceedings, Fergus and his tormentors engage in a kind of absurd contest of wits, in the course of which every aspect of Fergus's straying from the fold of family, church and state is examined.[30]

One of the ironies of the novel is that, although Fergus manages to dismiss the ghosts of his past, at the end he is still saddled with the very real plights of his present life, and the question remains whether he has moved into a position where he can resolve these. What is clear is that he succeeds in shaking off the crippling impact of his father. The longing of the exile figure for a past time and place takes the form of a lament for the father, although fathers in Moore's fiction are notorious for quickly writing off wandering sons as failures. It is not surprising, therefore, that Fergus's first and last visitor is his father, who in the end tells him tautologically: 'If you have not found a meaning, then your life is meaningless.'[31] But Fergus is finally capable of demythologising his father and accepting him as a man, releasing him from the roles of tyrant and god. Running through many of the confrontations is the theme of personal betrayal of family, friends, church and state, and these betrayals invariably involve women, most importantly Elaine Rosen, a woman in relation to whom Fergus feels a sense of guilt because he had forgotten her. The book ends with the acceptance of isolation in subjectivity and of the unapproachable independent complexity of those persons who have played the leading roles in Fergus's private inner drama.[32]

The novella *Catholics* (1972) is informed by two conflicts that ultimately combine to express Moore's idea that miracles are essential to religious faith. One conflict centres on the antagonism between the old liturgy and the new, ecumenical liturgy; and the other focuses on Abbot Tomás O'Malley's loss of faith, which has been the result of a visit to Lourdes, where Tomás became aware of the hollowness of the religion industry, and which has led him to refrain from praying for quite some time.

The antagonism between the liturgies is firmly established at the outset. Father Kinsella, emissary from the ecumenical headquarters in Amsterdam, is dressed in an informal and, according to traditional notions, unpriestly fashion. Because of his unorthodox clothes, he is not accepted by Brother Padraig, who tells him: 'You don't look like a priest. I just can't imagine you as one.'[33] It is certainly not accidental that Father Kinsella is rejected by the namesake of Ireland's patron saint, St Patrick. In a metaphorical sense, Father Kinsella is rejected by Ireland, the people and their religious leaders, because they regard all that Kinsella represents as blasphemous. By means of fishing-symbols, Moore establishes the monks of Muck Abbey as true followers of Jesus Christ. The monks are fishermen; they have recently cleaned up the water, so that it is no longer polluted (cf. p. 8). The new, ecumenical ideas have polluted the Christian faith, whereas for the monks of Muck, by adhering to the old Latin Mass, which relies on a belief in miracles, the water has been cleansed once more. The Abbot, Tomás O'Malley, wears 'a fisherman's sou'wester hat' (p. 30) and has 'the look of a sea bird, a fisher hawk' (p. 31). Significantly, Father Kinsella never gets into the fishing boat sent to bring him to Muck. He arrives and leaves by helicopter.

The ecumenical movement, in addition to being characteristic of such — in Moore's view — superfluous matters as 'inter-penetration of Christian and Buddhist faith' (p. 39) as well as of politicking instead of religious considerations, has abolished the old belief system by decreeing that the priest must say Mass in English and not with his back to the congregation. But the new Mass is seen by the monks as sacrilegious 'playacting and non-sense': '[...] this new Mass isn't a mystery, it's a mockery, a singsong. [...] some entertainment show' (p. 42). Father Matthew makes the point even more forcibly:

> Because the Mass is the daily miracle of the Catholic Faith. The Mass, in which bread and wine are changed into the body and blood of Jesus Christ. Without that, what is the Church? [...] Without a miracle, Christ did not rise from His tomb and ascend into heaven. And without that, there would be no Christian Church. (p. 71)

What Moore seems to imply is this: what use are ecumenical reforms if they are contrary to the people's ideas and, more importantly, if they are detrimental to Christian belief? Probably the most severe criticism levelled at the ecumenical reforms involves, firstly, the fact that the monks have done more for the Christian faith by re-introducing the Latin Mass after realising that the new Mass would empty the churches, and, secondly, that, even though the monks have helped establish faith, they are made to say Mass in English simply out of political considerations (cf. p. 58).

Tomás O'Malley is, true to his Christian name, depicted as a Doubting Thomas. At Lourdes, 'the tawdry religious supermarket' plunged him into 'the hell of the metaphysicians: the hell of those deprived of God' (p. 68). He has spent his time at Muck not as a holy man but 'a very secular man' (p. 83). Yet, he is an able leader of men, a competent abbot, an intelligent and intellectual man, a lover of books and, significantly, a person who has immense respect for the faith of others. For he has re-introduced the old Latin Mass out of consideration for the spiritual well-being of his people. As he explains to Father Kinsella:

> I said to myself, maybe the people here are different from the people in other places, maybe they will not stand for this change. After all, what are we doing, playing at being Sunday priests over there on the mainland, if it's not trying to keep the people's faith in Almighty God? (p. 54)

The Abbot is no iconoclast; he means well. What he did was not done for cheap private interests and a hunger for the sensational. Ultimately, though, he is prepared to observe his orders from Father General because he believes in discipline, as he admits to Father Kinsella (p. 53). He criticises Father Walter for being partly responsible for organising a vigil aimed at making God intervene in favour of the old Mass, and he orders Father Matthew, the most fervent supporter of the vigil, to go to bed on the grounds that '[w]hen you were ordained as an Albanesian monk, you made a solemn promise to God to obey your superiors' (pp. 70f.). Consequently, in the end he tells Father Kinsella: 'I will do as I am bid' (p. 81) because 'it is my duty to obey' (p. 82). After Kinsella has left, he tells the monks: 'From now on, the new Mass will be said, in English, here and at Cahircivey. The altars will conform with liturgical changes and will face the congregation [...]' (p. 86). Tomás is aware, of course, that this decision will meet with opposition, particularly from Father Matthew, and, as if to substantiate Moore's idea that a belief in miracles is essential to faith and hence the old liturgy and doctrine are the most viable ones, Tomás counters Matthew's resistance by bidding the monks to church in order to pray: 'A miracle', he told them, 'is when God is there in the tabernacle. [...] Prayer is the only miracle' (pp. 88f.). With this, however, Moore plunges Tomás again into the void: 'He entered null. He would never come back. In null' (p. 89). And he prays again for the first time after a long silence.

In *The Great Victorian Collection* (1975), Anthony Maloney, assistant professor of history at McGill University in Montreal, checks into the Sea Winds Motel in Carmel-by-the-Sea, California, and during the first night there he has a dream in which he envisages an enormous collection of Victoriana. This collection consists of objects that Maloney has seen or read about in the course of his studies. When next morning he looks out the window of his motel room, he finds his dream come true. For outside on the parking lot of the motel a variety of stalls exhibiting precisely the objects he dreamed of are arranged in a number of rows.

This unprecedented state of affairs gives rise to a series of events through which Moore launches his mild attack on the peculiar phenomena that have come to be associated with art as well as certain social occasions that art brings about.

The first thing that happens to Maloney and his Victorian collection is that the news media exploit both of them. One Frederick X. Vaterman, up to that point in time doomed to a mediocre life as a small-time journalist, senses that the Great Victorian Collection offers him the opportunity to make his dream of being 'a great newspaperman in the American tradition'[34] become reality. Experts are flown in to assess the collection and establish whether the exhibits are fakes or originals. Needless to say, they are unable to agree. Psychiatrists develop an interest in Maloney. Dr I.S. Spector, of Vanderbilt University, conducts a series of interviews with Maloney in order to determine his psychic make-up as well as to capture, from a scientific vantage point, the agonies that Maloney, on account of his Great Collection, is going through. Furthermore, one Hickman conceives the fantastic plan to build a Great Victorian Village three miles east of the Collection. The village is intended to accommodate the prodigious crowd of visitors who come to view the Collection. Ironically, after some time, most certainly meant as a bitter comment on the excesses of art reception, people are more interested in the village than in the Victoriana.

Whereas the commercialisation of art is unmistakably the object of Moore's critique as far as many of the incidents delineated are concerned, two other important, if not the most salient, thematic aspects of the novel are, firstly, the question of what the Great Victorian Collection stands for and, secondly, Maloney's personal development. The two aspects are related to one another, involving, as they do, the universal issue of the relationship between a work of art and its creator. The Great Victorian Collection is clearly a metaphor for art in general and the creation of the Collection by Maloney an artistic act of the imagination. Notably, Maloney has his dream in a location 'which is sometimes described as an "artists' paradise"' (p. 4). The Collection, despite contrary opinions by experts, is an original creation: 'I have made this Collection come to life,' says Maloney. 'No one has ever done anything remotely like it before' (pp. 10f).

Moore's point about the relationship between a work of art and its creator appears to be that the creator is bound to become the victim of his own creation. Maloney tells Dr Spector in one of their sessions: 'Well, I used to think that, because I dreamed up the Collection, it belonged to me. I was responsible for it. But now I'm beginning to think it's the other way around' (p. 194). The only way for the creator/ artist to redeem himself would be to create something new. However, even then, the process of becoming dependent upon one's own creation would begin afresh. The inversion of roles, to call it that, is made complete ultimately in that a work of art will, under normal circumstances, outlive its creator. In Maloney's case, the Collection attracts, and will go on doing so, large numbers of visitors, even after Maloney's premature death. Dr Spector rightly concludes his report — and incidentally the book as well — by stating: 'The extent to which it will outlive the man who created it [...], is, of course, beyond the range of our predictions' (p. 213).

After Maloney has relished the initial fruits of his artistic success, his main endeavour is, in fact, to break out of the vicious circle brought about by the inversion of roles inherent in any relationship between creator and his work: 'The answer is, of course, for me to bring another dream of mine to life. That would solve all my problems' (p. 100). But all he manages to achieve is to dream up what he calls the 'television dream'. The television dream is preceded by two noteworthy occurrences. For one thing, Maloney grows dissatisfied with his creation, realising that there is no life in it (p. 123). This realisation, for another, has been greatly influenced by the fact that he has become sexually attracted by Mary Ann, his self-appointed secretary. Maloney's decision to renounce his Collection (p. 124) and the concomitant deterioration of the Collection are effected either by the intrusion of erotics into art or, more likely, by an unwillingness or inability on Maloney's part to reconcile the dark 'animal' side of his self with his artistic intentions. Interestingly, the dark, erotic side of the Victoriana was not only officially banned from Victorian society but has likewise been shut away from the present-day visitors.

No matter what Maloney undertakes, he is incapable of attaining his goals. He is as impotent to dream a new dream as he is to copulate with Mary Ann. Moore links the two issues, as becomes evident from Maloney's interpreting his restless touring from one place to another as a running away from both the Collection (p. 149) and the bawdy television dream (p. 167). Maloney is unable either to satisfy Mary Ann or to have a liberating new dream because he finally emerges as a total victim of the Collection: 'His manner of falling in love with Mary Ann was another symptom of his curious fate. There could be no longer any real life for him — no life at all from the Collection' (p. 166). In the end, the work of art takes complete possession of the artist. Maloney dies, presumably from exhaustion from trying to escape his creation. Within the hour, the news media around the world report that the Collection still stands (p. 212).

*The Doctor's Wife* (1976) represents a questionable achieve-ment, despite the blurb's claim that '[t]his is the sort of novel, so rare nowadays, that engages the reader'.[35] One could even go further and claim that *The Doctor's Wife* is in many ways an execrable book. Thirty-seven-year-old Mrs Sheila Redden, on her way to Villefranche, stops for a day in Paris, where she meets an American in his late twenties. Before you can say 'Jack Robinson' she falls into bed with the young stud, who has a sexual organ the length of your arm. The account is peppered with juicy scenes for those who go in for that sort of titillative matter; but all in all, it lacks the ideational profundity that most of Moore's other books possess. The reason why Sheila Redden embarks on her adulterous affair is left too uncompelling (she has submerged her aspirations in a dull marriage) and ultimately too too vague (the devastating power of sudden, highly erotic love). Apparently, she is set on her course by a statement of Georges Pompidou's she comes across in a magazine: 'the future is forbidden to no one' (p. 36). Yet, will that really do? The attempts of her doctor-husband to get Sheila back (he wants to have her deported if she goes to the States with her lover, Tom Lowry, on grounds of her having two psycho-logically unstable members in her family) are equally uninspired. The weakness of the book is finally manifested in its indecisive ending: Sheila refrains from following Tom Lowry to Vermont, opting instead, it would appear, for a modest, though liberated life in London and being 'like the man in the newspaper story, the ordinary man who goes down to the corner to buy cigarettes and is never heard of again' (p. 6).

*The Temptation of Eileen Hughes* (1981) is, in a sense, a companion piece to *Judith Hearne*, marking an attempt on the part of Moore to return full circle to his native Belfast.[36] Eileen, a Belfast shopgirl, is a younger version of Judith, succeeding where Judith failed. She escapes the clutches of Bernard McAuley, her wealthy employer, who is frantically infatuated with her; she also escapes the machinations of Bernard's nymphomaniac wife, Mona, who tries to buy off Eileen. When she encounters an American public relations man, Eileen declares her independence from the McAuleys, taking another job and going home to her mother. In terms of narrative technique, the account is rendered by the contrasting streams of consciousness of Eileen, her mother, and Mona.

*Cold Heaven* (1983) is a page-turner if ever there was one. The novel is the spookiest of Moore's thrillers ; but it is a thriller dealing with a profound moral and religious issue. Marie Davenport's husband, Alex, is pronounced dead after a boating accident in France. Yet he mysteriously disappears from the hospital morgue and returns to the States, where he has physical relapses into death, or near-death. Marie is a Catholic-educated atheist who for a year has refused to make public an apparition she had of the Blessed Virgin, who informed her she wanted a shrine on a rock off the California coast near Carmel. Furthermore, she has been conducting an extra-marital affair for some time with a friend and colleague of Alex's, without having had the pluck to tell her husband. The plight of Alex is understood by Marie as a divine attempt to put pressure on her. Eventually, though, after a series of harrowing experiences, Marie is let off the hook by God in that a nun is allowed to experience the apparition also. This permits Marie to leave her husband for her lover. As John Wilson Foster notes,[37] this seems quite an outlandish, possibly silly framework of plot. But Moore devised it in an attempt to continue his investigation of moral action, which is the crux of his recent books and which is distinctly an antidote to the moral simplicities of a good deal of contemporary fiction.

   *Black Robe* (1985), a historical novel with a topical ideational significance, essentially deals with a clash of two diametrically opposed world views and religious beliefs. Moore explains in his 'Author's Note' that the book was inspired by a discussion of Francis Parkman's (1823–1893) *The Jesuits in North America,* which he came upon in Graham Greene's *Collected Essays.* In it he learned about Father Noel Chabanel's journey to the Jesuit mission in the Huron country in 1643. Father Chabanel detested the Indian life. He believed that the Devil whispered in his ear suggesting he procure his release from these barren revolting toils and return to France. Yet Chabanel refused to listen and he bound himself by a solemn oath to remain in Canada to the day of his death. Moore moved from Parkham to the *Relations*, the voluminous letters that the Jesuits sent back to their superiors in France. What struck him most about the material he perused was precisely the clash of worlds:

> The Huron, Iroquois and Algonquin were a handsome, brave, incredibly cruel people who, at that early stage, were in no way dependent on the white man, in fact, judged him to be their physical and mental inferior. They were warlike; they practised ritual cannibalism and, for reasons of religion, subjected their enemies to prolonged and unbearable tortures. Yet, as parents, they could not bear to strike or reprove their unruly children. They were pleasure-loving and polygamous [...]. They despised the 'Blackrobes' for their habit of hoarding possessions. They also held the white man in contempt for his stupidity in not realizing that the land, the rivers, the animals, were possessed of a living spirit and subject to laws that must be respected.[38]

Moore goes on to note that he

> was made doubly aware of the strange and gripping tragedy that occurred when the Indian belief in a world of night and in the

power of dreams clashed with the Jesuits' preachment of Christianity and a paradise after death. (p. ix)

To Moore, the novel is an attempt

to show that each of these beliefs inspired in the other fear, hostility, and despair, which later would result in the destruction and abandonment of the Jesuit mission, and the conquest of the Huron people by the Iroquois, their deadly enemies. (p. ix)

In Moore's hands, Father Chabanel becomes Father Paul Laforgue, who has been ordered by his superiors to travel, with a party of Algonquin hunters ('The Savages') and their families for protection and a French boy named Daniel Davost for company, to the Jesuit mission Ihonatiria in the Huron country, where trouble is brewing because The Savages there believe that the 'Blackrobes' (their name for the Jesuits) have brought a sickness that is killing most of their people. Father Laforgue must embark on a journey of terrible peril, travelling by canoe through hostile territory in a race against winter snows. He must eat the stinking Savage food and huddle with them at night in their makeshift shelters. Not until Laforgue sinfully and willingly witnesses Daniel copulating with a Savage girl does he realise that he has to save not only the souls of the Savages and the soul of his countryman, but his own soul as well, and this in the face of his hopes that he will prove worthy of a martyr's death — his principal reason for embarking on a venture to save a small outpost for France and for Faith.

In Daniel's view, the Savages are truer Christians than he and Laforgue will ever be. 'They have no ambitions. They think we are mean and foolish because we love possessions more than they do. They live for each other, they share everything, they do not become angry with each other, they forgive each other things we French would never forgive' (p. 101), he says. 'I know all that', Father Laforgue replies. 'I know it, and it fills me with shame.' Daniel goes on to point out that the Algonquin believe "in the mysteries of this land and these forests. It is there that they find their spiritual strength. [...] They believe that all things have a soul: men, animals, fish, forests, rivers'; and Laforgue counters: 'That is because Belial rules here' (p. 101). When Daniel explains that they

believe that at night the dead see. They move about, animals and men, in the forest of night. The souls of men haunt the souls of

animals, moving through forests made up of the souls of trees
which have died,

Laforgue comments: 'But what childish reasoning!' However, Daniel
cogently and promptly remarks: 'Is that harder to believe in than a
paradise where we all sit on clouds and look at God? Or burn forever in
the flames of hell?' (p. 102).

Of course, there is excruciating cruelty involved in the behaviour
of the Indians, as when the Iroquois attack Laforgue and Daniel together
with the Algonquin hunter Chomina and his family, butchering
Chomina's little boy and throwing the chopped-up body into a cooking
pot. But there are at least two key sections in the novel that seem to tip
the balance decidedly in favour of the Indian belief. One concerns the
series of scenes after Laforgue and his party have been captured by the
Iroquois. Chomina is mortally wounded and Laforgue, fearing for
Chomina's soul, wants to baptise him. But Chomina raises objections,
arguing:

> But my people are not baptized with this water sorcery. Therefore
> they are not in your paradise. Why would I want to go to a paradise
> where there are none of my people? (p. 165)

Being told that he should be looking forward to living in paradise after
death and to leaving this vale of tears, 'this world which is the world of
night' (p. 184), Chomina remarks:

> No man should welcome death. [...] What shit you speak. Look
> around you. The sun, the forest, the animals. This is all we have.
> It is because you Normans are deaf and blind that you think this
> world is a world of darkness and the world of the dead is a world
> of light. [...] If you have come to change us, you are stupid. We
> know the truth. This world is a cruel place but it is the sunlight.
> And I grieve now for I am leaving it. (pp. 184f.)

The second section comprises the incidents after Laforgue has arrived
at the mission. Riven by doubts about his faith as a consequence of his
experiences and his own personal failings, Father Laforgue is compelled
to admit to himself that his desire for martyrdom was a sinful mistake.
He also asks himself: 'Why have I ceased to pray?', and he realises that,
if he believed the eclipse of the sun, which has frightened the Savages

into submission, to be the hand of God, he would be left 'in the same murk of superstition as the Savages themselves' (p. 224). The hasty manner in which Father Jerome baptises the Huron people that live at the mission, an insidious blend of bigotry and sophistry aimed solely at salvaging and securing a couple of hundred souls for the Christian God, is highly questionable, not least because the ceremony is conducted without the Indians having been properly instructed. One of the Huron leaders makes the essential point well when he asks Father Jerome: 'Why do you not respect that we serve different gods and that we cannot live as you do' (p. 230). Father Laforgue himself unequivocally questions the whole procedure:

> Why are these baptisms but a mockery of all the days of my belief, of all the teachings of the Church [...]? Why did Chomina die and go to outer darkness when this priest, fanatic for a harvest of souls, will pass through the portals of heaven, a saint or martyr? (p. 241)

Though aware that the Huron people, as Christians, would lose their way and be destroyed (p. 243), Father Laforgue nonetheless goes ahead with baptising the 'uncomprehending' (p. 246) Indians; but he does so with the firm resolution to spend the rest of his life among them and with a regained belief in God. In the end, he is able to say a 'true prayer [...]: "Spare them. Spare them, O Lord. Do you love us? Yes."' This may be a victory for Father Laforgue; yet it is incontestably a pyrrhic victory, as Moore implies in his 'Author's Note'.

Told exclusively from the point of view of its protagonist, Cardinal Bem, *The Colour of Blood* (1987) pits a rational, pragmatic Christianity against nationalist–Catholic fanaticism. The Cardinal, Primate of a Soviet-bloc country, finds his reading of St Bernard of Clairvaux interrupted by an attempted assassination. He had sustained years of peaceful relations between a Marxist government and his Church, though lately, despite its mistakes, the Church has assumed the greater power over people's minds. Because of the concordat Bem has made with the government, he has earned the distrust of religious extremists. Later kidnapped by fanatics who plan to make his disappearance seem the work of the State in order to foment revolution, he manages to escape and, maintaining a fine balance between co-existence with the secular authorities and collaboration, he thwarts a plot to make the Jubilee celebrations of the martyrs at Rywald the catalyst for revolt. Facing the assassin's gun while administering Communion, he raises the host to signify his acceptance of death and the will of God. The novel is a thoroughly taut and thoughtful thriller that portrays a man of unquestioning religious faith, as distinct from the narrowness of mind evinced by the clergy of Moore's Belfast novels.

The 'Troubles' in Northern Ireland, or so *Lies of Silence* (1990) suggests, are the outcome of ineradicable bigotry among the poor working classes, both Protestant and Catholic. Michael Dillon, manager of the Clarence Hotel in Belfast, is estranged from his wife, Moira, whom he married above all for her good looks. He has been having an affair with a young Canadian woman who is working for the BBC. Before he can tell Moira that he is planning to leave her, their house is invaded by masked IRA men who, keeping his wife hostage, force Dillon to deliver a bomb to his hotel to assassinate the Reverend Alun Pottinger, who will be the distinguished speaker during a commemorative breakfast organised by the Orange Order. Accidentally, Dillon glimpses the face of one of the IRA men, and he is torn between saving his wife's life or the lives of many people who will be the victims of the bomb blast. Dillon believes that ninety per cent of the people of Ulster, Catholic and Protestant, just want to get on with their lives without interference by men in woollen masks, and he feels anger at the lies that have plagued his birthplace with a terminal illness of injustice, 'lies of silence from those in Westminster who [do] not want to face the injustices of Ulster's status quo'.[39] Yet when it comes to the crunch, he shirks from helping the police solve the case. Unlike Moira, who looks upon the incident in terms of her father's view of the IRA:

> And who are they for? [Moira's father asks Dillon.] Themselves! And who's for them? Nobody, except some stupid Yanks who know nothing' about what's goin' on here, and a few of my people, people born in the Falls Road and places like that.... And the worst of it is, it's people like us, ordinary Catholics, who are the only ones who can stop them. Instead of that we're helpin' them to go on destroyin' this country because we're too stupid to see the truth. And too frightened of them gettin' back at us. (p. 136)

Moira is determined to speak out against the IRA in an effort to take what she considers a first step in the direction of putting an end to the IRA atrocities. She even ventures to talk about her harrowing ordeal on television. Dillon's position, on the other hand, is this:

I mean, it's all very well to play Joan of Arc, but I don't want to be sitting here waiting for some gunman to walk in the door of this place and blow us all to smithereens. (pp. 161f.)

His well-dramatised problem, in this tautly plotted novel, full of incident, is whether to opt for safety and refuse to identify the IRA man and live a contented life in England with his mistress. Much pressure is put on him by his mistress, by his wife, and by a priest who is an uncle of the IRA man. After wavering between following Moira's example or remaining silent, he at length decides not to testify. But it is already too late: the IRA burst into his London flat to kill him. 'They raised their revolvers. They were not wearing masks. This time, there would be no witnesses.' (p. 251).

Moore had exploited the compositional formula of the thriller before for purposes of dealing with issues metaphysical (*Cold Heaven*), religious (*The Black Robe*), and political (*The Colour of Blood* and *Lies of Silence*). He did so again in *No Other Life* (1993). Even though his stature as a novelist is indisputable, yet as with quite a few writers who publish a book every year or every other year, there are jewels and there are rhinestones. Thus, for instance, a novel like *The Mangan Inheritance* (1979) fails to impress, if only because the concatenation of events is too predictable. When the American James Mangan journeys to Ireland to find out whether he is a descendant of the poet James Clarence Mangan (1803–1849), he encounters a red-haired wench who is also a Mangan; the young woman immediately causes James's virile member to spring to life, and it would indeed be an undiscerning reader who would not instantly foresee that the member is allowed to rise to the occasion some pages later when James and the girl are frolicking about in a huge bed. James discovers a family line of debauchery, child molestation, incest and second-rate poetry. Excitement turns to fear. A daguerreotype of the earlier Mangan, which bears an uncanny resemblance to the present-day James, is broken, symbolically releasing him from a now loathed inheritance. His return to his father's deathbed asserts his acceptance of the normative values of ordinary life and its responsibilities. Whatever Moore is doing, he always shows himself to be a tenacious storyteller and a marvellous creator of scintillating characters.

This is again the case in *No Other Life*, the first-person account of Father Paul Michel, a Canadian missionary on the desperately poor Caribbean island of Ganae. Father Michel rescues a little black boy from abject poverty and sets him on the road towards a dramatic and dangerous future as a revolutionary Catholic priest and, later, as the first democratically elected president in a land of dictators and doom. Jeannot, as Father Michel calls him, is young and brilliant, a messianic orator, who urges his black brethren to rise up against their oppressors. His sermon is always the same: rise up, cast off your chains. You, the poor, will inherit this island. The Vatican is alarmed, fearing a schismatic church in Ganae; the cynical Ganaen bishops are enraged; the mulatto rich and the ruling junta are prepared to stop at nothing to destroy Jeannot. Is he a saint or a rabble-rouser? His followers regard him as the messiah; Father Michel himself is quite unsure of Jeannot's true motives. As Diderot remarked, between fanaticism and barbarism there is only one step. The violence of the poor and the counter-violence of the military powers escalate. Jeannot's fiery speeches send thousands to their deaths.

While no doubt offering a solidly wrought sequence of events, the extensive middle section of the novel, detailing the political turmoil and Jeannot's embroilment in it, his efforts to escape the moves of his enemies and so forth, flags a bit in the long run. *No Other Life* would be something of a middle-of-the-road political thriller with, possibly, a topical appeal, if it did not contain this most notable issue: Father Michel's mother, on her deathbed, says to him: 'There is no one watching over us. [...] When we die, there is nothing. [...] There is no other life.'[40] And he asks himself later: 'Why did God fail her at the end?' (p. 75). Jeannot comes to realise that Christ was a leader who did not lead. Finally forced to cooperate with his political enemies, he once more addresses his multitudinous followers in these terms:

> You and only you
> With the help of God
> And the memory of the dead
> Can bring about our freedom (p. 202)

'When you can no longer see me', he goes on to say, 'when you can no longer find me, I will be with you', and steps down from the rostrum, disappearing in the throng never to surface again.

Now, ten years to the day since Jeannot seemed to vanish from the earth, not much has changed. There has been no revolution: an ungovernable rage and resentment consume the lives of the poor. Candles are lit daily to Jeannot's memory. Home-made shrines containing crude images of Jeannot may be seen at country crossroads and on the barren hillsides. The political system is still totally corrupt. The poor are its victims. Is there no one watching over us? Is there no other life?

*The Statement* (1995) represents a routine performance, showing Moore hammering out yet another novel according to the thriller pattern. Pierre Brossard, now in his seventies, used to be Chief of Second Section of the Marseilles region of the *milice*; he was condemned to death *in absentia* by French courts in 1944 and again in 1946, and further charged with a crime against humanity in the murder of fourteen Jews at Dombey, Alpes-Maritimes, 15 June 1944. In 1989, after forty-four years of delay, legal prevarications, and the complicity of the Catholic Church in hiding him from justice, a professional hitman, presumably hired by some secret Jewish organisation, is on his trail. But Brossard is an old hand, possessing an invincible warning system, and so he manages to shoot first and kill his adversary. A second hitman is sent. Meanwhile, Brossard's case has been transferred to the gendarmerie. Madame Annemarie Livi, a *judge d'instruction*, is in charge, and she engages one Colonel Roux to find the old man. The question that occupies Madame and Roux is: how could the President of the Republic be persuaded to sign a pardon for a thug like Brossard? Repeated attempts by the Catholic clergy alone could not have done the trick. There must have been some help from the Elysée Palace. Before too long, everyone is chasing everyone else: the hitman is chasing Brossard; Roux is chasing Brossard and the hitman, and a group of politically powerful people with a manifest interest in having Brossard liquidated are throwing all kinds of spanners. Influential organisations, such as the Direction de la Surveillance de Territoire, the Chevaliers de Ste Marie, or the Fraternity of St Donat — which has chosen to follow Monsignor Lefebvre, the quondam Archbishop of Dakar — busy themselves with pulling strings.

But perhaps only a spoilsport would divulge the intricate ramifications of the plot, let alone give away the ending. Suffice it to note that *The Statement* is a technically accomplished novel, a good read, as they say. But judged against Moore's former achievements, for instance *Judith Hearne*, *I am Mary Dunne*, *The Great Victorian Collection*, *Cold Heaven*, and *Black Robe*, *The Statement* is largely devoid of any noteworthy ideational deep structure. It has really little to say about cases like Pierre Brossard's or, for that matter, Klaus Barbie's; nor has it anything original to offer about corruption in high places or otherwise. The book is all surface. Interspersed in the terse, swift-moving narrative are passages of interior monologue. Most of the main personages, at one point or another, silently converse with themselves. It is a familiar device, of course; but here it leaves the impression of having been grafted on without any strict thematic necessity. The many textual units geared towards establishing Brossard's stalwart faith in God somehow fail to convince as instances of mental turmoil: they read like so much hot air. These, however, are the only compositional shortcomings in a book that looks as if it had been written with an eye to being turned into a film.

It is surely rather unfortunate that the last serious novel Moore published in his lifetime (he died in 1998), *The Magician's Wife* (1997), is his weakest. Yet what in comparison with the other respectable narratives must be considered a somewhat inferior performance is by Moore's own standards still of a quality that lesser writers are hard put to attain. Until the last, Moore remained a superb story-teller. And yet, *The Magician's Wife* has its flaws. Much of the writing is oddly wooden. The story is presented in a series of set pieces: Emmeline Lambert at home in Tours; Emmeline and her husband at one of the French Emperor's *séries*; the two in interview with the Emperor; Emmeline arriving in Algiers; Emmeline visiting Colonel Deniau in his house in Algiers, etc. In between there are *longueurs*. There is little sense of place and Emmeline herself remains vague and at times tiresome.

The novel is based on an historical incident that Moore came upon in a letter written by Flaubert to George Sand. The French armies had returned in 1856 from a victorious campaign in the Crimea. Napoleon III planned to complete his conquest of Algeria by subduing the southern Berber tribes the following spring. But disquieting news reached him from Algeria, where a holy man, a *marabout*, was about to reveal himself as the long-awaited Mahdi who would lead Islam to triumph over the infidel. Reluctant to deploy his weary armies, Napoleon III conceived an extraordinary plan: he would send out Houdin, France's great magician, from whom Houdini later took his name. By his miracles Houdin would discredit the *marabout*, whose paranormal skills lay mainly in faith healing. What passed in Europe as legerdemain would be seen by the Arabs as god-given supernatural powers. The project was crowned with success. The uprising did not take place, and in 1857, as planned the French gained the whole of Algeria, the French presence in that country ending as late as the summer of 1962 when Algeria declared its independence.

Moore's fictional version of these events is seen through the eyes of Emmeline, wife of Henri Lambert, the magician. Bored and lonely she sits sewing in her room while her husband, the genius and impresario creates new miracles in the dungeon-like basement of their country house. Emmeline knows that her husband loves her, but it is a love without physical substance. Then all of a sudden everything is changed. Napoleon III invites the couple to one of his fabled *séries*, a weekend-long house-party. In her new clothes Emmeline gains confidence, responds to compliments and begins a tenuous flirtation. She is shocked by the cynicism and artificiality she notices around her, but she has acquired an appetite for adventure and is happy to accompany her husband on the Emperor's preposterous project. In Algeria, Emmeline continues her flirtation with the handsome officer of the *Bureau Arabe*, but falls more seriously in love with Africa. 'Believe me, it [i.e. the Sahara] will change your life', she is warned.[41] She finds herself profoundly moved by Moslem worship. Most of all she is affected by the refrain 'Everything comes from God'. Almost overnight her spirit is refashioned. Timid and hitherto subservient, she becomes outspoken and independent, challenging the course of events and attempting to manipulate fate by disclosing the Emperor's project to the *marabout* and revealing her husband's allegedly supernatural powers for what they really are. Ultimately, however, she is thwarted by her failure to understand the infinite gradations of that credo 'Everything comes from God': the *marabout*, despite having been let into the secret, refrains from initiating the uprising, thus making the subsequent French victory possible.

The main deficiency of the novel lies in the fact that Emmeline's transition from timorous mouse to audacious heroine is too swift and too arbitrary to be credible. Her husband's tragedy — he is shot at and wounded and seriously incapacitated, so that he will never be able to perform his magic tricks again — is, by contrast, barely delineated, but far more compelling. The sudden momentum of the last fifty or so pages highlights the paucity of the rest. For almost the entire length of his career as a writer Moore was able to prove himself an exceptional wizard with words. It was only at the very end that his magic failed him.

# JOHN MCGAHERN

The world depicted in John McGahern's novels and stories is peopled with characters who are suffering from an urgent sense of loss — loss of health or loss of human love and affection. Both kinds mostly lead to a loss of faith and trust. As a consequence, often a heightened awareness of the emptiness and futility of human existence makes itself felt which forces the characters into emotional and intellectual isolation, into inner exile. In addition, the novels and stories focus on the themes of death, suffering, pain, love and sexuality, in particular the destructive power of sexuality. The basic frustration of McGahern's characters comes from the conflict between their instinctive needs and their drab environment. A life whose expectations cannot be fulfilled leads irresistibly to withdrawing into one's self, as in the case of Reegan in *The Barracks* (1963), if not to a sad desire to dominate and break the will of others, as Mahoney does in *The Dark* (1965).[1]

The repressive impact of the Catholic Church on life in Irish society is the target of strident criticism. The father–son conflict is a prominent feature of life in the family. In terms of literary influences, the names of Proust, Chekhov, Joyce and Mauriac are recurrently evoked by critics. Admiration is widely expressed for McGahern's empathic and deliberately low-key style of narration, his disciplined and unpretentious presentation of narrative details, as well as his sure-handed deployment of interior monologue and flashback, for example in *The Barracks*.

*The Barracks* covers the last sixteen months in the life of Elizabeth Reegan, focusing above all on the ordeal the woman undergoes after the discovery of cysts in her breasts, which are diagnosed as cancerous. It is an ordeal that leads her through disappointment, isolation, despondency and desperation, while at the same time helping her gain insight into her own life and the sense of life in general. In so doing, the novel charts Elizabeth's development from an existence characterised by discontent, unhappiness, futility and monotony, a lack of purpose and a hatred of her husband, Reegan, to moments, longer or shorter, of happiness, contentedness, redemptive resignation and a positive emotional commitment to Reegan. At one point, she reflects:

> Sometimes she'd think how lucky she was to have found Reegan,

to be married to him and not to Halliday, where she and he would drive each other crazy with the weight and desperation of their consciousness.[2]

Her relationship with Reegan is riven in the extreme. He is an insensitive bully of a man, with his 'intense pity for himself' (p. 11) and his aggressiveness, which results from his ongoing fights with his superior, Superintendent Quirke. Upon coming home in the evening, he is full of his bottled-up problems, and his character is nicely expressed in the following description: '[...] Reegan's voice stabbed into the quiet of the big barrack kitchen, harsh with mockery and violence' (p. 18). One after another, the other policemen, Casey, Brennan and Mullins, arrive and Reegan again and again recounts the clash with Quirke, making it 'become more extravagant, more comic and vicious since the first telling' (p. 17). The evening in the kitchen grows into a 'litany of truisms' (p. 23), becomes a 'brute clash of ego against ego' (p. 24):

> Examples began to be quoted, old case histories dragged up for it to end as it began — with nothing proven, no one's conviction altered in any way, it becoming simply the brute clash of ego against ego, any care for tolerance or meaning or truth ground under their blind passion to dominate. And the one trophy they all had to carry away was a gnawing resentment of each other's lonely and passing world. (p. 24)

She married Reegan because she was no longer 'content to drag through with her repetitive days, neither happy nor unhappy' (p. 14). The bitter irony of course is that the marriage forced her out of the frying pan into the fire, making her put up with an incomparably greater repetitiveness and humdrum existence, a 'drudgery she [can] barely face' (p. 35). For her husband, she believes, she is no more than a 'housekeeper' (p. 12).

The monotony of life in the barracks is formally expressed by the fact that the first three chapters all end with the description of an evening, with chapters 1 and 2 corresponding closely in the Reegans' saying of the Holy Rosary. Chapters 2 and 3, furthermore, open with the Reegan family getting up in the morning: 'The alarm clock woke her out of a state that wasn't deep enough to call it sleep' (p. 34) and: 'They rose into another white morning [...]' (p. 62). It is only with chapter 4, in which Elizabeth is taken into hospital, as a result of which the daily monotony of life in the barracks is broken, that the similarity of chapter beginnings and endings disappears.

Still, shortly after her release from hospital at Christmas time, Elizabeth experiences an intense sense of happiness. She feels that her life amidst the members of the Reegan family is filled with purpose:

> The day passed quickly for Elizabeth, her whole attention absorbed in the cooking of the dinner; she'd forgotten her sickness in looking forward to their enjoyment; the excitement of the children about her, asking her so many questions, telling her so much about their presents. (p. 151)

Later, when confined to her sick-bed, resignation as well as dissatisfaction and disappointment with her life make themselves felt again. She is constrained to admit to herself that she and Reegan have actually led lives apart from each other. She still has kept the roll of money that would allow her to leave Reegan for London whenever she wanted or found it necessary to do so: 'Their lives were flowing apart and she was alone and it was somehow sad and weepycreepy' (p. 96). To be sure, she confesses to Reegan that she is still in possession of the money (p. 126), but that alters next to nothing in the order of things. *The Barracks*, thus, also concerns itself with the terrible isolation of the marital partners. Reegan is intent upon making enough money in order to be able to quit the police. He is completely unaware of the state his wife is in: 'He never noticed how drawn and beaten Elizabeth looked: she'd have to collapse before he'd ever notice now' (p. 156). His greed for money to enable him to leave the police force has grown to desperation: 'Reegan saw nothing. All he saw was turf saved and the money that'd give him the freedom he craved' (p. 165).

Repeatedly, Elizabeth feeds into memories of Halliday, the man she loved before she came to know Reegan. With her illness getting worse and her suffering more intense, she becomes aware of the futility of her life and of the gap that has separated her from her husband. But she also begins to believe that she has been an utter failure:

> She watched him get ready to go [...]: she could do nothing, and yet she felt she'd failed him somehow, something at some time that she could have done for him, and that she had failed to do, though she could never know what it might have been and all she was left with was a sense of her own failure and inadequacy. (p. 145)

Moreover, she acutely feels the triviality and worthlessness of her own person:

> Her thoughts could begin on anything for object and still it trav-
> elled always the same road of pain to the nowhere of herself [...]
> (p. 146)

In view of her impending death, palpable reality has lost all sense and purpose. 'The whole mess of her life' takes on the character of a 'shocking comedy' (p. 134). Her time with Reegan was wasted on an inexorable lacerating of one another:

> They all lived on each other and devoured each other as they
> themselves were devoured, who would devour whom the first
> was the one question. (p. 173)

Yet, on the other hand, Elizabeth receives an impression of the mystery of life. Faced with the nothingness after death, she begins to regard life as a beneficial gain, a great gift to be deeply enjoyed:

> There was such deep joy sometimes, joy itself lost in a passion of
> wonderland in which she and all things were lost. [...] She had
> come to life out of mystery and would return, it surrounded her
> life, it safely held it as by hands; [...] she'd be consumed at last in
> whatever meaning her life had. Here she had none, none but to
> be, which in acceptance must be surely to love. There'd be no
> searching for meaning, she must surely grow into meaning as she
> grew to love, there was that or nothing and she couldn't lose. [...]
> All the apparent futility of her life in the barracks came at last to
> rest on this sense of mystery. [...] She accepted its absolute sway
> over her life [...] And if the reality is this: we have no life but this
> one — she could only reflect and smile [...] (p. 174)

The blurb of *The Barracks* notes: ' [...] *The Barracks* should be a sad book: in fact, it has a haunting, liberating power [...]'. The quotation above may suggest what that liberating power consists in: its note is one of trust, confidence and contentedness. '[...] we have no life but this one', and therefore all resentment, all hatred is an offence against life.

But *The Barracks* is also the novel about Reegan's obsessive endeavours to leave the hated police, which he associates with subjugation and humiliation. The last chapter shows Reegan arriving at his goal, when he holds his own against Quirke, after having written his resignation. In its depiction of Elizabeth's suffering, *The Barracks* is at once a deeply distressing and indeed liberating book that gains in impact by juxtaposing Elizabeth's fight for her life and Reegan's fight against Quirke, the one a quintessentially existentialist fight and the other a petty fight. Reagan sees his own case in such an existential dimension that he has no time to discern the full horror of his wife's plight.

When *The Dark* was published in 1965, the book was immediately banned in Ireland under the Censorship Act, not only for employing the f-word on its very first page, but more so for incorporating masturbatory scenes. As a consequence, McGahern, who at the time was teaching in a clerically controlled school in the archdiocese of Dublin, was jockeyed out of his job without explanation. He moved to London, working on building sites and as a part-time teacher.

*The Dark* situates its adolescent main character in two conflicts, in both of which he has to assert himself. One is the conflict with his father and the other consists of an inner struggle between a positive approach to life, in which the joys of life may be enjoyed to the full, and a fear of death and the Last Judgement indoctrinated by the church, as a result of which the protagonist must renounce the joys of life and embrace the priesthood. Both attitudes are associated with a symbolic figure: woman representing the temptation in life, and the priest standing for 'the priesthood of Christ' (p. 95) and the renunciation of woman, a turning to God, which, in a way, is seen as equalling death in life, and the abnegation of life.

The father—son conflict, which is at times also widened into a conflict with the social environment, shows itself predominantly in the diverse kinds of repression that the father exercises over his son, which culminate in the incestuous relationship into which the father forces his son (cf. chapter 3). In the middle part of the novel, the fatherly repressions are replaced by comparable repressions at the hands of Father Gerald. They are considered comparable because, like Mahoney, Father Gerald shares a bed with the boy. There are, however, no sexual advances; instead the priest makes the young man confess his major juvenile lapse, masturbation, which makes him feels deeply degraded: '[...] he was cutting through to the nothingness and squalor of your life, you were now as you were born, as low as dirt' (p. 54). Father Gerald's is a more subtle variety of repression for mortifying the adolescent sinner: '[...] shame, what must the priest think of you every time he looked at you any more' (p. 56). It is itself replaced by yet another form of repression, which the protagonist experiences when a lecturer, following his little quirk for asserting authority, throws him out of the Physics Theatre (pp. 138f.).

The most conspicuous characteristic of the father–son relationship is a blend of hatred and love, which pervades the whole novel. At the beginning hatred is uppermost. The boy is disgusted by the nightly advances of his father. He hates him for the brutality that makes him resort to the severest measures of punishment for even slight mistakes or lapses, for instance when the boy lets the word 'fuck' slip out. But he also despises his father for his continual grumbling and carping as well as his incessant accusations. The first chapter shows how the father punishes the children; the second has them retaliate by refusing to play a game of cards with him.

Occasionally, however, the boy's hatred of his father gives way to affection, even love, for example during the scene in the hotel (ch. 26). Mahoney's behaviour in the restaurant, his bragging about the scholarship his son has won, his brutal treatment of the waiter, his inability to eat properly with knife and fork — all this the boy registers with 'resentment' and 'hot embarrassment' (p. 116), and he asks himself: 'Why had the father to try and bulldoze everything through by brute force?' (p. 117). The attestations of love that Mahoney provokes by feigning an attitude of understanding, thus camouflaging the fact that their relationship is actually one of dispute and strife, the boy finds insufferable. And yet at the end of this day of celebration, cycling home with his father, he feels he wants to laugh about one of his father's old jokes and say to him: 'You are marvellous, my father' (p. 119). In the last chapter, father and son again lie together in bed, this time in a guest-house in Galway, after the decision has been taken that the boy will not go to university but to the ESB. The situation of course recalls the comparable one in chapter 3. Here, though, all aspects of sex are missing. The text notes: 'Memories of the nightmare nights in the bed with the broken brass bell came, and it was strange how the years had passed, how the nights were once, and different now, how this night'd probably be the last night of lying together' (p. 141). The difference between past and present marks the development the protagonist has undergone. Hatred and disgust have given way to affection, even love, and the son can finally say: 'I wouldn't have been brought up any other way or by any other father ' (p. 142).

More significant than the father–son conflict is the protagonist's inner struggle. In a world of patriarchal, clerical and societal repressions, the boy is searching for the right way in the dark of his adolescence. There is, on the one hand, his 'dream of flesh in woman' (p. 24), woman as the personification of all temptations in life: '[...] your hunger was for a woman, mirage of total marvel and everything in her flesh' (p. 41). It is a dream that gradually becomes coupled with a hankering after a bourgeois life: 'Dream of peace and loveliness, charm of security: picture of one woman, the sound of *wife*, a house with a garden and trees near the bend of a river [etc.]' (p. 61). On the other hand, there is the fear of purgatory, inculcated by an education that is grounded on the doctrines of the Catholic Church, a fear that orientates one's entire life to one's death: 'The moment of death was the only real moment in life; everything took its proper position there [...]' (p. 51). The thought of death, of the possibility of becoming guilty beyond redemption through making the dream of 'flesh in woman' come true, has the main character entertain the intention of becoming a priest. But the realisation of this intention falls through on account of his own personal shortcomings. The church would refer to it in terms of one of the Seven Deadly Sins: lust, manifest in his sexual fantasies and his masturbating: 'You'd no control over your lusts and if you hadn't how could you stay a priest?' (p. 41). He feels haunted by the 'respective hypocrisy' (p. 40) of his life, 'anguish of the struggle towards repeated failure' (p. 40). We are here in very close proximity to the Stephen Dedalus of *A Portrait*. The exhortations given to the boy in college by 'the priests from the various orders in search of vocations' (p. 94) are often 'too close for comfort' (p. 94), like Father Arnall's hell-fire sermon. Such exhortations, naturally, lead to the wish to counteract eternal damnation by the decision 'to give your life into that death' (p. 95). But that would mean: 'the death already accepted in life, the life already given into His keeping before it was required, years before, in your youth' (p. 94). His dream of 'flesh in woman' would never become reality. In the end, though, the dream wins out, and the protagonist gives up the idea of becoming a priest.

At the same time, in addition to solving his inner, or moral, conflict, the boy is struggling to discover what could pathetically be called the sense of life. The Reverend Bull Reegan used to rail down from the pulpit against the moving force behind people's conduct: 'Security. Security. Everyone's looking for security' (p. 101). Urban life in Galway confirms the truth of the Reverend's words for the boy: 'Everyone wanted as much security and money as they could get' (p. 128), and he comes to understand that '[l]ives were lived through in this rat hole of security, warding off blows, dealing blows, one desperate cling to stay

alive in this rat hole; terror of change [...]' (p. 101). The desire for security
and the concomitant feeling of being free are finally responsible for the
protagonist's decision against a promising university career and in favour
of accepting the job with the ESB. He may also be afraid of failing in
his studies, as he admits to his father (p. 139). But the decision is not
completely devoid of a note of desperation. When he has to take the
decision, the protagonist is not mature enough to weigh the pros and
cons of the two options. Mahoney is no help. The advice of one of the
Deans of Residence brings little clarity in the matter. The boy is in the
end as much a 'drifter' as he was at the height of his moral conflict.

Yet, the decision to turn his back on the university comes as no
surprise. It is anticipated when, as a boy, he works with his father in the
fields after the exam and experiences 'extraordinary peace and richness'
(p. 109). This suggests the significance of nature in McGahern's world
of fiction, as an antidote to the city. It likewise suggests that the
protagonist seems to be able to find peace and happiness in manual
rather than in mental work. Lastly, work in the fields seems to help him
find his place in life. Here he appears to come into his own: 'He was a
man. He was among men. He was able to take a man's place' (p. 110).
He also, significantly, notices that his father 'has grown old. Hard to
imagine this was the same man who'd made the winters a nightmare
over the squalid boots, the beating and the continual complaining' (p.
111). He feels that he is now not only a match for his father, but that he
could take his place.

*The Leavetaking* (1974) is certainly McGahern's weakest book. It falls
into two parts, the first one showing the narrator-hero, Patrick, coming
to terms with the symbolic shadows that have haunted the greater part
of his life and the second focusing on his beloved, the American Isobel,
a person quite comparable to Patrick in that she too has to shake off
the shadows which have made her life a misery. The problem is that
these two parts are not adequately balanced. The Isobel skein and the
London days are too long in comparison with Part I; for, in the final
analysis, *The Leavetaking* is clearly Patrick's story. Isobel comes into it,
first and foremost, because she is the woman he is devoted to. But in
Part II the spotlight is so dominantly on her that Patrick is almost pushed
off the stage. Isobel's altercations with her father are exceedingly long-
winded and lend an indefensible weight to these two characters.
Moreover, Part II is, in terms of narrative technique, much more
conservative than Part I. In the former, the stream of recollections
remains more or less uninterrupted, whereas in the latter a great number

of flashbacks activate different levels of time and effect a touch of the unconventional.

When working with his translator on the French edition of the novel, McGahern became only too aware of these and other shortcomings and produced a revised edition.[3] The changes he introduced are undoubtedly for the better, with much of the slack writing and melodrama of the first attempt ruthlessly excised. Many self-indulgent ruminations on the protagonist's early sexual adventures are jettisoned, and Isobel's ludicrous father, Evatt, is made to play a less prominent role. Regrettably, even these authorial economies fail to achieve the intention, avowed in the Author's Preface, of integrating the book's two parts. It remains, even after such extensive alterations, a work split down the middle, in which McGahern still fails to reconcile the troublesome 'disparities' that he defines in the Preface, 'the remembered "I"' and 'the beloved, the "otherest"'.[4]

*The Leavetaking*, in generic terms, represents a cross between a novel of consciousness and an *Entwicklungsroman*. The story unfolds in the mind of the narrator-protagonist, on his last day at a Catholic school in Dublin, where he has been working as a teacher and from where he is about to be dismissed for moral reasons, his offence being that he was living with a woman in 'unholy' matrimony. It is largely a narrative about the mental and emotional development of Patrick, who feels that his life has been overshadowed in diverse ways: by the influence, or rather by the memories, of his mother; by an experience of a sense of loss and helplessness in the face of her death; by his failed promise to her to become a priest; by his longing 'to enter the mystery of the lovely and living flesh of woman',[5] which prevented him from keeping his promise, all this regarded by him as an act of betrayal; and finally by Ireland, this priest-ridden country with her dubious morals. Through his love for Isobel and his refusal to give in to the false moral laws of Catholic Ireland, he eventually succeeds in escaping the influence of these shadows.

The present is closely related to the past, and *vice versa*. The present state is seen as a result of past events. The unfolding of the past is motivated by the fact that Patrick is about to be dismissed from his job. He is made to reflect on his life up to this day. In Part I, his youth and adolescence, his unhappy family life, in particular his mother's marriage and her illness and premature death, caused by a pregnancy her husband in an egotistical fit of sexual desire forced upon her. The last day frames the memories and frequently interrupts the steady progress of recollecting. In most cases, the memories are associatively linked to the last schoolday experiences. Thus, for example, meeting the headmaster generates thoughts of his interview nine years previously (pp. 13f.). Looking at the girls' school where 'the one with black hair teaches' (p. 25) whom he loved makes him recall his mother's question: 'Who do you love most in the world?' (p. 25). Or memories of his parents' honeymoon in Howth have him recollect how he and his lover looked for rooms in Howth. Love in Part I is mainly associated with his mother; in Part II it is at first related to love affairs of a more or less purely sensual nature, but then also to his mother inasmuch as he is looking for a woman who resembles her, and finally it is related to Isobel, who is set in contrast with his mother.

Shadows acquire the quality of a leitmotif. They open the novel and permeate the entire book. At the beginning, it is the shadows of the gulls, with which Patrick appears to be obsessed, recurrently noticing them floating 'among the feet on the concrete as [he] walks in a day of [his] life' (p. 9), the last day at the school in Dublin (cf. pp. 9–11, 19–21, 23–25, *passim*). Equally, other shadows are hanging over the narrator's life, shadows of his youth, his family, his mother, of the guilt at having wasted the hour he could have spent with her when she lay dying: '[...] the living face [he] had a whole hour to look on and threw away' (p. 78). The last day at the school, the narrative frame in other words, represents a leave-taking from the influence of some of the shadows: '[...] by the evening the life would have made its last break with the shadow and would be free to grow without warp in its own light. [...] A terrible new life was beginning, a life without her this evening and tomorrow and the next day, and the next day forever' (p. 82).

Isobel is likewise haunted by shadows, the shadows of her previous life, of unhappy marriages her father forced upon her, of liaisons and, most prominently, of her father himself, the latter constituting a direct parallel to the mother's shadow over Patrick. Isobel has, like Patrick, died many small deaths (cf. p. 105), and, like Patrick, she has been trying 'to walk into [her] own life' (p. 133). This she finally manages through psychoanalysis and the reading of Freud (pp. 130f.).

Lastly, there is the shadow of priest-ridden Ireland, which makes itself felt when Patrick decides to go to Ireland with Isobel, partly in order for her to escape her father's influence. He knows full well that they cannot stay there for long because in the eyes of the Catholic Irish they are not properly married, the wedding not having taken place in church. But Patrick is determined to 'see it through this time to the last amen' (p. 182). Once back in Ireland, he quickly learns '[w]hat a small country Ireland is, where everybody who is not related knows someone who knows someone else you share an enemy or friend with' (p. 182). Father Curry, on that last day, puts forward the decisive accusation:

> If it got out that I let you go on teaching up there after what you've done there'd be an uproar. The Archbishop wouldn't stand for it. The parents wouldn't stand for it. I couldn't stand for it. [...] Tell me this one fact. What entered your head to do such a thing? Didn't you know it was flying in the face of God? (p. 190)

Having afterwards returned home, he and Isobel make love and become one in the act of lovemaking, thus symbolically conquering the shadows:

> The odour of our lovemaking rises, redolent of slime and fish, and our very breathing seems an echo of the rise and fall of the sea as we drift to sleep [...]. (p. 195)

The relation between the lovemaking and the sea echoes the opening of the novel, where the narrator states that he believes 'that the first constant was water' (p. 9). His love for Isobel, then, is associated through this reference to water, the sea with the notion of a constant, of permanence. Concepts of love again play a significant part in McGahern's next novel, *The Pornographer*.

*The Pornographer* (1979) has met with a rather mixed reception, and critical considerations of the novel have rarely managed to give it its full due as an important achievement in McGahern's career.[6] It is therefore that the book will be discussed here in some detail.

The main point to be noticed about *The Pornographer* is that the novel charts a journey, in the figurative sense, that the unnamed first-person narrator undergoes as he matures from a composer of smutty pornographic stories to a serious-minded writer of autobiographical fiction. *The Pornographer* is, in a manner of speaking, his very own book. At the close, the narrator finds himself in a situation that recalls Marcel's in Proust's *À la recherche du temps perdu*:

> I tried to say something back but I couldn't. And in the silence a fragment of another day seemed to linger amid the sweeping wipers, and grow: the small round figure of my uncle getting out of the train away down the platform, childishly looking around, the

raincoat over his arm, at the beginning of the journey — if beginning it ever had — that had brought each to where we were, in
the now and forever.[7]

That other 'day' refers to the opening of his reminiscences,
describing how he met his uncle, who had come to visit his terminally ill
sister in hospital, at the railway station in Dublin:

> By the time the carriages themselves had jolted to a stop the plat-
> form was already black. When eventually I saw his small round
> figure far down the platform, childishly looking around, the rain-
> coat over his arm, 'A wise man always carries his coat on a good
> day' [...]. (p. 9)

That the whole account is rendered with hindsight becomes apparent
especially from certain reflexive passages, such as this:

> The superstitious, the poetic, the religious are all made safe within
> the social, given a tangible form. The darkness is pushed out. All
> things become interrelated. We learn sequence and precedence,
> grown anxious about our own position in the scheme, shutting
> out the larger anxiety of the darkness. There's nothing can be
> done about it. There's good form and bad form. All is outside. (p.
> 238)

Here is another one:

> The womb and the grave...The christening party becomes the
> funeral, the shudder that makes us flesh becomes the shudder
> that makes us meat. They say that it is the religious instinct that
> makes us seek the relationships and laws in things. And in be-
> tween there is time and work, as passing time, and killing time,
> and lessening time that'd lessen anyway [...]. (p. 30)

The passages may have a wiseacre note to them: 'By the time I left I no
longer felt the vulnerable single person that has to take on suffering and
death. We upholster ourselves' (p. 114), and they may occasionally seem
mystifying; but they are none the less central to how the narrator himself
assesses his own development and how he looks upon the inter-
relatedness of the religious, the poetic (or artistic), and the mystical. Sex
and art are regarded as equally grounded in mysticism, and if 'the religious

instinct [...] makes us seek the relationships and laws in things', then the same is true of the artistic instinct.

The superstitious, the poetic, the religious are all secure within the social context, given a tangible form. The darkness is pushed out. All things become interrelated. This is what the narrator comes to learn, and his autobiographical narrative throws into relief why it is that, having started out as a rather unfeeling perpetrator of pornographic stories and an exploiter of women much in the sense of his own 'sexual athletes', in the end he can say of himself: 'What I wanted to say was that I had a fierce need to pray, for myself, Maloney, my uncle, the girl, the whole shoot' (p. 252).

*The Pornographer* is permeated by contrast, thematic as well as motif contrast. Life in the city, as centred upon the narrator, his friend and the customer of his pornographic effusions, Maloney, as well as his lover, Josephine, is pitted against life in the country, represented here by the narrator's aunt and uncle and Nurse Brady. The narrator's relationship with Josephine is brought into sharp contrast with his relationship with Nurse Brady. Birth and death, the 'womb and the grave' (p. 30), are juxtaposed: Josephine gives birth to the narrator's child while the narrator's aunt lies dying. Secretly visiting his aunt in the ward in the middle of the night, the narrator passes through the maternity ward and thinks: '[...] all those women were waiting to give birth, to their own death' (p. 175). When his aunt is finally sent home from hospital, the narrator says to Nurse Brady: 'There's only two telegrams to wait for. A birth and a death.' (p. 224) The manner in which the narrator treats Josephine is clearly distinguished from the manner in which he behaves towards his ailing aunt. There is the significant difference between art and life, expressly propounded by Maloney and at first not understood and felt by the narrator himself; and there is the contrast between the figure the narrator cuts in the first half of the book and the one he cuts in the second half. There are, moreover, some oppositions that, paradoxically, also build up likenesses, such as sex and the religious as well as sex and death. Thus in the retrospective view of the narrator, the sex act is likened to death:

> Death must sometimes come the same way, the tension leaving the body, in pain and not in this sweetness and pride, but a last time, the circle completed, never having to come back to catch the flying moment that was always the same, always on the wing. (p. 57)

As for the overall structure of the book, Denis Sampson has persuasively shown how the narrative is organised in what he terms 'movements' — five movements and an 'overture', the latter, for example, comprising the first six episodes up to the moment the narrator is about to enter the dance hall. Sampson also quite correctly draws attention to the many echoes and repetitions that pervade the novel. One such echo or repetition is constituted by the fact that both women, Josephine as well as Nurse Brady, when he meets them for the first time at a dance in the Metropole Hotel, have dark hair and wear a blue dress. Or he waits for Nurse Brady under Clery's clock (p. 209), which is also where he once waited for Josephine.

The narrator empathically cares for his dying aunt, visiting her regularly in hospital and charitably supplying her with brandy to alleviate the pain. And yet, at the beginning and throughout the first half of his account, the narrator presents himself as one of 'the dead of heart' (p. 13). He was once in love with a woman before encountering Josephine, but the woman refused to marry him and gave him his marching orders. Now he is associated with life in the city, where the evenings stretch 'ahead like a long empty room' (p. 20), where 'everything [is] fragmented' (p. 63) and no genuine sense and purpose is to be found. Country people the narrator knows — and of course he himself is a country boy — get 'dwarfed in the city' (p. 93). He is during the greater part of the narrative at least until he becomes disgusted by his own pornographic writings under Maloney's influence. After all, it is Maloney who tells him what to write (cf., for instance, p. 28). Maloney is the cynical publisher of pornographic magazines who subscribes to the notion that 'Ireland wanking is Ireland free' (p. 25). He once had ambitions to be a poet. When he was ditched by the woman he was in love with, he felt humiliated and strangely enough, given his ideas concerning art and life to be considered shortly, wrote a long poem in rhyming couplets about his experience. 'He had been in love, had failed in love, and out of the loss had grown the poem' (p. 27). In his cynical way, he seeks to make the narrator follow the pattern of how he himself was eventually caught in marriage (cf. p. 133).

Before entering the Metropole, where he will meet Josephine — or that is not quite correct, for notably, it is not really before entering the Metropole that he reflects on the 'womb and the grave' (p. 30) — this reflection belongs not to the character who is about to embark on a sexual affair, but to the narrator while he is penning his autobiographical narrative, turning his life into art. Here once more is the entire reflection

The womb and the grave... The christening party becomes the funeral, the shudder that makes us flesh becomes the shudder that makes us meat. They say that it is the religious instinct that makes us seek the relationships and laws in things. And in between there is time and work, as passing time, and killing time, and lessening time that'd lessen anyhow, such as this going to the dance. (p. 30)

The last sentence aptly characterises the narrator's life in the city before he strikes up with Nurse Brady: passing time, killing time, and lessening time, marking a life that consists of a series of accidents outside any law.

Maloney warned the narrator against the confusion between art and life:

Art was art because it was not nature. Life was a series of accidents. Art was a vision of the law. Rarely did the accident conform to the Idea or Vision, so it had to be invented or made anew so that it conformed to the Vision. In short, it was life seen through a personality. Which brought us to the joyous triumph of all art. For, though life might be intolerable or sad, the very fact of being able to bring it within the law made it a cause for joy and celebration. Or to put it more crudely, though in this particular autobiographical case the girl was lost, it was through the particular loss that the poem had been won. (p. 27)

This notion, together with another of Maloney's views: 'Above all the imagination requires distance [...]. It can't function close up' (p. 21), is of especial import for the narrator's maturing process. For at first, he is incapable of creating such a necessary distance. Having finished yet another episode involving the sexual gymnastics of Mavis and the Colonel, the narrator feels 'flushed' getting up from the typewriter. 'Nothing', he reasons, 'holds together unless it is mixed with some of one's own blood' (p. 24). The next time, he again is 'flushed, [his] flesh excited again by the play of Mavis and the Colonel in the mind's eye' (p. 50), and he has grown 'inflamed enough [himself] to want to lie down with any warm body' (p. 51). But after Josephine has gone to London and taken up with her old friend Jonathan, whom he hopes will marry her, the narrator starts getting fed up with his pornographic stuff (cf. p. 124). Even so, he has to distinguish between art and life, or nature, as

outlined by Maloney. At this point he may be disgusted with his Mavis–
Colonel stories, yet he conflates his personal experiences and his
pornography, making the journey of his pornographic puppets to the
Shannon exactly mimic the trip he and Josephine took there (pp. 158ff.).
None the less, after having had a liberating experience with Nurse Brady,
he finds himself in a position where he can say: 'I was entering a new
life' (p. 218).

There is a strong link between sex and the religious. Mavis moans
while having sex with the Colonel: 'O Jesus [...] Fuck me, O fuck me, O
my Jesus' (p. 23). The sexual act is seen by the novel-writing narrator in
terms of a mystical experience. He assesses his first sexual encounter
with Josephine thus:

> Within her there was this instant of rest, the glory and the awe,
> that one was as close as ever man could be to the presence of the
> mystery, and life, the caged bird in its moment of pure rest be-
> fore it was about to be loosed into blinding light [...]. (p. 39)

As Sampson argues, this spiritual ecstasy is here associated with the
traditional Catholic image of the soul's release from the cage of the
body, and it appears to be conditioned in part by thoughts of the
conundrum of time and eternity.[8] The sexual experience becomes
elevated through biblical and literary echoes to a sense of mystical union
that diminishes the importance of the physical release:

> We were both the tree and the summer. There was no yearning
> toward nor falling away. We were one. It was as if we were, then,
> those four other people, now gone out of time, who had snatched
> the two of us into time. For a moment again we possessed their
> power and their glory anew, pushing out of mind all graveclothes.
> (p. 42)[9]

Still, the narrator approaches Josephine in the Metropole in terms of
his pornographic stories: 'a hot, fierce burning ache — the Colonel and
my Mavis again — grew to bathe in this warm living flesh beneath my
hands' (p. 36). He feels like a sexual athlete and she, to him, is 'a wonderful
healthy animal' (p. 34). He tells her from the first that '[l]ove has nothing
got to do with it. I'm attracted to you' (p. 38). In the end, he makes the
following sentiment into a 'scapular' that he keeps about his body
whenever he has dealings with Josephine:

> Everybody must feel that a man who hates any person hates that person the more for troubling him with expressions of love; or, at least, it adds to hatred the sting of disgust. (p. 137)

It is indeed a sentiment that fittingly sums up the narrator's attitude towards Josephine in the second half of the book.

Thirty-eight-year-old Josephine evinces a typically Catholic approach to the sexual act. After a somewhat abortive first experience with a married man, who post-coitally was more interested in the racing results than in her, she repeatedly convinces herself that she does not 'feel guilty or anything' (p. 41), regarding her demeanour as natural while increasingly accusing the narrator of having been corrupted in his attitude to sex by his pornography (cf. pp. 81, 86, 96). It would be quite unfounded to follow one's possible initial inclination and look upon her as a victim of a cold-hearted sexual predator. She is no victim. She is quite clear-headed in the pursuit of her aims. The narrator never tells her that love is involved and clearly points out that he would never marry her if she found herself pregnant. Furthermore, she in a way tricks him into the precarious situation by refusing to use contraceptive measures and deceiving him about her unsafe period. At one moment, the narrator senses that Josephine may think in these terms: 'You're the sort of person who needs a woman [...]; you're the sort of person who's ripe for plucking. And I'm the one for the job' (p. 59). She is undoubtedly out to pick 'a winner' (p. 101). The narrator's medical friend argues that whether 'she knew it or not she wanted to get pregnant' (p. 107). And who is to say that the doctor is not right in diagnosing Josephine's case thus:

> Time running out? Get pregnant, and it'll be taken care of. Bored with life? Get pregnant, and it'll stir things up. Not getting enough attention? Get pregnant, and it'll bring an overdose of attention. (pp. 112f.)

The narrator wants to be and stay free. Thoughts of a marital life with Josephine in a semi-detached house revolt him (p. 103). Josephine, on the other hand, strives towards ensnaring him by repeatedly and insistently suggesting to him that he is a good person (cf. p. 148) and consequently cannot but marry her now that she is pregnant. When all her efforts fail to bring the desired result, she finally has pressure put upon him by her Irish friend and landlord, who beats the narrator up.

The novel opens with the uncle's arrival in Dublin. The uncle is immediately established as a down-to-earth, jovial, hard-working, reasonable and practical person: 'Why would I take the car — when you can sit back and the train'll take you. Then the other fella has to do the driving.' (p. 9). But he is also a braces-and-belt, canny man: 'A wise man always carries his coat on a good day.' (p. 9), and a man who is stoical in bearing suffering: '"Well," he cleared his throat. "How is the patient?" in a voice that would have been equally suited to asking me if I thought the Great Wall of China was likely to be around for long more.' (p. 10). He is finally a person who has 'the rude health of a tree of crows' (p. 13).

The aunt, upon returning home to the country from hospital, starts working in the garden, which, not having been tended for the two previous years, is a wilderness of weeds. This adds a kind of pastoral quality to the aunt's life as well as to country life in general, in addition to the stoical toughness the aunt shows in the face of her frightful predicament. 'She was tough', the narrator notes. 'There was nothing but to salute that proud hardness with a perfect silence' (p. 144) — a proud toughness that does not lessen when confronted with what is experienced as the transience of human life and the futility of human attainments. Referring to her garden, the aunt remarks:

> It's only after years that you got some shape on things and then after all that you have to leave. It's comical. You want to go on and you can't. (p. 144)

Importantly, it is with his aunt and uncle in the country that the narrator is 'happy [...] for five such days' (p. 147).

The black-haired nurse, tellingly, grew up in the country, on a farm outside Monasterevin. She is only twenty-three and in a sense better suited for a thirty-year-old man than 38-year-old Josephine. The place where she lives in the hospital grounds 'remind[s] you of the country' (p. 173), or so the taxi-driver suggests. She is associated with the aunt because she nurses her in the ward. The narrator's affair with her is the exact opposite to the Josephine affair. There is nothing of Mavis and the Colonel about it. They may have had sex, but priapic grappling features nowhere in the description of the relationship. Instead, this is how the narrator refers to his making love to Nurse Brady:

> This body was the shelter of the self. Like all walls and shelters it would age and break and let the enemy in. But holding it now was

like holding glory, and having held it once was to hold it — no matter how broken and conquered — in glory still, and with the more terrible tenderness. (p. 177)

There is, then, tenderness here, no matter that it is terrible tenderness, a quality that is never part of his copulating with Josephine. Equally noteworthy is the fact that the narrator refers to Nurse Brady as 'a young woman rooted in her own life' (p. 209). He freely admits to her that he has got another woman pregnant, and, significantly, he introduces her to Maloney and the world he represents in order 'to show her that it was not just that one thing I was after' (p. 213), thus demonstrating that he means to integrate her fully into his whole life. It is with Nurse Brady that he feels he is entering a new life. He is, as he tells Maloney, now thinking of proposing marriage to her and coming back to live in the country (p. 250). Finally, it is Nurse Brady who teaches him that the main obligation in establishing viable and profound human relationships is to attend to people. Near the close of his account, he pins down the dilemma of his past life in the following way:

By not attending, by thinking any one thing was as worth doing as any other, by sleeping with anybody who'd agree, I had been the cause of as much pain and confusion and evil as if I had actively set out to do it. I had not attended properly. [...] Broken in love, I had turned back, let the light of imagination almost out. (p. 251)

The poetic quality of the book he has written and offered to the reader, Marcel-fashion, proves that he has been successful in letting the light of imagination in again.

It may now become intelligible in what sense Maloney's view of art and life has a specific bearing on the narrator's own case. The narrator's life is clearly a series of accidents, and in writing this series down he makes it anew so that it conforms to the vision of the law. His art as represented by the narrative at hand is life seen through a personality. Therein resides the joyous triumph of all art. Because he is finally able to bring his experience within the law, this makes it a cause for joy and celebration. And it is with this in mind that one may understand why at the close the narrator feels 'a fierce need to pray, for myself, Maloney, my uncle, the girl, the whole shoot' (p. 252).

*Amongst Women* (1990) is McGahern's masterpiece, as a number of

critics have argued.[10] It is an immensely compelling novel, in respect of
its ideas perhaps not as demanding as *The Pornographer*, but highly
admirable in its narrative performance. *Amongst Women* offers a
penetrating critique of patriarchy as the refuge of the socially ill-adjusted
and emotionally immature man, and asks probing questions about the
cult of the family. Moran, its principal character, has transformed his
inadequacies into a show of strength by making his home his castle.
Denied a role as founding father in the Irish state, he has set up his own
dominion.[11] Patriarchy in *Amongst Women* derives from patriotism. Moran,
a hero of the War of Independence, who has failed to make a successful
career in the Irish army in peacetime, directs his frustrated drive for
power into a diminished form of home rule.[12] A strong, redoubtable,
even tyrannical man for most of his adult life, who has deliberately kept
himself apart from society at large, he is in the narrative present, near
the end of his life, ironically shown as being fussed over and, in being
fussed over, dominated by the women in his life, his wife and his three
daughters. The novel makes this plain at its very opening:

> As he weakened, Moran became afraid of his daughters. This
> once powerful man who was so implanted in their lives that they
> had never really left Great Meadow, in spite of jobs and mar-
> riages and children and houses of their own in Dublin and
> London. Now they could not let him slip away.[13]

Or during the wedding reception, Rose and the girls are aware that '[t]hey
were mastered and yet they were controlling together what they were
mastered by' (p. 46). He may have ostensibly been in control as far as
the life of his family was concerned, but surreptitiously he has, for the
greater part, been manipulated by his wife and by his children. This
becomes apparent in his courtship of Rose, for instance. For all his
local notoriety as a strategist in the War of Independence, Moran
exercises very little control in the manner of his marriage. He is
continually outmanoeuvred by Rose, who mounts a shrewd, tactical
campaign to flush his interest in her into the open and to compel him
to proceed when he would prefer to retreat or delay.[14]

In all, *Amongst Women* shows the destructive legacy of political
evolution: the channelling of frustrated energies and ambitions into
petty authoritarianism and violence, the invocation of Catholicism to
support a domestic reign of terror, the maiming of a succeeding
generation through denial of individuality and insistence on conformity.[15]

More specifically, *Amongst Women* tells the story of the Moran family, who live at Great Meadow in the west of the Irish midlands. The narrative is divided into thematic blocks or episodes: Moran's courting of, and marriage to, Rose, his second wife; the gradual breaking away of the children from, in particular, their father; Maggie's departure for London, where she will work as a nurse; the school exams of Mona and Sheila and their subsequent move to Dublin; Michael's sexual initiation at fifteen with 22-year-old Nell Morahan, come home from New York for a few months; Michael's revolt against Moran when threatened with brutal flogging, and his flight to London; a hay saving incident, during which the family, with the exception of Luke, experiences a powerful feeling of bonding; and finally Moran's illness, death and burial.

The opening episode treats of the daughters' efforts to revive an old ritual, and the fact that it is a ritual that is to be revived is quite noteworthy. For, as will be seen, Moran's entire life is governed by ritual. The ritual in question at the beginning of the book is concerned with the celebration of Monaghan Day, the end-of-February fair in Mohill. By celebrating this day, the daughters hope to uplift the mood of their dying father. The second episode effects a flashback to one of the many other Monaghan Days on which Moran's old guerilla comrade, McQuaid, used to pay a visit to Great Meadow. The two men revel in memories of their days of glory during the War of Independence. But in the course of this visit there is disagreement because McQuaid chooses to take sides with Moran's estranged son, Luke, who, after having been fiercely flogged by his father, escaped to London. Accustomed to winning and having the last word in all things, Moran experiences this disagreement as an act of defeat. The daughters never really knew why McQuaid's visits were discontinued, and consequently they fail to see the futility of their efforts.

Having cut his connections with McQuaid, Moran decides to court Rose, a woman in her late thirties. He says it is for the good of the family, but essentially the decision is grounded on very personal considerations: as a counter-measure against an impending fear of loneliness. For Rose, life with Moran means the start of a new life; but Moran's behaviour quickly makes it obvious that for Moran himself nothing will change. His feeling of security and stability in life is the consequence of a repertoire of routine actions, most conspicuous among which is the saying of the rosary at night. Most of the episodes into which the book is divided have in common that they, in exemplary fashion, display instances of ritual routine, or recurrence. Everything joins up into a chain of incessant repetitions. The linear, or consecutive, manner of presentation suggests the flow of life, the inevitable process of change, by, for instance, featuring the growing-up of the children. Moran, on the other hand, tries to stay the passing of time.

The reasons for his conduct are many. There is, to begin with, his loss of power over his first-born son, Luke, and Luke's unflinching assertion of his independence, both of which have severely shaken Moran's own sense of manliness, a sense rooted in his experience of violence and death during the guerilla war. Moran loves Luke more than his other children; but his feelings for him express themselves in anger and resentment, and his inability to re-integrate Luke into the family is for Moran a permanent source of pain. Moreover, Moran is haunted by a fear of death. His inability to love is clearly seen in connection with his schooling in hatred as well as with his ability to kill during the war. His stern bitterness is directed against, among others, the Irish Free State. His disappointment in the new Ireland for which he himself fought has made him detest the war that brought independence. He tells his daughters: 'Don't let anybody fool you. It was a bad business. [...] The whole thing was a cod.' (p. 5). Even though as the head of the family he displays the air of a devout Catholic, Moran is deep down motivated by the feelings and thinking of an outcast and his instinctive vulnerability to anything that comes from outside the family unit. Moran is an utterly disillusioned hero, who is sustained solely by his desperate clinging to the fiction of family. In the remarkable scene of hay saving towards the close of the novel, the family, in a manner of speaking, succeeds in outwitting the terrible tyrant Time — the time until the rain sets in.

Moran is an uprooted and intensely insecure person. He has failed to find a suitable place and purpose in life in post-revolutionary Ireland. 'For people like McQuaid and myself', he tells his daughters, 'the war was the best part of our lives. Things were never so simple and clear again. I think we never rightly got the hang of it afterwards.' (p. 6). He is deeply dissatisfied with the progress of events in Ireland after the war. As he himself puts it: 'Sometimes I get sick when I see what I fought for.' (p. 15). To McQuaid he petulantly argues: 'Look where it brought us. Look at the country now. Run by a crowd of small-minded gangsters out for their own good.' (p. 18).

Much of Moran's behaviour is conditioned by a desperate desire to preserve the *status quo* and keep the family together as a bulwark against change:

[...] families were what mattered, more particularly that larger version of himself — *his* family; and while seated in the same scheming fury he saw each individual member gradually slipping away out of his reach. Yes, they would eventually all go. He would be alone. That he could not stand. (p. 22)

Moran is afraid of the world outside Great Meadow, a world signifying change. He tries to shun contact with people other than the members of his family, 'feeling vulnerable in the face of the power that rested in the hand of the outside' (p. 77). When the girls come home from London and Dublin, they bring 'the bracing breath of the outside, an outside Moran [refuses] to accept unless it [comes] from the family' (p. 93).

Moran is, as John Cronin has noted, a brilliantly imagined character.[16] He coldly tells his daughters: 'The closest I ever got to any man was when I had him in the sights of the rifle and I never missed' (p. 7), and he admits: 'I was never much on the lookout for kindness' (p. 139). Moran enthrals and terrifies his family. His moods swing dangerously between brief joviality and intense rage. Even Rose is not immune. As Cronin suggests, on one occasion, when he vents his fury on her, the image employed by McGahern reminds us that we are in the presence of a killer:

> Then one evening as she was tidying the room he said as quietly as if he were taking rifle aim, 'There's no need for you to go turning the whole place upside down. We managed well enough before you ever came round the place.'

Later, in another memorable image of savagery and pain, Moran, while mowing, shears the legs from under a hen pheasant concealed in the meadow. This excruciating image of the dying bird, so casually and unintentionally slain, gathers into itself all the novel tells us throughout of Moran's muddle of pious family concern and perilously destructive rage.[17]

Moran obviously derives from Reegan of *The Barracks*, Mahoney of *The Dark* and a number of other father-figures in McGahern's stories. He shares with Reegan his bitter dis-enchantment with the Irish Free State for which he fought only to find that the heady days of national struggle resulted merely in 'some of our johnnies in the top jobs instead of a few Englishmen'. His flogging of Luke and attempt at flagellating Michael recall the brutal opening scene of *The Dark*, and, like Maloney,

Moran represents a dangerous blend of loving father and domestic tyrant.[18]

Fear and love are the emotions that, inseparably interwoven, are regarded as holding the family together. Rose and the children live in permanent fear of Moran, and their constant efforts on his behalf are an expression of their desire and need to see in him a person they can love; they thus also convince themselves that he is loveable. Great Meadow is an almost holy place; returning to it satisfies the children's instinctive yearning for a belief in their own vitality. Rose personifies natural kindness. Her influence on a person such as Moran may be limited, yet she succeeds in creating an adequate breathing space for each of the children.

*Amongst Women* (the title being of course derived from 'Hail Mary') analyses the emotional restriction, the narrow sancti-moniousness and the patriarchy that characterised life in Ireland in the 1950s and 1960s. It offers a study of the intimidating and infuriating tensions as well as the appeasing rituals that weld the Moran family together so that the members may largely ignore the passage of time. Moran, house tyrant and loved father at one and the same time, is portrayed frozen in time and incapable of adapting to the changes that threaten his precarious position of authority. He attempts to convey a sense of permanence in a world in which change is paramount. The circular shape of the novel, brought about by the frame pattern of the narrative present and certain verbatim repetitions on the final pages of certain passages from the opening section, is a hint that the conundrum of time and eternity, the mystical wheel, is at the heart of McGahern's vision, here as in all of his fiction.[19]

# RODDY DOYLE

Roderick Doyle is quite conceivably the most successful contemporary novelist of his generation. Recently Gerry Smyth, in a study on 'the New Irish Fiction'[1] that groans under its prodigious weight of colonial and de-colonial theorising, assigned Doyle the central role within the context of the fiction produced in Ireland during the last two decades. 'Roddy Doyle', Smyth remarks, is 'one of the key modern Irish novelists' (p. 65). Perhaps that is correct. The question, though, is: key to what? 'Doyle's work is given a central place here', Smyth suggests as if in answer to our question, 'not on grounds of artistic value, commercial success or thematic typicality, although it could be argued that he rates highly on all three of these criteria' (p. 65). One must most energetically beg to differ with respect to the last part of this sentence.

But let us consider some of Smyth's further arguments. Doyle's excellence, we are told, partly resides in matters thematic.

> ...if there has been one overriding theme in Doyle's work to date it is the exploration of the relations between individuals and the collectives in which they find themselves, especially that collective known as the family. (p. 66)

But has not 'the exploration of the relations between individuals and the collectives in which they find themselves' been the overriding theme of the majority of novels since the tradition of narrative prose texts evolved? So what should be so special about Doyle's books?

> His representation of life as experienced by the Rabittes [sic], the Clarkes and the Spencers offers a range of perspectives on the ideology of the family as it operates in modern Ireland, and the serious challenges that were offered to that ideology as the 1980s slipped into the 1990s. (p. 66)

If that is true, then Smyth has regrettably failed to add that, judging by the strength(s) — or rather weakness(es) — of the 'Barrytown Trilogy', that representation has resulted in pretty small beer. Does Smyth seriously want to make anyone believe that a novel about the introduction of soul music into Irish life has anything noteworthy to say about 'the ideology of the family as it operates in modern Ireland'?

As for Doyle's excellence in terms of narrative technique, Symth notes:

> Since the start of his career, his work has been geared more to-wards 'showing' than 'telling', letting characters speak for themselves as far as possible. (p. 67)

Smyth goes on to make much of Doyle's reliance — almost exclusive reliance, one feels prompted to add — on the scenic method to the detriment of the summary, or descriptive, method, arguing that as a result of 'highly subtle effects through suggestion and narrative restraint' (p. 67), semantic gaps are left in what is told, gaps which the reader is called upon to fill in, so that the 'reader must become an active part of the meaning-making process' (p. 67). This is a rum argument. Every literary text worth its salt leaves gaps in what it proffers; this is a constituent characteristic of literary texts, as, in particular, the findings of reception theory have taught us. Without active reader participation, no literary work of art can ever come to life. All art is constituted in, and through, a communicative act between reader/perceiver/listener and text/painting/piece of music. As concerns Doyle's preference for 'showing', or the scenic method, for relying on dialogue instead of description, what Smyth considers a strength of Doyle's art may equally well be singled out as a cardinal shortcoming. There is evidence in Doyle's first four novels, up to *The Woman Who Walked Into Doors* (1997), that the author favoured the scenic method because he could not have been good at description even if someone had held a gun to his head. Which is to say, it is highly dubious that Doyle elected to write in this manner, even though he had it in him to write in a different style, for purposes of what Russian formalists would have termed 'making it new, or different'. Dialogue-based texts are no novelty, and more is the pity, as the examples of Ivy Compton-Burnett, Henry Green and others show. But Dame Ivy had something profound to communicate through this technique. Doyle, on the other hand, especially in the Barrytown trilogy, may have been aiming at transcending certain stereotypes, but he set up new ones that have greatly appealed to an undiscerning mass readership. This is the reason for Doyle's colossal commercial success: the novels are easy to read, easy to understand and, *pace* Smyth, they do not require sophisticated reader participation.

Doyle himself has remarked in a recent interview that

> inevitably people pick up my novels with all their dialogue and
> think, 'Oh, thinly disguised plays', which is just ignorance really.
> They're not aware of the difference in writing a novel and a play,
> they think that somehow because a novel has a lot of dialogue it's
> not really a novel.[2]

Well, actually, it is not quite that. Doyle is rather obviously begging the
question here by accusing his critics of ignorance instead of making
clear what aims he tried to achieve by means of this concentration on
dialogue.

*

Doyle was born in 1958 and grew up in the Kilbarrack area of Dublin,
the inspiration for his 'Barrytown' settings. He was educated at a national
school in Raheny, at St Fintan's Christian Brothers school in Sutton,
County Dublin, and at University College, Dublin, before working in
Kilbarrack as a teacher from 1979 until 1993. His literary career began
in 1987, when he and a friend formed a small press, King Farouk, to
publish *The Commitments*, which was later picked up by a London
publisher. The novel was turned into a most successful film by director
Alan Parker in 1991, with Doyle writing the screenplay. Doyle's second
novel, *The Snapper* (1990), was also turned into a film, directed by Stephen
Frears, and it also won critical acclaim. The third piece in the 'Barrytown
Trilogy', *The Van* (1991), was short-listed for the Booker Prize and also
filmed. In 1993, Doyle won the prestigious Booker Prize for *Paddy Clarke
Ha Ha Ha*.

Doyle has also written plays. His first one, *Brownbread* (which is
rhyming slang for 'dead'), was first staged at the SFX Centre, Dublin, in
September 1987. In it, three nineteen-year-old Dubliners kidnap an Irish
bishop because 'there was nothin' on the telly'. The play thrives on
quick-witted dialogue and coarse humour, as it pokes fun at modern
Dublin sensibilities. In 1990 his second play, *War*, was performed at the
SFX Centre. The setting is a pub, and the action features a quiz contest.
Again the piece offers witty dialogue and outrageous humour, but it is
not as convincing as *Brownbread*. His four-part play for television, *Family*,
was screened in 1994. It challenged sentimental stereotypes by focusing
on the emotional abuse of children by their violent fathers.

The 'Barrytown Trilogy' has earned Doyle efusive praise for his abrasive picture of contemporary Dublin.[3] If that praise is justified one must not forget to point out that in *The Commitments*, this picture is rather a microscopically small one. The novel treats of how the pop group of the title, under the leadership of Jimmy Rabbitte Jr, an ambitious young man, and under the tutelage of the trumpet-player Joey 'The Lips' Fagan, who claims to have played with the likes of James Brown, Otis Redding and Sam Cooke, want to bring soul music to Dublin. According to Jimmy Jr, the music of black America is also the music of working-class Dublin. The book has been highly commended for 'the candid dialogue and the author's ability to make the music lively even when all the reader has to rely on are the printed lyrics'.[4] A friend recommended *The Commitments* to me after the book had been re-issued by Heinemann in 1988, particularly, it turned out, because of his acquaintance with the author. I began reading it but gave up, I have to admit, halfway through, being firmly convinced that this represented a case of juvenile aberration. (Doyle's own characters would employ a four-letter word here.) The novel, I felt, if *The Commitments* was a novel at all, could not be taken seriously. To my shame, I still see no reason to revise my opinion. A Dublin publisher recently told me of a similar experience. He had bought himself a copy of *The Commitments*, but he had sent it windmilling over his shoulder at somewhere around page twenty. The copy was then picked up by his fifteen-year-old son, who just loved what it offered him.

Like its predecessor consisting mostly of dialogue, *The Snapper* focuses on Jimmy's twenty-year-old sister, Sharon, who, as a result of her having one night, in an utterly drunken state, engaged in priapic grappling with a married neighbour, is expecting a baby. The Rabbitte family, especially Jimmy Rabbitte Sr, stalwartly stand by Sharon and defend her against any invidious rumour during her pregnancy, as all await the arrival of baby Gina (in Irish slang 'the snapper').[5]

In *The Van*, Jimmy Rabbitte Sr and his friend 'Bimbo', both men having 'become redundant' at work (that is: they were fired), decide to invest in a 'Chipper van', called 'Bimbo's Burger'. The time is the summer of 1990, and all of Ireland is fanatical about the Italia '90 World Cup, which the Republic of Ireland team has qualified for. Reasoning that during the event no Irish person will have time to cook dinner, Jimmy and Bimbo expect to make oceans of money when the hungry soccer fans leave the pubs at closing time. But the business turns out a sorry failure. The partners have no business acumen. Further problems arise because Bimbo owns the van and Bimbo's wife wants to control the business. Eventually, a health inspector closes down 'Bimbo's Burger', and after a fistfight with Jimmy Sr., on whom he puts the blame for the shutdown, Bimbo drives the van into the Irish Sea. In spite of everything, though, Jimmy Sr and Bimbo remain the best of friends.

It is certainly true that, in a sense, *The Van* is the most complete work in the 'Barrytown Trilogy', and it is also correct to assert that the novel portrays a 'darker side of middle-class Dublin [are the Rabbittes really middle-class?] — being on the dole, sorting out family problems, and the struggle to feel needed'.[6] The question, however, is whether what Doyle chooses to show can qualify as a serious-minded analysis of contemporary life in Dublin, especially because the social problems engaged with are almost completely drowned by 'plenty of laughs'[7], the tone of the portrayal is too facetious and the picture of Dublin conveyed is rather fatuous. Again Doyle's method relies too heavily on dialogue couched in the idiom of the Dublin working-class and prodigiously peppered with scatological expressions. Quite a few reviewers and critics have raved about what they see as the vitality and freshness of Doyle's style, and they have praised the great variety of socio-economic phenomena highlighted by the author in conjuring up his characters' lives. But most of this is just silly hype. On the strength of the trilogy, it can justifiably be said that the thematic interest of Doyle's *oeuvre* is quite shallow.

Perhaps the best that may be noted about the thematic weight of Doyle's trilogy is this: the central theme of *The Commitments* is the search for personal identity. The members of the band, with the possible exception of Joey 'The Lips' Fagan who is of a more advanced age, are striving to discover their own potential and find the right course their life should take. Thus for Jimmy Jr., the wish to be in a band represents an effort to distinguish himself from others ('Yis want to be different, isn't that it?', p. 6). Coupled with this is of course the idea of acquiring recognition and achieving financial success ('Yis don't want to end up like [...] these tossers here. Amn't I right? [...] Yis want to get up there an' shout I'm Outspan fuckin' Foster', p. 6). In one way or another, the young men undergo an individual process of finding themselves.

The three girls, Nathalie, Bernie and Imelda, the 'Commit-mentettes', are somehow different. They realise quite early on that as far as their singing is concerned more is expected of them than they were hitherto able to achieve. 'They'd been in the folk mass choir when they were in school but that, they knew now, hadn't really been singing' (p. 34). All

three win remarkable self-assurance in the course of the book. They are
forced to step into the limelight and assert themselves, which is
something that they would not have been able to accomplish at the
outset. They like to sing on stage, but being a member of 'The
Commitments' for them means having fun and escaping the drabness
of their daily lives. Unlike their male colleagues, they do not really undergo
a process of discovering their identity.

The themes of family and gender mark *The Snapper*, as the account
focuses on Sharon's relationship to her father and on the reaction of
the neighbours to Sharon's pregnancy. Jimmy Sr, in his turn, faced with
his daughter's condition, finds himself constrained to define his
relationship towards Sharon as well as his own role as father anew. He is
made to realise by the event that he did not previously waste one thought
on what that role entailed. He therefore is not actually in a position
where he needs to re-define an appropriate stance as father; instead he
has to discover such a stance in the first place. In the beginning, though,
he confines his fatherly obligations to cracking feeble jokes, especially
at his children's expense. Matters of education mean nothing to him.
Consequently, he leaves it to his wife, Veronica, to tell the two junior
girls the facts of life to prevent them from ending up in Sharon's
predicament. Gradually, though, Jimmy Sr changes his attitude. The first
serious conversation ever between Sharon and him is brought about
not least because Jimmy Sr becomes aware of the significance that the
topic of child abuse has for the media. Moreover, he determinedly begins
to defend Sharon's honour: 'I'm not havin' some fat little fucker insultin'
any of my family' (p. 83), with the personal pronoun 'my' taking on
especial import.

Of course, in all this Jimmy Sr is at first thinking more about himself
than Sharon. This is made evident when he is sitting in the kitchen and
reflecting on recent events:

> [...] his life was being ruined because of her. It was fuckin' terri
> ble. He was the laughing stock of Barrytown. It wasn't her faul
> — but it was her fault as well. It wasn't his. He'd done nothing. (p
> 147)

But during the third conversation he has with Sharon (pp. 161–64)
Jimmy Sr, who shortly before had regarded himself as the victor becaus
Sharon had been willing to take all the blame, grows sentimental and
appears ready to accept his responsibilities: 'They were both laughing

They'd both won' (p. 163). Reconciliation between father and daughter has thus been truly established.

Yet there is a second effect on Jimmy Sr. With the help of a manual he begins to learn about female anatomy and about the fact that sex is more than 'ridin'. That he speaks to Sharon about such matters has various reasons. He cannot talk things of that nature over with his wife; his sons would laugh at him; but he feels safe with Sharon. The newly won intimacy between father and daughter is thereby confirmed. Furthermore, Jimmy Sr makes an important discovery in connection with Sharon's pregnancy: '[...] when yeh look at tha' pictures, righ', an' then the later ones, an' then the born baby growin' up — Well, it's a fuckin' miracle, isn't it?' (p. 179). Jimmy Sr has six children, but only now, just before becoming a grandfather, does he realise what a miracle the coming into being of human life is. It is for this reason that he considers himself

> a changed man. A new man. [...] He had done a lot of thinking since then. And a lot of reading, and looking at pictures. [...] There was more to life than drinking pints with your mates. There was Veronica, his wife, and his children. Some of his own sperms had gone into making them so, fuck it, he was responsible for them. But, by Jaysis, he'd made one poxy job of it so far. [...] But from now on it was going to be different. (p. 193)

Sharon herself learns to adopt a new attitude towards her father. The relationship between Sharon and Jimmy Sr reflects the relationship between modernity and tradition. She personifies the modern young woman of the 1990s, while her father is still caught in traditional convictions. Additionally, Sharon develops into a mature woman and mother, which fact becomes particularly apparent in the scenes featuring Sharon and her female friends, who only appear as a group, never as viable individuals.

*The Van* reviews Jimmy Sr's volatile personality, his inability to resolve conflicts and his notions about male behaviour and male identity. But Jimmy Sr is shown here as an active person who can prove whether he is actually able to profit from the experience gained in *The Snapper* and whether he has in fact changed into a different man, as he proclaimed in the pervious book. The later novel, furthermore, tackles the themes of unemployment and male friendship.

There is something to be said for the contention according to which it was only with *Paddy Clarke Ha Ha Ha* and the subsequent two novels that Roddy Doyle emerged as a novelist to be taken seriously, and this not just because he adopted a more sophisticated narrative technique. *Paddy Clarke Ha Ha Ha* signalled a change in approach that has come to full fruition in *The Woman Who Walked Into Doors*: narrative description began to take up more space and the tone of the books started to become darker and darker. Most notably, the social abuses, defects and miseries he now depicted were incomparably more compelling.

The events in *Paddy Clarke Ha Ha Ha* are rendered from the perspective of ten-year-old Patrick (Paddy) Clarke, who, together with the members of his family, among them his brother Francis ('Sinbad'), lives in Barrytown. Paddy and his friends like to fool around on building sites, lighting fires and bedaubing walls. They mess about in the barn of a farm and jump into the sea. The older boys take it out on Paddy, and Paddy retaliates by taking it out on Sinbad. At school, Paddy claims that one of the men who signed the Irish Proclamation of Independence, one Thomas J. Clarke, was his grandfather. But Thomas J. Clarke, as the teacher points out, was executed by the British on 3 May 1916. A headline in a newspaper makes Paddy believe that World War III is imminent. So he discusses with his father the question of whether there will also be war in Ireland. In a letter to Santa Claus he asks for a pair of Adidas soccer boots. In short — Paddy reports about his everyday experiences; his two friends, Liam and Aidan, whose mother died prematurely and whose father howls like a dog at nights in the garden from grief; incidents at school; games of cowboys-and-Indians; his enthusiasm for Father Damien, a missionary who devoted his life to the lepers; his love of books; visits to the cinema; the purchase of a car. And now and then Paddy, more in passing as it were, notices that his parents have rows and shout at each other.

A sewerage system is installed and Paddy gambols in the ditches. He and the other boys play soccer matches and watch the final of the European Cup on television; they discuss the matter of what fish fingers are made from, play with a dog and build a wigwam. Paddy is given a bicycle and learns how to ride it. He becomes a member of a soccer team, Barrytown United, and he locks Sinbad in a suitcase. One of his schoolmates drowns and the whole school attend the funeral. Paddy and his friends watch a butcher doing his work. Finally, Paddy wins a medal in a race.

Yet, despite all the distractions that life has in store for him, Paddy is compelled to realise that things at home are changing for the worse

One morning, he finds the breakfast table in a mess. The dishes from the supper of the night before have not been cleared away. His mother offers the explanation that she did not have the time. But Paddy knows the real reason to have been a row between his parents. The rows become more frequent. Eventually, the father hits the mother. From that point onwards, Paddy tries to stay with his mother as much as possible, so as to prevent his father from maltreating his wife once more. Paddy simply cannot understand his parents' behaviour. 'I loved him. He was my da. It didn't make sense. She was my ma.'[8] Again and again, the parents have fights and Paddy regards it as his duty to put an end to the fights or to prevent them in the first place. Then one morning, the mother does not get up at all; she stays in bed for two solid days. Paddy does not know whether she is ill or whether her behaviour is the consequence of a violent quarrel. He is utterly confused. In the end, the parents fight incessantly, and Paddy and Sinbad can hear the infuriated voices in their bedroom. He tries to stay awake whole nights, believing that in that way he will be able to forestall the fighting. At school he falls asleep from overtiredness. One night, the father returns home drunk. But the parents of some of his friends likewise have rows, and as a result they move from the area. Paddy senses that his family will be the next to decamp. He thinks of running away, but he stays on, knowing that he is helpless. 'Why did people not like each other?' (p. 257), he asks himself. He has a fight with his best friend and after that is ostracised by all the other boys. In the end, the father moves out after another terrible row, and the kids in the street start shouting:

– Paddy Clarke –
Paddy Clarke –
Has no da.
Ha ha ha! (p. 281)

Doyle shows how ten-year-old Paddy tries to explore the reality of his existence and make himself at home in it with almost febrile curiosity and a carefree thirst for action. Inevitably, he also comes face to face with the dark, seamy sides of life, or rather the kind of life he is forced to lead in the particular social milieu he grows up in, and Paddy reacts to this with helplessness and a sense of pain and loss. The recreation of Paddy's childhood, regarded by some as 'superb',[9] gives the impression of being quite random and repetitive. That randomness and repetitiveness might well be in accordance with Paddy's way of gaining experience. After all, it is he himself who is telling the tale. And yet there is also Henry James's view, as expressed in the Preface of *The Spoils of Poynton*, according to which life is all inclusion and confusion and art is all discrimination and selection.[10]

As in the 'Barrytown Trilogy', especially in *The Van*, the family is again the focus of attention. If we saw the institution coming under pressure in the preceding novel, in *Paddy Clarke Ha Ha Ha* we see it cracking and falling apart. Gerry Smyth has argued:

> The dysfunctional family is a symptom of an increasingly disjointed society, for the confusion Paddy feels with the onset of his parents' break-up is anticipated by the confusion already confronting him at the social and cultural levels.[11]

The remark may be to the point. No doubt, the Clarkes are a dysfunctional family; but it remains arguable whether Doyle has succeeded in sufficiently characterising, and giving shape to, that 'increasingly disjointed society'. Paddy is like most ten-year-olds — confused at the social and cultural levels. Clearly Doyle's attention to the details of a young boy's life is impressive. Without resorting to sentimentality, he re-creates the honest thoughts of Paddy, who may be slightly more sensitive and aware than most children of his age. Doyle also manages to steer clear of spoiling the narrative with 'witty adult observations'.[12] All this is clearly in favour of the book. Yet, the social and societal factors responsible for the decline of the family unit in the Ireland of the late '60s are allowed to remain too much in the shadow. They are at best implied, but that is rather inadequate for a novel with socio-critical pretensions.

Perhaps the most appropriate explication one can offer of Paddy's story is to suggest that Paddy's experience moves from sufficiency to inadequacy. At the start, Paddy is suffused by feelings of possession and belonging. 'We owned Barrytown, the whole lot of it. It went on forever.' These gradually give way to a sense of displacement and isolation. As Gerry Smyth notes,

> If Barrytown, like Ireland, was a country, then like Ireland in the 1960s it was soon to have the myth of national possession and self-sufficiency shattered. The fields and cows disappear, newer and bigger gangs take over, and Paddy finds himself boycotted by his former friends because of the social stigma attached to the break-up of the family.[13]

*Paddy Clarke* is, to a large extent, a novel about lost childhood. The novel is subtly divided into two skeins, one focusing on the world of children and the other on the world of adults. The former is characterised by the fact that all things make sense or that sense can, sometimes by means of fabricated explanations, easily be established. The latter, the adult world, behaves contrary to this. Here a wide gap can be found between essence and appearance. 'World War Three Looms Near' (p. 24) turns out to be nothing but a sensational headline in some newspaper; George Best's signature is not a real autograph (p. 137); Santa Claus does not exist (p. 31); and if you claim at the age of eight or nine that God has spoken to you, your parents will argue with you (pp. 52f.). The world of the grown-ups does not make sense to Paddy. There he can connect nothing with anything. If he occasionally succeeds, then this happens more by way of coincidence than otherwise, possible at times as a result of what Paddy has learned in school (p. 26). Explanations are either too seldom or too inadequately offered by the adults. Yet communication between the grown-ups and the children is fraught in both directions. Thus, for instance, Paddy is unable to tell his mother what he did not like about the zoo (p. 140), or why he does not want her to wash all the venetian blinds: 'I couldn't explain it; it was kind of a secret' (p. 164). This state of affairs seems quite normal. It only develops into a kind of emotional helter-skelter after the fights between his parents make themselves felt. The more chaotic and senseless the situation at home becomes, the more his relationship with his friends gets out of joint. Paddy tries to be like Charley Leavy (p. 250), in fact he forces himself upon Charley without much success, thus severing himself from his former group of friends. This attitude culminates in Paddy's fight with his best friend Kevin (pp. 272ff.). Paddy may win the fight, but he does so by losing his friend. In the end, the other boys boycott and ridicule him by shouting:

> — Paddy Clarke —
> Paddy Clarke —
> Has no da.
> Ha ha ha!

Doyle has subtly delineated Paddy's loss of childhood against the background of what may be called a broken pastoral. The Barrytown of the trilogy is just being built in *Paddy Clarke*. The houses in which Paddy and his friends live were erected in the open countryside. Such suburbs seem like a modern pastoral idyll. But it is a broken one. The only farm, Donnelly's, is a ruin; the farmer has moved to the new farm (p. 111) with his family and his animals; we are not told where that is. The fields have remained untilled; they now serve Paddy and his mates for running around in them. The act of running appears to symbolise limitless freedom. Yet Paddy calls the fields 'untouched' (p. 116). They are untouched because they are no longer in use. They are also untouched as yet by the building of the Corporation houses. At the close of the book harmony and idyll are no longer feasible: the last fields have been built upon; Paddy's parents have separated, and Paddy himself is made into an object of derision. In conjunction with the use of the broken pastoral notion, Doyle has employed the motif of the North American Indian. It permeates the narrative, signifying Paddy's yearning for unbounded freedom, on the one hand, while at the same time pointing at a similarity between the way Paddy loses his pastoral idyll and the way the Indians lost theirs.

Most critics are agreed that *The Woman Who Walked Into Doors* is Doyle's most convincing novel to date. The narrative is in the form of a heart-rending, deeply agonising monologue. It is not a soliloquy, because Paula Spencer is trying to communicate with someone about her miserable existence. Doyle tries to show, through Paula's words and point of view, the contradictions thrown up by the acts of violence, the guilt, self-hatred and victimisation that she has to suffer in addition to her husband's physical assaults.[14]

Paula notes of herself: 'I'm a sucker for romance'.[15] Her life with Charlo Spencer may have begun as a romance, but it certainly did not end as such. This is what happened to Paula when she first met her future husband:

> I swooned the first time I saw Charlo. I actually did. I didn't faint or fall on the floor but my legs went rubbery on me and I giggled. I suddenly knew that I had lungs because they were empty and collapsing. (p. 3)

They danced, and Paula comments: 'I put my head on his shoulder. He had me' (p. 4). He was 'the King' for her, and that made her someone, 'Not a Queen or a Princess, just someone. It was a start. It filled me' (p. 54). But now Charlo is dead. A year after Paula threw him out of the house, he was shot by the gardaí when he tried to make his get-away during an abortive attempt to extort money from a bank manager. Charlo was holding the man's wife hostage in their house. Suddenly he saw Special Branch men closing in on the area and he lost his cool and killed the woman. He ran off to the stolen car and climbed inside. Then he remembered that he was incapable of driving a motor car, never having possessed a car himself or ever had any driving lessons. He was shot while he was trying to get out of the vehicle. Before Paula met him, Charlo had been in prison for robbery. But he was a builder; he had a job. Paula is going over her memories in order to come to terms with her plight.

In her recollection, she tries to convince herself that she had a happy childhood and a loving, caring father, both of which her sister Carmel denies (cf. for instance p. 11). Carmel herself got married when she was seventeen. She would have married anyone just to get out of the house (cf. p. 47). The entire misery probably began as early as Paula's childhood, despite her insisting upon the following:

> Once upon a time my life had been good. My parents had loved me. The house was full of laughter. I'd run to school every morning. (p. 56)

Wishful thinking, more likely than not. For reality would seem to have been quite different. There was, for instance, the fact that where Paula grew up young girls were easily called sluts, whether they liked it or not.

> Where I grew up [...] you were a slut or a tight bitch, one or the other, if you were a girl — and usually before you were thirteen. You didn't have to do anything to be a slut. If you were good-looking; if you grew up fast. If you had a sexy walk; if you had clean hair; if you had dirty hair. [...] Anything could get you called a slut. My father called me a slut the first time I put on mascara. (pp. 45f.)

Paula was a slut before she was a proper teenager, before she knew anything about sex, before she even left primary school. 'My father said it, fellas said it, other girls said it, men in vans and lorries said it' (p. 47). The first time she went with a fellow was when she was only eleven. A long string of other fellows followed. Still she insists: 'It was great then, that year or two, from ten to eleven or so. It was all fun' (p. 82). Yet, she is clear-eyed enough to add: 'But it got complicated after that, and nasty'.

There was also no happy running to school. School was a nightmare.

The teachers, if they were not perverts, were either stupid or bored or women, and the only good thing about the women teachers was that they did not mess around with Paula and her fellow-pupils. School made her rough; she was not that way before she started there. 'Now I had to act rough and think dirty. I had to fight. I had to be hard' (p. 35). It makes little difference that she adds: 'maybe it all happens anyway, when you're growing up, no matter where you are'. Most probably things of that nature do not happen 'no matter where you are', but most likely they do occur in the second-lowest class, 1.6, where Paula ended up, eventually 'wanking a good-looking thick in the back of the classroom' (p. 41).

A good while later (notably enough there is no mention of her ever having worked), she was swept off her feet by Charlo. Charlo and Paula got engaged not least in order to spite Paula's father, who was against the liaison, hating Charlo and calling him a waster, a criminal. Does one dare add: who would blame him? No matter, Paula contends that after their wedding they were happy, for a while. She could see a smile on Charlo's face that said: I love you and I want to rip your clothes off. 'A smile that said We're going to live happily ever after. He believed it. I believed it' (p. 134). Their honeymoon in Courtown was a great success. She can still vividly and lovingly remember details of their mutual experiences in Mrs Doyle's guest-house (cf. p. 154), and plenty of sex, though little tenderness. At one point, she expressly states: 'We were very, very happy' (p. 167).

Yet things started to go downhill not long after the honeymoon. And then he started to hit her. She had said that there was a smell on his breath, and 'whack' was the answer. She went to a doctor: whack again. He followed her. 'There's nothing wrong with you; what's your problem? Whack. And I loved him when he didn't do it; I loved him with all my heart. He was so kind. He just lost his temper, sometimes' (p. 158). In her retelling of her abuse, she always wavers between criticism of her husband and self-accusation, between self-assertion and subjugation. When it happened, she had told him: '– Make your own fuckin' tea' (p. 169). More often than not, she feels that it was all her own fault:

> But sometimes I can't help thinking that I could have avoided it, I could have been cleverer. I could have made that fuckin' tea. [...] it wouldn't have killed me. He'd had his moods before. I'd seen them. I recognised them. I could have seen it coming. Instead, I provoked him. And now, here I am.

— Make your own fuckin' tea. (p. 169)

She goes even further to note in parenthesis:

> (I keep blaming myself. After all the years and broken bones and
> teeth and torture I still keep on blaming myself. I can't help it.
> What if? What if? He wouldn't have hit me if I hadn't...[...] (p.
> 170)

Charlo kicked Paula up the stairs and he kicked her down the stairs. He
burned her, scalded her, threatened her, thumped her, raped her for
seventeen years. She became the woman who walked into doors, a
euphemism for a battered wife. And all these seventeen years she was
craving attention, interest, understanding and compassion. But no one
seemed to care. 'Ask me ask me ask me', she repeatedly pleads (for
instance p. 187). It is a desperate cry for help. 'Broken nose, loose teeth,
cracked ribs. Ask me' (p. 187). Yet, all that people did — the doctors,
the neighbours, even her own mother and father — was ignore her,
look through instead of at her:

> I could walk through crowds. I could see all these people but they
> didn't see me. They could see the hand that held out the money.
> They could see the hand that held open the door. [...] They could
> see the mouth that spoke the words. [...] But they couldn't see
> me. The woman who wasn't there. The woman who had nothing
> wrong with her. The woman who was fine. The woman who
> walked into doors. (p. 187)

She goes on to remark:

> My mother looked and saw nothing. My father saw nothing, and
> he loved what he didn't see. My brothers saw nothing. His mother
> saw nothing. [...] The woman who kept walking into doors. (p.
> 187)

But when did it all start? At one point Paula says that Charlo started
beating her up after he had lost his job (cf. p. 192). But she then reasons:

> I could rest if I believed that; I could rest. But I keep on thinking
> and I'll never come to a tidy ending. [...] Why did he do it? No real
> answers come, no big Aha. (p. 192)

It is all such a frightful mess, such terrible confusion.

> He loved me and he beat me. I loved him and I took it. It's as simple as that, and as stupid and compli-cated. It's terrible. (p. 192)

Yet, on another occasion she suggests that Charlo hated her for being pregnant, for not being his little Paula any more — 'and he drew his fist back and hit me' (p. 163). To escape her misery, she flees into daydreams featuring the likes of Robert Redford or Bruce Willis (p. 58) or imaginary men — a barman, a plumber or an electrician (p. 100): 'I ran away in my dreams' (p. 210). She also withdraws into alcoholism. She started to drink because drink helped; drink calmed her down; drink gave her something to search for and do (cf. p. 212). It was as simple and as complex as that. One of her sons died, 'cot death' (p. 84), or so she imagined, once when she was absolutely plastered, and she swore never to drink again. But she could not give up the booze:

> I am an alcoholic. I've never admitted it to anyone. (No one would want to know.) I've never done anything about it; I've never tried to stop. I think I could if I really wanted to, if I was ready. (p. 88)

But she has not been ready yet, not even now after Charlo's death while she is putting her plight into words. The picture she conveys of herself now is this:

> She'll be thirty-nine in two months' time. Give her a mirror, and some make-up and a half-hour, and she'll make herself look thirty. See her when she's getting out of bed and she'll look fifty. She's an office-cleaner; she gets two-fifty an hour. She does houses as well in the mornings. [...] She has four children. She is a widow. She is an alcoholic. She has holes in her heart that never stop killing her. (p. 43)

She is still on the bottle. Sometimes she simply has to get out, cannot stand it any longer — the dirt, the emptiness, the stuffing coming out of the furniture, and nothing in the fridge. 'I can't cope. The urge. The bottle. I have to get out' (p. 103). Hers is a terribly miserable existence. At times, she would like to see someone worse off than herself; but she can only get comfort from the telly, the reports from the Third World on the News or pictures from Sarajevo. '[...] but they all seemed to have good warm clothes' (p. 10), she notes. Her own children never had such clothes.

The point about Paula is that in the end, after seventeen years of walking into doors, she is still capable of mustering enough strength to survive: she can still pick herself up.

> I never gave up.
> I'm here.
> I picked myself up. I washed the blood off my face. I put
> on the kettle. (p. 205)

As one critic has suggested, at the end of the book Paula is half in and half out of the door, an image that represents the threshold between self-control and subjection.[16] She has reclaimed her role as mother and homemaker, even though she may still depend on alcohol to carry on. 'I could never get past the door' (p. 209), she writes. But she finally had the will and the power to hit Charlo over the head with a pan and throw him out of the house. 'It was a great feeling. I'd done something good' (p. 226). This, significantly, is the last line of her searching account.

Paula's story is of course not structured in the chronological fashion in which I have presented it. It rather hopscotches about among Paula's recollections and conveys the impression of having been penned in random fashion, just in the way in which her memories assail her. The only conspicuous features that seem to effect a rudimentary sort of compositional patterning are certain recurrent passages which appear to treat of traumatic key experiences. Here are two such passages. The first describes the moment when Paula found herself on the floor after having been hit by Charlo, presumably the first time he did so:

> I knew nothing for a while, where I was, how come I was on the
> floor. Then I saw Charlo's feet, then his legs making a triangle
> with the floor. He seemed way up over me. Miles up. I had to
> bend back to see him. [etc.] (pp. 5, 175)

The second one concerns the fact that the doctor she went to see, hoping to get help from him and be able to express her devastating grief, did not care in the least:

> The doctor never looked at me. He studied parts of me but he

never saw all of me. He never looked at my eyes. Drink, he said to himself. I could see his nose moving, taking in the smell, deciding. (pp. 23, 164, 186)

The apparent randomness of the design shows that what Paula has put to paper *are* memories. She herself states:

That's the thing about memories. I can't pick and choose them. I can't pretend. [...] I can never settle into a nice memory, lie back and smile. (p. 197)

A little further on, she appropriately notes:

It's all a mess — there's no order or sequence. I have dates, a beginning and an end, but the years in between won't fall into place. (p. 203)

It is an excellent way of characterising Paula's approach and of supplying a *raison d'être* for the book's structure.

*The Woman Who Walked Into Doors* is meant to be Paula's work. She has written it, thereby proving that she is capable of exercising control. We find her in a position where she is able to tell her story. That she is responsible for the account becomes apparent through a number of metadiscursive comments. Thus at one point she declares in parenthesis: '(It kills me writing that and reading it — *I could never afford good shoes for my kids.* I don't put all the blame on him either.)' (p. 10). Gerry Smyth sees the effect of introducing the metadiscursive comments as follows:

I would suggest that Doyle's introduction of the metadiscursive aspects [...] is a way of defamiliar-ising the narrative, not in order to alienate the reader from Paula's plight, but rather to highlight the issues of authority and responsibility which are the actual themes of the novel. In effect, the text is asking the reader a series of questions. Can language describe violence? How does literature relate to the 'real'? Can a person tell the story of his or her own life? How reliant are notions of identity and character on textual devices? Can a man tell a woman's story? It is indicative of Doyle's skill that when he employs formal defamiliarising techniques [...] the effect is to heighten rather than mitigate the message of the novel.[17]

There are rather a lot of questions here that the metadiscursive statements allegedly ask, and while some of them do make some sense ('How does literature relate to the 'real'?') others are quite silly ('Can a man tell a woman's story?'). Nor do the remarks really defamiliarise the story. They merely throw into relief the fact that Paula is in authority; she is the implied authoress — a woman who has acquired the skill to write impressive passages such as this:

> I walked to the end of the cul-de-sac. There were cars in front of most of the houses. People in; someone was looking — there had to be somebody. Looking at a wet woman in her daughter's jacket. There was a small park at the end of the road and another road at the other end of it, to the left. That must have been where they'd parked their car, Charlo and Richie Massey. I wasn't going to go over there. (Does blood leave a stain on cement?) In front of me, to the right, over a bunch of bluey-green trees, there was a beautiful house, like a castle. A really beautiful thing with two round roofs shaped like cones. And windows in them. A gorgeous-looking place. People lived in that. There was a weather cock on top of the highest roof. It wasn't moving. I don't think I'd ever seen a weather cock before, or noticed one. Arrows pointing four ways. People lived in there, had bedrooms in that roof. The trees in the park were in round groups. They looked old but the place seemed brand new. No cracks in the paths, no dog dirt. I looked over at where I thought Richie Massey had parked the car. I could feel nothing. [etc.] (pp. 145f.)

The metadiscursive statements provide comments on Paula's very own procedure, without aspiring to the status of postmodernist metafictional claptrap. Instead, these comments lead to the cardinal question of what Paula is trying to achieve by committing her experiences to paper. Once again, Paula herself supplies the answer:

> (I'm not. What Carmel says. Rewriting history. I'm doing the opposite. I want to know the truth, not make it up. [...]) (p. 57)

Her writing constitutes a sense-making process. It is an effort to get at the truth, to come to grips with her own life. Repeatedly, she admonishes herself to adhere to 'Facts' (cf. for instance p. 104). Or she notes:

> I'm messing around here. Making things up; a story. I'm begin-
> ning to enjoy it. Hair *rips*. Why don't I say He pulled my hair?
> *Someone is crying. Someone is vomiting.* I cried, *I* fuckin' well vomited.
> [...] I don't want to make it up, I don't want to add to it. I don't
> want to lie. I don't have to; there's no need. I want to tell the
> truth. Like it happened. Plain and simple. (pp. 184f.)

Her entire account represents an utterly honest attempt to understand
her life, to face the truth and not seek consolation in alcohol. By the
same token, she wants to understand why after seventeen years of abuse
she still loves Charlo:

> I loved him when I was throwing him out. I loved him when
> Gerard [the Garda who came to tell her of Charlo's death] rang
> the bell. I love him now. (p. 24)

Paula may still, as she admits, occasionally need a drink, but the fact that
we find her capable of writing her story down and not straying from
the facts marks another decisive step in her efforts to become the woman
who can walk past the door.

The cover design of Roddy Doyle's latest novel to date, *A Star
Called Henry* (1999), may serve to deconstruct the marketing design that
the publisher has thought fit to deploy presumably on account of Doyle's
enormous sales figures. The author's name is printed on the dust-jacket
in bold red letters over one inch long, whereas the book's title is given in
slim white letters barely a quarter of an inch tall. This must be taken to
mean that a potential buyer is intended to go for the book not because
it is by Roddy Doyle *and* a new narrative offering, in which case the title
should have been represented in a manner more akin to that of the
author's name, but first and foremost because it is by Roddy Doyle and
never mind its contents. Perhaps this is as it should be, for *A Star Called
Henry* is, in the final analysis, an execrably bad novel.

What is Doyle up to in *A Star Called Henry*? He has written a historical
novel about the Irish Republic's first twenty-two years in the twentieth
century, reviewing, in particular, the politico-historical events during
the Easter Rising, the War of Independence and the founding of the
Free State and pointing out, for instance, that the Volunteers in the
GPO were a bunch of rosary-clutching gobshites:

> Some of the Volunteers had their beads out and were down on

their knees, humming the rosary. [...] Like a come-all-ye, the prayer was taken up by other men [...], down on their socialist knees. I took my eyes from the street for a few seconds and watched Connolly across the hall, grinding his teeth; I could almost hear them crumbling above the rosary drone. Pearse was in a corner, on a high stool, his head in a notebook; he was mumbling as well. Collins, to be fair to him, looked ready to go in among them and kick them back to earth.[18]

The leaders, such as Pearse (with 'arms [that] had no more muscle than his poetry', p. 124), Collins ('[Collins] loved his horseplay. As long as he was the horse.', p. 198), de Valera and others were no more than Catholic capitalists ('- Catholic and capitalist, Henry. It's an appalling combination', p. 116). In short, the Irish Fight for Freedom only replaced one exploitative government with another that turned out to be no less exploitative, without any interest whatsoever in the poor and socially underprivileged, who, before and after the Big Historical Change, got it equally squarely in the neck. Thus Doyle has, bravely enough, written a chapter of revisionist Irish history, for which act he has got it, and will continue to get it, in the neck himself. This is of course deplorably unfair, but must be expected if someone debunks the political and historical holy of holies of any given country as a mere myth. In all fairness, though, Doyle should not be excoriated for having a snipe at the hallowed founding fathers of the Irish Republic, but rather for the manner in which he has gone about the business. *A Star Called Henry* is an exasperating novel principally because Doyle's iconoclastic act of revisionism in the end fails to work and that is due to the flawed manner in which its protagonist, Henry Smart (*nomen est omen*), and by extension Doyle himself, has rendered his story.

But first, what of that story? The novel is divided into four parts. Part I deals with Henry Smart's childhood. Born into the Dublin slums of 1901, Henry is the son of a one-legged bouncer-cum-jobbing-hitman, who worked at Dolly Oblong's brothel and also settled scores for her partner, the mysterious Alfie Gandon, obligingly bumping off Gandon's enemies, preferably with a clout from his wooden leg, and getting rid of the bodies piece by piece in the rivers, streams and canals of Dublin environs. His mother, Melody, married at sixteen, after having walked into her future husband, causing him, being utterly stocious with drink and holding himself up on a number seven shovel because he was missing his wooden leg, to fall to the ground. She helped him get up and hobble along, and soon enough the two of them wound up before a priest to be married. Melody succumbed to consumption and alcoholism by her early twenties. When Henry was five, she became too sick to look after her children, and Henry took to the streets together with his eighteen-month-old brother Victor, shouting 'Fuck off' at King Edward V when he was parading the city in July 1907. For three years, the two boys lived under boxes, in hallways and on wasteland:

> I had Victor, my father's leg and nothing else. I was bright but illiterate, strapping but always sick. I was handsome and filthy and bursting out of my rags. And I was surviving. (p. 70)

Henry eked out a living by turning his hand to everything from ordinary thieving to rat-catching and mutilating cattle to order. On the day of George V's coronation, little Victor died, and Doyle has him expire in a way worthy of a Victorian weepie.

Cut to Easter 1916 and Part II, which focuses on certain events during the Rising. Henry is now fourteen and wearing the uniform of the Irish Citizen Army. The incidents highlighted confirm the view that much, if not all, that happened was of the Keystone Cops variety, such as when Henry remarks:

> We marched out across Sackville Street [now of course O'Connell Street]. Behind me, the horses pulled two lorries, full of our pick-axes, crowbars, sledges — weapons for the working men's war: Connolly's idea of urban warfare was tunnelling, knocking down walls, advance and retreat without having to go out into the rain — our few extra rifles and pistols, boxes of cartridges, bayonets, hatchets, cleavers. We marched straight across the wide street and felt the power as we stopped the trams and cars and people gaped and wondered. There were British officers outside the Metropole Hotel. They were used to marching Paddies. They laughed and one or two of them waved. (p. 94)

What is actually told of the occurrences during the Easter Rising amounts to pretty little if assessed within the context of an historical novel: the confusion inside the GPO and the mayhem on the street outside (looting, real fireworks set off by kids who had broken into Lawrence's toy and sports bazaar, the shawlies' attack, Lewis and Vickers and Maxim guns that kept going at the GPO, the eventual escape from the GPO into

Henry Street via a building backing onto it, the unconditional surrender, the killing of a few rebels, Henry's get-away through a manhole and some waterways under Dublin, and, not to be forgotten, Henry's copulating with his former teacher Miss O'Shea, whom he subsequently married and whose first name he — and the reader — never learns:

> I was falling onto my back when it happened. I'd been pushed on top of a high bed made of blocks of stamps, sheets and sheets of the things, columns of them, sticky side up. I was stuck there with my britches nuzzling my ankles as Miss O'Shea grabbed my knees and climbed on top of me. (p. 119)

Generally speaking, the description of the events inside and outside the GPO is somewhat chaotic, lacking a discernible *raison d'être*. At best, it might be said that, yes, this is exactly what they were — chaotic. And yet, one must be forgiven for suspecting that Doyle has not got it in him to offer more. One side-effect of this kind of narrative procedure is that it puts a strain on the reader to concretise in his imagination what is being told.

Henry finds himself in the General Post Office along with a collection of largely middle-class revolutionaries. He is convinced he is fighting to avenge the wrongs suffered by his family and his class and to create a glorious new world. But he is forced to realise that the Volunteers and most of the revolutionaries are Catholic, Anglophobic, stupid and petit bourgeois ('We were fighting a class war. We weren't in the same battle at all as the rest of the rebels', p. 107). They abhor the looters out on Sackville Street and they detest the shawlies who beat a path to the G.P.O. door in search of the pensions of their men folk, who are on the Western front. The Volunteers ('the poets and farmboys, the fuckin' shopkeepers', p. 103), who cannot understand how poverty determines behaviour, see these women and their men as pro-British traitors:[19]

> The women weren't giving up. I could see some of them, climbing over their friends to get at the door. A bunch of shawlies they were, all shapes and ages under their black hoods; they'd come down from Summerhill and I knew why. They were here to collect their allowances. Their men were over in France, or dead under the muck. And the shawlies wanted their money. (p. 101)

In Part III, Henry goes underground and comes to live with Piano Annie,

who was one of the shawlies. He becomes a docker, working under a
fat dwarf as stevedore who is in the habit of fornicating with the wives
of all the men he presides over. Henry is made to shovel coal and
phosphorite. His granny, who miraculously acquired the ability to read
at Henry's birth, has meanwhile progressed to *Don Quixote* and *Confessions
of an English Opium Eater* (p. 162). One of Henry's overriding interests is
to find out who Alfie Gandon is, for whom Henry's father killed off a
number of men. One day Henry bumps into Jack Dalton, who will later
become an influential member of the government of the Free State.
Dalton tells him of the revolutionary plans for the New Ireland. But
Henry senses that from his own point of view there is a good deal
amiss about these plans:

> [...] it struck me even then [...] that his Ireland was a very small
> place. Vast chunks of it didn't fit his bill; he had grudges stored
> up against the inhabitants of most of the counties. His republic
> was going to be a few blameless pockets, connected to the capital
> by vast bridges of his own design. (p. 171)

Still, Henry finds himself ready to die for Ireland again, but now it is a
version of Ireland 'that [has] little or nothing to do with the Ireland I'd
gone out to die for the last time' (p. 171). He becomes a Volunteer,
joining the First Battalion, F Company. It is the time of Michael Collins,
and before he can bat an eyelid Henry is sworn into the Irish
Revolutionary Brotherhood, and he goes to stay in the Irish Midlands,
training IRA volunteers in Rusg, in the course of which activity he meets
Miss O'Shea and in September 1919 they marry, and together they
conduct a kind of Bonnie-and-Clyde terror campaign, setting the
Midlands ablaze in the name of Irish freedom. He is next made one of
Collins's Twelve Apostles and stiffs dozens of spies for his boss (none
of them real spies, it turns out, just men with minds of their own whom
the Republican Movement could not tolerate.)[20]

 In Part IV, Henry is in Kilmainham Gaol. But he manages to escape
with the help of Miss O'Shea. It is now the period of 'executions and
counter-executions, reprisals and counter-reprisals' (p. 310), and for much
of the time Henry and his wife are on the run. One day, he encounters
a rebel leader called Ivan, whom Henry himself had trained in the
Midlands. Ivan is quite an influential man now, and he, without so much
as a by your leave, tells Henry to call off his wife, who through her
campaigns is ruining his business by 'interfering with free trade' (p. 316):

Nobody works without the nod from Ivan. A sweet doesn't get sucked without a good coating of the profit ending up on Ivan's tongue. I'm a roaring success, boy. (p. 315)

And when Ivan remarks: 'I'll be ready to lead my people into a new Ireland', Henry counters: '— And it'll be very like the old one' (p. 315). A short while later, Henry is shown his very own death warrant by another of his former revolutionary cronies, and after crossing 'Ireland in the groundwater' (p. 328) for months and after having been able to see his daughter, somewhat oddly named Freedom ('Saoirse'), Henry, now aged twenty, flees to Liverpool.

The picture that emerges of the Irish Fight for Freedom during the first two decades of the twentieth century, as of the Free State, is none too complimentary, to say the least. The members of the RIC and the G-Division as well as the soldiers, the Black and Tans and the Auxiliaries were not the monsters of Republican lore. They were just hard-nosed men who did a job and they did their job well. The founding fathers of the Republic had no vision and no genuine commitment to improving the lot of the Irish people. The glorious uprising, with its hundreds of dead people, achieved nothing more than the transfer of power to a questionable group of men who founded parties with Gaelic names that have milked the common men ever since.[21] Henry Smart takes part in some of the key events in Irish national history, but being a member of the underprivileged class he comes to the awareness that he has never been a true part of that history. In Doyle's hands, the grand patriotic narrative is tainted with a sharp sense of human frailty. Smart's sympathies lie unequivocally with his own social class. He is a disciple of James Connolly and a soldier in the socialist revolutionary Irish Citizen Army. In the end, though, he is compelled to admit that Irish socialism was interred with Connolly's bones and that the subsequent leaders had not the faintest interest in social justice or people like him. Under the cloak of Irish national liberation, the main concern of most of the influential revolutionaries did not extend much beyond merely changing the personnel in Dublin Castle, beyond painting the pillar boxes green and ensuring the continued sanctity of private property rights. The Irish revolution, as depicted here, is far too true to be good. It is shown riven with petty jealousies, murderous passions, anti-Semitic prejudice and ruthless self-advancement. 1916 was ultimately a bourgeois affair, since very little changed for those who had very little in the first place. When, towards the end, a former rebel leader and erstwhile friend of Henry's presents Henry with his death warrant, Henry asks:

> — Why?
> — Well, he said, if you're not with us you're against us. That's the thinking. And there are those who reckon that you're always going to be against us. And they're probably right. You've no stake in the country, man. Never had, never will. We needed trouble-makers and very soon now we'll have to be rid of them. And that, Henry, is all you are and ever were. A trouble-maker. The best in the business, mind. But — (pp. 326f.)

Post-revolutionary Ireland is run by men like Alfie Gandon, who now spells his surname Ó Gandúin. During the War of Independence, he was Mister Gandon, a businessman, a Home Ruler and a Catholic. Later someone says of him:

> He's a giant in this city [...]. Property, transport, banking, Corpo. He's in on them all. He's a powerful man, Henry. And a good fellow. There's more widows and orphans living off that fella's generosity than the nuns could ever handle. And he doesn't like to boast about it either. Chamber of Commerce, Gaelic League and a great sodality man. (p. 189)

When Dáil Éireann is formed in 1919, Alfie Gandon or Mr Ó Gandúin becomes Minister of Commercial Affairs and the Sea (p. 209). During the Great War, he is said to have very quickly 'become respectable, the party of the parish priests and those middle-class men cute enough to know when the wind was changing. It was the party of money and faith' (p. 207). When the Free State is born, he is holding down two ministries (p. 328), 'a national politician, of a nation eager to prove itself to the world' (p. 336). But Henry Smart realises that while he was training country boys for the IRA, his fellow revolutionaries were adding letters to their names: Michael Collins MP, Denis Acher MP, Alfred Gandon MP, Jack Dalton MP. He may have been bang in the middle of what was going to become big, big history, and he may have been 'one of Collins's anointed' (p. 208), but actually he was excluded from everything. None of the men of the slums and hovels ever made it onto the list. 'We were nameless and expendable, every bit as dead as the squaddies in France. [...] We were decoys and patsies. We followed orders and murdered' (p. 208)

All this naturally amounts to a powerful debunking of the shibboleths of the 1916 Rebellion, the War of Independence and the Civil War. The pity, though, is that Doyle should have elected to cloak his devastating critique as he did. It is done in a manner that, for various reasons, beggars credulity. To begin with, it is not a good idea to have a radical exposé of the shibboleths of a most crucial period in Ireland's history — and one that is intended to be taken seriously — presented by a foul-mouthed narrator who is inevitably bound to discredit whatever he is offering through his utterly unreliable way of telling it. Doyle presumably chose such a narratorial voice because, as his previous novels show, he is good at it. Yet the problem is that too much Doyle codology is thereby permitted to enter into the account for it to be convincing. Moreover, the character of Henry Smart is, in many ways, too good to be true. Here are a few examples of how he presents himself:

> I was a broth of an infant, the wonder of Summerhill and beyond. I was the big news, a local legend within hours of landing on the newspaper. (p. 22)

> I had charm and invention. Women saw the future Henry under my crust and they melted; they saw a future they wanted now and badly and knew they'd never get. They wanted to touch me but couldn't, so they patted little Victor instead. (p. 65)

> I was six foot, two inches tall and had the shoulders of a boy built to carry the weight of the world. I was probably the best-looking man in the G.P.O. [...] My eyes were astonishing, blue daggers that warned the world to keep its distance. (p. 89)

> My eyes were blue and fascinating whirlpools, they could suck in women while warning them to stay well away, a fighting combination that had them running at me. (p. 108)

Why should this be so? Dashing, intelligent, irresistibly handsome (curiously the terrible privations of his early life had no adverse effect on his development), he is physically almost perfect. This contestable state of affairs is mitigated only by Henry's very patchy moral sense, though we are led to believe that he will come good in the end. Also why should his birth be surrounded by preternatural events? The midwife who delivers him finds that her hands mysteriously tingle ever afterwards.

Additional miracles occur. His illiterate crone of a grandmother strangely acquires the ability to read: 'Granny Nash [...] picked up the *Freeman's Journal* and discovered that she could read' (p. 22). Finally, baby Henry's 'shite' is collected every evening and transported to Lady Gregory's rose-bushes at Coole Park (p. 23).

Why, to continue, has Doyle seen fit to people his novel with so many grotesques, like Piano Annie, with whom Henry shacks up after the Rising, or the priapic dwarf? Henry's female counterpart, Miss O'Shea, becomes another legendary figure, battling valiantly for personal and political liberty by pedalling around on a bicycle with a machine-gun fixed to its handlebars. Gifted with superhuman fortitude, she carries the wounded Henry to safety when her arm is riddled with bullets. Black and Tans and Sinn Féiners alike detest her unwomanly presumptions. Only Henry approves of her demands for sexual parity. Book-perusing Granny Nash is another oddity, at one time seen reading two books at one and the same time (p. 117).

The entire business with Henry's father's wooden leg is simply too risible. For example, during the Anglo-Irish war Henry wields his only legacy, the said wooden leg, to tremendous effect, and murders merrily in the name of Cathleen Ní Houlihan. Henry's childhood is so grim that its poverty makes the world of Frank McCourt's *Angela's Ashes* look like sheer blooming luxury. The fetid details of slum life in Dublin and torture and barbarity in the city's prisons are supplied in great profusion, but squalor and savagery keep being smothered under facetiousness. It is rather whimsical to have Henry's father and then Henry after him make their escapes from the rozzers and soldiers 'be the water', meaning via the subterranean waterways of Dublin, Harry Lime fashion. The sex-scene in the GPO during the Easter Rising is a laugh, and it puts a completely new complexion on the meaning of the term Easter, erm, Rising. The death of little Victor puts one in mind of Oscar Wilde's remark that one must have a heart of stone not to laugh at the death of Little Nell in Dickens's *The Old Curiosity Shop*. Certain aspects of Doyle's revisionist account, although mildly amusing, are out of place in an attempt of this sort that wants to be taken in earnest. Thus Henry claims:

> I'd played *The Last Post* at the grave of O'Donovan Rossa the year before. The history books will tell you that it was William Oman, but don't believe them: he was tucked up at home with the flu. (p. 90)

Or take his contention that when the famous photograph was taken of de Valera after the surrender, he, Henry, had been standing next to the great man:

> The photographer was a bollocks called Hanratty. [...] The first time I saw the photo my elbow was in it, but even that went in later versions. No room for Henry's elbow. [...] If Hanratty had moved his camera, just a bit to the right, just a fraction of a bit. I'd have been in. (pp. 138f.)

The idea may be designed to underscore Henry's conviction according to which there was no real place for the poor in the Irish Fight for Freedom, and yet the same point could have been made in a less flippant manner. Lastly, why should only the poor and underprivileged have been decent during the time and events in question?

It could probably be argued that Doyle has peppered his narrative with all those imbecilities in order to forestall critical reactions against his reading of Irish history. After all, he may point out, this is not really his own interpretation of the events during those crucial twenty-odd years in the twentieth century, but that of his foul-mouthed protagonist who alone is responsible for the shortcomings and inconsistencies singled out here. But such an argument simply will not wash. *A Star Called Henry* is the first novel in a projected series of three entitled *The Last Roundup*. Quite conceivably, there are any number of readers who cannot wait for the next two books to appear. But I definitely can.

# DERMOT BOLGER

Dermot Bolger was born in Finglas, a suburb of north Dublin, on 6 February 1959. His mother (who died in 1969) was the daughter of a Monaghan farmer, and his father (now retired) was a sailor. Bolger attended St Canice's Boys National School and later Beneavin College, both in Finglas. In 1977, after finishing school, he spent a year trying to establish a community arts group, Raven Arts, staging festivals. To finance the project, he found a job in 1978 as a factory hand in a plant producing welding rods, an experience on which his first novel, *Night Shift* (1985), was based. In 1979, he started work as a library assistant, mainly working on mobile libraries on the outskirts of Dublin, until 1984, when he became a full-time writer and publisher. In 1979, he had founded the Raven Arts Press, which published some of his own books of poetry, his first novel, work by then-unnoticed writers such as Paul Durcan and Matthew Sweeney, as well as various anthologies that he edited: *After the War Is Over* (1984), the Irish writers' protest at the visit of Ronald Reagan; *The Bright Wave/ An Tonn Gheal* (1986), the first dual-language anthology of contemporary Irish-language poetry; *Letters from the New Island* (1987–1989), a polemical series of pamphlets on Irish politics and culture. He closed down the Raven Arts Press in 1992 and is now executive editor of New Island Books, which, among others, brought out his editions of *Selected Poems of Francis Ledwidge* (1992) and *Ireland in Exile* (1993), the first anthology of writing by Irish authors living outside Ireland.

When Bolger was fifteen, Anthony Cronin recognised his talent and got him published in *The Irish Times* and *Profile*, an anthology of new Irish writers. Since then, he has brought out collections of poetry, for instance *The Habit of Flesh* (1979), *Finglas Lilies* (1980), *No Waiting America* (1981), *Internal Exiles* (1986), and *Leinster Street Ghosts* (1989). He has had plays produced in Dublin and elsewhere: *The Lament of Arthur Cleary* (1989), which won the Samuel Beckett Award, the Stewart Parker BBC Award, and Edinburgh Fringe First; *Blinded by the Light* (1990), which won the O.Z. Whitehead Prize; *In High Germany* (1990); *The Holy Ground* (1990); and *One Last White Horse* (1991). He has also published six novels: *Night Shift* (1985), which won the AE Memorial Prize; *The Woman's Daughter* (1987), which won the Macaulay Fellowship, was short-listed for the Hughes Fiction Prize, and appeared in an extended version

in 1991; *The Journey Home* (1990), which was short-listed for the Hughes
Fiction Prize and in 1992 for *The Irish Times*/Aer Lingus Prize; *Emily's
Shoes* (1992), *A Second Life* (1994), and *Father's Music* (1997).

One of the themes that seem to fascinate Bolger is how the past
impinges upon the present. Thus, in the poems of *Leinster Street Ghosts*
he deals with the presences that people leave behind. All who have passed
remain as imperceptible witnesses. They are the people who have been
written out of history. Bolger's work is an attempt to preserve the
memory of wasted lives so that they may not have been in vain. The
poems in the other collections — for instance, in *Internal Exiles* — reflect
Bolger's concern for life in Ireland today, yet again seen against the
background of historical influences. Thus a second thematic interest
that runs through his work is with analysing what he seems to see as the
societal aberrations in post-colonial Ireland, quite frequently in
juxtaposition with an almost Yeatsian idyllic past of rural Ireland.

*A Dublin Quartet* (1992), a collection of four of his plays, paints a
grim picture of modern urban life in an Ireland poised on the uneasy
edge of the European Community. In *The Lament of Arthur Cleary*, which,
like *The Holy Ground* and *One White Horse*, is indebted to surrealist stream-
of-consciousness theatre, Bolger offers a lament for a man who cannot
understand that the Ireland he left to go and fight on the Continent has,
upon his return, become a completely different and more dangerous
place, one run by crooks, property agents, modern-type gombeenmen
and drug pushers, where people feel uprooted, exploited, dispossessed,
and homeless. *The Holy Ground* presents the ruminations of a middle-
aged woman who has poisoned her husband because he stole her youth
and left her childless. *One Last White Horse* treats of how a young married
father, as a result of the poverty-stricken existence he is forced to lead,
becomes a heroin victim.

With *The Journey Home* (1990), Bolger appears to have aimed at the
class of fiction latterly known as 'dirty realism', much in vogue in the
US and written by such writers as Richard Ford and Cormac McCarthy.
In the terminology of Irish criticism, this form of narrative discourse
is also referred to as 'Northside Realism' (much to the chagrin of Bolger
and the other artists involved).[1] In *The Journey Home*, Francis Hanrahan,
Hano to his friend Shay, is on the run. Thugs hired by the grandsons of
one of Ireland's revolutionary heroes, Pascal and Patrick Plunkett
(property developer, moneylender and Junior Government Minister),
are on his heels. With Hano is Katie, or Cait, a street waif Shay has
befriended. Shay has obviously been killed. Flash forward to three days

ahead. Hano and Cait are at the end of their journey home. Home they have found in a dilapidated house in the country. After having made love, she has fallen asleep and he promises 'just this last time [to] bring back Shay to life'.[2] From this point on, the narrative develops three skeins, one describing the actual journey home, the second giving an account of Hano's life and friendship with Shay, and the third — for no apparent reason typeset in italics — offering strange material connected with Cait (or is it the dead Shay?) and grown decidedly dropsical with overeager efforts to bring in a poetical note.

Hano, nourished by childhood images of the rural Eden his father has told him about, grows up as a shy child of grey suburban streets. His first job lands him in the Voters' Register's office where he meets Shay, who is 'like a light switched on in a projector' (p. 24). (The quotation is just one specimen of Bolger's odd similes, comparisons and metaphors.) Shay introduces Hano to a grey Dublin underworld of nixers and dole, the description of which has tempted Bolger to lay it rather heavy on the reader, as horrors galore alternate with assorted vices and numerous instances of social as well as political corruption. What is wrong with the build-up of that world is that it involves too much telling and not enough showing. The description of office-life, Friday night's drinking, going on the spree, in fact Hano's whole initiation through Shay — all this is laboured, repetitive and prolix. Instead of achieving his intended effects by a matter-of-fact narrative style, Bolger has sought his salvation in an almost Elizabethan-esque blood-and-gore-and-guts technique, leaving no stops unpulled. Little surprise, then, that on top of his multifarious criminal leanings Pascal Plunkett should turn out to be a homosexual sod who makes an unequivocal pass at Hano.

The only time Hano had seemed at home was with an old woman in a caravan when he was still quite young. The woman represents 'a part of that barbarous race who had once controlled the land' (p. 182), a stalwart counterpoint to the industrialised Europeanised present-day Ireland. Needless to say, Hano and Cait journey towards her. And they find her — in spite of the fact that, having already been ancient when Hano saw her first, she must now be as old as Methuselah. Equally needless to say, when they arrive at the caravan Hano feels a sense of coming home. The caravan and the place where it is located are home because they do not represent the past, a fossilised rural world, as Hano had believed; he now senses that they are 'the future, [...] our destination, [...] nowhere' (p. 291). 'I never understood it until now', says Hano, 'soon it will be all that's left for the likes of you and I [*sic*] to belong to'

(p. 291). Such meretricious moralising and metaphorising, together with the italicised sections that appear to eff the ineffable make the novel hard to bear. Worst, though, is when Bolger, on the last three pages of the book, strives to milk his Hano–Shay story for some general comment on the state of affairs in present-day Ireland. In essence, this comment makes the point, almost Celtic Revivalist in kind, that the old Ireland, rural, racy, and rustic, is gone beyond retrieval. Home is lost. A Europeanised world is taking over.

There is anger in this novel as in others by Bolger, but this anger and the writer's proclivity towards subversiveness deplorably backfire. Declan Kiberd, for one, has sharply criticised Bolger for this aspect of his work:

> [...] the writing of Bolger and his colleagues was considerably less subversive than it sometimes took itself to be. In its underlying sentimentality about its youthful subjects as victims of social tyranny, it grossly exaggerated the malevolence and the importance of priests, teachers, politicians. Although it prided itself on its realistic engagement with the sordid aspects of Dublin life, it may have un-intentionally ratified the old pastoral notion of rural Ireland as real Ireland.[3]

It may be frequently difficult to agree with Declan Kiberd, particularly as concerns his opinions in *Inventing Ireland*, but here, for once, he surely has a point.

The extended version of *The Woman's Daughter* (1987) relies on the same questionable policy of employing three different skeins, without there being any intrinsic necessity for the division. The text also features imbecilities of quite a preposterous sort.

The reviewer in the *Sunday Tribune* felt that *The Woman's Daughter* was 'one of the essential Irish novels, certainly of this decade, and possibly of many others'.[4] Big words, forsooth, considering that in the final analysis the book represents quite pretentious stuff. What precisely it tries to express, the narrative itself seems to be uncertain about.

The opening is rightaway aiming at a poetical note:

> There is a city of the dead standing sentinel across from her window. Through the gully between them a swollen rivulet is frothing over smooth rocks brimming with the effervescent waste of factories. Within its boundaries grey slabs of granite are flecked with

shards of mud as sheets of rain churn up the black pools that nestle in the webbed tyre tracks.[5]

Walter Allen, discussing the achievement of Virginia Woolf as a writer, points out that she is often seen as 'a poet who used the medium of prose',[6] and he goes on to stress that she is 'at her weakest where she is most consciously the poet'. To his mind, the celebration of time in *To the Lighthouse*, like the interludes in *The Waves*, 'suffers from the usual faults of prose-poetry. It seems overwritten and pretentious'. Now, while it would be quite ridiculous to compare Bolger's writing with Mrs Woolf's, Bolger, too, most conspicuously strives towards prose-poetry, and there is likewise discernible, in the opening passages of *The Woman's Daughter*, a strenuous effort at a celebration of time, no less overwritten and utterly pretentious.

This is the first of three voices that feature in the account. Additionally, there are such curiosities as an official report about the titular woman and a letter by a neighbouring couple who are concerned about what is going on in the woman's house; but these only represent empty ploys. This initial voice subsequently appears to strive towards investing the story with some kind of mytho-historical significance, as when it states:

> This is the spot where the archers' horses paused first by the stream. They shook their manes that were caked with mud and lowered their noses towards the water. The king rode past with his lieutenants and stopped to examine the trees which the saint had planted there. [etc.] (p. 13)

What all this has to do with the story about the woman's daughter is not clear at this stage in the narrative; in fact, it remains somewhat unclear even at the very end.

The story of the woman's daughter is told by a second, omniscient-like voice that comments on the woman's daily activities, for example. And there is a third voice, a first-person perspective, meant to be the woman's very own. Now thirty-five years of age, she seems to be addressing her daughter, trying to explain about the past:

> [...] the story will begin, narrated over and over, part by part, as if some key that had been mislaid in all the other tellings might suddenly glint in the light of this one. Again and again the faces,

the actions, the voices of this house, as if the recounting could somehow exorcize them. Always she begins it for the girl whose mute eyes show no recognition. (p. 12)

That story concerns a woman who has hidden her illegitimate daughter in her house for some sixteen years, until a plumber found her out. It all began with the family moving into the area, into the house. At school, the girl had difficulty with her name. 'Sandra' was unacceptable, so she was called 'Brigid', far more suitable than her outlandish real one. Soon the mother dies, and the father, broken by the loss, does not much care about the daughter and her brother, Johnny, with whom she becomes involved sexually. Johnny disappears for shame, and Sandra agonises over her lost lover. Then the father suffers a stroke and dies, while she gives birth to a daughter, whom she hides in a room in the house:

> What could I do? You're not normal, you're not right in the head. I don't know the word — autistic, retarded? But there is something wrong. How could I bring you out of the house? I'd be in jail, Johnny would be in jail, and you would be locked away in some hospital. (p. 80)

Part III begins with a section featuring a first-person point of view:

> I can still sense it here, feel it in my blood, as it flows beneath this roadway. Thirty years since last June the stream has been buried — I remember coming up from my cottage that morning to watch the workmen smoothing over the tarmacadam [...] (p. 199)

The stream mentioned is later identified as the crystal rivulet that lends the title to this part and is intended to carry symbolic meaning. But who is this 'I'? Not the woman of Part I. Presumably the pronoun refers to an old man, Turlough:

> The joints stiffen in this weather, I've to rest and catch my breath after every twenty strides but I can see my destination now after all these empty years. (p. 199)

Then the narrative comes to focus on some youngish boy, apparently led by his grandmother into the woman's house. Later, lying in bed, he is haunted by what he has experienced there. His name is Johnny, but he s not the Johnny of Part I. Turlough wishes to leave everything to him:

> It's yours now, Johnny, I'm lost in this expanse, the metal bridge
> and concrete paths, the shuttered shops and supermarkets. I'm
> ready to join that list of ghosts, I'm part of them already. (p. 207)

Obviously, he knows about the woman and her daughter. Could he,
after all, be the Johnny of Part I? Then the juvenile Johnny makes love
to his girlfriend, Kathy, and while he is buggering her he thinks of the
woman's daughter. Is she the woman's daughter? Not very likely, even
though a certain reflective section featuring Kathy would seem to suggest
his possibility. She is caught in a burning cottage, thinking:

> And I looked up at the small lights of the houses around me and
> knew that these were all my people: the woman and her daughter
> caged in their room, Joanie's father coughing alone through the
> night, the lovers seeking out darkened corners, the gangs littering
> up the alley-ways [...] These were all my people, their stories, their
> lives,[...] passed into my care to be recorded with the tens of thou-
> sands gathered from over the centuries. (pp. 239f.)

In the end, Part III would seem to echo Part I. There is the Johnny
duality, and Kathy partly relives the titular woman's fate.

*The Woman's Daughter* is about memory, about communal archetypes
that, figuratively speaking, like the rivulet of Part III, flow from
generation to generation, even if undergound, encompassing the King
and his lieutenants and all subsequent people and their fates — the
stories and lives passed into the care of the remembering consciousness.

It is a powerful theme, no doubt. But Bolger's handling of it is
flawed to a considerable degree. There are too many unnecessary
mysteries. Parts I and III link in too inadequate a fashion. The
grandiloquent reference to that 'city of the dead standing sentinel' reads
like an attempt on Bolger's part to point the reader's nose at some
profound symbolic significance that, alas, is not there at all. Moreover,
the narrative is fraught with imbecilities — of a linguistic nature, such
as: '...if he found Johnny and I [*sic*] playing with them', and of a technical
kind; for instance, every so often one encounters passages such as this
one:

> johnny johnny sing for me, make the coat-hangers play: shake

the plates around the house and make mammy go away. johnny
johnny is my friend, he will come out to sing, when mammy goes
off to work and thinks she has locked me in [and so on and so
forth] (p. 79)

Nearly everyone knows doggerel of that sort. But need one incorporate
it into a novel?

For the extended version of *The Woman's Daughter*, as distinct from
the 1987 Raven Arts edition, Bolger has sandwiched a lengthy middle
section, entitled 'Victoriana', between the original two parts. It features
two stories of obsessive sexual attraction that are held together by a
number of thematic and motivic parallels. For example, the crucial sex-
scenes in both strands are juxtaposed (cf. pp. 128f.), and so are the
situations in which the man in each story falls asleep in his lover's
bedroom. Or there is the fact that both girls are deranged.

One narrative strand offers the first-person account of a late-
nineteenth-century tutor. He is the son of a poor family. A scholar
who calls himself Hegerty, takes him into his care and teaches him Latin
and Greek. His subsequent education is conducted by priests, and in
the end he comes to act as tutor in a Big House, where he becomes
infatuated with a servant-girl, Bridget, who invites him into her bed as a
protection against the demons that terrify her. Later she is locked up in
an asylum. He now is given to wandering in the environs of the place
thinking of Bridget and his own wife and daughter. The other strand
treats of a present-day 31-year-old librarian who strikes up a relationship
with a fellow librarian, a promiscuous young woman named Joanie, who
lures him into her bed as an act of revenge on her grandmother.

In addition to the motivic links within 'Victoriana', there are echoes
in it of the first and the third parts of the novel, which, although they
may appear slightly contrived, help coerce the book into a whole. Thus
for instance, Joanie shows her lover the estate where the woman of Part
I locked her daughter up (p. 92), and Part III tells of Joanie's first sexual
relationship with the young man who discovered the terrible secret of
the locked bedroom and is still haunted by the image of what he saw. In
'Victoriana' he is seen loitering on the fringes of things — a demented
bloated figure. Old Turlough, who is central to Part III, puts in a couple
of appearances as a young boy in the tutor's tale.

The newly added stories, essentially on account of their parallels,
seem to strive towards underscoring the 'message' that is so pregnant in
'The Crystal Rivulet' section: history flowing on like the eponymous

rivulet, repeating itself in subsequent generations. Lest the reader should not take the hint, Bolger has his tutor figure ruminate:

> I am so aware at this moment, as I listen to her last reluctant cry fading into a pattern of sleep, that I suddenly know that I am just one moment in history, one of an infinite line of fathers who watched at evening's end their children drift to sleep. They stretch behind me and before me, I as much a speck in their minds as they are in mine. (p. 91)

Again, it is an appealing idea, but one that Bolger has not succeeded in putting to adequate effect. Declan Kiberd is certainly right once more when he notes:

> In his attempt to give a voice to the voiceless of Irish history, Mr Bolger cannot sufficiently discipline his own tones to allow those of his characters to establish themselves and come through. The thesis is all [...][7]

Part III especially is fraught with needless sermonising: Bolger is stating too much and rendering too little. Contrarily, 'Victoriana', barring that passage quoted above, eschews tub-thumping. Its stories are told in a lucid, straightforward manner and not in that frantic and obfuscatory fashion which, in 'The Woman's Daughter' section, puts quite a strain on the reader. 'Victoriana' may well be among the most convincing pieces of fiction Bolger has written so far.

Nick Hornby, reviewing *The Woman's Daughter* in *The Sunday Times*, opined: '[...] this is nothing less than an attempt at the definitive late-twentieth-century Irish novel'.[8] This is nonsense of course, like those imbecilic claims according to which Bolger is a new Joyce. If he were, he would get his nominatives and accusatives right and avoid questionable similes, such as this one: '[...] their characters already formed as surely as if lava had slid across the nursery while they slept and hardened into rock around their white skin' (pp. 116f.). In a portrait, Bolger is quoted as saying that he wanted *The Journey Home* 'to be like Dickens or Graham Greene, full of characters and subplots'.[9] If that is all that Dickens' and Greene's novels are, full of characters and subplots, than Bolger may have succeeded. But of course they are not. They are products of high-class craftsmanship and artistic excellence, the two utterly essential prerequisites for worthwhile writing. In the same article, Bolger has admitted to hating 'the assumptions of high art, and the literary novel'. What may be wrong with these only philistines know. Perhaps Bolger's capacity as a writer would quite considerably be improved if he managed to overcome his hatred and acquired some of that high-class craftsmanship and artistic excellence.

In *Emily's Shoes* (1992), Michael McMahon has been haunted for years by the same dream: that he has killed someone, and he wonders whether there is 'something in the past which [he is] hiding from [himself]'. He may have been hiding the fact that he failed to bid farewell to the girl, Maggie, who meant so much to him in his youth, when he left Ireland for Canada. Or there may be the faceless figure of his seafaring father, whom he never got to know. Or there may be his mother's untimely death. Michael appears to be entangled in a web of guilt and haunted by a sense of loss and bereavement. He goes to live with his Aunt Emily in Birmingham, and there he develops an overriding penchant for women's shoes. He is imbued with 'a longing, a hunger', the source of which he cannot trace. But when he touches Emily's shoes, 'that yearning [seems] to stop'. Part II relates his affair with Maggie, which once again ends in loss; and Part III, tied up with Part I through motific echoes, tells of his relationship with a woman, Clare, over whom a sinister priest holds sway. Finally, all ends not too badly when Michael and Clare, almost like Leopold and Marion, find each other on Howth Head. The shoe fetishism and the complex guilt-loss bereavement syndrome are not worked out convincingly enough, and the disruption of chronology as well as the experimental use of typography looks grafted on.

In *A Second Life* (1994), Dublin photographer Sean Blake is clinically dead for several seconds after a car crash. He experiences the powerful sensation of being drawn towards a blissful afterworld, only to find his progress blocked by the haunting face of a man he only partially recognises. He is resuscitated and rather reluctantly adjusts to the gift of a second life: at the age of six weeks, he was taken from his mother when, as an adolescent girl in rural Ireland in the 1950s, she was forced by nuns to give up her baby for adoption. Sean embarks on a quest for his real mother, sifting through the madeleines of his memory and bits of dreams, recalling the places in his past life stimulated by photographs, and conducting research in the dust-covered archives of the Botanical Gardens. It is also a quest for his own identity. In parallel manner, his mother, now at an advanced age and her wits overpowered by curious sensations concerning her son's accident, is in search of Sean, whom she herself had called Paudi. With the help of various people, including an aunt in England, who tells him that his mother died two weeks prior to his arrival, Sean is able to identify the convent in which he was born. He severely reproaches the nuns for their despicable conduct at the time, and there would appear to be in the accusation some of Bolger's own anger at a deplorable period of Ireland's history. But as one nun rightly puts it: 'Unless you rid yourself of this anger you'll pass it on.' Whether Bolger intends to pass on any anger is debatable, as is the issue of whether — as the blurb claims — Sean Blake's story, in fact, succeeds in exposing a festering wound from Ireland's past to shed light on a changing modern country, exploring how we must not only retain the past but also try to redeem it.

It would be altogether defensible to have chosen *The Journey Home* for more extensive treatment. After all, Bolger came to some prominence with the publication of the book, and the novel helped establish that particular brand of recent Irish fiction labelled 'Northside Realism'. It therefore marked what could be regarded as a notable stage in the development of the Irish novel since 1945. Instead, I have singled out *Father's Music* (1997), for several reasons. *Father's Music* shares a number of both thematic and compositional features with other Bolger novels and may, in a way, be considered a summation of Bolger's *oeuvre* to date. Once more a past is evoked and the manner in which that private past impinges on the present life of the protagonist is thrown into relief. That protagonist is, yet again, in search of a parent, which search is also a means of finding self. Reminiscent of *The Journey Home*, we are offered an analysis of the corrupt and criminal side of life in Dublin, and we find that sinister world juxtaposed with a rural part of Ireland where old standards and values, and above all truth, have been preserved. But in *Father's Music*, Bolger has somewhat ameliorated his anger against social tyranny and diminished the malevolence of politicians. He has, furthermore, eschewed ratifying the old pastoral notion of rural Ireland as real Ireland, even though he is at times on the brink of falling into that trap again where he treats of Donegal and the traditional music still practised there — father's music. What he has not quite managed is to avoid sentimentality altogether, especially as far as the ending of the book is concerned. Lastly, the story he tells is in many ways the most impressive and arresting he has so far concocted. *Father's Music* offers not, as the blurb claims, a good psychological thriller, but a mildly passable one. The question, though, is how the efforts at writing such a class of narrative may collude with an attempt at a serious-minded analysis of the Dante-esque inferno of present-day Dublin. And all this is not to say that the novel is completely devoid of deficiencies, some of them familiar from his previous books.

Twenty-two-year-old Tracey Evans is living a promiscuous, free-spirited life in London. Brought up in her grandparents' house in Harrow, where her mother was prey to recurring illnesses and finally the victim of cancer, she fled to the capital after her mother's demise. Her father was an Irish fiddler in his fifties, who deserted his wife soon after the birth of his daughter. Now, in London, she enters into a sexual relationship with a married Irish businessman, Luke Duggan, in his forties, who turns out to be the brother of a notorious Dublin criminal. Luke and Tracey meet every Sunday in a hotel near an Irish Centre off the Edgeware Road. But it is while having sex with her lover that Tracey is assailed by memories of her maimed past — memories involving the copulating of her mother and father, her life in Harrow and, in particular, the way she mutilated herself when fourteen by scratching and bruising her arms with long-grown fingernails: a cry for help and attention. On one of these Sundays before meeting Luke, she buys an Irish newspaper and discovers an article reporting a '*Dublin Gangland Murder*' (p. 78). A photograph shows a man who resembles Luke, and Tracey knows the murdered man to be Luke's brother Christy. Luke decides to go to Dublin and asks Tracey to accompany him there. We are back in Bolger's sinister Dublin underworld:

> When robberies became common in Dublin and security tight-ened, Christy Duggan had orchestrated bank raids which paralysed isolated country towns. The police could never prove anything despite twenty-four-hour surveillance for two years, but [...] eve-rything about the Duggans was common knowledge. People knew even when Christy's gang were making a hit because he would drive up and down outside police headquarters. Libel laws meant his name never appeared in the papers, which referred to him as 'The Ice-man'. (p. 51)

It is a world of terror that Bolger moderately manages to evoke, as when Tracey is described walking down a menacing street. This street is in London, to be sure, but it could be anywhere in Dublin:

> I kept walking after taking the film back, turning down streets I would normally never take after dark. The pubs were packed with

drinkers as rock music blared from upstairs windows. It was almost closing time. Twice I nearly went into a bar and then stopped myself. It wasn't like me to lack the confidence to venture somewhere alone, but tonight I felt unable to adopt a mask. A taxi passed, braking hard to take the corner. There were shops covered by street shutters except for an Indian restaurant with no customers. I sensed the waiter eyeing me from the lit doorway. I walked quickly to escape his gaze and turned left, intending to circle back towards my flat. But when I got down the street I found it was a cul-de-sac. The last streetlight was a flickering blue as the bulb spluttered out. There was a walled laneway, dividing the street from the high rise flats beyond it. [etc.] (p. 38)

Tracey accompanies Luke to Dublin, and there gets involved with the heavies. Luke is made to sort out Christy's financial problems, with assorted thugs demanding money that Christy allegedly owes them. Christy has built himself a reputation in Dublin:

[...] all sources agreed that Christy Duggan was biding his time and studying Dublin's emerging crime scene. His first major heist was a robbery which had been staked out for months in advance by an inner-city crime boss known as Spiderman. Duggan, who sometimes acted as a driver for Spiderman, stole the outline of the plan, modified it to eliminate weaknesses and rounded up several associates of a Coolock criminal nicknamed Bilko to make a pre-emptive strike a week before Spiderman was due to stage the robbery.

That heist was still officially the second biggest in Ireland's history. The biggest occurred just two days later, leading to calls for the resignation of the then Minister for Justice. Christy Duggan was again responsible, this time using four minor associates of Spiderman to carry out a mail robbery, which Bilko had been planning for months, on the Dublin-Belfast express train. (p. 102)

He may have been 'The Ice-man', but he died bankrupt. His wife and children are living in a grandiose house in Howth that Luke bought for his brother.

Tracey wanders around Dublin, while a ginger-haired youth, Al by name and one of Luke's nephews, is keeping an eye on her. From that

point in the novel onwards, Bolger takes occasion to lay it on quite thick
at times, as Tracey is torn between Luke and Al. Dublin is a place where
people pop acid tabs and Ecstasy pills, and so does Tracey during a
night out with Al and his pals. As a result, she suffers a bad trip. And
every so often, what she experiences reminds her of certain incidents
from her past, when, aged eleven, she visited Ireland with her mother in
search of her elusive father. Thus, in the course of her bad trip, staggering
down Fishamble Street, she recalls being sexually abused by a man who
forced her to perform oral sex on him. Her grandmother, later, could
never understand why she brushed her teeth twenty times a day. Or she
is reminded of the time when she fell in with a gang of street urchins,
looting and stealing in the Henry Street area. She had run away from
her mother and was eventually found and taken back to Harrow by her
grandfather. The past constitutes a hurt within her that she has never
been able to articulate (cf. p. 139). Since she was eleven, she has wanted
people to stop asking her to be someone she could not be anymore (cf.
p. 156), and she senses that she can be herself with Luke. She realises
that

> I could tell Luke things I had never been able to tell anyone. [...] It
> was enough that I had finally found somebody I could trust, if
> and when I was ready. (p. 164)

All would be well, if it wasn't for Al, who constantly casts doubt on the
veracity of Luke's statements. And that is not the only problem. There
is hardly a brutal act, some gross stroke of fate, some turn of the screw,
that Bolger does not employ.

More people are killed, such as a thug who tries to press money
from Luke, and Al is suspected of having perpetrated the crime. Or did
Luke do it himself? That at least is what Al insinuates. Later Al's own
father, Luke's other brother, is shot near Waterford. Tracey's grandmother
has been rendered a vegetable as a result of a stroke and has asked her
husband to put an end to her miserable existence. Luke of course
organises a gun. But in the event, neither Tracey's grandfather nor Tracey
herself are able to fire the gun into the paralysed woman's head. In a
conversation with Grandad Pete, Tracey learns that Lily, her
grandmother, was raped by her alcoholic father, whom she looked after,
and that Lily had a child, Tracey's mother, as a result. Finally, Luke himself
is murdered, with two shots to the head, in Donegal by a motorcyclist.
The killer is subsequently identified as Luke's niece, Christine, the

daughter of Christy Duggan. She committed the deed as an act of revenge on her uncle for sacrificing his brother in his criminal dealings. There is a police raid and there are any number of reminiscences, particularly on the part of Luke, of an exceedingly impoverished childhood and a humiliating time in a borstal in Donegal. And Tracey gets deeper and deeper implicated in a situation where she finds it increasingly difficult to trust Luke. Was he really behind all those despicable doings, supervising them from a safe distance in London? Was he the brains of the Duggan gang or was he only picking up the pieces that others left behind? In short: did he tell Tracey the truth or was he, as Al contends, shame-facedly lying through his teeth? Was he really only using everyone, not least Tracey herself?

Before and after the scene in the hospital room, in which they try to kill the grandmother, Tracey and her grandfather have a long conversation, actually the only intense conversation she has had with him. One of the main focuses rests on the fate of her missing father. According to Grandad Pete, Frank Sweeney left his wife of his own accord: 'No one kicked him out. It was he who left her' (p. 266). Towards the end of the book, after Tracey has encountered her father in Mrs Cunningham's pub in Donegal, Mrs Cunningham reveals to her that her father stayed away from England not least because Tracey's grandparents threatened him with jail if he ever set foot in that country. So lies apparently also characterise, have always characterised, Tracey's life with mother and grandparents in Harrow.

It would appear that truth, honesty and authenticity are associated with and only to be found in remote rural Donegal, where Tracey's father, Frank Sweeney, has been living for the last twenty-two years. During a taxi drive, Luke and the taxi driver talk about traditional Irish music, and the two men enthuse about certain musicians. During the conversation, it transpires that the taxi driver used to know one Proinsías Mac Suibhne, a brilliant fiddle player from Donegal. He may be none other than Tracey's long-lost father. Subsequently, the taxi-man implores Tracey: 'If there's any chance he's your Daddy, then you should meet him just once, at least to tell him his wife is dead' (p. 193). After an old concertina player has divulged the truth about Proinsías Mac Suibhne to Tracey, and even Luke has urged her to go to Donegal in search of her father: 'I'm asking for nothing else, except that at least you'll remember me as the man who found your father' (p. 276), Tracey decides to make the effort. Of course, she finds the man and hears him sing and play his fiddle. Unfortunately, the reunion of daughter and father is not satisfactorily handled by Bolger. Tracey learns that, contrary to what has been conveyed to her by her grandparents, the relationship between her mother and her father was a happy one, and before the reader can have any intimations as to how the reconciliatory meeting between father and daughter may be rendered, the novel ends with the rather laconic remark: 'We both went to speak at the same time, neither of us knowing what we would say' (p. 388).

The business about whether Tracey is able to see through the chameleon-like nature of Luke and discover the truth about him:

> All I had against Luke was Al's word. Luke had once told me that Al was jealous of him. I wondered could he have invented everything from spite and even tipped off the police after all? (p. 344)

— in other words her wavering between believing him and distrusting him, is in the long run plain mystifying. The problem is that most of the characters appear to be telling lies. Why should she trust Al? Why should she believe her grandfather? In fact, Mrs Cunningham would seem to be the only reliable person Tracey speaks to. In the end, one ceases to care about whether Luke is a crook or a decent man. Aberrations are piled high, and at times Bolger is asking rather much of the reader to suspend his disbelief. The ending borders on the sentimental and does not provide a successful close to the story. Bolger has relied once again on thematic, or motific, echoes as in previous novels. To name only one such echo, Tracey more or less mimics her mother's affair with Frank Sweeney, through her affair with an Irishman twice her age. This becomes apparent, for example, when she tells her grandfather: 'You think I'm making the same mistake as my mother', and little does it signify that he replies: 'There's no comparison. [...] Your father was far older. He was like your mother, for the birds. And besides, he was a gentleman' (p. 296). But those echoes and motific recurrences add no noteworthy thematic dimension to the narrative. And in case anyone may wonder why Christy Duggan was nicknamed 'The Ice-man', here is the salacious explanation: Luke once brought a copy of *Playboy* home from London. There was an article on multiple orgasms. It said the best trick was to pop an ice-cube up your girlfriend's arse just as she was coming. Poor Christy was always susceptible to what he read in magazines. The trick did not work in his case, more is the pity.

This novel, like a sizeable portion of his remaining *oeuvre*, evinces that Bolger can at times be quite a sloppy writer. The book is riddled with split infinitives. Of course, there are cases where a split infinitive may express more precisely what one wishes to say. But the following example is simply silly: 'The kids had stopped smashing things to silently watch' (p. 112). In addition, there are two disconnected participle constructions within the first paragraph that are rather a disgrace for someone who boasts in the 'Introduction' to his *The Picador Book of Contemporary Irish Fiction* that he has refused to place 'these writers in any tradition of Irish writing — beyond the obvious one of generally using the English language far better than anyone else...'[10] Here they are:

> My breath comes faster as his hands grip my buttocks, managing to rub his shoulder against the walkman's volume control.
>
> The beat is inside my head from childhood, imagining an old shoe strike the stone flags and the hush of neighbours gathered in. (p. 3)

Bolger is of course not a Londoner, for otherwise he would know that one says 'a hotel off *the* Edgeware Road', because that road leads to Edgeware just as the Oxford Road leads to Oxford. And it should be 'I went to *the* Elephant & Castle', and not 'I went to Elephant & Castle'. Do writers these days no longer have editors?

But is Bolger not wonderful! He has recently devised a novel, *Finbar's Hotel*, in seven chapters, each one penned by a different writer, and the devious thing about the whole enterprise is that the reader is kept guessing as to who wrote which section. And guess he, or she, surely will. That is possibly the main attraction of the book. For the story, or rather stories, told are none too compelling. They are not too bad, to be fair, but one would not give one's right arm for any of them.

Benny is spending a night in Finbar's away from his wife and family to experience a bit of the action, to see what he has been missing out on. All he gets for his troubles is a bloody nose. Two sisters meet in Room 102 and discuss family problems, in particular the fraught relationship between one of them and their mother, while they gradually get soused. In Room 103, a loud-mouthed young man is staying with the cat of his former lover, who has given him the boot, and he wants to kill the cat in an act of revenge. In the end, he leaves the animal with a woman he chats up and misleads the cat owner, who is on his trail, into thinking that he drowned the cat in a suitcase in the river. Room

104 accommodates the son of the erstwhile owner of the hotel, who has come to persuade the night manager, who as an adolescent had an affair with his sister, to go and see her one more time, because she has been unable to forget him. The woman in Room 105 has been told that she is dying of cancer; she takes up with an American tour guide, a man more sinned against than sinning; they spend the night naked in bed together, but without going the whole hog; in the morning the man has left, and after breakfast she goes back to her husband in Galway (or was it Cork?).

In Room 106, there is a woman who has lived in the States for a considerable period of time; she has had numerous affairs and in fact is looking for another one for that night; memories of a man she used to know in Dublin still keep haunting her, and in the end she phones him to ask him to come to Finbar's. He never shows up; yet she is content, confident that she will fall in love. Finally, in Room 107, a notorious criminal, who has stolen valuable paintings, including a Rembrandt portrait of a woman, is waiting to clinch a deal with two Dutchmen. However, for various reasons, the deal does not come off.

The chapters are quite convincingly interconnected. Thus, for instance, the man from Room 107 meets the woman from the States in the bar and pilfers the ledger she has with her. This makes her confront the man in the company of three policemen in chapter 7, which incident in turn persuades the occupant of Room 107 to make his get-away without having sold the Rembrandt.

So far so good. But the vexing question *is*: who wrote which chapter? It is no doubt perfect tomfoolery, yet I will stick my neck out and make a guess. If Bolger or some of his collaborators learn of my suggestions, they will probably laugh themselves silly. No matter, here goes.

In some chapters, I think, it is easier to identify the author than in others. (Guffawing from the Bolger front.) Anyway, chapter 6 would seem to have been written by Anne Enright. My assumption is based on the weirdness of the section's com-positional design. Such weirdness, or the fact that one can connect nothing with anything — to exaggerate the matter — has been one hallmark of Ms Enright's two books to date. Chapter 2 could be by Bolger himself, for it is characterised by his way of trying to be funny and shows a Bolgerian problem with commas, which marred part of the text in *The Journey Home*. Here is one example: 'What do you mean, Joe? There's nothing the matter with Joe. Joe's fine.' That comma before the first mention of Joe is wrong, because Joe is not being addressed here at all. But the author in question could also be Jennifer Johnston, principally on account of the dreadful attempts at stream-of-consciousness and the pathetic singing of hymns against the pounding of heavy metal music in Room 103. Pathetic behaviour of this sort permeates Ms Johnston's *oeuvre*, from *The Captains and the Kings*, *The Gates* and *The Railway Station Man* (where there is a glaring example involving an Aga) to *The Invisible Worm*. In the end, my money is on Ms Johnston.

Chapter 4 is by Bolger. By way of explanation, I should like to name what I consider the slight waywardness of the subject matter: all other chapters are about the occupants of the rooms, this one is above all about the night manager. I should furthermore like to point to the socio-political note of the section and to the split infinitives.

Now things get tricky. Upon mature consideration, as the man said, I would allocate chapter 1 to Joseph O'Connor, the sole reason being that here we have a cowboy who is looking for some Indians. Apart from that, the straining efforts to be funny, which the section shows, I would associate with O'Connor. O'Connor once wrote a review for *The Observer* of an Eric Clapton concert that was of the same ilk. Chapter 3 is a problem, and so is chapter 7. The authors I have in mind are Tóibín and Hamilton. So Tóibín's name goes to chapter 3, for the heck of it, and Hamilton's to chapter 7, for the hell of it. This leaves Doyle for chapter 5, the heavy reliance on dialogue underpinning the choice. Most of Doyle's novels to date, especially the Barrytown trilogy, would amount to little more than a couple of pages in length, if all the dialogue were excised. Which is another way of suggesting that Doyle has so far proved a dud at narrative description.

This, then, is my guess. The only pity is that the jury will say: *nul points*. So what?

# PATRICK MCCABE

Patrick McCabe came to prominence as a writer in 1992 with the publication of his extraordinarily arresting novel *The Butcher Boy*, which he adapted for the stage under the title of *Frank Pig Says Hello*. The play was premiered at the 1992 Dublin Theatre Festival to some acclaim. *The Butcher Boy* was recently turned into a well-received film by Neil Jordan. Another of McCabe's plays, *Loco County Lonesome*, was premiered with less success at the 1994 Dublin Theatre Festival. McCabe started his career writing short stories, one of which received a Hennessy Award in 1979. He also penned a children's story, *The Adventure of Shay Mouse: The Mouse from Longford*[1] and had plays broadcast on the BBC and RTÉ. For instance, *A Mother's Love Is a Blessing* was a TV drama on RTÉ in 1994. *The Butcher Boy* marked his third published attempt at serious fiction, after *Music on Clinton Street*[2] (1986) and *Carn*[3] (1989). Two of the thematic concerns that he has explored in his work are especially noteworthy. One is the effect of the modern world on rural Ireland, or, phrased differently, social changes in Ireland of the 1970s and 1980s; the other is the fathoming of abnormal mental states, which McCabe achieves with uncanny brilliance. The incontestable strong point of his narrative art is the immediacy and intensity of the narratorial voices employed in the majority of his books, for example in *The Butcher Boy*, *The Dead School* and *Breakfast on Pluto*.

The title 'Music on Clinton Street' refers to a line from the song 'Famous Blue Raincoat' by Leonard Cohen, whose music together with Jim Morrison's and Tabs of Acid's is evoked to render a specific lifestyle in the States to where the protagonist's brother, James, has escaped from Ireland. James's letters to Des convey the dismal and ruined existence led by a man who is unable to come to terms with his newfound freedom. Des himself is an adolescent adrift in the grey mortuary of Saint Xavier's Diocesan College, founded during the Famine by Joe Kilgannon, a most magisterial clergyman of unfaltering convictions and stern ideals. Now the college is presided over by the Junior Dean, Philip.

McCabe skilfully contrasts the past and the present, Ireland and the US; he furthermore blends the lives of Des, the Junior Dean and both their parents to evoke powerful portraits of rural Ireland throughout the century. Basically a state-of-Ireland novel, *Music on Clinton Street* aims at an examination of a society in violent and bewildering transition, of the conflict between the static old order, exemplified by the college, and the influx of transatlantic culture, which transformed Ireland in the 1960s and 1970s. McCabe introduced himself as an exciting new novelist with an assured and, at times, quite unique voice.

*Carn* (1989) charts a couple of years in the history of the market town Carn, 'half a mile from the Irish border', focusing upon a handful of characters whose lives become intertwined. There is James Cooney, who opens a meat processing plant in 1966 and causes the place to blossom again after it had almost died when the railway closed in 1959. Or there is day-dreaming Sadie Rooney, a dead ringer for Joyce's Gerty McDowell. Very compelling and moving, there is drug- and drink-sodden Josie Keenan, come back after years of serving in bars or pleasing men on the flat of her back in England, whither she escaped after a certain Vincent Culligan had made her pregnant; hallucinatory voices drive her to attempt suicide; however, the water is too cold and she fails to drown herself; later she is raped by a barman and finally burns to death in a house set on fire by IRA men.

One has to search long and hard in contemporary writing to find lives delineated with such empathy and in such an impressive manner as in *Carn*. The narrative style is extremely impressive and the effect is sheer delight. Here is how one of Sadie Rooney's days ends; she is lying in bed dreaming of Elvis: 'Then click went the light and out went the moon.'

The novel opens with a reference to an act of violence by a former IRA sympathiser. Nearer the narrative present, Benny Dolan's father gets embroiled in a comparable incident in the course of which his friend is killed. At the end of Part I, another atrocity occurs: a bomb goes off in Carn and a man is blown to smithereens. Then yet another explosion hits the town and Benny's friend is killed. As a consequence, Benny joins an IRA group who set fire to Josie's house, resulting in her death. Benny accidentally shoots an innocent inhabitant of Carn, Pat Lacey, who is running away from Josie's drunken antics. At Josie's and Pat's joint funeral, a man is spied among the mourners who is familiar to the people of Carn. He is Vincent Culligan, who at the beginning of the novel vanished from the scene, having got Josie with child. Before the meat magnate hits the town, the broken pump skits 'its umbrella of water all over the cracked paving slabs'. After he has closed down his plant and absconded to Spain, the broken pump again skits 'its umbrella of water across the cracked paving slabs'. Carn's history, thus, is seen as a process of eternal recurrence — an Irish eternal recurrence, with violence and murder figuring over-prominently.

Recent fiction has seen an astounding number of superbly drawn first-person narrators, as idiosyncratic, unreliable and, at times, as wicked as one can get: Patrick McGrath's Sir Hugo and Spider, Robert McLiam Wilson's Ripley Bogle, Graham Swift's Bill Unwin, John Banville's Freddie Montgomery, to name but a few. Now, in *The Butcher Boy* (1992), Patrick McCabe has added his extraordinary specimen. Francie Brady, now in an asylum for the criminally insane, tells of events that happened 'twenty or thirty or forty years ago' (p. 1),[4] when he got involved with the Nugents, in particular Mrs Nugent, who called the Brady family 'pigs'. Francie is the son of an alcoholic father and a mother who is in and out of the local mental hospital, 'the garage' in Francie's terms.

The Nugents are ordinary, respectable people, or so it would seem; it is only in the narrator's increasingly unhinged mind that they develop into despicable and punishable ogres. Francie's only friend is Joe Purcell, whom he met one day when hacking at the ice on a big puddle with a lolly stick. One of the mean tricks the Nugents play on Francie, according to his warped reasoning, is that they wean Joe away from him and foster a relationship between Joe and their son, Philip.

Francie runs away to Dublin, where he spends three shillings on a souvenir plaque for his mother bearing the legend 'A Mother's love is a blessing no matter where you roam'. When he returns he finds the kitchen sink piled with his father's empty pilchard tins, the mother having drowned herself. He breaks into the Nugents' house, imagining the while that he is humiliating Mr and Mrs Nugent by teaching them to behave like pigs: 'What else do pigs do?...Mrs Nugent? They give us rashers! Yes, that's very true but it's not the answer I'm looking for.' He wrecks the bedroom and leaves a giant 'poo' on the carpet, 'the best poo ever'. As a result, he does time in a reformatory run by priests. There he pretends to have religious visions and connives at the homoerotic fantasies of 'Father Tiddly'. After his release, he commits another break-in, is yet again sent to a home, during which time his father dies; and when he gets out, he grows into the holy terror of the town — a violent outcast. He finds work in Leddy's abattoir, slaughtering pigs with a captive bolt pistol and collecting the 'brock' from the hotel. The pig and the butcher have become one.

All Francie longs for is to go on living in a make-believe world of cowboys and hide-outs in the woods with Joe. But Joe, in the meantime, has grown up. He has discovered music and is a boarder at an expensive school in Bundoran, the very town where Francie's parents spent their honeymoon in a guest-house in which his father used to sing 'I dreamt that I dwelt in marble halls'. For Francie it seems to have been a happy and idyllic time. When he goes to visit the house, he discovers that the past was as wretched as the present. All the alleged acts of humiliation and injustice take on excruciating proportions in Francie's schizophrenic and paranoid mind, and in order that these haunting ghosts be laid, Francie knows he must take the captive bolt pistol to Mrs Nugent. The heinous deed and its aftermath are played out against a backdrop of the Cuban Missile Crisis and much local ballyhoo about an apparition of Our Lady. The use of such cultural details, possibly in order to lend wider reference to the Francie story, Irish-town-life-in-the-sixties fashion, jar a bit; or rather they fail to make full sense. At the end, Francie meets another inmate of the asylum with whom he begins to hack at the ice on the big puddle behind the kitchen, and tears start streaming down his face. The story has come full circle.

The Butcher Boy offers a deeply moving, really devastating account of loneliness, jealousy, evil and madness. It is utterly astonishing how McCabe has succeeded in penetrating the deranged mind of his psychopathic narrator. What at first seems the rather innocent logic of a difficult, emotionally crippled child surreptitiously develops into the fiendish, riotous ravings of a maniac. But the author craftily relieves the unashamed horror of his narrative by equipping Francie with a deadpan sense of humour of the blackest sort. For example, in the reformatory he comes upon 'a saint on every window-sill, such a shower of dying-looking bastards I never seen'. One woman in the town is said to have 'a grin swinging between her ears like a skipping rope'.

The title of the novel refers to a ballad, sung by Francie's mother, about a girl who hangs herself for her butcher-boy lover who deceived her, and it also refers to Francie himself.

One of the main questions that the narrative raises is this: why does Francie Brady's mind disintegrate? For disintegrate it certainly does. Does Francie become a psychopath, does he go insane for hereditary reasons? After all, his mother is in and out of the 'garage', being mentally and psychologically unstable. Or does McCabe put the blame for Francie's decline on social causes? One can rephrase the questions in the following manner: Are the Nugents as obnoxious in real life as Francie makes them out to be or only in his warped imaginings? McCabe appears to come down in favour of certain social causes in small-town Ireland in the 1960s.

The Brady family are regarded as 'white trash'.[5] That partly is what causes Mrs Brady to commit suicide and what has driven her husband to drink. Francie recounts his life from an institution for the criminally insane in order to make sense of it. During the difficult period, or in the no-man's land, between adolescence and manhood, Francie failed to discover his identity, failed to find his own voice. As a result, his world, to some extent, degenerated into ceaseless role-playing — local roles, such as the Bogman and Francie Brady Not a Bad Bastard Any More, and more exotic roles gleaned from popular culture, such as Algernon Carruthers and various Hollywood heroes. He quotes all, but is none of these characters. The ringing noises in his head, which start to take over towards the end of the book, represent the increasingly unmanageable clash of all these voices. 'Francie', as Gerry Smyth has noted,

> confronts the perfidy of discourse and the gap that always exists between representation and reality, but [...] he cannot breach the gap, and his identity begins to crumble under the strain.[6]

Whether Mrs Nugent is in fact the despicable, stuck-up person Francie suggests is difficult to decide; we only have his word as evidence. But Francie is an utterly unreliable narrator. Of course, his dice are loaded, which fact results in the totally ambivalent nature of the narrative. True enough, the Nugents are exiles returned from England. The headmaster of Francie's school introduces the Nugent son to the class in these terms:

> This is Philip Nugent [...] he's come to join us. Philip used to live in London but his parents are from the town and they have come back here to live. (p. 2)

There is in Ireland a tendency in such people to put on certain superior airs vis-à-vis the people they once left and have now returned to. On the other hand, such superior airs may often only have been projected onto those people from prejudice. The film is quite unequivocal on this score. In it, Mrs Nugent speaks in an accent more sophisticated than that of the other characters. So perhaps Francie is right when he notes: 'If only the Nugents hadn't come to the town, if only they had left us alone, that was all they had to do.' (p. 167) The Nugents may indeed have ostracised Francie and his parents. At any rate, Francie hates and detests them, above all Mrs Nugent.

In addition, he finds his world beset by institutions of one kind or another, curtailing the freedom that he believes he once possessed and which he seeks to regain in his hideout and his fantasies about the Wild West. There is the orphanage to which his father and Uncle Alo were sent as children; the 'garage' to which his mother goes for her depression; the borstal where Francie is sent after his first assault on the Nugents' home; the boarding school from which Francie is excluded and which consolidates Joe's betrayal; and there is the institution for the criminally insane where he has spent the last 'twenty or thirty or forty years' (p. 1) and from where he is telling his story.

Of course, the Brady family is 'dysfunctional', if that is the term. Hearing his father say to his mother: 'God's curse the fucking day I ever set eyes on you!' (p. 7) is hardly the help young Francie needs to develop into a well-adjusted young man. Then his mother commits suicide, and Francie has not been able to experience the gradual separation from her that would allow him to mature emotionally.[7] As Gerry Smyth perceptively argues:

> This leaves him stranded [...], but still fundamentally in thrall to the image of his mother. The remainder of the book becomes a search by Francie to find objects and relationships capable of replacing the replete identity he exper- ienced with his mother; but as this was only ever an imaginary relationship anyway, all such attempts are doomed.[8]

Uncle Alo, Mary and the 'good old days' evoked by the family celebrations on the occasion of Alo's visits, his parents' allegedly happy sojourn in the Bundoran guest house, his friendship and adventures with Joe, all are slipping further and further away from an increasingly unsatisfactory present. More and more, Francie's life becomes characterised by a deprivation of love. Towards the end of his time in the reformatory with the priests, Francie reflects:

> After that the days were all the same, they just slipped past, days without Joe without da without anything. I didn't have to worry much about getting the Francie Brady Not a Bastard Any More Diploma anymore after the Tiddly business for I knew they were going to let me go the first chance they got I was like a fungus growing on the walls they wanted them washed clean again. (p. 95)

First he loses his mother and he feels guilty for not having attended her funeral. In the borstal he is told: 'You're a bad and wicked and evil man and you broke your mother's heart didn't even go to the poor woman's funeral' (p. 203). Next his father dies and then he is deprived of Joe's affection and friendship. Even those who are supposed to take care of him and help him amend his ways, the priests, exploit him for their own ulterior purposes, like Father Tiddly. Francie sums up his own situation:

> I pulled at the grass along the edge of the bank and counted all the people that were gone on me now.
> 1. Da
> 2. Ma
> 3. Alo
> 4. Joe
> When I said Joe's name all of a sudden I burst out laughing. For fuck's sake! I said, Joe gone! How the fuck would Joe be gone!
> That was the best yet. (p. 163)

In the end, Francie feels like the girl in 'The Butcher Boy' song his mother used to sing and who herself identified with the girl: both of them fit to hang themselves.

Francie tries to make all the disparate voices battling in his head conform to some kind of coherent narrative that will explain how things got so bad.[9] But all he is able to achieve is a phantasmagoric jumble of nightmarish impressions towards the end of the novel reminiscent of the 'Nighttown' section in *Ulysses*. And so he takes the captive bolt pistol, or 'the humane killer' as the doc in the institution for the criminally insane calls it, to Mrs Nugent and kills her.

Significantly, at the close he finds himself 'hacking away at the ice on the puddle behind the kitchens' (p. 215), when he is approached by a fellow inmate who says: '[...] give me a bit of stick there like a good man', and the two of them start 'hacking away together beneath the orange sky'. The situation in which he came to befriend Joe has repeated itself. To the words of warning from his new-found pal: '[...] you'll tell none of the bastards in here. They'll only fill you full of lies and let you down', Francie replies: 'Oho! [...] don't you worry nobody's letting me down again!' 'Nor me neither!', the pal adds, 'now you said it!' (p. 215) It appears that Francie has discovered the affection he was hankering after all along and has regained his freedom. For he comments: '[...] it was time to go tracking in the mountains, so off we went counting our footsteps in the snow [...]', and he can end by remarking: '[...] me with tears streaming down my face' (p. 215).

The Butcher Boy is a most powerful novel for the reasons specified here. It is less impressive as a so-called state-of-Ireland narrative, as some critics, for instance Gerry Smyth, are inclined to view it. Symth discusses the book together with Roddy Doyle's novels and Dermot Bolger's *The Journey Home* as socio-critical analyses of Ireland in the 1960s, 1970s and 1980s. Social issues are no doubt addressed in *The Butcher Boy*, as the present explication has shown. But the account is ill-equipped for diagnosing social wrongs in small-town Ireland during the 1960s or 1970s for the simple reason that all that is offered is filtered through the bewildered, sick mind of a fiendishly unreliable narrator. Of course, Francie Brady is Irish, and *The Butcher Boy* is about life in an Irish small town. But ultimately the book possesses wider dimensions than purely Irish ones. It engages with the question of what makes Francie lose his mind, as well as the related one of what causes a person to slip into criminal insanity. At the same time, that mind and the unreliable nature of the discourse constitute the prime strength of *The Butcher Boy*.

*The Dead School*[10] (1995) is about two schoolteachers, Raphael Bell and Malachy Dudgeon, and how the twain met in St Anthony's School, Dublin, where Raphael was headmaster, in the 1970s. Two themes that run through the novel are the changing of traditional Irish values during the time in question and the dying of love.

Raphael grew up as a model child, head altar boy, top scholar tripping over himself with brains in St Patrick's Teacher Training College, Drumcondra. His father was killed by the Black and Tans, 'God Save Ireland!'. He is offered the post as headmaster of St Anthony's and marries the beautiful Nessa Conroy, 'Macushla!' Their son is stillborn.

Malachy is less fortunate. His youth was overshadowed by the fact that his mother carried on an affair with a cowman; his father knew and in the end drowned himself. Love went into the grave for Malachy. On top of that, he was bullied by older boys from early on. Then he strikes up with a woman, Marion, who has had an abortion. In his job at St Anthony's, he proves a sorry failure, not measuring up to Bell's standards. He is inappropriately dressed and becomes the laughing stock of his pupils. Worst of all, one day one of his pupils drowns during an outdoor exercise. Malachy is given the boot. His job had got on top of him anyway and, as a consequence, his relationship with Marion had deteriorated. Love went into the grave a second time. He leaves for London to live among dopeheads, 'the dopiest doped-out hippy in town', spends some time in a mental institution, and when his mother is taken ill, returns to Dublin.

Meanwhile Bell's problems are aggravated by Marion, who, as the leader of the Parents' Committee, throws all sorts of spanners in the works. His authority is undermined, or so he sadly believes. Early retirement might be a solution, a colleague suggests, but Bell opts for resignation from his position as headmaster. His wife dies and Raphael buries himself in his house, drowning his sorrows in whiskey. One day Malachy, in a drunken state, decides to pay a visit to Bell's house and avenge himself on the man who used to tyrannise him. But Bell attacks him with a pair of heavy iron tongs, and when Malachy comes to, he sees the former headmaster swinging from the ceiling. Or did he only imagine he was attacked? That Bell hanged himself is certain.

There are two things about *The Dead School* that are most impressive. One is the narratorial voice, which tells the intertwining stories of Malachy and Raphael with exceptional vividness and immediacy. The other is the manner in which McCabe succeeds in rendering the process of Bell's growing insanity after he has handed in his resignation and imagines he is still teaching in the dead school of his own house, as well as the way in which the set-upon Malachy succumbs to drink and drugs in London. All this happens in the excellent last third of the book. Of course, it is not at all surprising that the author of *The Butcher Boy* should excel at capturing abnormal mental states with such bravura.

But there are shortcomings, which is why *The Dead School* does not really match either *Carn* or *The Butcher Boy*. The narrator remarks at the opening that he is going to tell the story of two teachers and the things they got up to 'in the days gone by'. Throughout attempts are discernible to lay the blame for the demise of Raphael Bell and his ideals of education on social changes. Good Old Ireland, the Ireland as represented by 'The Walton Programme' on radio with its heritage of the 'songs our fathers loved', is gone for ever. One of the reasons why Bell goes down is that he feels he is fighting a losing battle against the likes of one Terry Krash and his radio and TV shows on which the quality of bras is brazenly discussed. Additionally, there are women such as Marion who have had abortions and carry condoms around with them and try to impose their newfangled ideas on the running of his school. That aspect of social change, though, is not especially convincing, there being simply not enough meat offered in the novel to sink one's teeth into.

Furthermore, the first two thirds of the book, up to the point where the two principal characters embark on their downward courses, is too long-drawn-out. Some editorial pruning would have improved the quality of the narrative. Which is to say, it would have benefited in the eyes of those readers who seriously care about fiction. Those who are interested only in a good read are well served by the book as it is. For they get plenty for their money. And that scintillating voice is just priceless.

*Breakfast on Pluto* (1998) shares a number of features with the earlier *The Butcher Boy*. The most conspicuous one is the narratorial voice, which, in its idiosyncrasy and immediacy, recalls Francie Brady's voice. Moreover, Patrick 'Pussy' Braden, resplendent in housecoat and headscarf, sits in Kilburn, writing his story 'The Life and Times of Patrick Braden', for Dr Terence, his elusive psychiatrist, reawakening the truth behind his life in 1970s Ireland and the chaos of his days in a country, Ireland, and a city, London, filled with violence and tragedy. Like Francie, Patrick essentially recounts the events in his life to establish sense and meaning. The root cause of the slings and arrows of Pussy's outrageous fortune is lack of love and a failing sense of belonging or home.

Patrick is born the illegitimate child of an Irish parish priest. He embarks on life by being 'dumped on a step in a bloody *Rinso* box'. Growing up under the drunken glare of a foul-mouthed stepmother, Whiskers Braden, he finds relief from his early misery by putting on lipstick, becoming attracted 'to the airy appareil [*sic*] of the opposite sex'[11] and imagining himself dancing with Efrem Zimbalist Junior and 'Lorne Green out of *Bonanza*' (p. 14). At school, his festering resentment against his father and the longing for his missing mother lead to essays such as 'Father Stalk Sticks It In!' (p. 10), and quite soon his abiding fury drives him to become a transvestite prostitute. He leaves his village of Tyreelin and his friends, Charlie and Irwin, for London. He screws with a boxer on the ferry to Liverpool, goes to Piccadilly, gets half-strangled by a punter, becomes a cabaret act performing Dusty Springfield and Lulu songs, 'sweetness pussy kit-kit, perfumed creature of the night who once the catwalk of the world did storm as flashbulbs popped' (p. 2). He next falls in with a landlady who babies him and dresses him up as her dead son and who acts as a mother-substitute for him. While appearing to be in control of his chaos, Patrick is driven mad by the wish to find his real mother, whom he has never known and will not find until the end. It is a desire that blends poisonously with ruminations about his priest-father. Patrick is fortuitously in a restaurant blown up by an IRA bomb, but afterwards hilariously blamed and incarcerated for the violent act. In prison, he has visions of how he, as 'the Lurex Avenger' (p. 155), punishes his father by setting his body on fire and burning down his church. He also dreams of avenging himself on the inhabitants of Tyreelin, 'which lay nestled on the southern side of the Irish border' (p. 7), and, notably, he envisages having breakfast on Pluto with Mumsy, as he calls his natural mother, far away from the madding crowd.

Sweetie-pie Patrick's predicament unfolds against the background of political and sectarian violence, especially early 1970s IRA violence. Thus the jubilee commemoration in 1966 of the 1916 Rising is evoked. On another occasion, thirteen people are reported shot dead by the parachute regiment in Derry (p. 39). We are reminded of Bloody Sunday, in other words. A Down's syndrome boy is shot in the Northern Ireland troubles (p. 47). Patrick's friend Irwin Kerr, who becomes an IRA activist, is murdered for allegedly having turned informer. Charlie, who loves him, suffers a breakdown as a consequence and takes to drink. A soon-to-be-married man is abducted, tortured and eventually killed by terrorists:

> In the final, brief seconds before he felt the Magnum placed against his temple, Pat wondered whether he and Sandra would have had a dog. He thought perhaps Sandra might have been against it but they would have agreed in the end. (p. 164)

A bomb goes off in a restaurant and another one in a disco pub. Discord, hatred — the opposite of love, as Leopold Bloom knew — violence and alienation loom large. Even the helpful psychiatrist, Dr Terence, eventually betrays Patrick by disappearing from the scene.

And in the midst of all, Patrick 'Pussy' Braden is hankering after a family, love, affection and searching for familial security. At one point, he imagines this scene:

> [...] lying there on your deathbed, the cancer or whatever it is, literally rampaging through you, and, from every corner of the world, in aeroplanes, ships, long-distance trains, all the children for whom, through thick and thin, you have broken your back, together now braving the elements [...] simply in order to be at your side. (p. 40)

He can die contented in the firm conviction that '[e]veryone would my children love for they themselves knew love and shared it' (p. 41). It is a knowledge that 'Pussy' Patrick cannot share. The love that he has experienced is an utterly corrupted one, hence the frantic search for Mammy. One chapter is headed 'Where the Fuck is my Mammy?' (p. 73). Near the end of his wanderings, once back in Tyreelin, he fancies he has really fallen in love with a man. Yet, that person has another woman, whose hair Puss sets on fire in a pub.

> It's just that somehow I'd managed to work it all out so perfectly in my mind, with him and me together at last in the house I'd always dreamed of, our *Chez Nous* picture on the wall. (p. 193)

But all this happiness is just in the mind. In real life, love has gone sour, has been degraded into mere sex, as proved by the case of the girl of fifteen who is made pregnant by a married man behind the creamery and whom Patrick tries to help:

> Maybe that explains why I couldn't get Martina Sheridan out of my mind. If it's all just an excuse and if I was only using her as an excuse to take my weepiness out on, I don't know. (p. 187)

Or take Pussy's career as a prostitute. Patrick's account in his 'Life and Times...' is a cry for help, affection and love and a document of alienation. In compositional terms, its short chapters hopscotch about somewhat, but then Dr Terence told Patrick to write it all down '[j]ust as it comes to you' (p. 3). The music of the 1960s and 1970s — including Don Partridge's song 'Breakfast on Pluto', which was a UK chart hit in 1969 — with which the book is seasoned, adds some local colour, for what that is worth. Above all, it helps build up that world of fantasy and make-believe into which Pussy Braden escapes from his unbearable, ashen existence.

# FOOTNOTES

## Preface

[1] Cf. L.C. Knights, *Exploration* (London, 1946).

[2] Cf. Malcolm Bradbury's brilliant debunking of post-structuralism and deconstructionism, *Mensonge*

[3] Cf. Declan Kiberd's quite idiosyncratic interpretation of W.B. Yeats's poem 'Leda and the Swan', in *Inventing Ireland* (London: Cape, 1995), pp. 312–15.

[4] See, for instance, Gerry Smyth, *The Novel and the Nation* (London and Chicago/Ill.: Pluto, 1997); Christopher Murray, *Twentieth-Century Irish Drama: Mirror up to Nation* (Manchester and New York: Manchester Univ. Press, 1997).

[5] Cf. Linda Hutcheon, *A Poetics of Postmodernism: History, Theory, Fiction* (New York and London: Routledge, 1988); Brian McHale, *Postmodernist Fiction* (London and New York: Methuen, 1987); Brian McHale, *Constructing Postmodernism* (London and New York: Routledge, 1992); Anthony Cronin, *Samuel Beckett: The Last Modernist* (London: HarperCollins, 1996).

## Samuel Beckett

[1] Samuel Beckett, *Proust & Three Dialogues with Georges Duthuit* (London: Calder & Boyars, repr. 1970), p. 103.

[2] Samuel Beckett, *Molloy* (London: Calder & Boyars, repr. 1971), p. 29.

[3] Samuel Beckett, *Ill Seen Ill Said* (London: Calder, 1982), p. 20.

[4] Anthony Cronin, *Samuel Beckett: The Last Modernist* (London: Bloomsbury, 1966), p. 375.

[5] *Ibid.*, p. 376.

[6] *Ibid.*, p. 378.

[7] Samuel Beckett, *Watt* (London: Calder, 1976), p. 88.

[8] Samuel Beckett, *Endgame* (London: Faber & Faber, 1958), p. 20.

[9] The French word 'merde' (shit) punningly replaces the German 'Erde' (Earth) in what originally reads: 'die Erde hat mich wieder' (the Earth has me back again) and is a quotation from Goethe's *Faust I*.

[10] *Ibid.*, p. 38.

[11] Cf. Vivian Mercier, *Modern Irish Literature: Sources and Founders*, ed. Eilís Dillon (Oxford: Clarendon Press, 1994), p. 325.

[12] *Watt*, p. 218.

[13] 'From an Abandoned Work', in Samuel Beckett, *Six Residua* (London: Calder, 1978), p. 19.

[14] See, for instance, John P. Harrington, *The Irish Beckett* (Syracuse, New York: Syracuse Univ. Press, 1991); Mary Junker, *Beckett: The Irish Dimension* (Dublin: Wolfhound, 1995).

[15] Vivian Mercier, *Beckett/Beckett* (London: Souvenir Press, repr. 1990), p. 21.

[16] Samuel Beckett, *Murphy* (London: Picador, repr. 1973), p. 6.

[17] Cf. Frederick R. Karl, 'Waiting for Beckett: Quest and Re-Quest', *The Sewanee Review*,

LXIX (1961), p. 668; Mandfred Smuda, *Becketts Prosa als Metasprache* (Munich: Fink, 1970), pp. 20–40. I am indebted to Smuda's perceptive arguments, some of which I have adopted here.

[18] Cf. Smuda, pp. 28f.

[19] Samuel Beckett, 'Dante...Bruno. Vico...Joyce', in *Our Examina-tion Round His Factification for Incamination of Work in Progress* (London: Faber & Faber, repr. 1972), p. 14.

[20] Cf. Smuda, pp. 35f.

[21] The novel was written in France during the war and finished in 1945.

[22] Samuel Beckett, *Watt* (London: Calder & Boyars, repr. 1972), p. 14.

[23] Samuel Beckett, *Proust* (New York: Grove Press, repr. 1957), p. 62.

[24] Cf. Ursula Dreysse, *Realität als Aufgabe. Eine Untersuchung über Aufbaugesetze und Gehalte des Romanwerks von Samuel Beckett* (Bad Homburg, Berlin, Zurich: Gehlen Verlag, 1970), pp. 30–3.

[25] Cf., for example, the reviews in Lawrence Graver and Raymond Federman (eds.), *Samuel Beckett: The Critical Heritage* (London, Henley and Boston: Routledge and Kegan Paul, 1979), pp. 122–136.

[26] Cf. Smuda, pp. 48f.

[27] Cf. Linda Hutcheon, *A Poetics of Postmodernism: History, Theory, Fiction* (New York and London: Routledge, 1988); Brian McHale, *Postmodernist Fiction* (New York and London: Methuen, 1987).

[28] The novel first appeared in French in 1950.

[29] Cf. Dreysse, pp. 51–2, where a perceptive analysis of the novel is offered. Some of the arguments I have adopted here.

[30] Cf. Dreysse, p. 80.

[31] Samuel Beckett, *Malone Dies* (London: Calder & Boyars), 1975, p. 7. The novel was originally published in French in 1951.

[32] Cf. Dreysse, pp. 91–4.

[33] Samuel Beckett, *The Unnamable* (London: Calder & Boyars, 1975), p. 7. The novel first appeared in French in 1952.

[34] Cf. Hugh Kenner, *Samuel Beckett: A Critical Study* (New York, 1961), p. 128.

[35] Cf. Dreysse, p. 118.

[36] Cf. David H. Helsa, *The Shape of Chaos: An Interpretation of the Art of Samuel Beckett* (Minneapolis: The Univ. of Minnesota Press, 1971), pp. 112f.

[37] *Ibid.*, p. 115.

[38] *Ibid.*, p. 118.

[39] *Ibid.*, p. 127.

[40] Cf. Dreysse, pp. 142, 145.

[41] Samuel Beckett, *How It Is* (New York: Grove Press, 1964), p. 7. The novel was originally published in French in 1961.

## Aidan Higgins

[1] Aidan Higgins, *Bornholm Night-Ferry* (London: Allison & Busby, 1983), p. 79. All further references to the novel will be included in the text.

[2] Cf. Ursula Mayrhuber, *Aidan Higgins: An Analysis of His Works* (Diss. Vienna, 1990), typescript pp. 172–232.

[3] Roger Garfitt, 'Constants in Contemporary Irish Fiction', in: Douglas Dunn (ed.), *Two Decades of Irish Writing: A Critical Survey* (Chester Springs, PA, 1975), p. 227. See also Robin Skelton, 'Aidan Higgins and the Total Book', *Mosaic*, X, 1 (1976), p. 31.

4  Cf. Skelton, p. 28.

5  Bernard Share, 'Down the Balcony, *Hibernia* (August 19, 1977), p. 16.

6  Anthony Kerrigan, 'Threads Flex, Hues Meeting, Parting in Whey-Blue Haze: Aidan Higgins and *The Balcony of Europe*', *Malahat Review: An International Quarterly of Life and Letters*, 28 (1973), p. 117.

7  Cf. Mayrhuber, p. 9.

8  Cited in Mayrhuber, p. 158.

9  Cf. Bruce Arnold's remark in *The Dublin Magazine*, V, 1 (Spring 1966), p. 79.

10  Cf. Vera Kreilkamp, 'Reinventing a Form: The Big House in Aidan Higgins's *Langrishe, Go Down*', *The Canadian Journal of Irish Studies*, XI, 2 (December 1985), pp. 27–38.

11  'Beckettwise and Unblooming. John Hall Interviews Author Aidan Higgins', *Guardian* (October 11 1971), p. 8.

12  Samuel Beckett, 'Letter from Samuel Beckett Concerning Manuscript of Story "Killachter Meadow"', *Review of Contemporary Fiction* (Spring 1983), p. 157.

13  Aidan Higgins, *Langrishe, Go Down* (London, Glasgow, Toronto, Sydney, Auckland: Paladin, Grafton Books, repr. 1987), p. 15. All further references are to this edition.

14  Aidan Higgins, 'Imaginary Meadows', *Review of Contemporary Fiction* (Spring 1983), p. 117.

15  Morris Beja, 'Felons of Our Selves: The Fiction of Aidan Higgins', *Irish University Review*, 3 (1973), p. 167.

16  Cf. Mayrhuber, p. 153.

17  Cf. Mayrhuber, p. 131.

18  Cf. Kreilkamp's remarks. The *Machtübernahme*, so called, actually took place on 30 January 1933; but it was in July 1932 that Hitler's political party managed to gain 230 seats in the *Reichstag*.

19  Eamonn Wall has published quite an interesting discussion of *Balcony of Europe* that considers the novel a postmodernist updating of Joyce's *Ulysses* and *Dubliners*, cf. Eamonn Wall, 'Aidan Higgins's *Balcony of Europe*: Stephen Dedalus Hits the Road', *Colby Quarterly*, 31, 1 (March 1995), pp. 81–7.

20  Cf. Douglas Sealy's remark in 'Scrap by Scrap', p. 1134.

21  Aidan Higgins, *Scenes from a Receding Past* (London: John Calder, 1977), p. 16. All other references will be included in the text.

22  See Mayrhuber, p. 117.

23  *Ibid.*, p. 117.

24  *Ibid.*, p. 204.

25  *Ibid.*, p. 204.

26  Aidan Higgins, *Ronda Gorge & Other Precipices* (London: Secker & Warburg, 1989).

27  Aidan Higgins, *Helsingor Station & Other Departures* (London: Secker & Warburg, 1989), p. 46.

## John Banville

1  John Banville, *Birchwood* (London: Secker & Warburg, 1973), p. 5.

2  John Banville, *Kepler* (London: Secker & Warburg, 1981), p. 191.

3  Ludwig Wittgenstein, *Tractatus logico-philosophicus* (Frankfurt: Suhrkamp, 1971), p. 115.

4  Francis C. Molloy, 'The Search for Truth: The Fiction of John Banville', *Irish University Review*, X, 1 (Spring 1981), p. 42.

5  *Ibid.*, pp. 42f.

5  *Daily Telegraph,* 8 February 1973.

[7]   Cf. Molloy, p. 39.
[8]   John Banville, *The Newton Letter* (London: Secker & Warburg, 1982), p. 50.
[9]   Cf. John Banville, *Doctor Copernicus* (London: Secker & Warburg, 1976), p. 239.
[10]  *Ibid.*, pp. 238f.
[11]  George O'Brien, 'Goodbye to All That', *The Irish Review*, 30 January 1990, p. 89.
[12]  Vladimir Nabokov, *Lolita*, ed. with preface, introduction and notes by Alfred Appel, Jr (New York, Toronto: McGraw-Hill, 1970), p. 61.
[13]  John Banville, *The Book of Evidence* (London: Secker & Warburg, 1989), p. 3.
[14]  John Banville, *Doctor Copernicus* (London: Secker & Warburg, 1976), p. 209.
[15]  I wish to acknowledge my indebtedness for this argument and other points to Mr Donal O'Donoghue.
[16]  Rainer Maria Rilke, *The Notebook of Malte Laurids Brigge* (Oxford: OUP, repr. 1984), pp. 19f.
[17]  John Banville, *Ghosts* (London: Secker & Warburg, 1993), pp. 243f.
[18]  Cf. 'Making Little Monsters Walk', in Clare Boylan (ed.), *The Agony and the Ego* (Harmondsworth: Penguin, 1993), pp. 105–12.
[19]  John Banville, *The Untouchable* (London: Picador, 1997), p. 57.

# Edna O'Brien

[1]   W.B. Yeats, 'The Circus Animals' Desertion', in W.B. Yeats, *Collected Poems* (London & Basingstoke: Macmillan, repr. 1978), p. 392.
[2]   Cf. Raymonde Popot, 'Edna O'Brien's Paradise Lost'; in Patrick Rafroidi and Maurice Harmon (eds.), *The Irish Novel in Our Time* (Villeneuve-d'Asq: PUL, 1975–6), p. 277.
[3]   Maurice Harmon, 'Generations Apart: 1925-1975'; in P. Rafroidi and M. Harmon (eds.), *The Irish Novel in Our Time*, p. 56.
[4]   Cf. Popot, p. 268.
[5]   *Ibid.*, p. 256.
[6]   *Ibid.*, p. 261.
[7]   *Ibid.*, pp. 273f. The quotations are taken from Popot.
[8]   Edna O'Brien, 'An Irish Childhood', *The New Republic*, II, 23 (1976), p. 27.
[9]   Cf. R. Popot, p. 280.
[10]  Christina Hunt Mahoney, *Contemporary Irish Literature: Trans-forming Tradition* (Basingstoke and London: Macmillan, 1998), p. 211.
[11]  The quotations can be found in Grace Exkley's study *Edna O'Brien* (Lewisburg: Bucknell University Press, 1974), pp. 13f.
[12]  Edna O'Brien, *The Country Girls Trilogy* (Harmondsworth: Penguin, repr. 1988), p. 27.
[13]  The novel was originally published as *The Lonely Girl* in 1962.
[14]  Edna O'Brien, *Girl With Green Eyes* (Harmondsworth: Penguin, repr. 1974), p. 7.
[15]  Edna O'Brien, *August is a Wicked Month* (Harmondsworth: Penguin, repr. 1975), p. 107.
[16]  Edna O'Brien, *Casualties of Peace* (Harmondsworth: Penguin, repr. 1971), p. 37.
[17]  Edna O'Brien, *The Love Object*, in *Seven Novels and other Short Stories* (London: Collins, 1978), p. 685.
[18]  Edna O'Brien, *A Pagan Place* (Harmondsworth: Penguin, repr. 1971), p. 19.
[19]  Edna O'Brien, *Night* (Harmondsworth: Penguin, repr. 1974), p. 7.
[20]  Edna O'Brien, *Johnny I hardly knew you* (London: Weidenfeld and Nicolson, 1977), p. 7.
[21]  Edna O'Brien, *The High Road* (Harmondsworth: Penguin, repr. 1989), p. 1.

[22] Edna O'Brien, *Time and Tide* (Harmondsworth: Penguin, repr. 1993), p. 3.

[23] Edna O'Brien, *House of Splendid Isolation* (London: Weidenfeld & Nicolson, 1994), p. 3.

[24] Edna O'Brien, *Down by the River* (London: Weidenfeld & Nicolson, 1996), pp. 264f.

[25] Edna O'Brien, *Wild Decembers* (London: Weidenfeld & Nicolson, 1999), p. 2.

[26] Cf. the publisher's blurb to the novel.

[27] Emily Jane Brontë, 'Remembrance', in Christopher Ricks (ed.), *The Oxford Book of English Verse* (Oxford: OUP, 1999), p. 446.

## Jennifer Johnston

[1] Seán MacMahon, 'Anglo-Irish Attitudes: The Novels of Jennifer Johnston', *Éire-Ireland*, X, 3 (1975), p. 141.

[2] Mark Mortimer, 'The World of Jennifer Johnston: A Look at Three Novels', *The Crane Bag*, IV, 1 (1980), pp. 88, 94.

[3] Heinz Kosok, 'The Novels of Jennifer Johnston', in M. Diedrich and Ch. Schöneich (eds.), *Studien zur englischen und amerikanischen Prosa nach 1920* (Darmstadt: Wiss. Buchgesellschaft, 1986), pp. 98–111.

[4] Cited on the dust-jacket of *The Old Jest*.

[5] Some vituperative virago saw fit to accuse me of misogyny for my criticism of Johnston's novels (cf. Christine St Peter, 'Jennifer Johnston's Irish Troubles: A Materialist-Feminist Reading'; in Toni O'Brien Johnson and David Cairns (eds.), *Gender in Irish Writing* (Milton Keynes/ Philadelphia: Open University Press, 1991), pp. 112–27.), which is utterly laughable; and when I reviewed — unfavourably I cannot but admit — *The Invisible Worm* for *Études Irlandaises* (June 1988), the editors rushed in Mark Mortimer and printed his very laudatory review directly after mine. I may at times, out of an unshakeable love for good writing and a strong detestation for bad, have phrased some of my statements too strongly; but it is not completely without some delight that I can note that neither Christine St Peter nor Mark Mortimer, the two critics who directly took issue with me, has anything to offer in the way of refuting or invalidating my points. See also Ann Owens Weekes, *Irish Women Writers: An Uncharted Tradition* (Lexington: University of Kentucky Press, 1990), p. 192.

[6] Jennifer Johnston, *The Captains and the Kings* (London: Coronet Books, repr. 1979), p. 139.

[7] Jennifer Johnston, *The Old Jest* (London: Hamish Hamilton, 1979), p. 11.

[8] Jennifer Johnston, *The Christmas Tree* (London: Hamish Hamilton, 1981), p. 129.

[9] Jennifer Johnston, *The Railway Station Man* (London: Hamish Hamilton, 1984), p. 1.

[10] Jennifer Johnston, *Fool's Sanctuary* (London: Hamish Hamilton, 1987), p. 132.

[11] Jennifer Johnston, *Shadows on Our Skin* (London: Hamish Hamilton, 1977), p. 97.

[12] Aldous Huxley, *Crome Yellow* (Frogmore, St Albans: Panther, repr. 1977), pp. 17f.

[13] Rainer Maria Rilke, *The Notebook of Malte Laurids Brigge* (Oxford, New York: OUP, 1984), pp. 18–21. There seems to be a mistake in the translation. For the original version reads: '...Denn die Erinnerungen selbst sind es noch nicht. Erst wenn sie Blut werden in uns...' Instead of rendering the first sentence thus: 'For it is *not* the memories themselves that matter', the English version has turned it into a positive statement: '...it is the memories themselves that matter'.

[14] Shari Benstock, 'The Masculine World of Jennifer Johnston', in Thomas F. Stanley (ed.), *Twentieth-Century Women Novelists* (Totowa/NJ, 1982), p. 192.

[15] *Ibid.*, p. 216.

[16] William Golding, 'A Moving Target', in: W. Golding, A *Moving Target* (London, 1982), p. 170.

[17] Early on, a character tells her lover that her mother is playing Gertrude at the Abbey. 'I think they open in about three weeks.' [Jennifer Johnston, *Two Moons* (London: Review, 1998), p. 41.] At the close of the narrative, the first night of the *Hamlet* production has just taken place.

## Julia O'Faolain

[1] *Not in God's Image* (London: Temple Smith; New York: Harper, 1973).

[2] Cf. Val Warner, 'O'Faolain, Julia', in James Vinson (ed.), *Contem-porary Novelists* (New York: St Martin's Press, 1982), p. 504.

[3] Harmondsworth: Penguin, 1982.

[4] Julia O'Faolain, *Women in the Wall* (Harmondsworth: Penguin, repr. 1978), p. 47.

[5] Cf. Maurice Harmon's comment in *Irish University Review*, 5 (1975), pp. 323f.

[6] Lalage Pulvertaft, 'Under Order', *TLS*, 4 (April 1975), p. 353.

[7] *Ibid.*, p. 353.

[8] Patricia Craig, 'Those Dying Generations', *TLS*, (13 June 1980), p. 674.

[9] Ann Weekes, 'Diarmuid and Gráinne Again: Julia O'Faolain's *No Country for Old [sic] Men*', *Ireland*, 21 (1986), pp. 89–102. I have, in what I offer, made use of Ms Weekes' findings.

[10] *Ibid.*, p. 91.

[11] *Ibid.*, pp. 91f.

[12] *Ibid.*, p. 99.

[13] *Ibid.*, p. 101.

[14] Julia O'Faolain, *The Obedient Wife* (Harmondsworth: Penguin, repr. 1983), p. 230.

[15] *TLS*, 23 July 1982, p. 807.

[16] Cf. cover comment of the Penguin edition.

[17] Julia O'Faolain, *The Irish Signorina* (Harmondsworth: Penguin, repr. 1985), p. 10.

[18] Julia O'Faolain, *The Judas Cloth* (London: Sinclair-Stevenson, 1992), p. 6.

[19] 'The State of Fiction', *The New Republic*, 5 (Summer 1978).

## William Trevor

[1] Mira Stout, 'The Art of Fiction CVIII: William Trevor', *Paris Review*, CX, 2 (Spring 1989), p. 134.

[2] Cf. Kristin Morrison, *William Trevor* (New York: Twayne, 1993), p. 6.

[3] W. Trevor, *A Standard of Behaviour* (London: Acabus, repr. 1982), p. 102.

[4] Gregory A. Schirmer, *William Trevor: A Study of His Fiction* (London: Routledge, 1990), pp. 4f.

[5] Cf. K. Morrison, p. 38.

[6] *Ibid.*, p. 169, note 2. Asked by Mira Stout, in the *Paris Review* interview, whether *A Standard of Behaviour* was his first novel, Trevor replied: 'That's really a fragment which was written for profit when I was very poor. Strictly speaking it is my first novel, written some time before *The Old Boys*, but *The Old Boys* was the first serious thing I ever wrote.' (Mira Stout, 'The Art of Fiction CVIII: William Trevor, p. 125.)

[7] Cf. Schirmer, pp. 17f.

*Ibid.*, p. 20.

*Ibid.*, pp. 21f.

*Ibid.*, p. 22.

*Ibid.*, p. 23.

K. Morrison, p. 39.

*Ibid.*, p. 40.

W. Trevor, *The Boarding House* (Harmondsworth: Penguin, 1968), p. 85.

Cf. K. Morrison, p. 43.

*Ibid.*, p. 43.

*Ibid.*, pp. 45f.

W. Trevor, *The Love Department* (Harmondsworth: Penguin, repr. 1970), p. 13.

K. Morrison, p. 47.

*Ibid.*, p. 47.

W. Trevor, *Mrs Eckdorf in O'Neill's Hotel* (London, Sydney, Toronto: The Bodley Head, 1969), p. 9.

W. Trevor, *Miss Gomez and the Brethren* (Harmondsworth: Penguin, repr. 1997), p. 26.

W. Trevor, *Elizabeth Alone* (Harmondsworth: Penguin, 1988).

Cf. K. Morrison, p. 29.

W. Trevor, *The Children of Dynmouth* (Harmondsworth: Penguin, repr. 1987), p. 7.

Cf. Schirmer, pp. 66f.

*Ibid.*, p. 68.

W. Trevor, *Other People's Worlds* (Harmondsworth: Penguin, repr. 1988), p. 12.

Cf. K. Morrison, p. 32.

W. Trevor, *Fools of Fortune* (Harmondsworth: Penguin, 1984), pp. 165f.

Cf. Vera Kreilkamp, *The Anglo-Irish Novel and the Big House* (Syracuse, New York: Syracuse University Press, 1998), p. 224.

W. Trevor, *Nights at the Alexandra* (London, Melbourne, Auckland, Johannesburg: Hutchinson, 1987), p. 71.

Cf. Schirmer, *William Trevor*, p. 134.

*Ibid.*, p. 135.

*Ibid.*, p. 135.

Cf. K. Morrison, chapter 6.

Cf. Schirmer, p. 156.

W. Trevor, *The Silence in the Garden* (Harmondsworth: Penguin, repr. 1989), p. 146.

Cf. Schirmer, p. 159.

Cf. V. Kreilkamp, p. 230.

Cf. Schirmer, p. 160.

Cf. for instance, Julia O'Faolain's review 'The Saving Touch of Fantasy', *TLS*, (21 May 1991).

The list of Trevor's work prefacing for example *Death in Summer*, his latest novel, groups *Two Lives* among the novellas. The reason for this remains somewhat obscure. For *Reading Turgenev* comprises 222 pages, whereas *Death in Summer* itself is only 214 pages long. So length cannot be responsible for regarding the first part of *Two Lives* as a novella. *My House in Umbria* covers 153 pages, and there are any number of narrative works of that size published these days that range as novels. It is for such considerations that *Reading Turgenev* and *My House in Umbria* are classified here as novels.

William Trevor, *Two Lives* (London: Viking, 1991), p. 1.

W. Trevor, *Felicia's Journey* (London: Viking, 1994), p. 200.

W. Trevor, *Death in Summer* (London: Viking, 1998), p. 61.

# Brian Moore

1 Cf. Hallvard Dahlie, *Brian Moore* (Boston: Twayne, 1981), p. 11. See also Peter Parker (ed.), *The Reader's Guide to Twentieth-Century Writers* (London and Oxford: Fourth Estate & Helicon, 1995), p. 517.

2 Cf. Dahlie, p. 44.

3 Brian Moore, *The Lonely Passion of Judith Hearne* (London: Flamingo, repr. 1994), p. 7.

4 Jeanne Flood, *Brian Moore* (Lewisburg: Bucknell University Press, 1974), p. 19.

5 *Ibid.*, p. 30.

6 Brian Moore, *The Feast of Lupercal* (London: Andre Deutsch, 1958), p. 12.

7 Cf. Flood, pp. 30f.

8 *Ibid.*, p. 30.

9 *Ibid.*, p. 31.

10 *Ibid.*, pp. 32f.

11 *Ibid.*, p. 33.

12 *Ibid.*, p. 32.

13 Brian Moore, *The Luck of Ginger Coffey* (Harmondsworth: Penguin, repr. 1977), p. 75.

14 Wallace Stevens, *Collected Poems* (London and Boston: Faber & Faber, repr. 1987), p. 64.

15 Flood, p. 70. For an opposite view, see H. Dahlie, pp. 68f. I should like to acknowledge my indebtedness to Jeanne Flood for my comments on the book.

16 *Ibid.*, p.66.

17 Brian Moore, *The Emperor of Ice-Cream* (Harmondsworth: Penguin, repr. 1987), p. 14.

18 Flood, p. 67.

19 Cf. Dahlie, pp. 68f.

20 Cf. Jo O'Donoghue, *Brian Moore: A Critical Study* (Dublin: Gill & Macmillan, 1990), p. 118.

21 *Ibid.*, p. 119.

22 Cf. Dahlie, p. 123.

23 Brian Moore, *I Am Mary Dunne* (Harmondsworth: Penguin, repr. 1973), p. 9.

24 Not seventeen, as Dahlie notes, p. 125.

25 Cf. Dahlie, p. 127.

26 Cf. Flood, p. 73.

27 For example on pp. 83f.

28 Cf. the many overt and covert references to some of T.S. Eliot's works, such as *The Waste Land* and *Sweeney Agonistes*; see Jeanne Flood, pp. 82f.

29 See Dahlie, p. 95.

30 *Ibid.*, p. 95.

31 Brian Moore, *Fergus* (Harmondsworth: repr. 1977), p. 170.

32 Cf. Flood, p. 87.

33 Brian Moore, *Catholics* (Harmondsworth: Penguin, repr. 1977), p. 18.

34 Brian Moore, *The Great Victorian Collection* (London: Cape, 1975), p. 25.

35 Cf. London: Corgi, repr. 1978.

36 Cf. James M. Cahalan, *The Irish Novel: A Critical History* (Dublin: Gill & Macmillan, 1988), p. 270.

37 Robert Hogan (ed.), *Dictionary of Irish Literature*, vol. II. (Westport, CN and London: Greenwood, rev. and expanded edition 1996), p. 857.

38 Brian Moore, *Black Robe* (London: Cape, 1985), p. ix.

39 Brian Moore, *Lies of Silence* (London: Virago, repr. 1992), p. 70.

[40] Brian Moore, *No Other Life* (London: Bloomsbury, 1993), p. 73.

[41] Brian Moore, *The Magician's Wife* (London: Bloomsbury, 1997), p. 128.


## John McGahern

[1] Cf. Henri-D. Paratte, 'Conflicts in a Changing World: John McGahern', in Patrick Rafroidi and Maurice Harmon (eds.), *The Irish Novel in Our Time* (Lille: Publ. de L'Université de Lille III, 1975–76), pp. 312, 316.

[2] John McGahern, *The Barracks* (London: Panther, repr. 1966), p. 127.

[3] Cf. Preface to the revised edition.

[4] Cf. John Cronin, 'John McGahern's *Amongst Women*: Retrenchment and Renewal', *Irish University Review*, XXII, 1 (Spring/Summer 1992), p. 172.

[5] John McGahern, *The Leavetaking* (London: Faber & Faber, repr. 1975), p. 85.

[6] Cf. Denis Sampson, *Outstaring Nature's Eye: The Fiction of John McGahern* (Dublin: Lilliput Press, 1993), pp. 137–39, where some of the conflicting responses are discussed.

[7] John McGahern, *The Pornographer* (London and Boston: Faber & Faber, 1979), p. 252.

[8] Cf. Sampson, p. 144.

[9] *Ibid.*, p. 144.

[10] Cf. John Cronin, 'John McGahern's *Amongst Women*. Retrenchment and Renewal', pp. 168f.

[11] Cf. Antoinette Quinn, 'A Prayer for My Daughters: Patriarchy in *Amongst Women*', *Canadian Journal of Irish Studies*, XVII, 1 (July 1991), p. 83.

[12] *Ibid.*, p. 81.

[13] John McGahern, *Amongst Women* (London and Boston: Faber & Faber, 1990), p. 1.

[14] Cf. A. Quinn, p. 84.

[15] *Ibid.*, p. 79. Denis Sampson offers a perceptive analysis of the novel in *Outstaring Nature's Eye*, to which I should like to acknowledge my indebtedness for some of my own arguments.

[16] Cf. J. Cronin, pp. 175f.

[17] *Ibid.*, pp. 175f.

[18] *Ibid.*, pp. 174f.

[19] Cf. Sampson, p. 220.


## Roddy Doyle

[1] Gerry Smyth, *The Novel and the Nation: Studies in the New Irish Fiction* (London, Chicago: Pluto Press, 1997).

[2] 'An Interview with Roddy Doyle, 16 September 1996', in G. Smyth, *The Novel and the Nation*, p. 110.

[3] Cf. G. Smyth's evaluation.

[4] 'Roddy Doyle' entry in: R. Hogan (ed.), *Dictionary of Irish Literature*, vol. I. Westport/ Conn., London: Greenwood Press, 1996, p. 377.

[5] Cf. Bernard Share, *Slanguage: A Dictionary of Irish Slang* (Dublin: Gill & Macmillan, 1997), *s.v.* 'Snapper', p. 264.

[6] 'Roddy Doyle' entry, p. 378.

[7] *Ibid.*, p. 378.

[8]  Roddy Doyle, *Paddy Clarke Ha Ha Ha* (London: Minerva, 1994), p. 191.
[9]  For example, by Dermot Bolger, cf. the blurb.
[10]  Henry James, *The Spoils of Poynton* (Oxford and New York: OUP, 1982), p. xxxix.
[11]  G. Smyth, p. 79.
[12]  'Roddy Doyle' entry, p. 378.
[13]  G. Smyth, p. 80.
[14]  *Ibid.*, p. 85.
[15]  Roddy Doyle, *The Woman Who Walked Into Doors* (London: Minerva, 1997), p.41.
[16]  Cf. Smyth, p. 209.
[17]  *Ibid.*, p. 87.
[18]  Roddy Doyle, *A Star Called Henry* (London: Cape, 1999), p. 111.
[19]  Cf. C. Gébler's review.
[20]  *Ibid.*
[21]  *Ibid.*

## Dermot Bolger

[1]  Cf. Gerry Smyth, *The Novel and the Nation: Studies in the New Irish Fiction* (London, Chicago: Pluto Press, 1997), p. 76.
[2]  Dermot Bolger, *The Journey Home* (London: Viking, 1990), p. 5.
[3]  Declan Kiberd, *Inventing Ireland* (London: Cape, 1995), p. 609. For a similar criticism, see Gerry Smyth, pp. 76ff.
[4]  Quoted in an advertisement of the novel in *The Sunday Times*, 23 June 1991, BOOKS: p. 10.
[5]  Dermot Bolger, *The Woman's Daughter* (London: Viking, 1991), p. 3.
[6]  Walter Allen, *Tradition and Dream* (Harmondsworth: Penguin, repr. 1971), p. 42.
[7]  Declan Kiberd, 'The Children of Modernity', *The Irish Times*, 22 June 1991.
[8]  *The Sunday Times*, 7 July 1991, BOOKS 4.
[9]  Mary Holland, 'Looking into Finglas and Beyond', *The Observer*, 2 June 1991, p. 54.
[10]  *The Picador Book of Contemporary Irish Fiction*, ed. Dermot Bolger (London: Picador, 1993), p. xxvi.

## Patrick McCabe

[1]  Patrick McCabe, *The Adventures of Shay Mouse: The Mouse from Longford* (Dublin: Raven Arts Press, 1985).
[2]  Patrick McCabe, *Music on Clinton Street* (Dublin: Raven Arts Press, 1986).
[3]  Patrick McCabe, *Carn* (Nuffield, Henley-on-Thames: Aidan Ellis, 1989).
[4]  Patrick McCabe, *The Butcher Boy* (London: Picador, 1992).
[5]  Cf. Gerry Smyth, *The Novel and the Nation: Studies in the New Irish Fiction* (London and Chicago: Pluto Press, 1997), p. 82
[6]  *Ibid.*, p. 83.
[7]  *Ibid.*, p. 82.
[8]  *Ibid.*, p. 82.
[9]  *Ibid.*, p. 83.
[10]  Patrick McCabe, *The Dead School* (London: Picador, 1995).
[11]  Patrick McCabe, *Breakfast on Pluto* (London: Picador, 1998), p. 8.